M W
& R

WHERE THE JOBS ARE

Career Survival for Canadians in the New Global Economy

COLIN CAMPBELL

MACFARLANE WALTER & ROSS
TORONTO

Macfarlane Walter & Ross
37A Hazelton Avenue
Toronto, Canada M5R 2E3

Canadian Cataloguing in Publication Data

Campbell, Colin, 1948–
    Where the jobs are: career survival
for Canadians in the new global economy

Includes bibliographical references and index.
ISBN 0–921912–69–2

1. Employment forecasting – Canada.   2. Labor
market – Canada.   3. Vocational guidance – Canada.
I. Title.
HD5728.C35 1994   331.12'3'0971   C94–931391–2

Printed and bound in Canada

To my mother,
Hazel Jean Tomlinson

CONTENTS

FOREWORD

As a career counsellor and secondary school teacher for almost 20 years, it has become clear to me that helping a student find a career that matches his or her aptitudes, values, interests, and temperament is only half the battle. It is equally important that the student embark on the job hunt fully informed about the hiring prospects in his or her area of interest. And if the targetted career field is static, the student must be encouraged to explore the most attractive alternatives. Knowledge of the job market and the flexibility to act on that knowledge are essential.

To survive in today's uncertain job market, it is vital that we recognize and understand the forces that are rapidly altering our lives—the events and innovations that are reshaping the world. It is my hope that this book will illuminate and explain those economic, demographic, and geopolitical trends that will affect employment in Canada in this decade and into the next century.

This book seeks to answer a number of important questions: Which industry sectors will survive and thrive—and where in the world will they operate? What business practices and organizational structures will companies adopt in order to be competitive—and how can job hunters recognize these well-positioned companies? What are Canada's strengths and weaknesses in the global playing field? And what personal skills are required to develop a career strategy, market oneself to prospective employers, and anticipate changes in the workplace?

Given the technological advances that are driving and accelerating the economy, an individual's employment prospects will largely depend on his or her ability to plan strategically and to prepare for the opportunities that will arise from change. Use this book as a guide to a wide variety of traditional and new career markets at the company, industry, and country levels—and as a tool for taking control of your career and future prosperity.

The writing of any book requires both opportunity and inspiration. Without the encouragement of David Studd, head of Special Services at the Scarborough Centre for Alternative Studies, this work would not likely exist. I wish to thank my career assessment co-op colleagues, Robin McMullen and Irene Tilston for their abiding moral support and advice, Jan Walter, president of Macfarlane Walter & Ross for believing in the need for this book, and Diane Forrest and Liba Berry for their invaluable editorial contribution. My thanks to George Brown, the Toronto regional economist, and the liaison department of Employment and Immigration Canada for allowing me to use important job-related statistics and data. And as always, I am grateful for the love and patience of my wife, Nansi Laing, and the inspiration and advice of my mother, Hazel Jean Tomlinson.

INTRODUCTION

The future holds many difficult choices for Canada and its citizens. Until recently, most Canadians could ignore developments taking place elsewhere in the world and take comfort in the security of our rich natural resources. But now that this inheritance is largely depleted and what remains is diminished in value, we must find the means to survive in a very different world.

Many Canadians are facing terrible crises: older workers find themselves casualties of change as companies downsize, go bankrupt, or send jobs out of the country altogether; younger workers discover that they can no longer just quit school and find a ready job behind a counter or on the shop floor. With unemployment likely to remain above ten percent throughout the 1990s, time is running out for those out-of-work Canadians who are exhausting their unemployment insurance benefits, all the while becoming even less employable as education and job- experience prerequisites escalate. Even individuals with years of specialized education or advanced training are often unable to find jobs in their areas of expertise. Confused and frustrated, Canadians wonder what the future holds for themselves, for their children, and for the country itself.

To survive economically, we must learn to predict the future. Impossible? Not really. Once the trends affecting change are better understood, we can make fairly accurate predictions to help us plan a viable career strategy. Observation allows us to identify the forces revolutionizing business and industry. By examining the competitive practices of our most successful international neighbours—those countries with the lowest unemployment rates and highest increases in standard of living—we can determine what sorts of changes to expect, along with the implications of those changes for Canada and its work force. We also need to understand the changes in the workplace created by technological innovation.

We are told that the recession of the early nineties has come to an end, yet Canadian unemployment figures are still daunting. All recoveries are slow because employers want to be sure that a recession is over before they hire additional staff. But this has not been the usual boom-and-bust kind of recession that typically occurs at the end of a normal seven-year business cycle. During a traditional recession, businesses rarely indulge in large capital expenditures: cash flows are down, companies are deeply indebted, and there is plenty of underutilized equipment waiting to be used once the economy picks up. However, in 1992 in Canada and the U.S., computer and office machine production increased over 30 percent, achieving the highest growth rate since 1984. Accompanying this increase in technology spending is a significant rise in productivity, economic output (gross domestic product)—and unemployment. According to Philip Cross, Statistics Canada's director of current analysis, "As recoveries go, these are highly unusual trends. Traditionally, when people think of recovery, they think of job and income improvement. This is certainly different."

What is wrong with this picture? The answer: a jobless recovery. In purely economic terms, Statistics Canada's pronouncement that the recession is over is true. But such declarations give little comfort to those who still can't find jobs because, quite simply, technology has replaced people. Labour-intensive manufacturing jobs are obvious candidates for automation; not so obvious are positions that require the processing of information—in middle management and administration, for example. Today, these positions are disappearing, and the process has only begun. Not surprisingly, according to a 1993 Gallup poll, 41 percent of Canadians currently employed believe they will lose their jobs.

Studies published in the early eighties revealed that 25 percent of North Americans were employed in jobs that were expected to last for 20 years or more; for workers over 30, the figure was 40 percent, with the percentage higher for individuals employed by large companies. This notion changed dramatically in 1992 when many big international companies laid off thousands of workers: Mercedes-Benz AG, 27,000; International Business Machines Corporation (IBM), 40,000 in 1992, 25,000 in 1993; and Philips Electronics Ltd., 40,000 since 1990. Between 1979 and 1992, the Fortune 500 companies laid off a total of 4.4 million employees or 340,000 annually. Sadly, despite our current high unemployment rates, there are 600,000 to 800,000 high-paying jobs available in Canada which cannot be filled for lack of candidates with the appropriate education, experience, skills, and training. This represents the highest job vacancy rate in nearly 20 years.

How did this contradictory situation come to pass? A hundred years ago, Egerton Ryerson in Canada and Horace Mann in the U.S. introduced universal public education, thereby creating an enormous economic advantage for North America: an educated work force. But today the world has caught up, and in some cases surpassed us, in education and training. For example, for every 10,000 people, Japan has 535 engineers, the U.S. has 139 engineers, and Canada has 50. Mexico and the Philippines now graduate four times as many engineers, as a percentage of the population, as Canada does. According to David Wilson, professor of adult education at the University of Toronto, Korea, Singapore, and Brazil all have skills-training programs that are far superior to those available in Canada.

Clearly, where Canada's education system was once a strength, it is now a limiting factor. Germany's giant electronics firm, Siemens AG, would like to quadruple its 3,000-strong Canadian work force, but the company is frustrated by the shortage of appropriately trained Canadians. Remember that high-skill jobs do not necessarily demand college or university training. The U.S. and Canada graduate a far larger percentage of college- and university-trained workers than any other industrialized country, yet both have been outperformed economically by countries with superior secondary educational systems, notably Germany and Japan. This is reflected in the fact that the top ten percent of graduating high school students in the U.S. have math abilities that are only as good as the bottom ten percent of their Japanese counterparts. Canada's educational disadvantage is exacerbated by a secondary school dropout rate of 33 percent compared to Germany's less than five percent and Japan's two percent. The combination of high dropout rates and inferior skills training has had a profound effect on those not employed in the high-skills areas.

Although 35 percent of the school population eventually attends a post-secondary institution, only 50 percent of those who attend actually graduate. This does not augur well for the future when you consider that by the year 2000, 58 percent of all new jobs will require more than 12

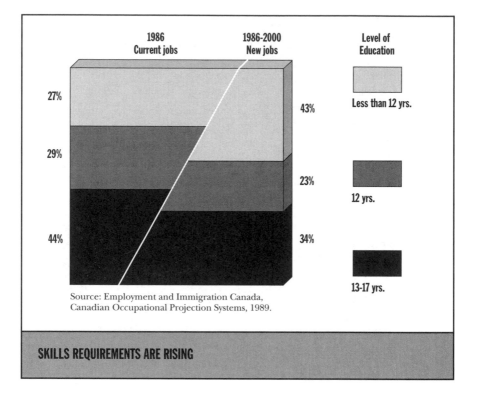

1986
Current jobs

1986-2000
New jobs

Level of
Education

27%

43%

Less than 12 yrs.

29%

23%

12 yrs.

44%

34%

13-17 yrs.

Source: Employment and Immigration Canada,
Canadian Occupational Projection Systems, 1989.

SKILLS REQUIREMENTS ARE RISING

years of training and 40 percent will require a minimum of 17 years of education.

Most high school students are largely unaware of the economic and demographic realities they will face when they leave school. Few graduates realize that if present trends continue, they can expect to earn 25 percent less in lifetime income than students who graduated 15 years ago. Between 1973 and 1986, families headed by parents in their low- to mid-twenties saw their annual real income (adjusted for inflation) drop by 28 pecent, while single-parent mothers experienced a 33 percent decline in real earnings. If we examine these figures in the context of education levels, we find that young men who failed to graduate from high school suffered a 42 percent drop in earnings; those who did graduate saw their income drop by 28 percent. College and university graduates were the only group that kept pace with inflation.

In the past, the connection between learning and income may not have been as evident as it is today; once upon a time, you could make $20 an hour in low-skilled, blue-collar manufacturing jobs. These well-paid jobs have either been automated or, if particularly labour-intensive, relo-

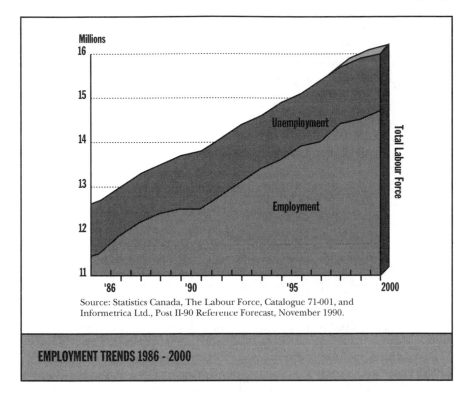

Millions

Source: Statistics Canada, The Labour Force, Catalogue 71-001, and
Informetrica Ltd., Post II-90 Reference Forecast, November 1990.

EMPLOYMENT TRENDS 1986 - 2000

cated to low-wage countries. Over the past ten years, many U.S. companies have moved their operations to Mexico, Thailand, Malaysia, South
Korea, and other Asian countries. Even the Japanese have improved their
export competitiveness by producing approximately 40 percent of their
parts offshore.

For the unskilled worker in Canada and the U.S., the service sector,
which currently employs 70 percent of the work force and accounts for
90 percent of all job creation during the 1980s, has become the major
source of employment. Not surprisingly, the entry-level salary for these
largely low-skilled jobs is correspondingly low and the chances for promotion or further training often negligible.

Today, as many as three million people, or 25 percent of the Canadian
work force, support themselves in low-paying, part-time, temporary or
seasonal jobs with an average annual income of $13,166 in the late eight-
ies compared to $30,370 for regular, full-time workers. In the future, only
those with high-level, hard-to-replace skills will be employed full-time.
Individuals with lower-level skills will be hired either on a part-time or
contractual basis so that companies are free to employ or lay off workers,

without incurring the expense of personnel benefits. Since 83 percent of the working population never completed a post-secondary education, there is no shortage of unskilled workers. The shortage is in the number of low-skill jobs.

But why can't government just create jobs as it did during the Great Depression? The answer to this question lies in the much-publicized government deficit and its implications for future government spending. Although Canada's economy will improve over the next few years and some reduction in the deficit may be expected, governments will be forced to constrain their spending. This will have significant implications for welfare, unemployment, education, training, and health care budgets. Canadians will have to come to terms with diminished government services and support of all kinds, and job creation programs on the scale of those seen during the depression will be impossible to rationalize. The relatively high interest rates will slow business investment and growth and the taxation required to service the deficit. Many companies and skilled workers will choose to leave Canada for countries with lower interest rates and taxes, and with better long-term prospects for industrial growth and career advancement. Crime rates will escalate in the larger urban areas as the economically disenfranchised express the frustration and anger that typically accompany a sense of hopelessness.

As troubling as these developments may be, their impact will be small compared to another inevitable phenomenon—the spread of information technology that will radically change the way business is structured and conducted. Geographical and time barriers will simply disappear. With transportation, telecommunications, and information processing costs declining, all exporting companies will be in some shape or form multinational. Thanks to fax machines, computer networks, on-line information and marketing services, electronic mail, and videoconferencing, 25 percent of all Canadians now work out of their homes. In the not too distant future, many Canadians will be competing with other equally well-qualified prospective employees around the globe, with the job likely going to the applicant who will accept the lowest wage. IBM, for example, contracts out software jobs to some of India's 300,000 highly trained programmers. These workers are paid about $400 a month and they can receive or transfer information instantly via satellite. India's software business increased by 72 percent in 1992.

In ten years, electronic money transfer will replace currency as we know it and most major purchases will be made from an individual's home and not at a retail outlet. This change alone suggests that the commercial landscape will be very different and that job hunting will become a journey akin to Alice's in Wonderland. To paraphrase the Red Queen, you will need to run in order to stand still. But before you rush into the future with no plan of action, take time to examine and consider the following trends, and make your decisions accordingly:

- Increasingly, levels of education, experience, and training will dictate income levels, as well as type and length of employment.
- More and more, part-time work will replace full-time work; by the end of the 1990s, between 50 percent and 75 percent of all jobs will be part-time; workers will be hired on a contractual or temporary basis.
- Work arrangements will become more flexible; individuals will work out of their homes and will be able to conduct business from virtually anywhere in the world.
- Borders between countries will become essentially meaningless since investment, jobs, and employees will move to the most competitive countries.

This maze of change will present new challenges for job seekers. More than ever before, you will have to pay attention to trends in technology, how business and the workplace operate, national and international economics, as well as shifts in your chosen field of work. But despite the difficulties, with awareness and flexibility, you can find a path for yourself. This book will help you do it.

THE INFORMATION TECHNOLOGY REVOLUTION

- **That's Entertainment**
- **The Retail Trade Transformed**
- **The Information Explosion**
- **The Vanishing Paper Trail**
- **When Cash Goes On-line**

Every industry is going to change dramatically. None is going to escape the power of the information technologies. The once-separate spheres of computers, telecommunications, entertainment, and consumer electronics have merged. Tomorrow, added to that list will be medicine, health care, transportation, retailing, and most other industries.

JOHN MAYO, PRESIDENT, AT&T BELL LABORATORIES

Information technology has finally reached a critical mass and is poised for a period of explosive development in virtually all domains...and [with its] offspring will create tens of millions of new jobs throughout the industrialized world.

CEDRIC RITCHIE, CHAIRMAN, BANK OF NOVA SCOTIA

When someone asked Lech Walesa what had caused the collapse of the Eastern European Communist empire, he pointed at a television and said, "It came from there." When we consider how much information is communicated by the world's one billion television sets and how powerful information itself can be, we begin to appreciate Walesa's cryptic reply. The information revolution has brought about major shifts in political, social, and economic power, changing the way we live, play, and do business.

Already we've seen the beginnings of this revolution, with cable television, computers, cellular phones, and fax machines. With fibre optics, digital compression, and interactive high-definition television (HDTV) just around the corner, we are about to witness the convergence of sound, image, information, software, and animation. And once all information can be put into a common computer language or "digitized," *all* media can be merged. What follows is a brief portrait of some major technological innovations along with speculation on how they will change our lives. Only by understanding this revolution can we hope to understand the transformations in the workplace and in the way business is conducted and what we, as individuals, need to do to survive and prosper in the future.

That's Entertainment...

Technology is already having an enormous impact in almost every aspect of the entertainment industry. This won't only affect how we spend our leisure hours in future; the entertainment industry will become a major

---

YOUR VERY OWN HOLODECK

How many of us have dreamed of traveling in space or meeting historical characters, all while sitting in the comfort of our living rooms? *Virtual reality*, the programming of video to appear as 3-D images with which the viewer can interact, will allow us to step into three-dimensional worlds whose only limitation is the power of the imagination. Invented to improve flight simulation, virtual reality allows pilots to "virtually" fly a newly designed but as yet unbuilt aircraft over any terrain in the world. Before long, virtual reality will be standard practice in testing and training, as well as a major boost to the entertainment industry.

employer, with dramatic shifts in products and how those products are produced. Plus, technology that is developed for the entertainment industry will also be applied in other fields. The changes we see now to jobs and corporate structure in this industry will soon be felt in others.

Applying new technology to the entertainment industry has created major business opportunities. Canadian companies have become experts at developing and using technology to create special effects for the movies. The Toronto software company, Alias Research Inc., produced the morphing software for *Terminator 2* that turns one figure into another before our eyes; SoftImage, a Montreal firm, created the 3-D graphic software that brought to life the running dinosaurs in *Jurassic Park*. The National Film Board, a developer of leading-edge technology throughout its 55-year history, is working on digital image systems that will eventually lead to desktop filmmaking.

Video games are also a big moneymaker. Over one in four Canadian households own at least one of the three Nintendo products retailing for $55 to $85 each and that require hardware costing $100 or more. In 1991, Nintendo Company, Ltd.'s $4.4 billion in retail sales surpassed the gross profits of any movie studio in North America. According to David Sheff, author of *Game Over: How Nintendo Zapped an American Industry, Captured Your Dollars and Enslaved Your Children*, video game sales generally exceed those of the entire North American movie industry, and Nintendo's imports account for roughly ten percent of the U.S. trade deficit with Japan.

Sales figures indicate that teenagers prefer video games to music recordings and rock concerts. Sega's "Sonic Hedgehog 2" game made more money on release than the bestselling rock music compact disk of 1992 over the entire year. In response to this trend, Peter Gabriel released the first rock CD-ROM (compact disk—read only memory)—a compact disk containing different kinds of information in different formats—in the fall of 1993; it includes a video game, promotional information, and stored sound, which allows the purchaser to create unique compositions on a computer using bits of Gabriel's music. Educators, retailers, and corporate marketing departments are already using CD-ROMs to combine different forms of information for consumers to examine and manipulate.

The new technology will allow the entertainment industry to deliver what we want far more efficiently. Within five years, fibre optics—a cable material that can carry many times more information more quickly and cheaply than current cables—will relay digitized movies to theaters or homes. Compact disks of any album will be made on demand in a store, or at a vending machine, thanks to technology developed by IBM and the Blockbuster Entertainment Corporation, thus eliminating the need to stock prerecorded compact disks. This same technology can be used to produce video games, computer software, or most kinds of digital information within a matter of minutes. Ultimately, some form of pay-per-view, -play or -listen system will prevail, eliminating the need for the purchase or rental of videos, games, and compact disks.

By the year 2000, the interactive television business is expected to become a $6 billion (U.S.) industry with 40 million subscribers in North America, or 50 percent of the current viewing public. Hewlett Packard Ltd., Radio Shack, and Apple Computer, Inc. are investing heavily in the appropriate hardware and software. Time Warner Inc., the largest media company in the world and the second largest cable television operator in the U.S., is building a full-service network which allows cable TV viewers to order movies from an extensive library of films, shop interactively, and play interactive video games. Similarly, Interactive Network Inc. of Mountain View, California, offers a service whereby the viewer, having paid $199 for the necessary equipment and a monthly subscription fee of $15, can hook up to 120 daily events or play the latest video game, comment on current affairs, or become a home Jeopardy contestant. Eventually, interactive television technology will allow the viewer to vote for the most valuable player, solve a murder mystery, play along with game shows, voice their opinions to Geraldo, Phil, and Oprah, and balance their bank accounts, all through their television screens. Even newspapers and magazines have become interactive as they go on-line, allowing consumers to respond to articles, ask quesions, and use software that gathers and organizes information of interest.

The Walt Disney Company spent roughly $300,000 a minute to make *The Little Mermaid* and *Beauty and the Beast*. Computer animators can now produce these same movies for less than $200,000 a minute. According to James Cameron, director of *Terminator 2*, set lighting can be enhanced in the darkroom, turning the sky a different colour or removing an actor's crow's-feet. Eastman Kodak Company and Tristar are developing 3-D "previsualization" of entire feature films before a single frame is shot, at a cost of only $15,000 monthly for labour, software, and computers. Before long, entire sets will be built in computers. Even actors may be replaced by "synthespians" created from stored libraries of gestures and expressions much the way digital sound sampling has taken the place of musicians. By now, most of us have seen commercials in which long-deceased movie stars converse with celebrities who are very much alive—these effects come from such stored libraries of images. In 1986, Ted Turner bought MGM studios to acquire 3,600 movies in the RKO, MGM, and Warner Brothers film libraries; these films will be digitized and their images used again in television, films, print media, amusement parks, and computer and video games.

In the arts and entertainment business of the future, there will probably be fewer jobs for those on the "performance" side—actors and musicians—and more on the technological side—software applications, maintenance and design. For example, the role of the stuntman or stuntwoman will virtually disappear, as stunts are achieved through computer simulation. With over 500 television channels in our future, there will be countless openings for commentators, media critics, editors, directors, scriptwriters, special effects experts, graphic artists, makeup artists, programming directors, and administrative, marketing, and support staff.

THE ELECTRONIC JOB SEARCH

Pounding the pavement in search of a job will soon be a thing of the past. In the future, job seekers will turn to interactive TV or on-line information services such as Compuserve, Prodigy, and America On-line for the equivalent of today's classified ads. Split screens will allow many people to "meet" on-screen to do business. Job hunters will use computer billboards to find positions, forward resumés electronically, and set up on-line interviews. Resumés will have to include more detail about personality and preferences so that the prospective employer can better match people to teams, and interviewers may require a software applications test administered on-line. The candidate's ability to use telecommunications networks will figure prominently in hiring decisions, especially among companies interested in individuals who will work from home.

Many of these jobs will overlap since computerization has integrated several functions. In some settings, a single person can perform the lighting, sound, and camera duties. Although fewer people will be needed on a set, the expected proliferation of television channels will more than compensate for the fewer technicians needed. With makeup, lighting, sound, and camera work enhanced by computer after the initial shooting, postproduction will play a bigger role.

The Retail Trade Transformed

Why did Barry Diller, former head of Fox studios, pass up an opportunity to buy the NBC television network and acquire QVC, a home shopping network, instead? During a home shopping sales session, Diller watched as, in less than two hours, 19,000 customers ordered 29,000 Diane Von Furstenberg home furnishings and clothing items worth $1,200,000! On another occasion, he observed soap opera star Susan Lucci sell $500,000 in hair care products in a single hour. Today, Barry Diller's QVC shopping channel is extraordinarily successful, declaring profits of $20 million in 1991 and $36 million during the first nine months of 1992.

Home shopping is the beginning of an irreversible trend. Before long, specific television channels will be devoted to the direct selling of every type of merchandise or service, with anticipated sales reaching $100 billion by the end of the decade, compared to $360 million in 1986 and $1.3 billion in 1993. The next step in the home shopping revolution may involve the merging of a major multimedia giant with Diller's QVC. Such a merger would enjoy unlimited merchandising opportunities.

While the current channels, with their zircons, skin creams, and hair replacement products, may not look attractive to many consumers, technology and marketing support should eventually make home shopping a sophisticated, viable alternative to traditional retailing. Interactive high-definition television sets will allow you to manipulate a product on screen, looking at it from different perspectives or zooming in to examine a detail. It will be possible to acquire product information immediately, talk to knowledgeable sales representatives, and order directly from the manufacturer, who will have the item shipped to the consumer's door. Everything will be billed automatically and paid for electronically.

Retailers are already using the new technology to enhance mail order. Apple Computer, Inc., Electronic Data Systems Corporation, and

Redgate Communications Corporation are collaborating to distribute catalogues on disk to 30,000 CD-ROM drive users across the U.S. Combining sound, music, video, these CD-ROMs allow users to browse through 21 catalogues for 18 of the largest U.S. retailers.

Of course, consumers will still want to "kick the tires" of certain products before purchasing. Many manufacturers will send merchandise for consumer trial. Consumer events such as home shows and auto shows will be held more frequently, allowing potential customers to inspect major purchases in person.

Many of us will still buy small items, such as toiletries, or specialized products, such as high-fashion clothes, at the store. But the new approach to shopping will save money for both business and consumers by cutting out the middlemen—wholesalers, distributors, retailers. Ordering directly from the factory cuts the cost of storing slow-moving inventory. Manufacturers will have more opportunity to communicate directly with consumers about new products without a heavy investment in advertising. Customers need no longer pay the overhead of a retail outlet. As a result of these changes, some products will cost up to 50 percent less than they do currently, there will be a lot of vacant store space for rent, and many people in retail sales will find themselves out of a job.

Technology will also change the way real estate is sold. Already, real estate television channels allow prospective buyers to look through homes before deciding which to actually visit. The Home Plus channel in Toronto draws 632,000 weekly viewers who turn it on three days a week for up to 20 minutes a day. Royal LePage Real Estate Services Ltd.'s InfoHome 2000 provides an on-line, multiple-listing database, which house hunters with a computer modem hooked up to their telephones can search by neighbourhood, price range, and architectural characteristics. Using computer assisted design (CAD), Aareas By Design Inc., an Ontario computer graphics company, transfers 3-D architectural computer drawings to videotape, allowing customers to walk up to the front door, open it, enter the foyer, and inspect the living room, dining room, and kitchen before going upstairs to look at bedrooms, bathrooms, and closets. The video blends live footage with animated computer design so that parents can even watch their children playing in the backyard. Eventually, consumers will be able to design their own homes on a virtual reality tour that allows them to make changes to the landscaping and architecture.

Mass production, the first great revolution of this century, allowed companies to churn out identical products at low prices. Now computerization is making it possible for them to produce customized products at competitive prices. In Japan, for example, the National Bicycle Industrial Company builds made-to-order bicycles which can be delivered within two weeks. The company offers 11,231,862 variations on its base models and charges only a ten percent premium over ready-made models. Computer assisted design and computer assisted manufacturing (CAD/CAM) and robotics offers greater flexibility in manufacturing. Products can be easily designed or changed on-screen; manufacturing robots are then instructed, by computer, what changes they need to make to the production process. Once technology allows manufacturers to produce only as much as customers are ordering, large inventories will disappear, as will many warehousing jobs, while the number of product delivery jobs will increase. Delivery companies that can provide speedy service will flourish.

Television advertising will change dramatically once television becomes interactive. In the past, commercials were broadcast during program breaks; then, VCRs and picture-in-picture options allowed the viewer to skip advertising messages altogether. As television channels proliferate, advertisers will be able to target their messages more accurately to consumers who, by the very channel and program they're watching, are almost certainly interested in the product. With interactive television, consumers will ask for product information when they want it. As a result, new jobs will be created for consumer information consultants or brokers. Instead of consulting consumer magazines, the customer will seek out the advice of a product evaluation service. The ability to acquire specific product information, along with unbiased evaluations, will make for a better informed and more powerful consumer who can no longer be seduced by a famous brand name alone.

The Information Explosion

We are bombarded with information at an ever-increasing rate: the amount of new information being generated doubles every five years. Computers have helped to create this explosion, and fortunately, computing power has also increased exponentially to help us process it. Hitachi (Canadian) Ltd. and Texas Instruments Inc. are collaborating to develop 256-megabit DRAM (dynamic random access memory) chips which will hold the equivalent of more than 11,000 pages of text. By 1999, it is estimated that microprocessor chips will have 100 million transistors each, 3,000 times the capacity of the largest chip in 1980. With fibre optics in place, it will be possible to carry all of North America's long distance calls on a single line of optical fibre!

In 1993, the then federal communications minister, Perrin Beatty, called upon telecommunications companies to work with government to create a "data superhighway"—a nationwide information-sharing system that would take advantage of these new technologies—by the year 2000. The major obstacle to this initiative is the setting of standards that will allow existing microwave, satellite, and fibre optic systems to communicate with dedicated federal government and banking data networks. But with more people in Canada hooked up to telephone and cable systems than anywhere else in the world, the benefits of compatability would be immediate. Both business and consumers could communicate with anyone, anywhere, anytime, to do their banking, file tax returns, and perform a multitude of other services. In the U.S., it is estimated that consumers would spend over $2 trillion on the data superhighway over the next ten years, on everything from home-delivery pizza to a round-the world cruise.

Just as it will make retailing more competitive, the new information technology can save money and create greater efficiency. For example, Supply and Services Canada used to send out 140,000 documents annually requesting bids from Canadian businesses interested in government contracts. By hiring Information Systems Management Corporation to run an on-line bidding service, the department now saves $1 million a year and the government suppliers are receiving better information.

To help cope with the information explosion on a more personal level, Matsushita Electric of Canada Ltd., Philips Electronics, Motorola Inc., AT&T, and Sony of Canada Ltd. have joined Apple in the development of the personal intelligent communicator, a cordless phone that acts as a fax machine, appointment diary, electronic notebook, beeper, message sender, and modem that will allow it to communicate electronically with other computers. Motorola has developed Mobile Networks Integration Technology software which allows a computer user to dial in to his or her computer by cellular phone and send data anywhere, or anytime. Companies and information services have installed automated fax-on-demand software allowing customers to receive faxes by calling an 800 number. Internet, an international on-line service connecting universities, libraries, and other major institutions saw its use by individuals increase from 50 percent to 80 percent in 1993; approximately 25 million subscribers worldwide are active users.

Similarly, the Canadian Network for the Advancement of Research, Industry and Education (CANARIE) is spending $1 billion over the next eight years to improve the computer network that allows Canadian researchers in government, universities, and corporations to share information.

Technology has transformed education and training by making information almost universally accessible. Consider the following networks and on-line services: Canada's Electronic Village network unites educators across Canada; Ontario's O-Net links researchers provincewide; the Community Learning and Information Network (CLIN) in the U.S. uses local schools as the focus of community training and education; Epos International in Europe offers telecommunications services like E-mail or satellite link-ups for education, public subscription services, commercial software packages, and a European network that offers televised extension courses (distance learning). As these services demonstrate, there is a worldwide trend to making all forms of communication and services available to anyone with a cable or telephone line, a computer and a modem.

Accessible on-line services means that before long, students will have the option of taking their classes at home. Distance learning will reduce the cost of post-secondary education and training, and make both more widely available. Because many primary- and secondary-school students will be handling their assignments interactively at home, parents will be in a better position to measure progress and monitor problems, and parents and teachers will be able to work more productively as a team. For example, the Interactive Channel operated by IT Network already gives parents in Michigan daily information on homework and other learning activities that pertain to their child. In an era of rapidly expanding and accessible knowledge, everyone will be become a teacher and learner throughout life.

The Vanishing Paper Trail

A variety of new technologies have allowed business to become more efficient but at the same time have wiped out many traditional jobs. For example, at the Department of Consumer and Corporate Affairs, patent searches are now conducted electronically, and the administrative and clerical staff who once processed and filed literally mountains of paper have disappeared. Many such jobs have been taken over by machines that carry out transactions without human intervention. A dramatic illustration is computerized stock trading. If you compare a snapshot of the trading floor in 1989 with a recent photo, you will notice a marked decline in the number of floor traders; computerized trading has put them on the jobs-endangered list. The popular fax machine—a recent Gallup survey of Fortune 500 companies shows a fax rate of 428 pages a day for the average company, a 43 percent increase over 1992—has cut deeply into post office and courier business.

The voice automation market is a $1 billion-a-year industry and has drastically diminished the role of receptionist. By now, everyone has had some contact with this technology: you phone a company and a voice machine redirects your call. The fastest-growing aspect of this business is interactive voice response (IVR) which allows you to place orders, pay bills, or conduct banking transactions. In the U.S., IVR sales total over $500 million annually, while in Canada, it is worth $10 million and growing. IVR technology will become so sophisticated that in the future you will simply say, "Bob Smith, please," and the machine will instantly carry

---

THE ELECTRONIC SUPERMARKET

Cashier jobs are at risk at A&P stores, thanks to the introduction of self-checkout. The shopper scans his or her groceries, the prices are read out by a computerized voice, displayed on a screen, and tallied. The customer then takes the bill to a cashier. A bar code is placed on the produce and customers weigh it themselves. Any product that has not been scanned correctly or has an incorrect bar code for its size and weight is automatically rejected. While this process will not eliminate all cashiers, discounts for self-service will nonetheless attract many customers who have already accepted the bagging of their own groceries as a normal part of the shopping experience.

out the request. Voice recognition will transform the telephone into a powerful computer terminal capable of accessing large databases or carrying out any number of transactions.

Electronic data interchange (EDI) is another innovation that is improving efficiency while eliminating traditional jobs. EDI makes it possible for computers to talk directly to other computers and exchange information. Through EDI, products can be automatically reordered from suppliers, thereby reducing inventory, lowering costs, speeding delivery, and largely eliminating human error. For example, when a frying pan is purchased at the Price Club, a discount warehouse, the electronic cash register deducts a frying pan from the inventory. If Price Club stock is low, a computer reorders a shipment of frying pans from the supplier's computer, which in turn processes the order and sends the Price Club an invoice electronically. The supplier's computer also monitors the Price Club's inventory, and if stock is low, can ship items automatically. While EDI makes more competitive retailing possible, it also means job loss.

The EDI Council of Canada reports that over 4,000 Canadian companies currently use electronic data interchange (24,000 in the U.S.). Food companies, drugstores, and automobile manufacturers were among the first to embrace EDI, but the heaviest user is Supply and Services Canada which used to spend about $750,000 in paper and postage annually. Revenue Canada estimates that 80 percent of Canada Customs clients will be using EDI by the year 2000, which will save 100 million pieces of paper a year. Even the faxing of written information will eventually be replaced by EDI.

EDI is making the consumer's life much easier as well. If there's something you need, you can deal with one computer, which will pass on your request or information to the appropriate computer to get further information, make a booking, or fill out a form. For example, individuals subscribing to on-line information services such as Compuserve can enter American Airlines' Sabre reservation system and shop for flights, book seats, and make hotel reservations, all on-line. The Ontario Ministry of Transport now has kiosks in convenient public locations where you can renew your driver's license at any time of the day through EDI.

However, the most exciting new computer technology, according to over 80 percent of engineers surveyed by *Electronic Engineering Times,* is neural networks. Neural networks consist of computer software that can process many different sets of information at once—for example, following the ups and downs of various stocks on the stock market—and recognizing patterns in that information. Neural networks are also capable of learning, as long as they are provided with feedback about the results of any decision they make. For example, they might look for patterns—even very subtle patterns—in the movement of stocks and learn to better predict how those stocks will behave. In fact, neural networks have outperformed the Standard and Poor's 500 stock index for each of the past five years. Ontario Hydro employs them to monitor power grids, customs officials use them with X-ray scanners to detect suspicious items in suitcases, and credit card companies have reduced credit card fraud by almost 50 percent through "neural nets" that note sudden changes in consumer spending habits. Neural nets have even become expert beer tasters at Labatt Ltd., where they can predict how a new beer recipe will taste without actually having to make the beer.

Neural networks are more capable than humans of detecting complex relationships. If attached to a machine, a neural net can tell you how well worn each part is, when maintenance should be performed, what is wrong with any part of the machine, and even when a part should be replaced rather than repaired. Ultimately, most training will take place with neural networks, since they can monitor your progress in learning, notice a pattern to your mistakes in thinking or problem solving, and show you other ways of mastering a skill. Clearly, there are many job implications for blue-collar workers and anyone who plays a monitoring and controlling role in industry. Fewer mechanics will be needed, and stock traders and teachers had better start looking over their shoulders. On the other hand, most of us will become addicted to the conveniences this technology will bring into the home. As Ian McGugan, writing about neural networks in *Canadian Business*, puts it, "They will make machines far more adaptive and human-like than their predecessors. Imagine stereos that automatically adjust bass and treble levels to suit your preferences and the music being played. Or washing machines that take into account load size and water quality without being told."

When Cash Goes On-Line...

One particularly interesting kind of information that will soon be transferred by EDI is information about money. It is estimated that the cost of issuing a cheque is between $10 to $30 when initiation, handling, authorizing, signing, mailing, and reconciliation are factored in. The City of Edmonton has seen its transmission costs drop to less than one-tenth of a cent per transaction by using EDI to transfer money directly into recipients' accounts.

Thanks to a variety of technologies, money is already moving more quickly through our economy, less and less of it in the form of cash. Banks have speeded up the process with automatic bank machines, on-line home banking, and overnight cheque clearing. Increasingly, money is changing hands electronically through charge cards, automatic payroll deduction or debit cards. Indeed, cash outside the bank accounts for only four percent of the gross domestic product compared with 13 percent 50 years ago. Obviously, fewer frontline employees—tellers, clerks, and middle managers—will be needed as this process continues.

Within ten years, it is possible that money will be replaced by a national electronic money system. Purchases will be deducted directly from your account via a debit card, and you will also be able to use that card to transfer money from your account to those of others, without ever touching paper currency or a chequebook.

This has obvious advantages for the government, since it will be able to automatically deduct the appropriate taxes from every transaction you conduct—a challenge to the underground economy, which is currently estimated at ten percent to 28 percent of the gross domestic product. With taxes more efficiently extracted, it is possible that taxation rates will be lowered, and Revenue Canada would collect a greater share of potential tax revenue instead of the 70 percent it manages to retrieve at the moment. Card holder identification will be made foolproof by a 3-D photo of the user embedded in the card. Even with the current technology, electronic 3-D identification is already 100 percent accurate. Obviously, there will be concerns about privacy, security, and technologies that will allow some people to evade the tax system and conduct illicit transactions. PGP—or "Pretty Good Privacy"—devices are already available to prevent the monitoring and tracing of financial transactions or information exchange. This has major implications for tax collection, trade, and organized crime.

BULLETIN BOARD

- The entertainment industry will be a major testing ground for the new technology, providing major business opportunities and transforming careers and the industry itself in the process.
- Television will become a meeting place for the sharing of commercial (and noncommercial) interests. There will be television channels devoted to every major type of merchandise, service, or interest.
- Wider accessibility to information will transform all forms of education and training.
- The new technology will change the way products are marketed and sold.
- EDI, neural networks, and other new computer technologies will have major implications for the job market, virtually eliminating many blue-collar and low-skilled office jobs.
- Banks, government, and law enforcement will be most affected by the changeover to electronic currency.

The Future is Now

While the technological revolution will transform our future, it is already affecting the way we shop, bank, renew our licences, and watch television. In the near future, the changes will be even more dramatic. Fibre optics, digitization, and interactive high-definition television will affect all aspects of our lives, including how we work and conduct business. In the entertainment industry, we see a shift in emphasis from performance creativity to creativity that makes use of increasingly complex technology. Technology will also speed up and reduce the costs of many different aspects of business, from marketing to research and development to financial transactions.

In the future, job security will come from career planning that takes into account how dramatically information technology will change the workplace, industry, and Canada's place in the global economy. If you can figure out how the revolution in information technology will affect hiring and firing practices in your field, you will be in a position to seize the many opportunities that any form of change creates. In finding rewarding career opportunities, what you know about the future developments revolutionizing the working world will be just as important as who you know. The chapters that follow will take a closer look at how the technological revolution, combined with global competition, will affect the workplace and how it does business.

CHAPTER TWO

THE CHANGING WORKPLACE

- **A New Way of Doing Business**
- **The Group-Based Workplace**
- **Employment in a Team-Based Workplace**
- **Skills for the Future**
- **There's No Place Like Home**

The revolution in the '80s was toward just-in-time inventory. The revolution of the '90s is toward just-in-time employment. Companies will use people only as they need them.

NANCY HUTCHENS, HUMAN RESOURCES CONSULTANT

No trade barrier will keep out the technological changes that are revolutioniz-ing work in the rich world.

THE ECONOMIST

Over the past decade, manufacturing and service industries have undergone major restructuring as a result of technological change and global competition. Many employees have been displaced and a number of functions traditionally performed in-house have been contracted out or automated. The walls separating departments are vanishing as companies assess their organizational structure for efficiency and productivity and focus on how best to serve their customers. According to a Royal Bank study by economist Frank Sweet, 165,000 jobs or 40 percent of all jobs lost between 1990 and 1992 were casualties of restructuring as opposed to the 9.5 percent lost due to restructuring during the 1981-82 recession.

Traditionally, companies were structured hierarchically. Each function of a company—marketing, finance, accounting, information services, production, or purchasing—had its own department, ruled by a manager to whom other managers reported, and other managers with less authority and responsibility reported to this "second" level of management. The various departments within the company operated as independent units with their own agendas, often failing to share information effectively. Often, they even acted as though they were rivals. At the bottom of the heap were frontline employees. Although it was usually these employees who had the most direct experience with the customer or the product or service the customer would buy, they had little power to serve that customer and little input into company decisions. It was upper management—the people farthest from the action—who made the decisions.

The system had its advantages, however. Individuals could specialize within a department and develop expertise, and the highly structured environment provided security and its own checks and balances. So the hierarchical corporation flourished, as long as markets were stable and competition was not too intense.

Then, in the 1970s, a major challenge from the emerging economies of the developing world forced western corporations to begin reevaluating how they did business with their customers. It's not that corporations didn't care what their customers wanted. But the company agenda tended to take priority, and corporate structures made it difficult for customers to be heard. We're all familiar with the experience of calling a company with a question or complaint and being passed up the line of authority until, if we're lucky, we finally reach someone with the power to deal with our concerns. Often, we never make it to that individual because a manager with that much seniority must be protected from the constant interruption of dealing with customers.

This rigid corporate structure created distance between the company and the individuals buying its products and services. The company produced what, in its mind, the consumers wanted, and the consumers dutifully bought—because there was little other choice. But when, for example, Japanese car manufacturers began to sell vehicles at lower prices with greater fuel efficiency, suddenly there was choice and consumers responded. Western companies realized that if they were going to hang on to their customers, they were going to have to change their attitudes to those customers. They would have to listen closely to what customers wanted and give it to them cheaply and efficiently—because if they didn't, someone else would.

Managers hoped that by introducing greater efficiency and cost savings, the new computer technology would make them more competitive. And indeed, there were improvements. The development of personal computers at low cost meant that the company could afford to give every employee a computer that would allow him or her to access information and work independently. "Open system architecture" meant that employees could also communicate with one another and work together via computer. Initially, however, each department acquired software designed specifically for its particular functions, and the software of one department was frequently incompatible with that of others. Access to the technology was often restricted to a few individuals.

Corporations gradually realized that while computers had certainly helped them make better use of their resources and reduce costs, there were more gains to be made. The overlap of systems and function components led to inefficiency, and lack of integration resulted in time delays, communication problems, and a myopic focus on aspects of a job at the expense of larger goals and, ultimately, the customer. Local area networks (LANs) helped address some of these limitations by connecting many computers to a single mainframe, thereby allowing employees to share equipment, printers, and information. LANs made it easier for workers within a department to form working groups, which were much more efficient on a number of levels. Unfortunately, the hierarchical structure had yet to adapt to the sharing of responsibility among group members.

Meanwhile, the competitive challenge—primarily from Japan, but from Europe and the emerging nations as well—continued. Corporations realized that in order to serve their customers and keep them loyal, they needed to give more power to the frontline employees who dealt directly with the customer. They needed to empower those employees to make decisions and solve problems, and they also needed to listen to those employees when planning new products and corporate strategy. Fortunately, the new computer technology made it possible to give those frontline employees more information, flexibility, and control.

Some management gurus have called this new structure the "inverted pyramid." Instead of being at the bottom of the hierarchy, the mass of frontline employees who deal with customers are now at the top, supported and coached by their managers. Others refer to the "flattened corporation," because the middle level of the pyramid—the middle managers who passed down orders and passed up information—is quickly disappearing. Regardless of the geometry, these individuals are increasingly working in teams, because what computers began, global competition made necessary. Compared to the old hierarchy, teams are responsive, adaptable, require less supervision, and generally work better in a business environment of constant change.

The new corporate structure requires a major adjustment in how we work. While in the past the idea of "teamwork" was encouraged, it was often little more than a pious wish in a highly competitive, hierarchical structure. Today each member of a team is given considerable power and expected to use it. Since all members of a team are evaluated and rewarded on the group's performance, it is in everyone's interests to work together. To perform effectively, the group must understand the goals of the project, set objectives, and assign responsibilities. This is best done with the assistance of an executive who can monitor the team's performance and make sure it has the resources it needs to get the job done. Team members must be supplied with appropriately compatible computer technology so that there is a coordinated flow of information between team members and outside contacts. And every member of the team is expected to solicit feedback from the customer on an ongoing basis.

A New Way of Doing Business

The technological revolution has implications not only within the corporation but in the way it relates to the rest of the world. Information used to pass from person to person slowly, weighed down by the geographic problems of relaying information. But once computers are networked to one another across companies, countries, and continents, everyone has access to more and more of everyone else's business. Customers, marketers, production, suppliers, suppliers' suppliers—all become interlinked into one vast hub of information that bounces back and forth. Information is no longer proprietary. Department and company boundaries become irrelevant.

Technology has not only freed information, it has freed the corporation to concentrate on what's most important. Software exists to perform most departmental, interdepartmental, and intercompany functions, leaving business to focus on the customer, while computers take care of everything else. Today, the two functions of business are to make the computers work better or the customer happier. All other business functions have been subsumed by the computer and telecommunications.

In an era of global trade, instant communication and low cost transportation, any business function can be performed almost anywhere at anytime. If you need accounting, someone in India will do it for you. Thus you may no longer even need an accounting department.

In future, businesses will evolve their own temporary structures as needed. Or as George Gilder, the U.S. futurist and economist, puts it, "Across increasingly meaningless lines on the map, entrepreneurs rush huge and turbulent streams of capital, manufacturing components, product sub-assemblies, process inventories, research and development projects, software programs, technology licenses, circuit-board schematics, and managerial ideas. Many of the most important transactions consist of electronic impulses between branches, subsidiaries, and licencees and defy every calculation of national exchange. This is not trade in the conventional sense. It is horizontal and vertical integration of industry across national borders."

In this new environment, collaboration among companies will become even more commonplace. Companies will create a new position—vice-president of external operations— which will involve developing, monitoring, and encouraging the many alliances that can be formed with other companies, while ensuring that corporate interests are not compromised in the process.

In the words of Peter Senge, author of *The Fifth Discipline: The Learning Organization*, "The twentieth century will be seen as a revolution—from seeing the world as one primarily made up of *things* to one that is fundamentally made up of *relationships*....That should be a cornerstone of any learning organization—understanding interdependency...It represents a totally different basis for designing strategy and policy."

Already, customers and suppliers are being given more direct access to a company's information systems. This not only strengthens the company's relationships with both groups, it significantly reduces its warehousing, ordering, inventory, and billing costs. For example, Kmart Corporation linked up its computer system with 200 suppliers, providing sales and warehousing information on-line in exchange for improved delivery service. Now its suppliers can better estimate future demand for the products shipped, Kmart reduces inventory through faster, more frequent deliveries, and customers are ensured that the products they want are available.

The Team-Based Workplace

As the following examples demonstrate, switching to a new corporate structure involves careful evaluation and planning and means major changes for employees.

Case Study 1: Shell Canada Limited

When Shell Canada set out to build a new lubricant plant in Brockville, Ontario, the company wanted a facility tailored for high productivity, flexibility, and short-run production that would attract overseas customers—a new market for the company. The company decided on a plan that would combine large-scale computerization with work teams.

All applicants for positions at the new plant were subjected to an elaborate screening process that tested them for ability and willingness to learn, technical skills, and aptitude for teamwork. They also had to undergo a battery of written tests, role-playing sessions, and problem-solving exercises. Only 20 of the 46 production-line workers from the old Shell plant were accepted; the rest were chosen from 1,200 outside applicants.

The plant itself combined five integrated computer systems which join production, supplies, warehousing, delivery and scheduling, and marketing. Of the 75 workers employed, 60 are team members who are divided into three self-managed "job families" responsible for bulk handling, warehousing, and packaging. Each worker or "team operator" has computer access to all plant operation information and is required to learn all the skills necessary in his or her job family as well as one skill in each of the other two families. Team members are expected to solve problems as they arise even if this requires complaining directly to suppliers. The teams hold responsibility for cost control, discipline, and scheduling of vacations and training. Annual salaries, based on the number of skills acquired, range from $26,196 for new team members to $45,588 for operators with six skills, regardless of seniority.

Less than half the former number of staff is required at the new plant, which produces as much as the larger, older plant it replaced; absenteeism is one-third the normal manufacturing average; the company has found customers in 44 countries in an industry where exports were a rarity until three years ago; and the plant can adapt its products to fit any customer's requirements.

Case Study 2: EBA Engineering Consultants Ltd.

EBA Engineering Consultants, in Calgary, Alberta, was a typical old-style organization: hierarchical, rule-bound, and conservative. The employees felt they had little power in their positions or in the running of the company, and management was perceived as overly controlling. Katharine Bondy, a management consultant at the Western Leadership Centre Inc., was hired to help change the situation. Senior managers were enroled in training sessions during which many admitted they had lost sight of their goals, partly because they had been working independently, often at cross-purposes. Bondy also found that the company was perceived by its clients as disorganized: customers did not know who to contact when problems arose.

Encouraged to solicit feedback from its clients, EBA set up meetings at which their customers responded with a number of proposals. Based on these suggestions, EBA made the following important changes: a single individual became the contact person for a particular client; employees were given more freedom to suggest and make changes within the organization; training programs to improve employee-customer communication were established for all staff; the divisions between departments were eliminated; and Friday-night beer sessions encouraged the staff to interact informally. Moreover, hiring practices were changed significantly to make sure that hirees were team players, with a personnel consultant participating in interviewing prospective employees and Ms. Bondy's firm administering psychological tests.

The reorganization of EBA resulted in better client-company relations, a happier work force, and greater productivity. The results have been so encouraging, in fact, that the company plans a similar restructuring for its British Columbia division.

Case Study 3: Unitel Communications Inc.

Unitel Communications, a large telecommunications company, had a problem delivering reliable communications services to its clients on time. Paradigm Consulting Inc., called in for advice, pointed out that the company's hierarchical structure was getting in the way of serving the customer. For example, it took more than 135 steps just to process a single order! President and CEO, George Harvey, recognizing the importance of a customer-first mind-set, focussed the company's energies on four main goals: building a modern communications network; reducing costs; revitalizing products and markets; and satisfying customer needs. The revamped structure created customer support groups organized according to type of client—finance, banking, for example—or geographical location. Order taking and support staff were relocated to regional offices in order to shorten the order-taking process. Three levels of head office middle management were eliminated and sales and product development teams were made directly responsible for customer and market needs. Before any product was changed, all of these teams had to be consulted.

As a result of these changes, the monthly failure rate of Unitel's lines went from 11 percent in 1989 to 4.1 percent in 1992, with the average amount of time needed to restore circuits reduced from nine hours to 3.2 hours. Thanks to increased sales and the elimination of 1,000 jobs, the company's income per employee has increased from less than $90,000 to $150,000 since 1989.

These case studies are typical of what has been happening to corporate hierarchies throughout North America: many employees were let go, particularly those unsuited to working in a less authoritarian environment; those who remained required retraining; each company's teams developed a stronger customer focus; and hiring practices were altered to reflect the communication skills necessary in the team-based workplace. While the companies involved are now more likely to survive and prosper in today's competitive marketplace, the adjustments for both management and employees have been substantial.

Employment in a Team-Based Workplace

Restructuring of the sort illustrated by the case studies discussed above will dramatically and inevitably alter the relationship between employer and employee. Traditionally, they had an almost cradle-to-grave commitment to each other in what was largely a feudal arrangement. Loyal time-servers were allowed to rise up the ladder of success, meeting challenges at each new level. If the company asked the employee to move, the employee moved; it was unthinkable to say no. Indeed, in a hierarchy, employees can be so focussed on pleasing the boss that the customer and the company suffer.

However, when the ladder of success is removed and structures flattened, middle managers cease to have any useful purpose and are let go. Although unemployment rose by 15 percent in 1991 as companies downsized, managers experienced a 55 percent increase in unemployment. According to Harvard Business School professor Michael Yoshino, "We're going to see hundreds of thousands of medium-level managers thrown out of a job in the next few years....Big organizations which were immensely successful in the 1970s and 1980s have grown fat and soft in the 1990s because of too little direction and too many managers who don't have any real purpose....You're going to see middle managers laid off who are 30, 40, and 50 years of age. All these well-educated, talented people will suddenly find themselves with nothing to do and no one willing to hire them."

If managers and professionals no longer have job security, will anyone have it? For most employees, the answer is no. Believe it or not, this prognosis is not necessarily depressing, especially for those who are well-trained and enjoy freedom, change, and challenge. Laid-off employees may become workers in the "virtual organization," a term used by futurist Frank Ogden to describe an organization that has no permanent employees, one that consists of a core group of experts who are hired for a short time to complete a project or until a new set of skills is needed for the company to maintain its competitive edge. Lower-skilled workers are hired for even shorter terms as the need arises. A movie crew is a good example of the virtual organization: it comprises camera people, makeup artists, set designers, and actors who collaborate to shoot a single film, then disperse once the project is completed.

George Handy, management professor at the London Business School and author of *Age of Unreason*, foresees a shamrock-shaped or three-leafed structure for the corporation of the future:

- One leaf comprises "insiders" or well-paid knowledge workers who are also the head office decision makers;
- The next leaf is made up of the specially trained workers and self-employed professionals who are hired on contract for the length of a project and then let go when their job is complete;
- The final leaf or hired-help division comprises the "technopeasants" or just-in-time work force, a low-skilled group that will experience short periods of employment and long periods of unemployment.

Companies are already well on their way toward hiring more part-timers. In 1975, only six percent of the Canadian work force was part-time; today, part-timers comprise 20 percent to 25 percent of the work force, and roughly a quarter of them would prefer to have full-time work. Statistics Canada estimates that 30 percent of workers fall into the "non-standard work" category: part-time, contract, self-employed, or anything other than employed full-time. By the end of the 1990s, it is anticipated that 50 percent to 75 percent of those working will be part-time.

Often, "downsizing" or "rightsizing" heralds a trend toward hiring more part-time staff. In a survey conducted in 1993 by Right Associates, 393 of 505 senior executives from 21 industry groups in North America said their companies had downsized within the past five years. In addition, according to Ross Finlay, president of the Technical Service Council, 22 percent of its 190 members hired contract workers for six-month to three-year projects, while 47 percent were continuing to "restructure." Even if they're not officially downsizing, some companies are trying to replace full-time with part-time staff, in order to have more flexibility to cope with future unknowns. Canada Safeway Ltd., for example, has offered generous severance packages to encourage full-time staff

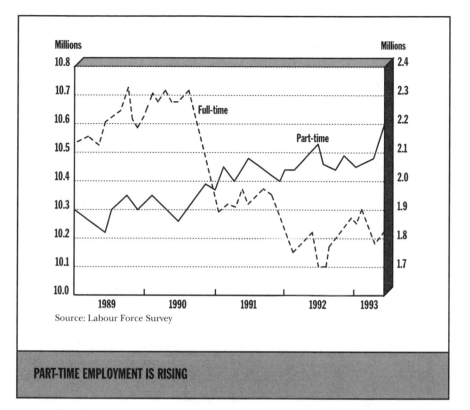

PART-TIME EMPLOYMENT IS RISING

to retire, hiring part-timers to take their place. A survey by Robert Half Canada Inc., also in 1993, found that 80 percent of the companies canvassed plan to increase their use of temporary staff whether they are growing or downsizing, and two-thirds expect to further decrease staffing in the future. Since the market value of pension fund assets has risen by 24 percent since 1991, pension surpluses have been used by companies to fund these early retirement schemes.

These new realities will call for new attitudes. The workers of the future will rely less on organizations and government, and more on their own skills, knowledge, and ability to adapt. They'll learn to treat employers as customers so that they have a better chance of being hired on for future projects. And they'll be more analytical about their potential employers, preferring to go after jobs in successful companies in expanding industries. As these companies prosper and expand, they will hire more "insiders," many of whom may well have been former contract workers. In addition, these companies will most likely renew contracts and employ casual labour for longer periods so long as they are expanding. As for all those middle managers who lost their jobs in the flattening of the corporate structure, according to Michael Yoshino, they'll partner with other unemployed managers and sell their services to their former employers. For example, Contract Management Resources is one of the many companies that fills the need for temporary high-priced managerial help. It consists of 40 associates who were former middle managers and who now work out of their homes. When companies do hire managers, they will look for different qualities than in the past. Managers will no longer act as commanders of the troops but as coaches, coordinators, partners, facilitators, feedback generators, skills builders, progress monitors, outcome evaluators, and information sources. They'll become more responsive to the needs of individual employees and of teams of employees. Management by intimidation will be frowned upon in this new team-focussed environment. Research shows that honesty, integrity, and a strong sense of self are the most valuable managerial assets. Instead of the old feudal arrangement—you work for me and I'll look after you—the new social contract between workers and management is based on mutual respect and benefit: the employee helps solve business problems for the company and its customers, and the company helps the employee realize his or her career goals. Organizations in which employees and management are working at cross-purposes are doomed.

In the team-based workplace, pay will be increasingly tied to performance and the changing market value of an employee's skills. In 1991, 38 percent of Canadian companies began substituting pay for performance in place of salaries to staff, compared with 24 percent in 1989. The days of the automatic across-the-board pay adjustment are gone. According to the Conference Board of Canada, 65 percent of Canadian companies had individual bonus plans in place in 1993.

Accountability will also extend to absenteeism, which now costs the Canadian economy $10 billion annually. In a recent Conference Board of Canada survey, one-third of the over 340 companies canvassed reported increased absenteeism since 1990. Toronto's public works department experiences a 19 percent absenteeism rate annually, which amounts to an additional expense of $26 million; and Toronto garbage collectors' 35 percent absenteeism rate means that one out every five workers is absent every day. Companies grappling with this problem have tried a number of approaches. Offering bonuses for good attendance, gimmicks such as weekly lotteries, or using software that tracks absenteeism and automatically generates reports for problem employees does not address the root of the problem. In future, the emphasis on individual responsibility and responsibility to the team, plus company programs that are sympathetic to employees' needs—such as flexible work hours, job sharing, and on-site daycare—should diminish the cost of absenteeism.

With so much riding on the qualities and performance of each employee, companies will use increasingly sophisticated techniques in the hiring process. According to career consultant Philip Jarvis of STM Systems Corp., it costs, on average, more than $25,000 to recruit, select, and train an employee to full productivity. In future, companies will screen and test potential employees more thoroughly than ever for their technical skills, leadership potential, personality, interpersonal skills, creativity, and problem-solving ability.

Today, companies hire individuals who "fit" their competitive and professional development needs. That is, rather than replace former employees with new ones in the same positions, companies use an employee's departure as an opportunity to restructure the position, keeping in mind the skills and strengths of existing employees and their ongoing professional development needs. In restructuring a position, management may even decide that functions traditionally performed in-house would be more efficiently and productively carried out from an employee's home. Technology has helped make this arrangement a viable alternative.

There's No Place Like Home

Technology is rapidly turning the home into an office. According to Thelma Moutrie, manager of national retail operations for Xerox Canada Ltd., the home office market is expected to grow from $5 million to $3 billion by the year 2000. Employers are realizing they can save money on office space if employees work out of their homes on days when it's not necessary for them to be in the office. Joe Greene, director of telecommunications research, International Data Corporation Inc., expects that by 1995, 400,000 Canadians will be telecommuting, if only part-time or informally. In Toronto, Ryerson Polytechnic University researchers found that 23 percent or two million Canadian households run home-based businesses. Approximately one-third of these workers had either been fired or encouraged to leave companies under early retirement plans.

In a variation of the home telecommuting arrangement, IBM recently introduced their "flexiplace" program which provided 900 of its 10,000 employees with technology that allowed them to work anywhere—from their cars, homes, mini-neighbourhood offices, and, in some cases, even from the offices of customers. Consequently, IBM saved $40 million in annual real estate costs and reduced its need for such facilities as cafeterias, meeting space, and boardrooms. The company now rents two floors of the Toronto-Dominion Tower instead of the 14 floors the company occupied prior to the flexiplace program. Although most of these IBM employees spend much of their time away from the office, communal offices are available in different metropolitan locations, with one work station for four employees. With videoconferencing costs likely to drop over the next few years, even the need for office work stations will disappear. Sales employees should be able to spend less time on the road, since they can deal with customers on-screen.

Companies have realized that approximately 25 percent of their assets are tied up in real estate; therefore, many are choosing to share offices with outside business people who need temporary space. According to an Industrial Development Research Foundation report, "Corporate Real Estate 2000," IBM has established such facilities for all of its British marketing and sales staff and is doing the same in 20 locations in the U.S. Andersen Consulting's 13 "just-in-time" offices shared by 70 management consultants saved the company $505,000 the first year the strategy was introduced. Ninety percent of respondents working in this kind of envi-

---

HOME-WORK STATS

According to a study by Hart and Associates, in 1993, 48 percent of home workers were full-time (usually run their own business), 25 percent were part-time, 22 percent took work home, four percent were telecommuting; 58 percent of the home business operators were 25 to 44 years old and 49 percent were located in cities with populations in excess of 100,000; 30 percent were located in rural areas. Most home businesses were in Ontario (41 percent); 19 percent were in Quebec;14 percent were in British Columbia; and 11 percent were in Alberta. The current growth rate of home businesses is 15 percent annually.

BULLETIN BOARD

- Downsizing will continue as firms increasingly contract out functions.
- Between 50 percent and 75 percent of the work force will be part-timers by the year 2000.
- There will be three types of workers: insiders, contract, and low-skilled hired help. Insiders will retain their jobs the longest, perhaps 5 years; contract workers will average 2 years; low-skilled workers, only one year.
- Employability will be based on education, experience, and marketable skills.
- An increasing number of individuals will work out of their homes, at least on a part-time basis.

TIPS

➤ Join an association related to the career of your choice and attend their trade shows or conferences. The local library has information regarding these trade and professional associations (see Chapter 5 for area-specific associations). Information is also available from on-line information services; join topic-specific computer forums.

ronment reported that the quality of their work did not suffer.

According to Linda Russell, senior partner with Telecommuting Consultants International, Inc., switching workers to telecommuting gradually increases productivity between ten percent and 35 percent, with an annual average saving of $8,000 per telecommuter. Workers don't miss the inconvenience, expense, and stress of traffic jams, parking, gas, automobile maintenance, or dry cleaning bills. According to B.C. Systems Corporation, the average telecommuter saves $1,700 in expenses and reduces travel by 3,000 kilometers. Many companies are realizing that they benefit as well and will often hire only those individuals who agree to work from home, at least part-time.

For the increasing number of men and women who are concerned about combining active careers with raising a family, working out of the home can be an extremely attractive option. The shift from manufacturing and goods-producing to a service-based economy generates many more opportunities to offer services from the home. And a more educated labour force will likely be amenable to accepting the responsibility, decision-making, and working-alone aspects of such arrangements.

For some jobs, "home" can be anywhere in the world. One can imagine many people choosing pleasant, even exotic surroundings. Real estate agents in Ontario's cottage country, for example, are already seeing increased sales to people who plan to live and work full-time at home in the country for companies in urban centres. With long-distance costs decreasing and companies going global, companies will be attracted by those workers skilled enough or willing to work for low wages out of their homes wherever they are located. Unless individuals are trained to work in the high-skill end of this market, they may find worldwide competition, even among home workers, intensifying.

CHAPTER THREE

THE COMPETITIVE EDGE

- **Competitive Companies**
- **Corporate Strategy**
- **Team Dynamics**
- **Restructuring, Outsourcing, and Suppliers**
- **Company Size and Alliances**
- **Research and Development**
- **Training and Competitiveness**
- **Working in Unionized Companies**
- **The Job Interview**

In the emerging flexible approach to manufacturing and in re-engineering of other corporate activities, it is controlled experimentation that is crucial—the search for an ever better way of doing things.

PAUL ROMER, UNIVERSITY OF CALIFORNIA AT BERKELEY

The pace of discontinuous change is staggering for most working people—they are struggling for context and for understanding of a whole new economic age.

LINDSAY MEREDITH, SIMON FRASER UNIVERSITY

We are all painfully aware of how daunting it is to find a job and hang on to it. When we are offered a job, we want to make sure it's with a company that will be around for a while, one in which we will have opportunities to develop our skills and advance our careers. The equation is simple: if the company succeeds, the employee succeeds. Today, job seekers need to be as selective in choosing an employer as the employer is in choosing an employee. To do that, you need to understand what factors will make companies successful competitors in the new economy.

Competitive Companies

One of the most important measures of a company's competitiveness is how productive it is. Productivity is the value of the goods or services divided by the cost of producing them. As productivity increases, the cost per unit of producing goods or services declines. By looking at an organization's productivity we can compare its current performance with its past record or with the performance of its competitors. If some companies in a particular industry are more productive than their competitors, the more productive will likely be the survivors; the others will fail because they'll have to sell their products or services at a higher price to cover the additional cost of producing or manufacturing the product or providing the service. The only way companies can compete and survive is by producing a unique product or providing a specialized service or by being price competitive if offering standard goods or services.

We can also measure a country's productivity by dividing the dollar value of the goods and services the country produces and sells—the gross domestic product (GDP)—by the number of people in the country. In 1992, Canada's productivity placed tenth in the world with a gross domestic product of $21,710 (U.S.) per person; Japan placed first with $32,018 (U.S.) per person. What accounts for the difference? These figures don't mean that the Japanese work 50 percent harder than Canadians, but they do tell us that they are 50 percent more efficient. The reasons for different productivity rates among countries are complex. However, one common reason that some countries are more productive than others is their use of technology. Technology—its quality and how effectively you put it to use—is crucial to productivity.

The greatest potential for productivity improvement is in the manufacturing or goods-producing sector because that's where the most technology is used. Aiming for greater productivity, manufacturers have been busily replacing workers with technology, which, if properly used, can perform certain jobs more cheaply and efficiently. Witness the staggering layoffs in manufacturing, or the number of companies going under because they cannot compete against manufacturers in other countries. In the 1970s and 1980s, when many international manufacturing companies focussed on fine-tuning their operations, their productivity increased by 3.6 percent a year. Motorola and Xerox now measure their defects in parts per million instead of percentages, and 3M has doubled its sales without having to increase its work force substantially.

Meanwhile, back at the office, productivity has been increasing by only 0.3 percent annually. The focus of the 1990s, therefore, will be on making administration and services more efficient again through the increased use of technology. Studies from the early nineties reveal that one task out of three in the office must be redone and most companies could reduce office staff by 15 percent to 30 percent without diminishing performance.

The trend toward improving productivity in the service sector will have far-reaching effects, since 97 percent of all new jobs created in Canada in the past decade were in the service industries—an increase from 79 percent of all new jobs in the 1970s.

Kathryn McMullen of Queen's University conducted a survey on work and technology that illustrates how important it is to look for jobs in companies that use technology to improve productivity. McMullen researched 224 companies over 1980-85 and 1986-91 and found that there were greater increases in employment in companies that began purchasing technology in 1980-85 than in those that started investing in technology in 1986-91. Average sales increases were 70 percent higher in the group that purchased during 1980-85, and companies that did not invest in technology at all experienced declining sales and had to lay off workers.

The demand for improvement in productivity often comes from major purchasing corporations. In 1993, the vice-president of General Motors informed the company's suppliers worldwide that they must improve their productivity by 60 percent and reduce their prices accordingly or General Motors would no longer use their services. Competitive survival, then, is frequently a function of productivity improvement.

Michael Porter, a Harvard professor and authority on competition, asserts that "a demanding market, rather than a welcoming or easy-to-serve one...underpins success."

With global competition heating up and trade barriers falling, the choices are clear: a company becomes more productive or folds. Remember this during your interview: ask about the company's plans for productivity improvement and how these changes affect the way the company does business.

Corporate Strategy

Another factor that plays a major role in a company's competitive survival and success is corporate strategy. Even an excellent product with strong marketing will fail if a company doesn't plan carefully. For example, everyone now vaguely remembers Beta VCRs manufactured by Sony of Canada Ltd. They were of higher quality than VHS tape systems. But Sony refused to license its technology to other VCR makers, preferring to market it exclusively so the company could hang on to 100 percent of the profits. The inferior VHS system was widely licensed. Consumers preferred a system that was available at competitive prices, video manufacturers responded by churning out popular movies on VHS tape, and despite Sony's hefty marketing muscle, Beta VCRs sank almost without a trace.

Licensing, of course, is only one of a multitude of constantly shifting factors in each industry. Trade magazines, newsletters, and articles in business magazines can help you understand what the major strategy issues are, how various companies are responding, and who the winners and losers are. Keeping an eye on the strategies of your employer and its rivals will help you decide if you want to remain in your current job or if you'd be better off joining a more competitive company. Just as companies need to remain nimble in responding to industry developments, so employees and job seekers should pay close attention to how corporate strategy may help or hinder their careers, and plan accordingly.

Team Dynamics

As discussed in the last chapter, many companies are restructuring in order to become more competitive—with varying degrees of success. It is important to understand and evaluate what potential employers are actually saying when they claim they've switched to a "team" structure.

In *The Post-Capitalist Society,* management expert Peter Drucker describes three team models. The first is the baseball team, with each player separately fulfilling his or her specific role, and assuming other players will cooperate by doing the same. This model works well in mass production organizations where each person is trained for and assigned a specific task that can be measured much the way a baseball player's statistics are measured. The analogy for Drucker's second team model is the symphony orchestra. Players hold specific positions and are directed by the conductor at all times. This model is flexible because it can respond as a group to change its direction or focus. Drucker compares his third model to a jazz quartet. Each player is very familiar with the other group members, and they play to complement one another with no outside direction. Since each player covers for the shortcomings of other players, this team is greater than the sum of its parts.

The traditional business was set up on the baseball team model; both the assembly line and the office depended on individuals fulfilling rigidly defined roles. The Japanese changed their automotive industry to the symphony orchestra model in the 1970s, and as a result, enjoyed substantial improvements in their speed in introducing and producing new cars. The U.S. auto industry, on the other hand, kept the less flexible baseball team model and as a result did not enjoy the same benefits as the Japanese.

However, innovations in information technology mean companies can now move to the jazz quartet model. Now that everyone on a team can access information, members can operate even without a "coach" or "conductor." Team members become interdependent and can provide one another with backup when required. When a prospective employer tells you the company has a team structure, they should be talking about the jazz quartet model.

One mistake many companies make is failing to match information technology to the new structure. For example, Bow Valley Energy Inc., Calgary, Alberta, switched to a team structure, but its information technology remained hierarchical. The company was still using mainframes that didn't allow for a flow of information between teams. Once the company started using high-powered desktop work stations instead of mainframes, information was more accessible to everyone, the company enjoyed greater productivity, and its information technology operating costs decreased by 40 percent.

Team success also depends on how responsive senior management is to the needs of the team. Unless a team has an executive willing to provide it with whatever it needs to get essential work done—and quickly—the team becomes discouraged and caught up in bureaucratic procedures.

Team size is also important. Typically, the Japanese employ small product development teams supported by senior managers, whereas Americans use large teams (often 200-400 workers) supported by junior managers. Any group larger than 150 tends to run into information and communication problems, particularly if the computer information technology used in the company is not compatible. Moreover, the speed and flexibility enjoyed by smaller teams means a company has gambled less of its resources on a given project. The Japanese, for example, can easily replace a model if it is not selling, unlike American companies, with their huge investment in large development teams which take longer to finish a project; the Saturn took an extremely long time to develop, and had the car been a failure, the company would have lost a substantial amount of money.

During your job interview, ask if the company is team-based and if senior management supports these teams. If you are already working for a company that is re-engineering to teams, analyze the dynamics of the team or teams you would be working with. Make sure the team has a mandate, that roles have been defined, schedules established, and measures of success determined. If you are working for a company that is downsizing but not switching to teams or some other less hierarchical structure, consider looking for work elsewhere. Many managers downsize just to cut costs and are not prepared to make the organizational changes that downsizing requires. When companies downsize this way, they often get rid of the wrong workers—the talented and knowledgeable employees whose loss will be expensive to the company in the long run. Managers focussing on downsizing often forget that the knowledge of their workers is a component in determining the company's long-run success. Once a company decides to downsize, it would be well advised to involve employees in making decisions about who goes and who stays. As it now stands, most people hear that they are about to be laid off through the grapevine. Avoid such companies at all costs. During your job interview, ask if the company has recently downsized and how much decision-making power employees had during the process.

When investigating a company that claims it is re-engineering, make sure that re-engineering *is* what it is doing. According to Michael Hammer, author of *Re-engineering the Corporation*, 50 percent of large corporations claim to be re-engineering, but on closer inspection, only 25 percent are actually doing it. Some companies confuse incremental improvement or continuous quality improvement with re-engineering. In Hammer's words, re-engineering is "a *radical* redesign of business processes for dramatic improvement." True re-egineering means that the entire structure of workflow has been altered to be more efficient and serve the customer better.

Because re-engineering significantly disrupts the balance of power in an organization, middle managers are often reluctant to promote changes that may very well threaten their jobs. Therefore, senior management must be decisive in seeing through the transformation to the end.

Companies with 100 or more employees or a minimum of $100 million in sales benefit most from re-engineering. Although smaller companies have successfully re-engineered, the advantages of reducing fragmentation and inconsistency are greater in larger organizations where departments may seem oblivious to their relationships to other departments or to the company as a whole. Re-engineering must be followed by continuous evaluation and improvement of the way the company operates. For example, Japanese workers are entitled to stop the assembly line or summon a supervisor at any point of the operation if they see a problem and then work as a team to solve that problem. Workers and management are then continually communicating and learning. This combination of improving efficiency, identifying weaknesses, and experimenting with new structures and methods characterizes successful companies of the future.

Restructuring, Outsourcing, and Suppliers

As part of the restructuring process, every job and function in the company is reexamined to see if it would make more sense to contract it out—"outsource" it—to some external company or individual. Tasks that have little to do with the core business of the company are typically outsourced, usually at a lower cost than it would take the company to do the job itself. This allows the company to focus on what it does best.

Peter Drucker uses the hospital as an example of the need for out-sourcing. Often maintenance is the largest cost in running a hospital. But since patient-care concerns are the hospital's core business, little thought is given to improving productivity in the maintenance department. No one involved in the central business of the hospital—doctors, nurses, administrators—has expertise in this area. Instead, the hospital might consider outsourcing its maintenance work to a company that specializes in maintenance. They know the business and they've focussed on doing what they know best. As a result, the hospital gets better, more cost-effective maintenance, and the staff of the maintenance company performs profitable, satisfying work. If these same individuals had been working as employees of a hospital maintenance department, it is unlikely that there would have been any incentive or encouragement for making significant improvements. Thus, companies have learned that outsourcing is frequently more economical and productive for all parties in the long run.

You would be wise to seek out companies that outsource all but their core area of expertise. Those companies have the brightest competitive future and offer a greater chance for promotion. If the company still retains departments that are not central to its areas of expertise, try not to get stuck there. Jobs in the core areas offer greater opportunities for promotion or for becoming an insider. And remember too that with larger companies outsourcing more of their functions, many jobs will emerge in companies that provide services such as maintenance, marketing, computer systems control, and consulting in a wide range of fields.

The challenge of competition has changed the relationship between suppliers and purchasing companies. Ideally, companies and their suppliers should be working more closely for the benefit of both. For example, Motorola has its own "university," and insists that all of its suppliers send representatives to its university at the suppliers' expense to improve their delivery of services to Motorola and to better forecast demand for their own products. This symbiotic relationship between suppliers and purchasing companies is already common in Japan and is becoming increasingly popular in the West.

Company Size and Alliances

In the past, corporate size and corporate success were almost synonymous. But in the world of downsizing, that equation is rapidly being eroded. For example, the share of the work force employed by Fortune 500 companies has decreased from 30 percent to ten percent over the past decade. Small business is widely touted as the biggest job creator. In this changing environment, what size of company offers the best opportunities and has the greatest chance for success?

Although small companies (up to 200 employees) may offer the most job opportunities, only 52 percent of new small companies survive beyond the third year. Even those that are initially successful often experience growing pains in shifting from an entrepreneurial to an administrative management style. In addition, small companies are more vulnerable than larger companies to intense competition once they grow beyond their initial market niche. On the other hand, in a small company, employees have a better chance of becoming insiders and get a broader range of experience and skills as the company struggles to survive. And if the company does succeed, those who were hired early on will become the key core workers.

The opportunities are certainly there, if you have the right skills. According to a 1993 *Profit* magazine survey of Canada's 100 rapidly expanding companies, employment in these mostly small- and medium-sized companies has grown from 2,436 to 15,452 within the past five years, a 534 percent increase. While the economy as a whole produced only 3.2 percent more jobs during this period, these companies increased their new positions by 311 percent. Rapidly growing companies are looking for employees who not only have technical skills, but who are entrepreneurial and have some of the managerial skills the employer may lack. Matching the right person with the right job is particularly important in fast-growth companies since that individual will very likely have to carry out a number of tasks independently yet work as an effective team member. In a small company, if one member of the team falls apart, the whole team may fall apart.

Although they may not be creating quite as many jobs as small business, medium-sized companies (201-500 employees) may offer more secure employment. They have the best opportunities for global growth since they have already expanded into diverse markets, at least geographically. These companies are very often more flexible than larger companies. For example, medium-sized companies tend to use smaller work teams than large companies, which means they can respond to problems or customize products faster than a big operation. They are probably more stable as a result and better positioned financially, operationally, and administratively to pursue global markets. To do so, however, they must usually form an alliance with another company in the foreign markets they hope to enter. The foreign company will know its home turf better than the exporting company, it will have the distribution channels and marketing know-how to penetrate the markets quickly, and it will possess the financial muscle to establish a significant market presence. However, negotiating and coordinating these alliances is a time-consuming business, so there will still be a place for large companies (over 500 employees), which have the resources to undertake major projects. All companies are susceptible to merger and acquisition in the long run, particularly smaller companies or those that are not doing well. A small company in particular takes the risk that the single product or invention that brought it success may be superseded by a similar or better product from a larger company with more marketing and distributing power. Therefore, being acquired by a larger company is often the best possible fate for a small company. However, employees of a company that's being acquired, or of the smaller company of two companies involved in a merger, are at most risk from an inevitable restructuring.

When we consider larger companies (500 employees plus) we almost invariably mean multinationals. Most large companies, especially in a country the size of Canada, are forced to look overseas if they are to continue to grow.

Multinationals are an important factor in our economic life. The United Nations estimates that there are 35,000 multinationals which control some 170,000 foreign affiliates. The largest 100 multinationals likely account for 40 percent to 50 percent of all cross-border assets and approximately 16 percent of the world's productive assets.

Multinationals have traditionally enjoyed a number of advantages over domestic companies. Their size gives them economies of scale in marketing, distribution, and manufacturing. And while brand names are less all-powerful than in the past, consumers still tend to purchase the brand-name products manufactured by a company that can afford large-scale advertising—Sony and Matsushita, for example—and provide long-term guarantees. Multinationals can spread their risk and seize a wider range of opportunities. A strike in one plant does not affect another in a different country, and a currency devaluation in one country can be offset by the rise in currency elsewhere. If North American markets are in a slump, but the Far East is expanding, multinationals can gear production to the expanding areas. If a country raises tariffs, sets import quotas, or erects other barriers, a multinational can get around them by starting up operations in that country.

Oddly enough, statistics show that locating in many countries is not as big an advantage to multinationals as many may assume. Only 54 percent of the sales revenue of the top 50 non-financial multinationals comes from exports on average. Given a choice, a multinational would usually prefer to remain in one country and just export to the rest of the world, since getting involved in other countries' ways of doing business is often complicated and expensive. However, tariff barriers, tax advantages or disadvantages, political considerations, local regulations, and other factors often force a company to establish a presence in other countries. As huge markets develop globally, however, most multinationals will become more truly multinational or more alliance-oriented in order to profit from those markets.

Although multinationals will always exist, alliances among medium and large companies can often substitute for multinational status. This, in fact, is often preferable. In his study, "The Global Corporation— Obsolete So Soon," Cyrus Freidham predicts that today's global company will be superseded to some extent by the "relationship enterprise," a network of strategic alliances among big companies, spanning different industries and countries, but held together by common goals that encourage them to act almost as a single company. For example, Canadians assume that our trade initiatives in Asia should be focussed on selling to Japan. We are overlooking a more practical approach: *linking* with Asian businesses in order to penetrate the key markets of both Japan and China. These competitive networks of companies would work as a team for the benefit of all.

Unlike smaller company networks which operate within a single country—the Japanese *kieretsus*, for example—relationship enterprises are corporate juggernauts, with total revenues approaching $1 trillion by early next century—larger than all but the world's six biggest economies. Freidham suggests that early in the 21st century, The Boeing Company, British Airways, Siemens AG, TNT, an Australian parcel-delivery company, and SNECMA, a French aero-engine maker, might together win a bid to build ten new airports in China. As part of this deal, British Airways and TNT would receive preferential routes and landing slots, the Chinese government would buy all state aircraft from Boeing-SNECMA, and Siemens AG would provide the air traffic control systems for all ten airports. This plan may sound farfetched, but consider this: Boeing, members of Airbus consortium, McDonnell Douglas Canada Ltd., Mitsubishi, Kawasaki, and Fuji are already talking about doing something similar to jointly develop a new super-jumbo jet; General Motors and Toyota are discussing the possibility of Toyota building light trucks in a General Motors plant; and the world's big telecommunications companies have banded together to provide a worldwide network of fibre-optic submarine cables. Although many multinationals will join together only to take advantage of a particular market opportunity, continued mutual success may encourage them to make longer-term commitments. For example, Unitel, in conjunction with its U.S. shareholder, AT&T, recently joined Japan's principal international carrier, Kokusai Denshin Denwa Co., and Singapore Telecom in an alliance called WorldPartners Association, its goal to increase one-stop shopping for any multinational's telecommunications needs. The alliance is in response to other alliances among competitors.

Research and Development

One motivation for companies to form alliances is to share research and development. For example, when IBM and Apple both found their products—IBM's DOS software and Apple's easy-to-use point and click operating system—threatened by Microsoft products, the two rivals agreed to cooperate on research and development to stay competitive with Microsoft.

Research and development has always been an important factor in corporate success—either doing your own or buying it from someone else—and it will be indispensable in the future. Take a look at the issue of new product development, for example. Part of the reason for Sony's continued dominance in consumer electronics is that it introduces four new electronic products daily. Fortunately for Sony's competitors, consumers demand a variety of products at various prices and in numerous styles. A market that diverse is too big for even a giant like Sony to con-

BULLETIN BOARD

- A company's competitiveness is defined by its productivity, industry strategies, company size, whether or not it has been effectively re-engineered to a less hierarchical structure, its employee training policies, its relationships with its unions, and the extent to which everyone's pay is tied to performance.
- Look for employment in companies with close-knit teams that have committed management support.
- Investigate large, growing corporations where career advancement includes worldwide possibilities.
- Investigate medium and large companies for research and development jobs.
- Initially seek out small growing companies, which will be the main sources of job creation in a world moving toward outsourcing functions; this is a good way to learn a broad range of skills before seeking employment in larger companies.
- Get as much education and training in an area of critical demand as you can, regardless of company size.

quer. But the situation will become even more pressured as customers get involved in "co-construction" or product development. In order to constantly develop new products that are better and cheaper than what came out last week, companies will have to form alliances or joint ventures, even with their competitors, simply to afford the necessary research and development. So, in looking for an employer, you'll want to focus on those companies that are committed to research and development and looking for creative ways to finance and share it.

Training and Competitiveness

The new structure of corporations, an environment of constant change, and the increasing need for flexibility means that training will be crucial to competitiveness. If a shortage of appropriately skilled workers exists in the marketplace, large companies must either train new employees or move to markets where trained employees are plentiful. Since it's not always possible to simply get up and move, companies often invest in

BULLETIN BOARD

TIPS

➤ Annual reports and prospectuses provide a good source of information about a company's competitiveness, as does the performance of its shares. However, read a company's information intelligently and don't rely only on traditional measures of performance. In *Shifting Gears: Thriving in the New Economy,* economist Nuala Beck recommends examining a number of less traditional or well-known measurement standards, such as the ratio between a company's stock price and number of patents, its *research-to-development ratio, research-to-patent ratio,* and *technology-to-spending ratio.* The higher the ratio, the more likely the company will survive in the future, since the more research, the more patents; the more patents, the more products; and the more products, the more future business. The *research-to-patent ratio* measures how productive the research spending is, while the amount of the company's spending devoted to purchasing technology is a measure of the company's overall commitment to entering the new information technology era. Since the new economy is where prosperity lies, it's also crucial to know what percentage of the company's business is directed to the new economy. Moreover, given the global competitiveness characteristic of these industries, you need to know the firm's *export ratio* (percentage of sales exported) and its *global market penetration* (world market share). The number of countries exported to and the size of these markets reveals the diversification of the company's risk and its potential for growth.

educating existing staff. Here, large corporations have an advantage because they're more likely to be able to afford training for their staff. A few examples: Uniroyal Chemical Ltd. recently introduced a three-year apprenticeship program in conjunction with Ontario's Skills Development Branch; the Canadian Imperial Bank of Commerce spends between $180-250 million annually on staff training; and employees of Canada West Insurance Company and The Canadian Surety Company receive a $1,000 bonus for attending classes one morning a week, $3,000 plus tuition for completing a three-year community college program, and up to $8,000 for becoming actuaries.

While a company's training policy may look impressive on paper, it is imperative that the operation actually do what it sets out to do—make you competitively skilled and the company more productive. Jim Clemmer, author of *Firing On All Cylinders: The Service/Quality System for High-Powered Corporate Performance*, believes that "most organizations use their training investments about as strategically as they deploy their office supplies spending...One of the biggest causes of wasted training dollars is ineffective methods...Another way of wasting dollars is failing to link training with organizational strategies and day-to-day management behaviour." Training must be followed up with on-the-job support, helping employees consolidate and build on the training. For example, for every dollar invested in training, Motorola achieved a $33 return in increased productivity in plants where there was management follow-up, but a negative return on investment in plants where there was none; Xerox found that trainees only retained 13 percent of their training if there was no follow-up.

A very effective approach to training is the "cascading" method employed by Finning Ltd. in Vancouver, British Columbia, the world's largest Caterpillar dealer: senior management is the first to receive service and quality training, and they in turn train those below them. To ensure everyone practises what they preach, Calgary's Western Gas Marketing Ltd. uses an appraisal system that makes managers responsible for ensuring the principles taught are applied on the job.

When you are considering a prospective employer, inquire about its training, follow-up, and evaluation practices.

Working in Unionized Companies

Unionized companies will probably not be the most promising places to work. As a rule, unions function best when the economy is stable or expanding, but during tough economic times, unions often have trouble protecting their members. Since unions will fight hard against lowering salaries so that a company can hire more people, chances of finding jobs in unionized companies are slim. Even if work in a unionized company is available, remember that seniority determines who stays and who goes: if you were the last one in, you'll be the first one out. Therefore, it may make sense for the job hunter to look for a job in a non-unionized environment.

If you are interested in working for a unionized company, whether as a union member or in management, be sure to research the company's history with the union. Bad management-union relations can seriously damage a company's competitiveness. Eventually, unions and management may have no choice but to cooperate—a refreshing change for both sides. If that happens, unions will place a greater emphasis on company training and may have to relinquish seniority in favour of proven competence as a means of deciding who stays and who goes during layoff periods. Ultimately, it's vital that unions not undermine a company's ability to remain competitive. That will require considerable flexibility on both sides.

The Job Interview

By researching a prospective employer, you can get a good idea of how competitive the company is. The job interview is another opportunity to investigate. If the company is well run, management will appreciate informed and intelligent questions and be impressed that you understand competitive issues.

KEY QUESTIONS TO ASK PROSPECTIVE EMPLOYERS

- How big is the company? What is its growth potential?
- Who are the company's major competitors?
- What is the outlook for the industry as a whole? What are the major determining forces affecting the industry's and company's future?
- How does the company measure its productivity? How productive is it compared with other companies? What plans are in place to improve productivity? What organizational changes are anticipated as a result?
- How is the company organized? Why has it adopted its particular structure? Is it typical of the industry? Does the company use teams? If so, what kind? Do supervisors, managers, and executives act as effective coaches and team leaders? What guidelines govern team operation?
- Has the company downsized recently? If so, how was this process conducted?
- What role does information technology play in the company? What changes are anticipated in the near future?
- Does the company outsource any of its functions or does it plan to in the future? If so, which functions and why?

- What is the company's relationship with its suppliers? What role does information technology play in the relationship? How could it be improved? Does the company "lend" employees to these companies?
- Has the company formed alliances? With which companies and for what reason?
- Does the company export? If so, to how many countries? If only to the U.S., why?
- How does the company's reward system work? Do reward systems encourage and reinforce high performance? Is pay based on performance? Is there an employee- and management-share ownership plan?
- What opportunities exist for promotion?
- If training is required, does the company provide it? What kind? Who does the training? Is senior management involved in follow-up? In what way?
- Is the company unionized? If so, what kind of relationship does management have with the union? Does the union encourage or accept workplace re-engineering or the introduction of information technology?

CHAPTER FOUR

WHERE THE JOBS ARE IN THE NEW ECONOMY

- **Industry and Product Life Cycles**
- **The Impact of Demographics on Employment**
- **The Focus on Customer Service**
- **Salaries**
- **Jobs in the New Economy**

The potential for inexpensive replication meant that early "knowledge workers"...like Colt or Ford could earn far more from the ideas that they created than even the best craftsmen could [from the articles they made].

PAUL ROMER, UNIVERSITY OF CALIFORNIA AT BERKELEY

If I introduce a new technology to create a market this morning, I'd better start working on ways to improve it this afternoon. If I don't, someone else will, and my market share will begin eroding by sunset.

RAYMOND SMITH, CEO, BELL ATLANTIC CORPORATION

n the last chapter, we examined what will make companies competitive in the era of technological revolution. Now it's time to look at what your actual career prospects will be.

In this chapter, we're going to examine where the jobs are in the "new economy," a term coined by economist Nuala Beck. In her book, *Shifting Gears: Thriving in the New Economy,* Beck points out that while most of us have been preoccupied with the recession, a major shift has happened in the way our economy operates. The industries Canadians relied on in the past to provide jobs—natural resources industries such as mining and forestry, for example—are no longer the main engines of growth in our economy. Beck estimates that 70 percent of Canadians are already employed in the industries that make up the new economy—such as telecommunications, computer hardware and software, robotics, and pharmaceuticals—and asserts that it is these industries that will drive our economic growth. Before we take a detailed look at each of these industries, let's consider some aspects of the "new economy" and how it will affect working life.

Every economic phase presents obstacles that have to be overcome before a subsequent phase can begin. Once these barriers are overcome—by making a process more efficient, inventing an entirely new process or substance, or enhancing a service of some kind—the rules of the economic game change and new sets of winners and losers emerge. For example, improvements in methods of transportation, communication, and delivery made trade between countries easier (satellite, planes, and computers versus cable, boats, and the mail) which made greater economic development possible and ultimately improved our quality of life. During the industrial revolution, the forging of steel helped make the machine age possible, which in turn helped make mass manufacturing a reality. And the discovery of the transistor paved the way for the invention of the computer chip and the dawning of the new information technology age.

Each of these changes, in turn, has a major effect on the job market, as we can see by looking at the development of the Canadian work force. A century ago, the largest single group of workers outside the home was on the farm. However, starting in the late nineteenth century, farm equipment became mechanized and more labour-efficient, causing the agricultural work force to diminish from 40 percent to four percent of the overall work force by 1975. The actual number of agricultural workers declined as well, so that by 1970 the industry employed only 25 percent as many workers as it did before 1930.

The biggest percentage growth in the work force has been among white-collar workers. In 1900, they formed only 20 percent of the work force, yet by 1965, approximately 50 percent were white-collar workers. And by 2020, over 75 percent of the work force will be white-collar—partly because of growth in the service industries.

Meanwhile, blue-collar jobs will almost disappear. So far, the decline in jobs in this sector, because of improvements in manufacturing technology, has been gradual (from a peak of 46 percent in the 1940s to 38 percent in the 1980s). But the downhill slide is gathering momentum. By 2020, blue-collar workers will represent only 20 percent of the work force, applying their skills to the maintenance and repair of automated machinery. Unlike the blue-collar workers of the past, these will be highly skilled college graduates trained in the use of sophisticated technology, more properly considered white-collar. Eventually, even these jobs will probably be decimated by technology. Indeed, Jean-Claude Paye, secretary-general of the Organization for Economic Co-operation and Development (OECD), predicts that eventually only two percent of those employed in developed nations will be working in manufacturing and just one percent will be employed in agriculture.

However, with the emphasis on information and technology, white-collar professionals should continue to be in demand, and a new group, "paraprofessionals," will emerge. With scientific knowledge doubling every six to ten years, professionals will have to acquire more specialized skills and delegate their routine duties to "paraprofessionals"—workers in the same field, but with less training. By the year 2000, it's expected that the number of paraprofessionals and professionals will exceed 20 percent of the work force, making these knowledge workers the most prominent segment of the work force as the more traditional manufacturing and labouring jobs continue to disappear. These new technicians are more technology-oriented than machine-oriented; they include medical technologists, materials scientists, nuclear technicians, broadcast engineers, air traffic controllers, and paralegals.

A more ominous change that may be in store for Canadians is the development of a two-tiered society of "haves" and "have-nots."

Economists worry that, as low-skilled, well-paid blue-collar jobs disappear, those with little education will be forced to take low-paying jobs in the service sector that may be part-time and offer no benefits or security— flipping hamburgers is the nightmare most frequently cited. Society will divide between well-paid, relatively secure "haves" and an underclass of "have-nots" who drift between jobs with little financial security and plenty of anger. Such a division would create major social disruption and a challenge to Canadians' traditional values of fairness, optimism, and community well-being.

Although the transition will be far from smooth or consistent, eventually all industries will be influenced by the explosion in technology. Traditional industries will incorporate new technology to become more competitive. And the various technologies have become businesses in their own right—think, for example, of the giant computer software companies that didn't even exist 20 years ago.

Industry and Product Life Cycles

Another important feature of the technological revolution will be a shortening in product life cycles. Products go through a life cycle comprising five phases: the growth or market acceptance phrase; the bandwagon phase; the peak or turning point phase; the declining phase; and the mature phase.

During the growth phase, consumers know about the product and its usefulness and are buying it in increasing numbers. Products such as CD-ROMs, multimedia products, new software, recycled paper products, transdermal drugs, environmental consulting, and fine wire currently fall into this category. During the next phase—the bandwagon phase— demand for the product is increasing and there are not enough companies to fully satisfy demand. The product's price tends to rise or level off as companies cash in on the popularity of the product. Many other companies jump on the bandwagon to try to get in on the higher profits realized during this phase. Video dating, video games, high resolution televisions, cellular phones, mutual funds, registered retirement savings plans (RRSPs) fall into this category. During the peak or turning point phase, the market is saturated with the product and growth slows. Too many companies are competing for the same customers in a shrinking market, and so prices fall. Products in this phase include Walkmans and their competitors, older established software, microwaves and—before too long—cellular phones. During the declining phase, sales and prices decrease as companies, desperate to hang on to their share of a shrinking market, slash prices. Everyone in the industry knows that a shakeout is in progress and that not all of the players will survive. This has been happening in the computer mainframe business. After the shakeout, the product enters the mature phase, when just enough companies have survived to provide products to meet demand. Prices are stable and growth is slow since the product has been around for some time, and business consists of satisfying existing demand, as in insurance and breakfast cereals, or is repeat business, as in automobiles, refrigerators, and stoves. Although growth is typically slow during this phase, it is possible to generate a new product life cycle by introducing new variations—a new form of insurance to protect software, for example—or by making improvements to existing products.

Industries as a whole also go through phases of growth and decline. For example, most of Canada's natural resource industries are in the declining or mature phase, while telecommunications and communications, medical technology, pharmaceuticals, biotechnology, environmental technology, software, video, and instrumentation are all in the growth phase. Almost all of the growth industries are technologically based. Thus, the driving force behind the new economy is technological innovation, which is creating new applications and decreasing the price of its key component, computer chips, while also making them more powerful; this, in turn, makes new applications possible, and so on, in a self-perpetuating cycle. Technology's capacity to continuously renew and upgrade itself means we are about to witness one of the longest self-sustaining growth cycles ever in these industries.

Ironically, that industrial growth cycle will be sustained by briefer and briefer product life cycles. With technology advancing by leaps and bounds, technological product life cycles are already becoming progressively shorter. The computer purchased a year ago is already obsolete by today's standards. Companies that rely on technology—virtually all of them, in future—will have to buy those new products in order to remain competitive. And the companies that produce the technology, if they wish to survive, will have to keep inventing newer or improved products in order to keep up with their competitors. The winner will be the company that can get the newest products to the market fastest and most often. According to a 1993 report by Ernst & Young on the computer industry, "More than half of Hewlett Packard's annual revenue ($16.4 billion U.S.) comes from products introduced over the past two years. Likewise, another North American electronics manufacturer attributes more than 80 percent of its annual revenue to products on the market three years or less."

With the development of each new product, there will be a race to produce the one that will set the standard. The company that owns and licenses the standard will dominate the market. For example, fear of losing out to each other or the Japanese in high definition television has driven western companies to cooperate rather than compete in their research and development. As a result, the Japanese, despite decades of research, seem to have been left in the HDTV dust—at least, for the moment.

The competition will be strongest in three different segments of the market: the content of digital transmissions (such as data banks, consumer services, music, books and movies); the delivery of information (over telephone lines, cable television, satellites, or other wireless networks); and the manipulation of information allowing consumers to select and customize the data they want (with operating software, personal computers, hand-held communicators, and television controllers).

Few will enter the race alone; instead, companies will form strategic alliances to share research and market expertise. The strategic alliance that gains the most market share by offering the right combinations of content, delivery, and manipulation, will control the product and service markets.

The Impact of Demographics on Employment

The technological revolution and the job opportunities it offers will also be affected by demographics—by the way various generations age and by the size of the population as a whole.

The so-called baby boom generation is an enormously influential demographic group and will continue to be the driving force in future economic growth. Baby boomers arrived on the scene in the 20 years following the Second World War: approximately one-third of Canada's population was born between 1947 and 1966, the greatest number in 1960. (The U.S. boomers are slightly older, born between 1946 and 1964 and peaking in 1957.) These unruly baby boomers were responsible for rock and roll, the hippie era, student protest, an inflated real estate market, a BMW lifestyle, and, now, cocooning and the championing of family values.

But while they may seem like a demographic monolith, in fact the baby boom should be seen as a range of age groups. Baby boomers are now between the ages of 27 and 47, with the largest group, those born in 1960, 34 years old. The group that appears to have had the greatest influence, the "Woodstock generation," was in fact only the vanguard of the boom—the ones who got there first and so had the greatest opportunities to build their careers and acquire wealth. The group cryptically called Generation X—those now between the ages of 26 and 35—actually represent the peak boomer years. Their large numbers are currently mirrored in their overrepresentation among those now unemployed.

Because baby boomers form such a large but segmented group, a company must try to find out what each sector of boomers is likely to want or need, and focus its marketing efforts on fulfilling these demands. For example, the real estate boom in the late eighties was driven by the first wave of boomers who were 40 years old and wanted to move up in the housing market, but only because, at the same time, there were enough younger boomers wanting to buy their first houses to support a boom. In future, the first wave of boomers will spend a lot of money on high-tech home entertainment and convenience items. The middle boomers will spend money on educational information technology for their kids, and the tail end of the baby boom will be the last ones to buy real estate over the next few years. They will also keep the baby product industry going until about the year 2000.

However, once we get to the "baby busters," people born between 1967 and 1980, the numbers drop. Those aged 15 to 24 declined by 20 percent during the 1980s. Indeed, there would be a shortage of workers at the moment were it not for immigration, which has more than compensated for this period of declining birth rates. The group born since 1980—the "baby boom echo"—has meant better profits in the children's market—clothing, toys, music, and books—and will continue to do so for all markets that follow these children as they grow. Eventually, however, this group will probably produce a surplus of young workers at the beginning of the next decade as they reach working age.

In the second half of the 1990s, we will see the beginning of a tidal wave of emptynester baby boomers as the first of the boomers reach 50. Already, between 1981 and 1991, the number of emptynesters in Canada increased from one million families to 1.5 million families; the number of childless couples rose 13 percent during the same time period to one million families. Consequently, although the total number of families increased 16 percent during this period, from 6.3 million to 7.4 million families, the number of families without children at home increased by 28 percent. This age group is already a powerful economic force. Statistics show that people who are over 50—26 percent of the population—purchase 43 percent of the new domestic cars and 48 percent of the luxury cars; they own 75 percent of all the North American financial assets; they account for 40 percent of all consumer demand; they spend more on health care and personal care products, gamble more, watch more television, join more clubs, and read more newspapers than any other age group; and they eat out three times a week on average. Emptynester buying power will increase as the boomer generation begins to reach 50 years of age in 1997.

What are the characteristics of emptynesters? They fall into two groups: pre-retirement and retirement. Pre-retirement emptynesters no longer have their children living at home and the children are no longer dependent on the parents for support. These emptynester parents, who are approximately 50 years old, are at their peak income-earning power and with the children gone and the mortgage minimal or paid off altogether, their household expenses are low. In addition, their own parents, many of whom were a generation of savers as a result of their having gone through the Great Depression, are nearing the end of their lives and are about to bequeath their life savings to their emptynester children. Consequently, this generation, known as "whoopies" or "well-off older people," will be the wealthiest generation ever until they retire. At the moment, the 50- to 64-year-old age group controls 45 percent of total personal wealth in Canada, with the value of their residences in excess of $230 billion, and their net worth amounting to $550 billion; yet they only represent 12 percent of the population. Over the next 30 years, this group offers an unprecedented marketing opportunity for companies that can offer them the kinds of goods and services they will surely demand.

What are those goods and services? The RRSP and mutual fund markets should triple by the year 2000 and will grow until 2025 and beyond. Pre-retirement emptynesters are sophisticated shoppers and will emphasize value rather than ostentation. No longer needing big homes in which to raise families, they will look to the condominium and townhouse market. Convenience services of all kinds will flourish—home delivery of groceries and quality-cooked meals, other residential services, such as landscaping, renovation and housesitting, and health services. You can expect the members of this generation to treat themselves to all those things they promised themselves once the kids were through college or university and had moved away. Thus, the travel and recreation market will grow, as will the market for luxurious—but not opulent— cars. Cosmetic surgery has increased by 70 percent since 1981. The sale of prescription drugs, eyeglasses, and bifocals are increasing as well, with self-diagnostic health care devices expected to be a $2.5 billion market in North America during the 1990s. Movie attendance by adults over 40 has grown by 81 percent in the past six years; this is the only age group whose attendance has increased. Continuing education has become more popular as, in growing numbers, aging adults take classes related to crafts and hobbies, as well as enrol in university courses. Moreover, many home businesses will be launched by boomers who change careers in their 50s. Post-retirement emptynesters, many of them women, are interested in similar products as the pre-retirement emptynesters, and many will have the leisure time to travel. As they age, they will also form a major market for health and home care.

Demographic effects vary from one region to another. For example, demographic factors will affect employment opportunites in health care in different parts of Canada. Quebec has an earlier average age of death and therefore fewer seniors to care for, so the province's health care system is not subject to as much strain as that of other provinces; Saskatchewan bears a greater health care burden than Quebec since more people live to a ripe old age and there are fewer taxpayers overall. Because the economic boom came later to Newfoundland, there are fewer young children so you will not find a Toys R Us located there, whereas in Saskatchewan the long cold winter nights seem to have led to a large baby boom echo. Unlike Canada, the U.S., New Zealand, and Australia, Europe did not experience a baby boom. Few children were born during the Second World War, for obvious reasons, and after the war many young Europeans emigrated to North America. Since the peak year for having children in Europe was 1939, companies hoping to take advantage of the emptynester phenomenon in Europe would find that on average the market is made up of people ten years older than their Canadian counterparts. In Japan, the fertility rate plummeted as a response to the dropping of the atomic bombs. In Russia, where the size of an individual's apartment was determined by the number of children in the family, birth rates stayed high, which led to high levels of unemployment among young people.

Even the dramatic changes occurring in organizational structures are partly a result of changing demographics. In the 1950s, the population was pyramidal in shape with fewer older people at the top, and corporate structures reflected that social reality. But since baby boomers have now reached the age where they might traditionally expect to be in charge, it's necessary to reshape the organizational structure to accommodate all the middle-aged executives who can't find room at the top. For these employees, career challenge and increased salary will come not by promotion but by lateral moves that offer the opportunity to acquire new skills and be rewarded for them.

Competitiveness, productivity, and prosperity depend in many ways on demographic-related factors. As noted by Christopher Patten, governor of Hong Kong, "You cannot afford to let your rate of population increase trim too much off your economic growth. Over the past 100 years, Japan grew at an average of four percent a year, almost four times the annual rate of her population increase." The point Patten is making is that the more a country produces, while still keeping its population low, the more there is for everybody. The Japanese made up for their lower fertility rate and the smaller work force that resulted by inventing robots and other labour-replacing technologies. In the process, they greatly increased their productivity and the wealth of the slowly growing population. (Although ironically Japan's real estate problems plus high food tariffs mean that many Japanese have a far less comfortable lifestyle than their western neighbours.) However, in a country where population growth is rapid, business tries to create economic growth by keeping wages low. The trouble is, while there may be more money coming in, there's also a growing population, and so there's still the same or less for everyone. A quick look at the populous Brazil, India, and China reveals how difficult it is to have economic prosperity match the rapid increase in population. Improvements in China stem as much from limiting families to one child as from shifting to a capitalist market-based economy.

The Focus on Customer Service

As discussed in Chapter 2, international competition has already forced corporations to put more emphasis on customer service. In the future, with the huge stakes to be won by capturing the public's heart with a particular product, and the ability to serve customers more effectively through technology, companies will continue to focus on the customer.

In the past, focussing on the customer too often meant seducing the unsuspecting and uninformed consumer into buying something unnecessary or inferior. Marketing continues to be haunted by the stereotype of the brash used car salesman. More recently, many service companies have developed the more positive have-a-nice-day variety of customer service. But while efforts to create a friendlier atmosphere should be applauded, true customer service is far more sophisticated.

In successful corporations, sales and marketing has already shifted its focus from trying to sell consumers products they don't need to finding out what the customer does need and providing the goods or services cost-effectively. Increasing global competitiveness demands that workers not only come up with innovative ways of meeting a customer's needs, but also that they anticipate problems and come up with solutions. Employees become intermediaries, informing customers about the value of their company's product while also convincing the company of the validity of their customers' needs. Even those employees who don't ordinarily deal directly with customers are encouraged to keep the customer ever in mind and constantly seek information on trends in demand. Companies that focus on customer needs find it much easier to make priorities clearer throughout the organization. The increase in outsourcing means that customer service will be an even bigger theme than in the past, as more and more companies begin to deal with one another on a customer-supplier basis. Meanwhile, information technology makes this shift in focus possible by taking on many of the ordering, accounting, processing, and internal and external communication tasks, thereby freeing up personnel for marketing, which is the wealth-generating side of the business.

The emphasis on customer service is good news for people whose main strength is in marketing and who may be wondering where they fit into a high-tech future. Indeed, customer service has become so important that often the fastest means of promotion is through the demonstration of sales and marketing ability. High-tech companies are interested in hiring individuals who are not only technically competent but who also have the attributes essential for selling: initiative, flexibility, good communications skills, energy, and versatility. According to recruitment coordinator Dave Uez of NCR Canada Ltd., sales is "the best route to senior management." Ken Gravelle, staff development manager for Xerox, echoes this belief: "Every one of our vice-presidents and all senior staff in every department, including personnel, have experience in the selling field."

At successful corporations, the importance of sales is reflected by thorough in-house sales training. Xerox sales recruits receive a minimum of six months of basic sales training before they go on to the company's international headquarters in Leesberg, Virginia, for three weeks of intensive training. According to Jo Currie, a contributing editor to *Career Options*, "IBM, NCR, and GE [General Electric] all have highly structured programs for new recruits, involving classroom time, on-the-job training supervised by experienced employees, and self-study. Salaries while training ranged from $28,000 to $32,000." The skills, education, or training that accompanies sales ability will vary according to the industry. The less technical the industry, the more likely that business graduates of various kinds will find entry-level sales positions. Since most entry-level jobs are available on small teams or in small businesses, job seekers would be well advised to develop an entrepreneurial spirit. Those who combine an entrepreneurial drive with advanced degrees in business and a technical area have an excellent chance of becoming vice-presidents of any growing smaller company within five years. Indeed, those with computer literacy and finance or marketing skills—the "gold collar workers"—often get to write their own job ticket.

Salaries

The technological revolution brings with it a host of factors that will influence salaries. However, many of the old reliable rules will still be around.

Salary will still be at least partially determined by: education or training level; experience; industry life cycle phase; competition; degree of leadership and responsibility; complexity of skills employed; individual performance; gender dominance in occupation area; industry unionization; comparative global salaries; corporate structure; and demographics.

In major cities, college graduates earn roughly $20,000-30,000 for an entry-level position; undergraduates, between $25,000-30,000; and postgraduates, between $30,000-45,000. Growth industries that require skilled workers are obviously going to pay more than mature industries that are trying to cut costs. In industries going through a shakeout phase, competition for jobs is the stiffest and salaries are likely to be lower as a result. In general, the lower the skills and training required in a position, the higher the level of competition. At the other extreme are many jobs that require high-skilled, experienced workers but cannot be filled because of a lack of qualified candidates. Anyone who can fit the criteria for one of these jobs can expect a healthy paycheque.

Governments, burdened by overwhelming deficits, will keep the salaries of government workers and other public service employees at current or reduced levels for some time. Certain jobs will simply be cut back, regardless of how much the public may need those services, creating an oversupply of workers that will keep wages low. For example, expect the pay for daycare and eldercare workers, health care aides, and registered nursing assistants to stay low, even though demand is likely to increase in these areas and the medical responsibilities in outpatient settings will expand to include services previously provided by hospitals. The salaries for these positions also reflect a gender bias, which has led businesses, institutions, and governments to pay lower salaries in careers dominated by women.

The more unionized an industry, the higher the wages will likely be. However, it will be increasingly difficult to find jobs in unionized companies, since management will try to replace experienced workers with technology, through restructuring jobs, or moving to a non-union setting.

More and more, non-unionized workers will find their salaries tied to performance, both theirs and the company's. The move to outsourcing and hiring temporary or contract workers is management's attempt to avoid permanent employee-related costs, such as pensions and workers' compensation, and to sidestep the formation of unions among their workers. Temporary employees will be paid only for what they can bring to the company, and they must hone their skills to survive. According to Massachusetts Institute of Technology (MIT) economist Lester Thurow, those with Third World skills will make a Third World wage.

Salary levels shift and change as companies re-engineer so that greater responsibility is assumed by frontline workers and middle managers disappear. In the past, an executive position implied greater responsibility and skill and automatically led to higher pay. In the future, it will be what a worker actually does to complete a project, rather than a title and the competence that's assumed to go with it, that determines his or her pay. Those who are willing and able to take on a variety of challenging knowledge-based tasks and play a leadership role will likely earn more than those who have more limited job descriptions.

In the flattened corporation, raises and promotions—and the higher salaries attached to them—are increasingly being replaced by lateral moves and non-financial rewards: more pats on the back, one-shot bonuses, and non-cash perks like counselling programs, training opportunities, flexible work schedules and casual dress rules. In a survey of 3,200 companies conducted in 1993 by William M. Mercer Inc., a compensation consulting firm, 60 percent of the companies surveyed now reward this way as opposed to 20 percent in 1988.

Demographics has played a large part in both hiring and setting salaries. Generation X undoubtedly feels that time was not on its side, whereas the early baby boomers grew up in a time of abundant opportunity and rapid salary increases. Ironically, the generation following Generation X is now in its teens and by the year 2000 will encounter labour shortages and rising wages in many new economy positions.

Jobs in the New Economy

Dividing jobs into "old economy" and "new economy" jobs does not necessarily mean that the former are vanishing while the latter expand. Old economy industries will apply new technology to keep themselves and their products competitive. We'll look at the job prospects for these industries in Chapter 5. For the moment, let's consider jobs in new economy industries—the telecommunications industry, the computer and software industry, instrumentation, robotics and research and development, medical technology, pharmaceuticals, biotechnology and health care, and environmental industries. Approximately seven out of ten Canadians are currently employed in information technology-based industries, which in turn support 120 different supply industries. These industries are largely in the growth phase, and all are underpinned by heavy investment in information technology and its applications. Despite their status as growth areas, these industries are extremely competitive because such potentially large global markets are up for grabs. These are knowledge-intensive areas, and require individuals proficient in science and technology. Although individual employers may rise and fall because of a high level of competition, long-term career prospects in these industries are excellent since all these industries will experience prolonged periods of economic growth and prosperity. These industries also afford opportunities for professional development and advancement and the possibility of moving elsewhere in Canada or the world, and although there is no guarantee of job security with a particular company, there will likely always be a job somewhere in the industry. Individuals employed in these new economy industries will only experience short periods of unwanted unemployment.

WHERE THE JOBS ARE IN THE TELECOMMUNICATIONS INDUSTRY

According to Columbia University's Center for Telecommunications and Information Studies, the global telecommunications industry is larger than either the computer or aerospace industries. It's a $700 billion business worldwide, with Canada cornering $21 billion of this market. Although it only represents 2.7 percent of our gross national product, the industry's annual growth rate is estimated to be six percent to seven percent, and is growing twice as fast as any other industry in Canada as a percentage of the gross domestic product. Not only do more people work in the communications and telecommunications industry than in the forestry industry in British Columbia, but the telecommunications industry is larger than Canada's petroleum and mining industries combined! The Department of Industry, Science and Technology reports that there are 185,000 people working in this field, the majority of whom live in Ontario and Quebec.

In 1992, the worldwide telecommunications equipment industry was worth approximately $110 billion (U.S.), with Northern Telecom Ltd.

holding a 7.5 percent share of the business. This industry manufactures terminal and mobile equipment, electronic components, switching equipment, satellite and microwave systems, transmission products, PBXs, telephones, and copper and fibre optic cables, employing 50,000 workers in Canada and generating $6 billion in business annually. Northern Telecom is the largest manufacturer of telecommunications equipment, and is responsible for supplying most of the nation's telephone terminals and central office equipment. This multinational corporation employs over 20,000 Canadians, most of whom live in Ontario, and has 50 plants located worldwide. The mid-sized companies in telecommunications manufacturing include Newbridge Networks Corp., Mitel Corporation, Spar Aerospace Limited, Toshiba of Canada Ltd., Motorola, and Gandalf Data Limited. Unfortunately, because many of these companies have been automating, their work forces have been

NOR-TEL JOBS

Many knowledge-intensive positions in the telecommunications industry will require university degrees. You would certainly need a university education to apply for the following high-tech positions were recently posted by Northern Telecom for its Data Networks business (global enterprise and public networks combining cell, router, and multiplexor functionality) and its Broadband data and switching markets (utilizing ATM, frame relay, and other broadband techniques). Indeed, you almost need a degree simply to understand the job titles: business development, commercial marketing, software implementation, software design, data communications object-oriented design and implementation, magellan performance engineering, real-time system design, system architecture, hardware design, high-speed interconnect, CAD-based ASIC and PCB design synthesis and simulation, network management, digital logic design, system testing, technical support, fiber optic interconnect design, protocol test methodologies, BIST DFT methods, ATM communication protocols, and routing protocols. System and software positions required experience with one or more of the following: data communications, real-time POSIX-based systems, C, C++, Declarative languages, Smalltalk, UNIX, Pascal, System Architecture, X.25, Routers, Bridges, Hubs, Multiplexor, and Network Architecture.

shrinking. So, where are the jobs in this industry?

Many telecommunications jobs will be available in companies that make extensive use of telecommunications equipment and services. These "end-users" include industries such as broadcasting, manufacturing, finance, newspaper publishing, health care, education, and retailing. A company's relationship with its suppliers, customer service, and operation management increasingly depend on a flexible communications system that is continually improving. Jobs in the telecommunications industry often vary according to what use the technology is put to within a company and the size of the company itself. While office administrators might oversee the implementation and operation of a local area network (LAN) or telephone switching system, a dispatcher for a trucking company might coordinate and monitor a fleet's whereabouts via satellite. Larger firms often hire specialists for particular aspects of the purchasing, managing, implemention, and training aspects of telecommunications voice and data systems. Canadian banks spend more than four percent of their revenue on telecommunications services and often hire dozens of workers to operate this technology. To appreciate the many telecommunications employment opportunities available in banking in Canada and internationally, one has only to think of the many electronic innovations pioneered by banks: electronic funds transfer, multibranch banking, home banking, automatic teller machines (ATMs) and, recently, imaging technology. The Hongkong Bank of Canada, whose parent bank is one of the ten largest financial institutions in the world, participates in six international ATM worldwide networks that provide customers access to over 100,000 machines; corporate customers can access global accounts electronically, then carry out any banking transaction worldwide; letters of credit can be created electronically by customers who can also communicate with their banks through electronic mail.

With more than $720 million spent on telecommunications research and development in 1992, many jobs will be available in this continually expanding field. Of the researchers hired in the industry in that year, 3,100 hold bachelor's degrees; 1,250, master's degrees; and 305, doctoral degrees. Jobs are also available for those with less training: 1,100 individuals provide administrative support and an additional 1,000 provide technical support. Remember, too, that there are many non-technical jobs associated with any growing industry, in such areas as finance, marketing,

BULLETIN BOARD

- **Job demand factors**: telecommunications is the fastest-growing industry thanks to the growth of computer networks and the globalization of trade.
- **Job growth areas**: electrical engineering; communications; technical support; end-user support; database support; education; operations; administration; law; sales.
- **Skills, abilities, qualities, education needed**: college diploma or university degree in electronic engineering, electronic engineering technology or computer sciences; strong logical and problem-solving abilities; systems thinking.
- **Job reduction areas**: telephone operators; switchboard operators; receptionists; information personnel; telephone order takers; telecommunications technology will also eliminate jobs in retailing and hotels relying on business travel.
- **Growth limiting factors**: adoption of common standards for data transmission; installation of optical fibre; ability to form alliances; and government regulations.
- **Issues:** the race to establish a global standard will lead to a breakneck pace of research and development. Who will win—telephone, cable or satellite companies? Pay close attention to ongoing developments.

administration, and data entry.

Given the convergence of a number of technologies, the telecommunications industry faces a challenging future. Telephone, cable, cellular, and television boundaries will disappear and so will some of the players in an inevitable industry shakeout. Indeed, a fierce struggle for survival is taking place at the moment, with companies being forced to globalize in order to meet end-user demands for one-stop worldwide service. Customers are increasingly demanding integrated services throughout the world. Competition has intensified now that customers are buying quality, low-cost communications equipment and materials worldwide. Since many manufacturers are having trouble generating the capital needed for research and development, many joint ventures and mergers and acquisitions are inevitable. When a competitor like AT&T has, in

BULLETIN BOARD

TIPS

> A certificate in telecommunications can be obtained from Ryerson University in Toronto or by taking the program on a part-time basis at a number of community colleges. College technology programs focus on the operation and maintenance of systems, whereas design and development positions require a combination of software engineering and electrical engineering. Other combinations of courses that have resulted from the merging of computers and telecommunications include information management and industrial engineering for application-related jobs, while information management and law prepares the job seeker for employment in regulatory agencies such as the Canadian Radio-Television and Telecommunications Commission (CRTC). Additional educational and training information can be obtained by contacting the Telecommunications Department, Ryerson Polytechnic Institute, 350 Victoria St., Toronto, M5B 2K3 or telephone 416-979-5000, ext. 6740.

> Industry journals such as *Network World* and *Computing Canada* are good sources of information about recent developments in this rapidly changing field.

CONTACTS

➤ Canadian Business Telecommunications Alliance
202, 15 Toronto St.,
Toronto, ON M5C 2E3
Tel. 416-847-2570 Fax: 416-865-0859

addition to its $15-16 billion equipment business, a $50 billion service business to draw upon for cash flow, obviously smaller companies can only survive if they band together to share resources.

With the industry globalizing its ventures, many companies like SR Telecom Inc. of Montreal export telecommunications systems to developing countries. Given the worldwide push to make telephones accessible to everyone, many companies will export telecommunications systems to developing countries. There will be plenty of opportunity for exporting to the many countries that will go directly to cellular and digital systems, skipping the copper wire telephone stage altogether. With this in mind, avoid seeking employment in companies that are largely domestic or that trade with only one other country. These companies will either go out of business or be subject to a merger or acquisition, which could mean that you get downsized out of a job. If you are about to join a telecommunications company, ask what its strategy is on joint ventures and future markets. For example, because Newbridge Networks anticipated the impending shift to multiplexors (sophisticated electronic switchers typically used by banks and other large institutions) six months ahead of its competition, it now serves 80 telephone companies in 60 countries, with exports accounting for 90 percent of its sales. It also developed its products around universal telephone company standards, making networks easier to divide among different customers, and has entered the ATM market, which is a future growth area.

WHERE THE JOBS ARE IN THE COMPUTER AND SOFTWARE INDUSTRY

While the computer and software industry surpassed the chemical industry in 1991 to become the largest in North America, with sales of $322 billion in the U.S., the next two years were not kind to it. It has seen profits fall, fierce price wars, flat sales, and thousands of jobs eliminated. At the same time, personal computer makers, such as Dell Computer Corporation, saw their quarterly sales rise by 129 percent and their profits by 77 percent. Similarly, profits for Microsoft. rose by 53 percent. According to *Career Pathways*, a U.S. career magazine, "Twenty years ago, there were 50,000 computers installed worldwide. Today, more than 50,000 computers are installed every day."

The products of the computer industry are becoming more or less interchangeable; witness the proliferation of hardware and software companies. Soon, the only differences between products will be price, profit margins, and marketing strategy. Dell is successful, for example, because the company sells its computers directly, not through a retailer or a sales force. As a result, Dell was able to keep prices lower than its competitors. It is unusual for an innovative high-tech business to produce such a uniform product; however, once a standard has been established, all products tend to conform to the standard. In the case of the personal computer market, the architecture of IBM computers became the industry standard for the clone market. Once an operating system becomes a standard, all software firms design their application software to conform to this standard. For this reason, the products are very much alike or commodity-like.

As discussed in the section on product life cycles, once the market stops growing, the focus shifts to cost cutting as a shakeout takes place. Revenues from the sales of computers for white-collar computer workers, who are the biggest users of computers, have been level in the U.S. since 1983, have just leveled off in Europe and Asia, and will level off in developing countries within a few years. This is partly because the price of computing power—memory size plus clock speed plus operating system efficiency plus software capability—dropped by at least 30 percent annually. As computer components became cheaper, thanks to research and development, more companies that produced clones could afford to enter the market, and profits fell with the increased competition. Although annual computer sales run at about $300 billion worldwide, most potential buyers already have a computer of some sort. IBM anticipates that the computer hardware business will not match world economic growth in general. According to a 1993 report on the industry by McKinsey and Co., a management consulting firm, "Just surviving will be a struggle and even many of today's healthy companies could become extinct."

The software and services side of the industry, however, are expected to grow 11 percent to 13 percent a year worldwide from 1993 to 1997. The software industry has more room to grow because of the infinite number of possible applications. The $60 million a year 3-D software market is expected to increase 30 percent annually over the next five years; 2-D software editing and special effects software, allowing home users to make their own movies, will be worth $450 million annually.

Of Canada's 150,000 software workers, two-thirds are in-house employees—working for banks, insurance companies, real estate firms, government, the wholesale and retail trade—and one-third are employed in the software industry itself, with growth rates of 20 percent annually anticipated for software companies and five percent for in-house software workers. There are companies that manufacture and market software such as Cognos Inc.'s PowerHouse database or Corel's draw products; approximately 12,000 individuals are currently employed in this area.

Other software companies may design "embedded software" which is needed for inclusion in other products. IBM and Northern Telecom are involved in this aspect, though this software is needed in all manufacturing sectors—CAE Electronic flight simulators and Spar Aerospace CANADARM, for example. Approximately 7,000 workers are active in this aspect of the industry. Information technology service companies such as DMR Group Inc. and SHL Systemhouse Inc. operate as systems integrators and project consultants, while smaller consulting firms undertake more specific application projects; there are 33,000 software workers in this field.

Even though IBM continues to lay off staff, the company is nonethe-

---

HOW THE CANADIAN COMPUTER INDUSTRY RATES...

In 1992, the Canadian computer industry earned $10 billion or roughly three percent of the world's information technology revenue, thereby putting Canada in seventh place. The hardware category earned $6.1, with mainframes declining five percent but single-user systems (networks) increasing three percent. The software industry earned $1.4 billion: application solutions, accounting for $360 million in revenue, grew by 18 percent; application tools grew by 16 percent and generated $470 million in sales; and system/utilities grew by 13 percent, for $590 million in sales. Overall, Canada came in ninth with respect to software sales. The services market, which consists of hardware maintenance and professional services (consulting and design, systems implementation, education, training, and facilities management) realized $2.5 billion in sales or a nine percent growth rate (professional services grew by 17 percent). Software Productivity Research Inc., a U.S. company which measures quality and productivity for clients worldwide, rated Canada's productivity in creating management information software—payroll systems, billing, and accounting, for example—fourth. Canada rates third in productivity of maintenance and enhancement of programs—restructuring, reverse engineering, and re-engineering old programs. Canada came in second in software quality and defect levels, but did not make the top ten in systems software, where Japan and the U.S. were first and second respectively. Overall, Canada is fifth, with Japan in the number one spot, and the U.S., seventh.

less hiring software workers. Software represents $2.8 billion in business for IBM. In Canada, 1,500 of its 10,000 employees work in the software side of the industry. The two software products IBM now specializes in are compilers and database managers, both of which are sold globally. Given that there are 140 million personal computer users worldwide and only 30 million large mainframe computer users, IBM will very likely shift its focus to the multitask work station side of the business.

Individuals who hold a master's degree in computer science or computer engineering will have very little trouble finding positions in the software industry. However, in-house software users are not necessarily computer-trained and, as a result, many will be laid off unless they retrain. The Chevron Corporation, for example, notified all 2,300 of its information technology workers in November 1992, that there would be a restructuring and that the company would require only 1,800 employees who could handle the newly adopted personal computers and networks. Fortunately, the federal government and many companies that use information technology plan to spend $12 million over the next three years upgrading the skills of 15,000 Canadian software workers. The knowledge and skills requirements of information service workers are similar to those of software workers, though at a lower technical level. These workers often perform a variety of functions that are not necessarily computer-related. Job titles include programmer, systems analyst, end-user support, project manager, and maintenance personnel.

Individuals interested in pursuing a career in the computer industry will need to continually upgrade their skills to keep pace with the latest developments. Two worldwide trends include the diverging of information technology companies into either technology manufacturers or technology providers, with some technology manufacturers moving over to become providers—Control Data Systems Canada and Unisys Canada Inc., for example—and the segmentation of the industry into value-added chain segments—support and maintenance, distribution channels, applications software, software tools and utilities, system software, processors, and peripherals—with intense competition in each chain segment. The increasing diversity and segmentation within the industry means individuals contemplating a career in the software industry must specialize. At the moment there is some confusion over job titles, but these are gradually being standardized. As with any growing and expanding industry, there are many spin-off job areas that do not necessarily involve programming. There are jobs for individuals who are skilled in administration, finance, law, client services, sales, and marketing. Job seekers interested in the marketing side of the industry should be wary, however; according to a report by the Information Technology Association of Canada entitled "Doing More With Less," hundreds of marketing jobs in the computer industry have disappeared now that U.S. parent companies are often assuming this function as a cost-cutting measure.

The training side of the software industry represents a job growth area. Since a shortage of appropriately trained software workers is anticipated in the future, community colleges and private training institutes have taken advantage of this prediction to offer crash courses in programming. The Institute of Computer Studies, Toronto, Ontario, for example, offers an immersion course which claims to condense a regular three-year college program into five months. Students are required to eat, breathe, and sleep computer training during their five months of computer boot camp. Many of the institute's graduates have been hired by companies like Bell Canada, Sun Life Assurance Company of Canada, Canadian Imperial Bank of Commerce, Air Canada, and Lotus Development Canada Ltd.

At Software Development '93 held in Boston, John Soyring, director of software development for IBM, announced that some of the best career prospects exist in object technology (OT) and distributed client/server computing. He made this claim because new hardware architectures such as Pentium and Power PC are now extending the capabilities of personal computers for use in distributed computing, as are digital signal processing (DSP) chips and asynchronous transport mode (ATM) network switching. Vendors are laying the groundwork for object technology and distributed computing by creating such standards as DCE (Distributed Computing Environment), DME (Distributed Management Environment) and CORBA (Common Object Request Broker Architecture). Other efforts in this direction include Open Doc, COSE (Common Operating System Environment), and Taligent, which is a combined project of IBM and Apple. Programmers who now begin developing software for these new industry platforms will likely find employment easily, given the head start they will have on other programmers.

According to Peter Ward, a corporate recruiter, the ideal applicant for many growth companies has five to 15 years of experience and is willing to work on contract. Eighty percent of the professionals he now hires are employed on a contract basis. Computer specialists are in short supply, according to Cynthia Lucas of Total EDP Services, a Toronto job placement agency. Shortages exist for SYBASE specialists, database analysts, programmer analysts, and systems analysts with two to six years' experience. Co-op program graduates are considered for these positions, but not college or university undergraduates without previous industry experience.

Training and service have become vital to companies with a desire to maximize their investment in computer technology. According to a research study conducted by Nolan, Norton, & Co., the information technology consulting arm of KPMG Peat Marwick Thorne, the actual cost of personal computing can be as high as $20,000 per machine per year as a result of a hidden cost of $6,000 to $15,000 from the amount of time employees spend showing one another how to get the computer to perform some task. Thus, with 55 percent of the employees in large organizations using computers, serving the information needs of companies will be a lucrative growth area. Xerox expects that by 1995, 50 percent of its revenue will accrue from offering computer services and software information. Employees would phone Xerox to have their software problems solved quickly, instead of wasting the company's time trying to solve a computer problem on their own.

By 1993, 52 percent of all computer sites had adopted open systems, compared with six percent in 1989. By 1995, it is expected that 78 percent of all computer sites will be using open systems. Using open systems directly translates into lower computer training costs. It stands to reason, then, that most companies will adopt open systems and increase spending on training, thereby creating more jobs for the computer literate in the process.

Most software applications jobs will come from solving generic business problems or from making information technology friendlier. Many small software companies get their starts by designing a broad-based application package that is geared to saving companies considerable sums of money over time. Numetrix Ltd. developed a software program for Kraft General Foods Inc. called Schedulex; this program tells Kraft precisely how much of each product the company should produce and in

BULLETIN BOARD

- **Job demand factors:** falling price of computer technology; increased power of personal computers; open system architecture allowing for networks within and among companies; compatible software; and, facilitation of information transfer.
- **Job growth areas:** the software industry and professional services areas; the entertainment industry.
- **Skills, abilities, qualities, education needed:** individuals with advanced skills and experience are eagerly sought by companies around the world; a university degree in computer science, accompanied by co-op learning programs, is strongly recommended; creative software solutions usually require a reasonably good knowledge of the application area—accounting, for example—so expertise in both software and an application area are a plus; business skills are an advantage since most software needs to be designed for new programs, products, services, and organizational forms; ability to work in a team and to solve problems creatively; patience; persistence; logical thinking; attention to detail; flexibility.
- **Job reduction areas:** order or information processing; middle management; information services for those who have not upgraded their skills; publishing and printing other than desktop; inventory staff.
- **Growth limiting factors:** low-cost software developers in India, Israel, Ireland, Mexico, Singapore, Hungary, China, and the Philippines.
- **Issues:** open system versus proprietary system products; increasing commodity-like nature of software and hardware making cost a critical factor; common or compatible technology with suppliers; operating system standards for personal computer and network markets; competition focussing on each segment of the value-added chain network.

what order, with the least amount of inventory, changeovers, and over-time. Manufacturers, hard hit by the recession, are also adopting this software as an industry standard so that they can stop and start production according to the competitive needs of companies, or for meeting the changing needs of consumers. Benchmark Technologies, on the other hand, has devised a software program called Integrated Software Processing Workframe (ISPW) which runs IBM mainframes so as to inte-

BULLETIN BOARD

TIPS

➤ When looking for training, opt for computer co-op programs, since graduates from these programs can usually find work much easier than those who have only taken courses.

CONTACTS

✍ Canadian Business Software Association
#202, 160 Frederick St.,
Toronto, ON M5A 4H9

✍ Information Technology Association of Canada
#402, 2800 Skymark Ave.,
Mississauga ON L4W 5A6 Tel. 416-602-8345 Fax: 416-602-8346

✍ The Canadian Information Processing Society
#205, 430 King St. West,
Toronto, ON M5V1L5 Tel. 416-593-4040 Fax: 416-593-5184

✍ Association for Systems Management
24586 Bagley Rd.,
Cleveland, OH 44138
(chapters in major cities across Canada)

grate different software being used on a mainframe; ISPW makes life easier for the computer programmer, who can apply the process to solve problems arising from the use of software written in different languages. The programmer does not need to be familiar with the different computer languages in order to solve glitches. Once successful, these programs quickly become industry standards.

The bridging of different proprietary computer systems to make them compatible will always be a growth area. When Adobe Systems announced a new software product allowing flawless communication among Apple Macintoshes, IBM-compatibles, and UNIX-based systems, its stock jumped $14 (U.S.) in one week.

Creativity is very often the passport to innovative software development. Fred Cohen, inventor of the phrase "computer virus," is currently working on harnessing the positive potential of these viruses, to create "vampire worms." The "worms" can be used to perform difficult computations after hours by utilizing available processing powers to carry program updates to every node in a network; reduce file corruption; perform hardware diagnosis, software upgrading, and garbage removal; destroy other viruses; and even flash subliminal gentle reminders onto a debtor's system, such as, "Please pay your overdue account at Virtual Reality Inc."

Job seekers must look at the software development industry globally when considering a career in this field. According to the World Bank, companies will often select more than one country when looking for software developers, with India chosen by 53 percent of the companies; Ireland, by 50 percent; and Israel, Singapore, Hungary, Mexico, China, and the Philippines, by 25 percent to 32 percent. India's software exports rose from $10 million during the 1980s to $144 million in 1992, with $350 million predicted by 1995 by India's National Association of Software and Services Companies. China's Electronic Industry Ministry anticipates software export growth from $12 million in 1990 to $200 million by 1995. Whereas Microsoft used to hire 153 of the 160 graduates from the top engineering schools in India in 1983 and bring them to the U.S., it now hires the same graduates but has them remain in India and pays them $400 per month (a UNIX programmer in North America makes an annual salary of $50,000 to $70,000). Data entry and processing jobs are migrating to these countries at an even faster rate, though eventually these jobs will be automated through the use of scanners.

WHERE THE JOBS ARE IN INSTRUMENTATION, ROBOTICS, RESEARCH AND DESIGN

The instrumentation industry is one of the most challenging job growth areas in the new economy. At the most fundamental level, this might include developing the technology used for tracking, distribution, security, and inventory control. Such automatic data collection devices—handheld decoders used to scan retail shelves and transmit inventory information by radio frequency to a computer database, for example—are fast and efficient and constitute significant savings for a company. At the high end of the instrumentation industry lie virtual reality and the most powerful computer chips. The developments in this area have been astounding; indeed, today there is more computing power under the hood of a car than the astronauts had during the first lunar landing.

Just as machine tools formed the basis of the industrial mass manufacturing era, electronic instrumentation is transforming every aspect of manufacturing. The average home already exploits microchip technology in thermostats, security systems, VCRs, microwaves, telephones, fax and answering machines, stereos and compact disk players, and personal computers. The transition from machine tools to instrumentation devices is evident in the size of the markets. In the U.S., the machine tool market is worth $4.2 billion annually compared to the $23 billion annual industrial control device market or the $40 billion modern instrumentation market. The high-tech world of robotics, computer controls, and laser technology has arrived.

Currently, Canadian researchers are working on developing robots with "intelligence systems" that will allow the robots to assist in such complex tasks as brain surgery or virtual reality computer animation. This is certainly a quantum leap beyond the market for all-purpose robots used to make cars or cut down trees. Japanese engineers at the Electrotechnical Laboratory in Tsukuba are letting the electrical hardware of the computer alter its own circuitry as it adapts to the environment. The appropriate task chips are allowed to reproduce or reconfigure more chips on an ongoing basis without needing rewiring for each new task or improvement. When small glitches occur, the robot merely reconfigures its circuits to overcome it. Programmable Logic Devices (PLDs), used to test prototype circuits, will populate a single chip, effectively putting many circuit designers out of business. For example, this kind of robot could work on the ocean floor carrying out a variety of tasks without constant supervision. In the future, robots will work as porters, house cleaners, restaurant workers, educational assistants, receptionists, library assistants, hotel workers, hospital workers, hazardous waste handlers, police workers in dangerous situations, minefield sweepers, firefighters, office-mail deliverers, space-based and earth-bound construction workers, security workers, short-order cooks, babysitters, cashiers, gas station attendants, and travel guest greeters.

Robots fall into three categories: fixed machines, which perform automatic repetitive tasks; field robots, which move around in unstructured environments and often carry out dangerous tasks; and intelligent robots, which employ artificial intelligence to solve problems. Automobile plants are the largest users of fixed robots to perform repetitive, assembly-line tasks such as spot welding, metal cutting, and painting. Component assembly of computers and electronic devices lend themselves to this kind of automation. Fixed robots, while perhaps the least exciting, pose the greatest immediate threat to manufacturing jobs.

While fixed robots have been used in Japan for a long time, circumstances in North America have not been conducive to the wide-scale use of robot technology. In Japan, investment capital was very inexpensive, labour in such short supply that it threatened Japan's export boom, competition among auto manufacturers stiff, unions helpful, engineers plentiful, and top-quality design and production methods a priority. In North America, on the other hand, complications in the 1980s arose as a result of union disagreements, the high cost of investment capital, a decline in new investment in manufacturing, the expense of redesigning factory floors to accommodate robots, and an abundant labour force. The original robots were also beset by problems typical of all products in the early stages of development and use. The upshot was that after some initial enthusiasm, robots were largely discarded among North American companies, while the Japanese have continuously upgraded their robot technology and captured a significant share of the auto market by reducing costs through automation. Nowadays, no manufacturing company capable of utilizing robots can afford not to. If used around the clock, a robot can pay for itself in one year. Factories increase their competitiveness enormously by automating. For example, after automating, Nissan Canada Inc. reduced the 11 months needed to retool its body assembly for model changeover to less than two months and at one-third the cost. The further automating of the FANUC manufacturing plant in Japan in 1982 eliminated roughly half the work force and tripled productivity.

Robots are cost-effective and increase productivity for a number of reasons: they do not require workers' compensation, sick days, vacations, overtime pay, medical plans, unemployment insurance benefits, or retraining programs, which taken together are often a company's largest uncontrolled cost. Moreover, robots do not require specific environmental conditions, they do not get tired, and they can be stringently controlled. "Because their movements are perfectly controlled, they do not waste materials—robot spray painters, for example, use up to 30 percent less paint than human workers," states Paul Kennedy, author of *Preparing for the Twenty-First Century*.

Robots are slowly gaining a foothold in all manufacturing endeavours. Countries that do not quickly adopt robotic technology will head into a long, and likely irreversible, period of manufacturing decline. But those countries that are quickest off the mark in developing and using robotic technology will see their standard of living rise and their economies prosper through export-led growth and increased foreign investment. In 1988, Japan had 176,000 of the 280,000 robots worldwide; Western Europe, 48,000; and the U.S., 33,000.

For a robotics revolution to take hold in any country, the key ingredients are a supply of knowledge workers and an abundance of investment capital. Unfortunately, Canada falls short in both respects.

The limiting factors in the development of robotics technology are computer- and software-related. Once computer chips increase in power and decrease in price—something they are rapidly doing—and artificial and neural software intelligence improve, we will see field robots and androids emerge. According to Maureen Caudill in her book *In Our Own Image: Building an Artificial Person*, "Within 20 years, we will have the knowledge and ability to build androids that look and act in a way most people will consider 'humanlike'....[and] will redefine the measure of mankind." Already "fuzzy logic" technology—technology that can handle ambiguity in meaning and concept yet make the best decision under the circumstances—is entering photography, psychological analysis, monitoring, medicine, and prediction and decision support systems. Even autonomously driven and operated armoured vehicles and flying robots have made their debut.

Before robots come to replace brain surgeons, the latter will be using virtual reality in the form of a probe that will "see" the tumor and tell the surgeon the angle of approach to excise it from the patient's brain. Moreover, medical virtual imaging will allow a doctor to actually see the three-dimensional position of a baby in the mother's womb as ultrasound images are converted to three-dimensional images. Even psychologists will use virtual reality in treating phobias and other mental illnesses. At the moment, surgical instruments are a $10 billion industry. With new developments in virtual reality applications, that number will quickly double. The medical significance of these developments is staggering.

As discussed earlier, the training possibilities and entertainment potential of virtual reality are seemingly endless. The training potential of

BULLETIN BOARD

- **Job demand factors:** the industry has a long period of growth ahead since it is in an early stage of its growth cycle.
- **Job growth areas:** robotics; fluid power and automation; control systems; advanced CAD/CAM and mechanical engineering; any area in need of sensing, monitoring, or control will be an applications growth area—environmental monitoring of ozone, gas emissions, water purity or radiation, for example; chemistry and physics research in laser technology
- **Skills, abilities, qualities, education needed:** creativity; problem-solving and decision-making skills; ability to understand how people interact with technology, along with the ability to translate this understanding into software; scientific curiosity; a high level of education, including, ideally, an electronic engineering degree combined with software expertise, plus an M.B.A.; or mechanical engineering with software and electronic expertise.
- **Job reduction areas:** robots will replace workers in performing many routine functions, particularly where danger, accessibility, or great strength are factors.
- **Growth limiting factors**: life cycle growth determined by cost, integration level, and power of computer chips; appropriate virtual, artificial, and neural software at a reasonable cost; overall cost of laser technology and robots.
- **Issues:** company policy regarding redeployment of those workers displaced; social upheaval as robots replace humans; conflicts with unions.

virtual reality has made the Pentagon's Advanced Research Projects Agency (ARPA) one of the biggest investors in virtual research. Tank warfare from the Gulf War is relived for training purposes, ground crew are taught how to manage aircraft, and pilots are taught how to fly in all weather conditions over different kinds of terrain and land at any airport. Approximately 75 percent of the $50 million spent in 1992 for nonmilitary applications by companies interested in virtual reality was in research and development. Most of the development capital was spent on "experiential prototyping"—a technology that simulates machine parts or

BULLETIN BOARD

CONTACTS

➤ Canadian Council of Professional Engineers
#401, 116 Albert St.,
Ottawa, ON K1P 5G3 Tel. 613-232-2474 Fax: 613-230-5759

➤ Canadian Council of Technicians and Technologists
(for Engineering and Applied Sciences),
285 McLeod St., 2nd Fl.,
Ottawa ON K2R 1A1 Tel. 613-238-8123 Fax: 613-238-8822

➤ Robotics & Automation Society
c/o Electrical and Electronics Engineers, Inc.
PO Box 1331,
Piscataway NJ 08855-1331 USA Tel. 908-981-0060 Fax: 908-981-0027

architectural layouts so that both clients and designers can explore proposed changes before proceeding with construction. For example, parts designed in AutoCAD can be assembled using Autodesk's Cyberspace Developer Kit which consists of a head-mounted display and an airborne or flying mouse. Virtual reality, however, is still in its infancy. As Ben Delaney, editor and publisher of *CybergEdgeJournal*, says, "Virtual reality is where personal computers were in 1979. Personal computers back then were slow. They didn't do much. They crashed a lot. But you could start to see the promise. Ten years later, everything has changed. Virtual reality may have a longer gestation period, but it has the same potential."

Even further down the road lies more sophisticated development in the area of laser technology. Although laser technology has been with us for a while and has entered the home in the form of compact disk players, applications of laser technology are just beginning to emerge. According to Katsumi Tanigaki, research manager for NEC Technologies Canada, "Chemistry and physics are converging, and lasers are at the crossroads." Chemists now use lasers to excite molecules, break chemical bonds, and grow crystals. Laser technology research currently focusses on creating higher-quality thin films for semiconductors, building materials with greater strength and durability, and transforming molecules into recording devices with a thousand times as much storage density as optical disks, and into high-speed optical switches for computers. Physicists currently make use of lasers to isolate atoms, slow them down and examine their behaviour. Eventually such research may lead to the creation of unique atom clusters that will form the basis of new materials, to compress and confine hot plasma in nuclear fusion reactions as a means of making them more efficient, and to construct high-intensity atom beams that will be essential tools in the making of micromachines or miniature devices that can be used as sensors and robots. Once these developments come to fruition, they will revolutionize robotics, pharmacology, product creation, industrial processing, and information technology. Although lasers are still too expensive and crude, manufacturing costs are falling and lasers are quickly improving in power, lifespan, and quality.

Universities and colleges now offer courses in robotics, fluid power and automation technology, control systems, computer assisted design and computer assisted manufacturing (CAD/CAM), laser technology, mechanical engineering, and electronic engineering. All of these fields will grow in importance as part of the instrumentation technology revolution that goes hand in hand with the information technology revolution. Sensing, monitoring, and controlling functions everywhere are increasingly being automated, as are the design processes. Thus, the customizing of applications is proving to be very affordable and the savings or conveniences realized are quickly appreciated. Careers in these fields will flourish all over the world. Individuals who combine software expertise with engineering training will easily find positions in research and development.

There will also be major opportunities in the electronics side of the field, including semiconductor design of integrated circuits.

While today the average Canadian interacts with an average of ten computers a day via cars, entertainment, appliances, and information technology, by the year 2000, an individual will be experiencing an average of more than 1,000 interactions a day. Moreover, every 18 months, silicon chips no larger than a fingernail double the number of components they can contain, thereby opening up endless and exciting possibilities for consumer, business, or industrial use.

WHERE THE JOBS ARE IN MEDICAL TECHNOLOGY, PHARMACEUTICALS, BIOTECHNOLOGY, AND HEALTH CARE

The world market for medical devices was roughly $81 billion in 1990, with an annual projected growth rate of seven percent to the year 2000. Some products can expect annual growth rates of 20 percent. The instrumentation market has already entered the medical technology industry with such technology as CAT scans, radial axial tomography, arthroscopic surgery, magnetic image resonance, and laser surgery, and will eventually enter all aspects of the industry. Despite the recession, the health care industry has been growing rapidly. Canada, which spends $66 billion annually on health care and treatment, has increased its number of diagnostic laboratories, treatment centres, walk-in medical centres, and other specialty clinics, which in turn has increased the need for diagnostic equipment, surgical instruments, pharmaceuticals and low-tech supplies such as surgical dressings. From 1984 to 1991, the aging boomer population created more jobs in the health care sector than in any other industry. As this generation continues to age over the next 15 years, it is expected that health care will rise from its current ten percent of gross domestic product to 15 percent. Encouraged by Bill C-91 which increases patent protection on drugs from ten years to 20, pharmaceutical companies are planning to spend $2 billion in research and development between 1992 and 1996, double the amount spent on research and development between 1987 and 1991. The demand for new diagnostic techniques, medical treatments, and new drugs is a result of the sheer size of the aging boomer population and the rapid technological advances made possible by computerization. With health care authorities trying to reduce costs by promoting greater use of ambulatory care services and shorter inpatient stays, pharmaceutical companies benefit as such strategies are conducive to increasing the use of drug therapy as a cost-effective means of patient treatment. The Canadian Medical Association reported that Canadians now spend over $11 billion on medication, thanks to the rising cost of drugs, which is more than the $10 billion they spend on doctor services.

Fortunately, the health care industry has brought together universities and pharmaceutical, biotechnological and medical companies in order to satisfy the demand for new or improved products and treatments. At the moment, says McGill professor Peter Macklem, in Canada the link between the health industry and academia is perhaps more evident than in any other country. Professor Macklem is also president of Inspiraplex, a federally sponsored "Centre of Excellence" that unites private business and medical research. Six of the 15 networks of Centres of Excellence focus on the health care industry. Both universities and business benefit from this arrangement, with universities getting the much-needed funds and technology transfer royalties for research, and business getting the innovative products the market is demanding. Furthermore, the presence of the networks has encouraged foreign medical companies to increase investment in Canada. For example, Merck Frosst Canada Inc. will be investing $15 million to create a research and development facility in Vancouver close to one the university centres of excellence. The University of Manitoba has done the same in attracting a British respirology company to set up nearby. In order to retain the benefit of research and development carried out in Canada, however, and to build a robust health care industry, Canada must create stricter technology transfer agreements. At the moment, technology initially researched in Canada is subsequently sent back to head offices in other countries where remaining research and development takes place.

Despite the growing demand for health care products and services, deficit-ridden provincial governments have curtailed medical expenditures. Hospitals, forced to do more with less money, are outsourcing many services to specialized clinics; professional administrators have replaced doctors in the running of hospitals, since the emphasis is on improving quality, cutting costs, and reducing the length of time a patient stays in hospital. Given that Canada ranks 18th out of 21 countries in medical cost control and 17th in system performance, health care industries will increasingly make greater use of information technology to improve medical productivity and efficiency. Computerization helps contain costs. Computerized inventory control can eliminate the needless waste of expired pharmaceuticals. On-line statistical information systems can measure the effectiveness of various administrative solutions, diagnostic, and surgical procedures, and treatment techniques. According to John Goudey, director of Ernst & Young's Life Sciences Division, "Cost containment and improved productivity are going to be the themes in hospitals and the health care industry [throughout] the 1990s. New technologics, especially information technologies, are going to help out in a big way." One need only consider that the over-40 crowd already accounts for 65 percent of all health care costs to realize the importance of cost containment as the boomer generation ages.

To cut costs, the ways in which medical services are delivered must be changed. Since doctors' services constitute the greatest expense in delivering medical services, attempts are being made to decrease the need for doctors in the health care system. Each additional doctor adds an estimated $500,000 a year to medical costs. Even though the population has increased by only 12 percent since 1983, the number of doctors increased by 38 percent. And today, there is one physician for every 450 Canadians, compared with one for every 860. Medical schools have been instructed to reduce enrolment. Forty-six percent of the doctors surveyed by an independent firm for the Canadian Medical Association supported reductions in medical school enrolments. It has been proposed that nurses take over some of the functions traditionally performed by doctors. Therefore, individuals interested in pursuing a nursing career would be well advised to obtain university degrees as part of their training. Nurses who specialize, become nurse practitioners, and obtain a master's degree will have very little trouble finding employment. Community college nursing programs will be eliminated and the number of nurses graduating is expected to decline as a result; instead, colleges will focus on courses for registered nursing assistants (RNAs) and health care aides as demand increases for these medical workers.

In 1991 there were 3.2 million Canadians over 65 years of age; by 2001 there will be four million individuals older than 65. The aging of the baby boom generation will mean increased demand for geriatricians, long-term care administrators, registered nurses with management skills, dietitians, physiotherapists and occupational therapists, eldercare workers, social workers, and recreational therapists. Jobs requiring minimal post-secondary school training include health care/nurses aides (who will make up 75 percent of the long-term care work force), cooks, laundry and housekeeping aides, maintenance workers, ward clerks, office coordinators, and admissions receptionists.

Since an aging population requires more medical testing, there will be increased demand for medical laboratories, which in turn will hire more lab technicians and assistants, radiologists, computer systems technicians, drivers and, in the short term, data entry operators. Individuals working in this environment will need to cultivate problem-solving skills, team skills, and measuring skills. Continuous learning and academic upgrading will be essential in this field as the simpler functions become automated.

Pharmaceuticals companies are also tailoring their research to meet the growing needs of aging boomers. People are expecting to live longer and are demanding products that will allow them to retain a 50-year-old lifestyle into their seventies. Since post-menopausal women comprise the fastest-growing segment of the Canadian population, many companies are developing drugs to treat the effects of menopause and osteoporosis. Research into ulcers, arthritis, endometriosis, cancer, Alzheimer's disease, and cardiovascular problems is also proceeding apace.

Normally, a new drug costs at least $250 million and takes ten years to develop. A new generation of computer software, however, is transforming the ability of researchers to visualize and design molecules. With computer-assisted molecular design (CAMD), molecules can be designed that behave in a specific way—to regulate pain or hypertension, for example. Now that biological research is revealing the detailed structures of target receptor sites the drug molecules must latch on to, it is easier to design molecules that fit properly. HyperCube Inc., a Waterloo, Ontario, software company, developed a sophisticated molecule builder capable of advanced analysis called HyperChem, which may become the industry standard for desktop molecular modeling since it is compatible with existing software.

In deciding which biotechnological companies to apply to, it's important to find out how many alliances the companies have with others in the field, particularly with large pharmaceutical companies. According to a 1992 study by Ernst & Young, 70 percent of all Canadian biotechnical companies have formed at least one alliance. The $200 million to $250 million cost of getting products to market requires such alliances. Medium-sized companies have usually formed over seven alliances, while the industry average is four. Alliances aimed at acquiring marketing and distribution expertise are becoming more important as competition is increasingly focussed on commercializing research and development results as quickly as possible. Cangene Corporation of Mississauga, Ontario, formed an alliance with Akzo Pharma, a Dutch pharmaceutical giant, which gave Akzo a licence to market Cangene's diagnostic technology, such as its AIDS diagnosing technology. Small research and develop-

BULLETIN BOARD

- **Job demand factors:** aging boomers' health concerns will dominate all aspects of the health care industry which is in its early growth phase.
- **Job growth areas:** research in medical instrumentation and pharmaceuticals; sales positions in medical instrumentation and pharmaceutical companies; registered nursing assistants; health care aides; physiotherapists; respirologists; speech pathologists; dental hygienists; occupational therapists; radiologists; home care registered nurses; operating and emergency room registered nurses; nurse practitioners; activation co-ordinators.
- **Skills, abilities, qualities, education needed**: pharmaceutical sales representatives must first acquire a science degree, then complete a pharmaceutical representative course; for positions with biotech companies, math, science, and computer literacy skills; managerial positions will require expertise in program planning, finance, human resources, policy development, project management, communication skills; the best jobs in the pharmaceutical and biotechnology fields combine at least one other area of expertise with pharmacology—for example, neuropharmacology or biochemistry plus microbiology; knowledge of software applications; nurses and RNAs at the moment require Grade 12 English and math and two senior sciences; medical students must complete a two-year premedical program for admission, with the exception of McMaster University, which includes non-academic criteria; all medical schools expect applicants to have some medicine-related volunteer experience.
- **Job reduction areas:** generic drug firms; doctors, except for specialties addressing the needs of the elderly—gerontology, cardiology, neurology, radiology, oncology, cosmetic surgery, urology; general nursing; middle management.
- **Growth limiting factors:** governments' ability to pay for services.
- **Issues:** patients becoming partners in the health care process; the legal implications to the cost containment or rationalization of services process; shift in emphasis to prevention of illness; effects of pollution on health; a variety of ethical issues prompted by advances in technology.

BULLETIN BOARD

TIPS

➤ For more job-specific information about occupations in health care industries, consult *Health Career Job Explosion* by Dennis Damp.

CONTACTS

✍ Canadian Medical Association
1867 Alta Vista Dr.,
Ottawa, ON K1G 3Y6 Tel. 613-9331 Fax: 613-731-9013

✍ Canadian Institute of Biotechnology
388 Albert St.,
Ottawa, ON K1R 5B2 Tel. 613-563-8849 Fax 613-563-8850

✍ Canadian Nurses Association
50 The Driveway,
Ottawa, ON K2P 1E2 Tel. 613-237-2133 Fax: 613-237-3520

✍ Canadian Pharmaceutical Association
1785 Alta Vista Dr., 2nd Fl.,
Ottawa, ON K1G 3Y6 Tel 613-523-7877 Fax: 613-523-0445

✍ British Columbia Society of Medical Technologists
PO Box 715,
New Westminster, B.C. V3L 4Z3 Tel. 604-942-1092

✍ Ontario Society of Medical Technologists
#600, 234 Eglinton Ave East,
Toronto, ON M4P 1K5 Tel. 416-485-6768 Fax: 416-485-7660

ment companies working on specialized technologies require alliances with well-established pharmaceutical companies to take advantage of the latter's capital and worldwide distribution and marketing networks. Similarly, the large pharmaceutical companies need the smaller biotechnical companies to provide them with leading-edge products in need of further development.

There will be an increase in medical specialization with the advent of newer technologies, treatments, and procedures; for example, there will be greater demand for rehabilitation specialists and radiation oncologists to serve the needs of an aging population. The entire orientation of health care is likely to shift to a more family- and community-based model. Greater emphasis will be placed on health protection and disease prevention. Given the move toward patient empowerment, high-quality physical and psychological environments will be demanded by everyone everywhere. This will mean more jobs for patient rights advocates, ergonomics specialists, community home workers, psychologists, psychotherapists, and alternative medicine deliverers.

Consulting jobs for M.B.A.'s and M.H.Sc.'s will proliferate in connection with planning, operational reviews, mergers, organizational development, utilization reviews, total quality management (TQM), continuous service improvement, service facilitation, and internationalization. Job seekers looking for managerial positions will require expertise in program and service planning, finance, human resources, policy development, organizational development, and information systems. Specialized abilities required include consensus management and project management as well as analytical, listening, and writing skills. Today, it is taken for granted that a candidate for a job in the biotechnology and medical fields has strong math, science, and computer literacy skills.

Many ethical issues are likely to arise in the future with respect to the rationalization of services—who gets what, why, when, where, and how much. These issues will also mean that the job descriptions of health care workers will need to be clarified, especially in sensitive areas.

In the short term, government debt will constrain health care growth at the expense of patients. In 1992, nine of the provinces froze their health care spending for the first time since 1965-66. Should this trend continue, a two-tiered system will emerge as more deinsured services are relegated to private coverage and the number of private clinics continues to grow as waiting times for crucial testing increases the health risk to the critically ill or those needing early diagnosis for therapy to be effective. Already there is a critical shortage of radiologists. Even now, 28 percent of health care funding comes from the private sector in the form of consumer purchases, drug plans, eye plans, and the cost of nursing homes. In either case, cost containment and rationalization will characterize the health care profession well into the future as aging boomers use health sevices in progressively increasing numbers.

WHERE THE JOBS ARE IN ENVIRONMENTAL INDUSTRIES

Canada's environment industry is expected to generate approximately $12 billion annually by the year 2000. Ironically, much of this is a result of

Canada's dubious distinction as one of the world's largest per capita users of energy and producers of garbage or waste material. Although the federal government's Green Plan, which promised to provide $3 billion in funding for research, cleanup, and public involvement programs, is about to go the way of most political promises, environmental industries will continue to grow on a worldwide basis simply out of necessity. Within 50 years, the world's population will reach a minimum of 9 billion regardless of efforts to curtail population growth. Economic output will likely be five times what it is today. Along with these developments will be worldwide shortages in renewable resources. Currently, environmental damage resulting from water, soil, and air pollution cost China over 15 percent of its gross national product. The World Bank estimates it would cost approximately $100 billion annually by the year 2000 just to provide developing countries with adequate water and sanitation services, or two percent to three percent of their gross domestic product.

Countries that postpone initiating environmental reforms will find that at some point, savings accrued in curtailing environmental damage exceed the cost of implementing environmental programs. Unfortunately, political will is sluggish in bringing about necessary reforms, perhaps because the payback period may be lengthy or the environmental damage not yet conspicuous enough. In the meantime, many companies are selling environmentally friendly products, services, or consulting advice to individual companies concerned about environmental costs or conforming to current legislation.

The environment industry is one of the fastest-growing industries in the western Canadian economy with an annual expected growth of between five percent and 15 percent over the next five years, according to a 1993 report by Sentar Consultants of Calgary. About 2,000 "green" companies were responsible for $1.8 billion in sales in British Columbia, Alberta, Saskatchewan, and Manitoba. The 20,000 people employed in the industry work largely in the service sector—predominantly consulting—in such areas as recycling, site remediation, and air quality. Only 15 percent of these companies derived their primary income from selling environmental products, and manufacturers of environmental products reported average sales of only slightly more than $2 million. In Ontario, environmental protection is a $2.5 billion industry employing 30,000 workers; of the 15,000 who work in waste management, over 50 percent have low- or medium-skilled jobs, and in environmental manufacturing, roughly 33 percent are employed as labourers.

On the scientific end of the industry, most environmental researchers hold doctorates in chemistry, biology, physics, engineering, and meteorology. In 1992, Environment Canada employed 200 doctoral-level researchers, and private environmental labs employed an additional 200. Typically, there is one B.Sc. engineer and two technologists—electronic, computer, biological, or chemical—who assist each researcher. In response to the demand for trained technicians to assist environmental researchers, community colleges offer two- or three-year technician and technologist programs, and many universities offer degrees in environmental studies. Hydrogeologists with an B.Sc, M.Sc. or Ph.D. in hydrogeology are in demand. They assess and design landfill sites, and are instrumental in environmental cleanup.

The industry also employs administrative support service personnel who must be knowledgeable in scientific terms and techniques, computer literate, and prepared to supervise technical staff.

A background in biology is a prerequisite for all environmental jobs as research shifts from the physical sciences to the impact that environmental corruption has on life forms. This change of emphasis has spurred growth in jobs involving environmental audits and impact studies.

As of the end of 1993, Ontario's educational institutes, construction and demolition companies, food service establishments, health care facilities, hotels and motels, manufacturers, multi-unit residential dwellings, office buildings, and retail shopping complexes are required to carry out waste audits and establish work plans, implement source separation of recyclables, and implement work plans so as to reduce unnecessary waste disposal. All audits and work plans must be updated annually and the work plans displayed for municipality or Ministry of Environment spot checks. Of the ten million tons of solid waste generated annually in Ontario, 60 percent is attributable to the commercial, industrial, and institutional sectors; clearly, many job opportunities will open in the handling and reduction of waste disposal.

Environmental companies are discovering that solving someone else's waste problems is a growing market. Eco-Tek Wastewater Treatment Inc., for example, recovers metals from the industrial waste water that used to be dumped into streams, rivers, and lakes. For companies employing the

Eco-Tec technology, the payback period of its investment is as short as three months. Philip Environmental Inc., which is in the business of cleaning up hazardous waste, saw its sales climb from $100 million in 1991 to $157 million in 1992. Consolidated Envirowaste Industries developed a speeded-up composting process to take advantage of rising tipping or dumping fees and the demand for fertilizer. Now that all provinces have planned to reduce landfill waste by 50 percent by the year 2000 (using 1987 as the base year), there are tremendous opportunities for companies of this kind. Bovar Engineering Products is involved in site assessment, waste disposal, medical waste disposal, and product research and development. By exporting pollution monitoring and control equipment to Latin American countries that are now in the process of developing environmental legislation, the company is anticipating a 20 percent annual growth rate.

Many corporations are also finding that they can enjoy significant cost savings by cutting energy costs. IBM now saves $200,000 annually in energy costs by using a cool storage system at one of its offices. Other companies realizing savings from similar initiatives include Xerox ($187,000), Bell ($250,000), Novacor ($200,000), and Oshawa Foods ($250,000). Inco Limited plans to save $1.6 million in annual energy costs through energy conservation, and autoglass manufacturer PPG Canada Inc. expects to save $656,000 yearly. Currently, energy performance contracting is a $70 million business. There are 25 energy service companies that design, implement, and finance the cost-saving energy technology in exchange for a percentage of the savings a company accrues. Since building owners do not pay for anything, the energy service companies assume all the risk. Many energy contractors, such as Tescor Energy Services Inc., have seen their operations double because of the potential savings to the company.

Land reclamation also presents many employment opportunities. In Canada, urban expansion and soil erosion has reduced farmland by 65 percent, with 54,000 hectare of farmland converted to concrete each year. Moreover, the water supply is becoming increasingly contaminated as farmers replace topsoil with chemical fertilizer. Environmental degradation will pose a serious problem for Canadians as the population continues to expand, and many jobs in the environment industry will emerge in an effort to contain damage growth rates.

BULLETIN BOARD

- **Job demand factors:** population explosion; stricter environmental regulations; potential for cost saving; landfill shortages; dumping fees; garbage collection costs; recyclable usages; water contamination.
- **Job growth areas:** marketing, administrative, auditing, finance, legal, public relations, technical and research job for business graduates who are technically conversant with a particular environmental area or who have technical diplomas in the relevant areas; cleanup jobs which do not require highly skilled workers; jobs with companies which want to find alternative use for waste products, save energy, eliminate toxicity, monitor pollution levels, or dispose of waste products; water-related sanitation jobs (e.g., hydrogeologists) have the greatest demand worldwide.
- **Skills, abilities, qualities, education needed:** computer and technological literacy; area-specific scientific and technical comprehension; ability to work in small teams and to prepare and present reports; precise data collection skills; good knowledge of environmental regulations; ability to work within a strict budget; ability to work independently; flexibility and patience.
- **Job reduction areas:** none.
- **Growth limiting factors**: affordability; government regulations; political will; ability of technological knowledge to keep up with need
- **Issues:** how long government action can be delayed by cutbacks; society's response to the impending results of environmental audits; continental and international pressure on Canada to improve environmental practices; determination of safe levels and potential "sunsetting" of environmental pollutants; search for safe alternatives to pollutants; waste management and prevention; success of green marketing.

TIPS

➤ For more information about environmental careers, consult *Environmental Career Guide* by Nicholas Basta, and to learn more about energy technology companies, take a look at the *Canadian Directory of Efficiency and Alternate Energy Technologies, the Canadian Environmental Directory 1994/95,* and *Get a Life: A Green Cure for Canada's Economic Blues.*

BULLETIN BOARD

CONTACTS

- Canadian Association of Recycling Industries
  #502, 50 Gervais St.,
  Don Mills, ON M3C 1Z3 Tel. 416-510-1244 Fax: 416-510-1248
- Canadian Association of Water Pollution Research & Control
  Canada Centre for Inland Waters,
  867 Lakeshore Rd., PO Box 5068,
  Burlington, ON L7R 4L7 Tel. 905-336-4598 Fax: 905-336-4858
- Canadian Environment Network
  PO Box 1289, Stn. B
  Ottawa, ON K1P 5R3 Tel. 613-563-2078 Fax: 563-7236
- Canadian Environment Industry Association
  Centre d'achats l'Acadie-Sauvé
  #232, 1400, rue Sauvé ouest,
  Montreal PQ H4N 1C5 Tel. 514-745-3580 Fax: 514-745-3582
- Canadian Environmental Auditing Association
  c/o Don Fraser, Ontario Hydro H6C7, 700 University Ave.,
  Toronto, ON M5G 1X6 Tel. 416-592-3208
- Canadian Environmental Equipment Manufacturer's Association
  #701, 116 Albert St.,
  Ottawa, ON K1P 5G3 Tel. 613 232 7213
- Canadian Environmental Law Society
  c/o Legal and Literary Society, Osgoode Hall of Law School,
  York University, 4700 Keele St.,
  North York ON M3J 1P3 Tel. 416-736-5027 Fax: 416-736-5736
- Canadian Society of Environmental Biologists
  PO Box 962, Stn F, Toronto, ON M4Y 2N9
- Canadian Water Quality Association
  #A201, 151 Frobisher Dr.,
  Waterloo, ON N2V 2C9 Tel. 519-885-3854 Fax: 519-747-9124
- Canadian Water & Wastewater Association
  24 Clarence St., 3rd Fl.,
  Ottawa, ON K1N 5P3 Tel. 613-238-5692 Fax: 613-238-5193
- Pollution Probe Foundation
  12 Madison Ave.,
  Toronto, ON M5R 2S1 Tel. 416-926-1907 Fax: 416/926-1601

At the moment, many companies have been successful because of growing export markets. American demand for green technology outstrips Canadian demand because of the stricter regulatory laws passed in the U.S. Consequently, Canadian companies such as SolarChem, which makes equipment to clean toxic chemicals from waste water, do little business in Canada. Undoubtedly, Canadian regulations will become stricter, creating opportunities for Canadian environmental companies, particularly in the area of waste associated with primary resource extraction and processing, such as sludges, slag, mine tailings, or unremoved clear-cut timber, which accounts for 98.6 percent of our waste problems.

Many imaginative ways of recycling products have formed the basis for new businesses that range from making graffiti-proof freeway walls from plastic pop bottles and used tires, to making plastic lumber. However, recyclable waste is only worth one-tenth to one-twentieth its initial value, with some items prohibitively expensive to recycle—polystyrene containers and utensils common to the fast-food industry, for example. In future, the focus will likely shift from recycling to developing non-polluting and easily reusable or disposable products.

Environmental concern has also entered the investment world. Approximately $14 million worth of mutual funds in Canada are directed to companies with a reputable environmental record. In North America as a whole, "green investing" represents a $600 billion market. Screening criteria include a company's air and water pollution record, its approaches to waste management, its recycling policy, and prosecution record. Eco-Rating International, a Zurich-based firm, has developed a ten-point system for rating a company's environmental performance, which includes its environmental sustainability and the ecological standing of its technologies among its rating categories. There is a green magazine for executives entitled *ECO* that outlines the costs that result from environmental damage, cleanup, and regulation.

Even natural resources companies, which are laying off frontline workers, have had to hire environmental personnel. According to a 1992 study by Employment and Immigration Canada, the pulp and paper industry will require up to 3,000 environmental workers by 1995. Ten years ago, Inco employed between 15,000 and 18,000 individuals in Ontario; in 1993, this figure dropped to 6,600. While Inco's work force was shrinking, its environmental department increased its hiring of engineers and individuals with degrees in physics, chemistry, biology, and forestry.

Other professions that will be in demand will be wildlife conservationists, administrators, secretarial staff, public relations and communications specialists, environmental planners and managers, lawyers, environmental accountants, architects, journalists, truck drivers, and pickers and sorters of garbage. Moreover, since many small companies in the industry are run by scientists and engineers who may lack expertise in marketing, human resources management, or strategic planning, many positions will open up in these areas. Already seven out of ten Canadian offices have waste reduction programs in place. Before long, every company will be hiring waste and energy management planners and consultants. Xerox has enhanced job descriptions to include environmental goals and has even reassigned territories for service representatives so they can take public transit or walk from one customer location to another.

The future of sustainable economic growth has become one of the most pressing issues facing the world, and the job market potential of this will likely expand faster than the world's population. The United Nations is considering sponsoring "environmental peacekeepers"—a team of environmental soldiers ready to fight ecological disasters anywhere in the world. Perhaps the most substantial job growth will occur in water sanitation, given that 80 percent of the diseases affecting the global population are attributable to contaminated or unsafe water resources. All countries facing large population growth will be in dire need of environmental monitoring, planning, and remediation. By the year 2000, India's population will exceed one billion despite its having one of the world's oldest population control programs. Thus, India, Asia, and Central and South America will provide employment opportunities in the environmental industry and will be insatiable export markets. As country after country tightens its environmental regulations, environmental-related jobs will become an extension of every company's or institution's responsibility.

As an industry, the environment has almost limitless growth potential. By the 21st century, no country will be able to afford not to be environmentally responsible without suffering irreversible damage to its natural resources. Quality of life is at stake in a smog-filled, ozone-depleted, litter-ridden, no-swimming world. Change has to occur; whether it will take place smoothly or chaotically remains to be seen.

CHAPTER FIVE

WHERE THE JOBS ARE IN THE SERVICE, MANUFACTURING, AND NATURAL RESOURCES INDUSTRIES

- **The Rise of the Service Economy**
- **Dynamic Service Industries**
- **Traditional Services**
- **Non-Market Services**
- **Careers in Manufacturing and Natural Resources**

In rich countries today, over half the workers in a typical manufacturing firm do service-type jobs—design, distribution, financial planning; only a minority make things on the factory floor.
THE ECONOMIST

The lines between the services and manufacturing industries are becoming blurred, and the notion that manufacturing is somehow more real or more productive than services is just not valid. While one cannot export a fine dining experience or a weekend at a resort, services *are* becoming increasingly "tradable." The fine dining experience or holiday retreat that attracts tourists amounts to importing trade. Such factors as deregulation and falling trade barriers will likely encourage trade in services, particularly to developing countries in need of finance, telecommunications, and consulting expertise. Over 60 percent of the gross domestic product of developed countries comes from their service industries, which also account for approximately 40 percent of the stock of foreign direct investment by the big five industrial economies— the U.S., Germany, Japan, France, and England. Manufacturing will diminish as a percentage of gross domestic product as labour-intensive industries move to countries that offer cheaper labor. Since there is more value added by inventing a software program or designing a circuit than by grinding out yet another auto part, high-wage, knowledge-intensive jobs will stay in countries with the best-trained work force. In the long term, as robotics and automation increasingly replaces workers on the factory floor, manufacturing will migrate to knowledge-intensive countries that are in strategic positions for the acquisition of raw materials or the distribution of finished products. When the automotive industry is completely automated, for example, companies will not have to move their factories to Mexico with its cheaper labour and proximity to the large U.S. market; they will simply locate in the U.S. where the product is sold.

Since the early sixties, the service sector has doubled in Canada and in nine other industrialized nations. Approximately eight million Canadians currently work in service industries such as finance, communications, real estate, transportation, community and personal services, and public administration. Of all jobs created since 1980, 93 percent have been in the service sector. By 1990, 72 percent of Canadian and U.S. workers were employed in the service industry as compared with 58 percent in 1960. While this increase is partly a result of the large number of women who have entered service sector industries and the greater demand for social services and household workers, the shift to knowledge workers accounts for the lion's share of this growth. Between 1978 and 1986, 32 percent of job growth in Canada occurred in service companies with 100 or more employees, and 58 percent in small service companies with less than 20 employees. The largest percentage of employment in small companies is characteristic of the traditional services—retailing, hospitality, amusement and recreation, and personal services. In terms of overall employment, most service jobs are in medium or large organizations—banks, insurance companies, and educational institutions.

The image of the service job has changed dramatically, no longer consistent with the stereotype of someone mindlessly flipping burgers or performing tedious clerical tasks. The information technology revolution is reducing—even eliminating—these mundane tasks as more and more of these jobs become automated. The most promising service sector careers are in the knowledge sector. In fact, over half the workers in the developed countries are engaged in the production, storage, retrieval, or distribution of knowledge—all areas that offer the most promising service sector careers.

While skills upgrading has been least significant in traditional services, large increases in retraining have been required in distributive, information, and non-market services such as government, education, health, libraries, and other noncompetitive services. The 1980s showed substantial activity in skills upgrading in the areas of finance, communications, insurance, the amusement and recreation industries, public administration, and health.

During past recessions, the service sector—except for the areas of retail and wholesale—was not severely hit by layoffs. Often there was a countercyclical trend in the non-market services as rising unemployment led to increased enrolment in education programs and the number of social services jobs increased to meet the needs of the unemployed, who had formerly been employed in the goods-producing sector of the economy. And while consumers were buying less, the service sectors did not suffer appreciably. This is no longer the case.

Like the manufacturing sector, service industries were hard hit by the recession. Corresponding to a decreased demand for manufactured goods or natural resources, was a decline in demand for services. The resultant slowdown of the economy, the lowering of computer prices, and the advances in information technology provided companies of all kinds with a perfect opportunity to restructure or downsize.

Whereas the 1970s and 1980s saw substantial productivity improvements in manufacturing, the 1990s will enjoy productivity improvements in the service sector on a very large scale. The heating up of global competition in the service industries—largely an outgrowth of the information technology revolution—made it mandatory that service companies use the new technology if they were to survive. With technology altering the flow and processing of information, companies had to find more efficient organizational structures so that they could run their businesses more competitively. Many traditionally secure service jobs began to disappear altogether. In the U.S., automation has reduced the number of new jobs created annually by approximately 700,000. Considering that NCR's 7780 work station is capable of processing cheques, remittance slips, and other documents at 500 items per minute, this hefty reduction is not surprising.

Public service jobs have also felt the impact of information technology, especially since bureaucracies, which need to continuously process large volumes of information are often the best candidates for productivity improvement. Cash-strapped governments have had to adopt labor- and cost-saving technology at the expense of many public service jobs. This approach has also been taken by large institutions like banks and insurance companies which have been forced to trim their operations. The information technology revolution has changed virtually every occupation in the service industry—usually for the better as workers are relieved of the more tedious aspects of their jobs through automation. While many jobs have disappeared, many new jobs have emerged, and with them, opportunities for workers to grow professionally. To survive in these new service jobs, an individual must become a knowledge worker, comfortable with information technology and conversant with software applications relevant to the service the company provides. Employees who can use technology to process information or raw data and who can communicate the results to others in the form of business plans, newsletters, annual reports, and direct mailings to clients will be indispensable to the company.

The Dynamic Service Industries

The dynamic services comprise two *producer industries*—finance, insurance, and real estate; and business services—and two *distribution industries*—transportation, communications, utilities, and the wholesale trade. These high value-adding industries are becoming key players in international trade. Over 20 percent of employees in dynamic services industries are dependent upon exports for their jobs.

Until teleconferencing and electronic highways become universal, most high-skilled jobs in the dynamic services will be located in large urban centres where well-trained individuals are available and the head-quarters or main divisional offices of goods-producing companies are found. Goods-producing companies, in fact, are the largest users of the dynamic services.

The interdependence between the dynamic services and the goods-producing sector is dramatized by the fact that in1985 a one-dollar output in each of the goods-producing industries, when added together, produced a total demand of 96 cents for finance and real estate services and 85 cents for wholesale services. The six service industries most dependent upon demand for the goods industries are utilities, finance, real estate, the wholesale trade, business services, transportation, and communications. In 1988, these dynamic services were responsible for 56 percent of the service sector's gross domestic product and 36 percent of the country's gross domestic product. In the past, this interdependency has led to a concentration of non-primary goods—that is, goods from industries other than agriculture, forestry, mining, and fishing—and dynamic services in urban centres, particularly the finance, insurance, and real estate industries. This was also the case for management consultants, architects, and urban designers, personnel and executive-search services, computer services, and engineering and scientific services, and to a lesser extent for legal and accounting services.

Once teleconferencing and telecommunications become universal, companies that traditionally locate their offices in urban centres will consider other options. The trend towards home businesses means that service industries can be located anywhere. Indeed, a knowledge worker could develop software on a sailboat crossing the Atlantic as expeditiously as in an office downtown. The migration of work to off-site locations has had the greatest impact in the knowledge-based service industries which do not have to be on-site to produce a result in the same way as, for example, a cleaning service has to.

In the past, routine information transfer could be easily handled electronically, but complex decision making required face-to-face contact. With the restructuring of companies to teams and the wider use of teleconferencing, all players can now meet face-to-face electronically. Thus, a worker's ability to operate both independently and as a team member is becoming a greater asset in the dynamic services. Moreover, as education, skills, and knowledge increases worldwide, and employers are in the position to hire globally, individuals will have job security only if they have more education, knowledge, experience, or skills than other workers in other parts of the world. Job seekers must keep this in mind when researching companies they may wish to work for, and only choose those that offer them opportunities to increase their skills and knowledge. The need to upgrade continuously is essential for career survival in a global economy.

PRODUCER INDUSTRIES: FINANCE, INSURANCE AND REAL ESTATE; BUSINESS SERVICES
Where the Jobs are in Finance

Finance companies have entered almost every arena of bank lending, including credit cards, mortgages, and real estate and commercial loans. Generally, these companies have been more successful than banks even though they lend to companies that banks would probably turn down, especially during tough economic times. In the U.S., finance companies increased business loans by 5.8 percent in 1991, while business loans granted by commercial banks fell by 4.7 percent. Why this trend? Finance companies are better able than banks to assess risk because they monitor the borrower's business more carefully. For example, if a finance company is lending money based on accounts receivable, it will likely check on the amount of goods shipped. As a result of their diligence, finance companies doubled business loans between 1985 and 1991, while bank loans increased by only 24 percent. Indeed, finance companies continued to be more profitable than banks throughout the 1980s.

Since lending is the primary business of finance companies, they will lend money even during a recession. With banks reluctant to lend to small businesses, there is more opportunity for finance companies to step in with business loans. Banks, conservative by nature, will not lend money without loan guarantees in the form of personal or business assets. Thus, Canadian banks would never have lent money to Bill Gates, president of

BULLETIN BOARD

- **Job demand factors:** businesses need loans to grow and compete globally.
- **Job growth areas:** marketing, financial planners, loan experts.
- **Skills, abilities, qualities, education needed**: decision making, problem solving, financial, marketing, analytical; college diploma or university degree in business is essential.
- **Growth limiting factors**: competition from banks and other lending institutions.

CONTACTS

- Asssociation of Canadian Financial Corporations
  Sussex Centre,#401, 50 Burnhamthorpe Rd. West,
  Mississauga, ON L4B 3C2 Tel. 416-949-4820 Fax: 416-896-9380
- Trust Companies Association of Canada Inc.
  #720, 50 O'Connor St.,
  Ottawa, ON K1P 6L2 Tel. 613-563-3205 Fax: 613-235-3111

Microsoft because software is not considered an asset by the banks. Canada has had a long-standing tradition of not supporting local entrepreneurships.

Individuals interested in the world of business and finance would learn far more working for a finance company than for a bank. Since most new businesses in the future will be small businesses, finance companies will likely grow to meet a demand for small business loans. And since marketing plays a vital role in the industry, marketing graduates with an interest in finance and financial products are frequently recruited.

Banking

As technology takes us closer to a cashless society, banks and banking will completely change. As deposit-taking institutions, banks will become computer terminals that process and record money transfers; tellers' jobs will be eliminated, as will the jobs of individuals involved in the paper-trail aspect of chequing and account reconciliation. In1992, the Canadian Imperial Bank of Commerce laid off 2,500 employees, and this is just the beginning. The number of bank branches will be reduced as home banking becomes more popular. The Royal Bank plans to close 43 of its 142 Royal Trust branches in 1994. Telephone banking services are becoming pervasive, with the Canadian Imperial Bank of Commerce offering LinkUp; the Toronto Dominion, Bankline; and Royal Bank, Ca$hTouch. Trust companies have entered the home banking market with Canada Trust's EasyLine, and mutual fund companies such as Altamira Investment Services Inc. are offering MoneyLine accounts that allow customers to buy and sell mutual funds and transfer money between funds and bank accounts by phone. Even Standard Life Assurance Company allows customers to purchase mutual funds over the phone on a 24-hour basis. Canada Trust's seventy-five 24-hour drive-through banking centres and 900 banking machines now account for 28 percent of all its banking transactions.

The banking industry will continue to shift its focus to areas such as mortgages, personal and business loans, insurance, and investment and financial planning. These markets will be aggressively pursued as a number of institutions compete with one another for their share of aging boomer retirement planning funds. Banks already control 32 percent of the RRSP market. But trust companies, insurance companies, credit unions, financial planners, and mutual funds organizations will compete to gain more market share in this growing area. Banks, however, enjoy a number of advantages over their competitors: widely dispersed distribution channels; well-developed information technology; proprietary customer financial information; years of client relationship building; financial and marketing clout; the stability and security associated with large institutions and international connections. The major obstacle banks will face is to overcome their atrocious customer service policies.

Increasingly, especially as aging boomers choose financial institutions with which to do their retirement financial planning, relationship building, convenience, security, and rates of return on investment are becoming central concerns. And although banks are perhaps best positioned to deliver these services, it is possible that their aloofness, arrogance, and complacency will drive customers elsewhere to do business. Banks will also have to become better at defining, managing, and pricing risk at all levels—from international banking to negotiating small personal loans. Their efforts to enter the insurance market will have a sobering effect in this respect, considering the losses incurred by many insurance companies. The banks are still recovering from the international bad debts left over from the days of abundant Saudi oil money that needed to be reinvested. Banks will need sophisticated financial expertise because most domestic businesses of the future will be small businesses with assets and potential that will not be as easy to quantify as in the past—software consulting, for example. In addition, banks will need to improve their rates of return on investments, or the more well-informed boomer investor may choose to use the no-frills trading and insurance services of the banking industry. Since banks can make a lot of money from the higher value-added financial planning that consolidates the various financial interests of aging boomers, it is imperative that these institutions offer a variety of products with different combinations of risk levels.

Although banks have been leary of lending to small businesses unless the loans are fully secured with hard assets, they are once again entering the area of mergers and acquisitions, which will play a key role in accelerating the globalization of trade. Often, negotiating such deals requires risk management skills that include an understanding of the international competitive banking industry, especially since banks, like insurance companies, will ultimately form joint loan-granting agreements for exceptionally large investment activities. Therefore, banks will have to hire a variety of financial and actuarial experts. Individuals interested in a career in the insurance industry will find banks hiring insurance personnel. Since the banking industry continues to make enormous investment

---

SERVICE WITH A SMILE ...?

A survey conducted by Marketing Solutions, a Toronto company that specializes in the financial services industry, indicated that few branch employees asked for a customer's name or offered their own, even when the customer was about to deposit tens of thousands of dollars. Over 50 percent of the 250 bank and trust branches surveyed failed simple customer service and investment strategy tests. Clients were expected to conduct their confidential business over a counter; questions to assess the client's financial situation and attitude toward risk were not asked; relevant advice was not given; phone numbers were not solicited, nor were follow-up calls made to assure clients that their financial interests were being taken care of.

in information technology, software and hardware maintenance employees will be required in large numbers. Job opportunities in international investment banking will emerge to meet the growing investment needs of Asian and Latin American economies and multinationals requiring worldwide integrated banking services.

In their need to better assess and manage risk, banks will become more involved in their loans to businesses and will spend more time visiting or closely monitoring their clients and playing a greater advisory role in the lending process. Managers and customer representatives will be called upon to upgrade their financial and business skills and improve their understanding of marketing and the marketplace.

The banking industry is acquiring increased information technology and developing greater expertise in insurance and financial planning. Banks will hire accordingly. To improve its customer service and to market its new products, banks will be anxious to hire more marketing and service-oriented personnel. According to Liz McLean, manager of recruitment with Toronto Dominion Bank in Toronto, "Whereas finance and related skills were important in the 1980s, marketing and creativity are big now.... We recruit for a *career* as opposed to for a specific job. The people we hire have the potential to move into many different areas of the banking world."

Trust companies will continue to experience a decline in business now that banks and insurance companies have been allowed to enter the financial services market. A consolidation among trust companies will

---

BANKING ON A JOB

Although Canada's major banks employ more than 172,000 people, only 8,919 full- and part-time employees were hired in 1992, down from 12,498 in 1991. According to Marie Gohier, manager of corporate recruiting for the Royal Bank, "We are hiring less than a few years ago, with numbers down 50 percent from 1989-90.... I don't think we'll ever see the numbers we had...in the late 1980s.... In 1989, 60 percent to 65 percent of our new positions were filled through external hiring. Today, that number is down to 30 percent to 35 percent." In 1994, the Royal Bank plans to eliminate 4,100 jobs.

BULLETIN BOARD

- **Job demand factors**: the move to the cashless society; boomer retirement planning; growth of small business and foreign banking opportunities.
- **Job growth areas**: financial experts and planners as well as insurance-knowledgeable staff; marketing and customer service-oriented positions; software and hardware maintenance staff.
- **Skills, abilities, qualities, education needed**: computer literacy; communication skills; creativity, problem-solving and decision-making skills; diploma or degree in business essential.
- **Job reduction areas**: all teller, paper handling, or account reconciliation functions.

Contacts:

➤ Institute of Canadian Bankers
Box 348, Exchange Tower,
#600, 2 First Canadian Place,
Toronto, ON M5X 1E1 Tel. 416-362-6092 Fax: 416-362-7705

---

likely occur, along with insurance companies acquiring a portion of the smaller trust companies, leaving only a few smaller trust operations to focus on well-defined niches—corporate trust services, for example—or smaller regional markets not well served by credit unions.

Where the Jobs are in Insurance

Next to the Japanese, Canadians purchase more life insurance than anyone else in the world. In 1991, 60 Canadian companies sold $154 billion in life insurance alone. In addition, 150 companies sold Canadians property and casualty insurance. However, this is an extremely competitive industry based on price and in the future there will not be enough business to support such a large number of companies. Moreover, revenues are down, with commercial property premiums dropping 3.6 percent in 1992 to $1.7 billion as a result of bankruptcies, business closings, and retrenchment. Investment income fell about $185 million to $2.4 billion; profits fell $100 million to $863 million; and, return of equity fell one percent to 7.7 percent over 1991 as interest rates dropped. The reinsurance business, which insures against natural disasters, is still reeling from its losses which in the U.S. alone exceeded $20 billion. And as mentioned above, banks are aggressively moving into the insurance business by taking advantage of the proprietary financial knowledge they have of their large client base.

Insurance premiums of all kinds are about to rise. In Canada's reinsurance market, premiums will rise by as much as 19 percent as opposed to 40 percent in the U.S. As predicted by environmentalists, violent storms are on the increase, with the ratio of claims and expenses to premium income rising by 110 percent in 1991 and 117 percent in 1992. Environmental considerations are creating new problems for insurers with the 1988 Piper Alpha explosion and fire that cost insurers $1.4 billion, and the 1989 Exxon Valdez oil spill that set them back $425 million.

Following the large increases in liability insurance premiums between 1985 and 1986 and the setting of very restricted coverage limits coupled with larger deductibles, 30 percent of those seeking insurance abandoned the traditional insurance market and developed other approaches such as reciprocal pooling—as in the case of school boards that insure one another rather than buy insurance—or captive corporate-owned insurance companies in which large firms own insurance companies— typically located in Bermuda for tax reasons—which they use for self-insurance. In 1992, this kind of self-insurance was up 18 percent, and in the commercial risk financing market, self-insurance rose to 30 percent in 1993. With coverage restrictions bound to increase further, this trend will likely continue.

Financially, insurers are not in good shape, with many liquidating higher-interest bonds in order to cover current losses. Therefore, they can only invest their premiums at lower interest rates. The real estate slump incurred huge loan losses for insurers and undermined the availability of quality commercial mortgages for investment purposes. Since 35 percent of all assets held by insurers resides in real estate and mortgages, the financial damage will likely lessen in the short term, with no additional drop in value likely from such occurrences as bankruptcies and mortgage defaults now that the economy is slowly recovering. However, dividends to participating policy holders have diminished; operating costs have been cut, often meaning staff layoffs; and new information technology must be purchased so as to compete with banks, which were faster off the mark in adopting new technology. To make matters worse, fraudulent claims, which account for the ten percent to 20 percent of the $12 billion that insurers annually pay out, are rising at an annual rate of 12 percent.

Losses suffered by big insurance companies will diminish worldwide reinsurance capacity and force up prices in order to compensate. Many small- and medium-sized insurance companies are showing substantial losses in the current slow economy, with almost 20 Canadian companies currently for sale. To achieve solvency, there will be mergers, acquisitions, and strategic alliances, a broader-risk capital base, and greater market efficiency. As the market becomes more complex, with additional risks and outside competition, insurance companies are beginning to special-ize—travel, life, accident, property, for example—as part of a survival strategy.

Banks will either try to bypass the brokerage function and sell their own insurance or try to replace the brokers. Technology can help banks achieve this goal. For example, banks may wish to take advantage of Compulife Software. A computerized quote system used by many insur-ance agents, it surveys over 50 Canadian companies and displays the highest and lowest premiums based on the client's sex, age, and smoking habits. Banks could also use this software to fulfill the brokerage function for the more straightforward types of insurance. As mentioned earlier, banks have already entered the travel, accident, life, property, and casual-ty sectors of the insurance industry. Insurance companies may have to work harder at offering the consumer the more complicated products that banks are less likely to pursue, such as the growing need for insur-ance against software theft and other proprietary aspects of information abuse or loss. And, as consumers become more litigation-happy, there will be a conspicuous market for various liability products such as insur-ance for corporate directors.

Many insurance companies are trying to help clients avoid taxes by offering universal life policies that combine term life insurance and a sav-ings program. Given the shrinking under-45 market—the prime market for life insurance—and the declining growth in the life insurance mar-ket, insurance companies are exploiting the older boomer market's inter-est in investment and retirement products; this market is already growing faster than the life insurance market. Banks are also in hot pursuit of this market, though they have yet to consolidate the life, casualty, savings, and insurance markets.

Federal legislation allowing other financial service companies to become more like banks and investment companies, will result in a huge battle between banks and insurance companies for both insurance and investment business. Banks have already shown their predatory nature by taking over trust company and investment dealer functions. They will likely pursue the life, auto, and home insurance markets as well. In the short term, banks are forbidden from using their vast branch system and customer information to sell insurance, but this will change eventually.

The insurance industry is plagued by a worldwide overabundance of suppliers. Many companies—even medium-sized ones—are too small to effectively compete. To compete, insurance companies will have to join multinationals similar to those already dominating the property and casualty markets in Canada. Even multinationals are demanding one-stop multinational insurance to simplify their insurance needs. Since insurance companies are already earning lower rates of return than other financial sectors, a series of mergers and acquisitions will occur so as to gain the economies of scale and greater access to a larger capital base: Zurich Canada purchased the Travelers Insurance Company, and General Accident Assurance Company of Canada became the largest company in the general insurance market after acquiring the Prudential Life Assurance Company of England (Canada)'s property and casualty operations; the Manufacturers Life Assurance Company may convert its trust company subsidiaries into a Schedule 2 bank; Imperial Life Assurance Company of Canada has issued redeemable preferreds and Confederation Life Insurance Company offered subordinated debentures—both attempting to add to their capital base. Mutual life insurers, which are owned by their policy holders, may demutualize into public share holding stock companies in order to take advantage of the capital markets.

What job prospects does the insurance industry offer? Not yet fully exploited are insurance sales to women, a group which represents 52 percent of the market. Women often want more information than men and are happier dealing with female insurance representatives than their male counterparts. This represents a significant opportunity for women who wish to enter the sales or marketing side of the industry. With the

BULLETIN BOARD

- **Job demand factors**: growing need for new forms of insurance such as environmental or corporate responsibility insurance; bigger companies needed for reinsurance loss coverage; multinationals wanting worldwide coverage, necessitating the emergence of multinational insurance companies.
- **Job growth areas**: actuaries specializing in new areas of risk; opportunities for women selling insurance to other women; insurance jobs in banks.
- **Skills, abilities, qualities, education needed**: a firm grasp of more complicated products and knowledge in financial planning; a diploma in insurance; courses offered by professional organizations and institutes.
- **Job reduction factors**: downsizing as result of mergers and acquisitions.

CONTACTS

- Canadian Institute of Actuaries
  #1040, 360 Albert St.,
  Ottawa, ON K1R 7X7 Tel. 613-236-9196
- Canadian Institute of Chartered Life Underwriters & Chartered Financial Consultants
  41 Lesmill Rd.,
  Don Mills, ON M3B 2T3 Tel. 416-444-5251 Fax: 416-444-8031
- Canadian Life & Health Insurance Association
  #1700, 1 Queen St. East,
  Toronto, ON M5C 2X9 Tel. 416-777-2221 Fax: 416-777-1895
- Insurance Brokers Association of Canada
  #701, 181 University Ave.,
  Toronto, ON M5H 3M7 Tel. 416-367-1831 Fax: 683-7831
- The Insurance Institute of Canada
  18 King St. East, 6th Fl.,
  Toronto, ON M5C 1C4 Tel. 416-362-8586 Fax: 416-362-1126

financial product side of the insurance business growing, there will be a greater demand for financial planners. Mutual Life of Canada pays 30 financial planners to provide financial information to its sales agents and clients. New products—environmental insurance, for example—will require extensive risk assessment, which means more actuaries will be needed. Since actuaries frequently command annual salaries in excess of $100,000, this field is definitely worth considering.

Insurance companies will hire people with strong teamwork skills. In an attempt to reduce the distribution costs of premiums from 35 percent to 20 percent over the next five years, the Canadian Surety Company and Canada West Insurance Company, for example, have put employees in self-managed teams, which eventually will be recruiting their own members, setting their own priorities, and providing one-stop shopping for their clients' needs. Individuals interested in pursuing a career in the insurance industry are strongly advised to develop these skills.

Where the Jobs are in Investment

Money invested in RRSPs has more than doubled from $71 billion in 1987 to $148 billion in 1992, representing an annual growth rate of 16 percent. Banks have 32 percent of the RRSP market; trust companies, 20 percent; life insurers, 20 percent; credit unions, 13 percent; and mutual funds, 15 percent.

According to Hubert Fenken, an analyst with the Labor and Household Surveys Analysis Division of Statistics Canada, women's earnings, group RRSPs, and legislative changes have led to the RRSP boom. Women have been entering the work force in increasing numbers and, given their longevity, they are concerned about planning their long-term financial future, especially since the Canada Pension Plan is likely to dwindle as a source of future income.

In 1991, the number of RRSP contributors grew by 14 percent and total contributions by 30 percent as a result of legislative changes that raised contribution ceilings. The federal government encourages RRSPs as a replacement for the Canada Pension Plan by advising citizens of their RRSP limits in their tax return notices. Since it is one of the few significant tax breaks available to the average Canadian, many are taking advantage of it to escape from the ratcheting effect of continually rising taxes. A 1993 Gallup poll commissioned by Investors Group Financial Services Inc. found that 42 percent of Canadians plan to rely on their RRSPs for retirement income, with 33 percent citing other forms of personal investment and savings. Only 30 percent planned to rely on the Canada Pension Plan to get them through retirement. In 1993, 49.7 percent of the respondents held RRSPs compared with 39.1 percent in 1992. Of those respondents who did not have an RRSP, 25.9 percent planned to enrol in one by the end of 1994, compared with 18.8 percent in 1992. Among retired Canadians, only16.7 percent depend on RRSP income, while 66 percent rely on the Canada Pension Plan and 45.6 percent on company pensions. Of those preparing for retirement, 49 percent plan to invest their money in an RRSP and 41.8 percent viewed a house purchase as their preferred long-term investment.

Self-directed RRSPs through brokerages—individual-directed as opposed to institutional-run RRSPs—are growing even faster than conventional RRSPs now that boomers insist on a higher rate of return than those accrued by traditional deposits. According to John Kaszel, educational director at the Investments Funds Institute of Canada, "People are looking at the returns on mutual funds relative to the interest rates on regular deposits, and they're seeing the advantage of mutual funds. Even the more conservative mutual funds, which invest in bonds and mortgages, are outperforming deposits and GICs." Banks and trust companies have been aggressively promoting the benefits of investing in mutual funds, thereby further enhancing consumer education and awareness. However, only 28 percent of Canadians have ever invested in mutual funds and 75 percent are unable to identify any specific type of mutual fund. Of those investing in mutual funds, 23 percent reported switching to mutual funds as a result of falling interest rates.

The Investment Funds Institute of Canada reports that the total mutual fund assets in 1992 were $67.3 billion, representing a 35 percent increase over 1991. This reflects a 25 percent increase in net sales and a 75 percent appreciation of asset worth. In September 1993, mutual fund assets soared another 42 percent to $95.8 billion. Assets grew by four percent monthly, making mutual funds one of the fastest growing areas of the economy. The rush to invest in mutual funds is a result of the professional management and risk diversification available to small investors through mutual fund investment. The number of shareholders rose 22 percent over the previous year to 5.5 million. The volatility of the Canadian dollar encouraged many to use mutual funds directed to foreign bonds and income funds as a means of hedging and diversifying outside Canada. The foreign mutual funds saw the largest percentage growth as assets grew by 488 percent to $685 million by the end of 1992. Balanced funds, a mixture of stocks and bonds, rose 100 percent to $6.2 billion. A 1993 report by Gordon Capital Corporation sees the value of mutual assets reaching $474 billion by 2002. By 1998, the value of mutual funds is expected to surpass or equal the value of total personal bank and trust deposits.

Registered pension funds are the largest area of investment. In the U.S., banks account for only 6.4 percent of all the money raised annually. There are at least six pension funds which each raise more money than all the banks combined. In Canada, the 35 largest pension funds enjoy combined assets of more than $155 billion and represent about half of all the trusted pension assets under management in Canada. Pension funds are the biggest investors in the equity or stock markets, with many holding minority shareholder positions in numerous companies. However, pension funds typically seek out long-term investment opportunities much like the majority of mutual funds.

Where are the jobs in this industry? Most are in the growing mutual fund and RRSP markets. In fact, many individuals have struck out on their own as financial planners who offer to guide confused investors through the maze of RRIFs, RRSPs, estate planning and life insurance packages. There are many success stories: one M.B.A., unable to get a job after graduation, decided to sell mutual funds to teachers and netted $1 million in his first year!

The future looks bleak for traditional stockbroker jobs. These positions are very market-sensitive, and with the application of computerized trading increasing, individual investors will be able to carry out their own transactions before too long. The increasing sophistication of the boomer investor coupled with greater access to ever-expanding on-line information sources will change the standard stock-market way of doing business. The banks already offer no-frills trading through the Toronto Dominion's "Greenline" and other discount trading services that provide online service to investors through their personal computers. Investors can view quotes from all North American stock exchanges, U.S. options, and indices. These services can be customized to provide complete bid/ask prices, offer sizes, day's opening, high/low, last trade and data, spreadsheets, and real-time or historical graphs. No-load mutual funds will also contribute to the continuing erosion of brokerage commissions over time. Currently, pension funds are keeping the stockbrokers in business. The proportion of shares in the U.S. held by institutions rose from

20 percent in 1970 to over 50 percent in 1992, and will continue to climb—though more slowly—as baby boomers pour more money into their pension funds over the next 20 years.

Career opportunities will be available in mutual fund organizations and in the on-line information service fields which update investors on relevant developments. Banks and insurance companies will seek financial planning experts as they make more aggressive moves into these areas. Accountants and stockbrokers would be well advised to earn a Certified Financial Analyst (C.F.A.) designation to take advantage of the opportunities in mutual funds and other financial planning services—stocks, bonds, and annuities.

In a world of round-the-clock trading, factors like access to information, investor psychology, and timing will be decisive. Thus the market for investor and financial planning advice books and specialized trading services will flourish. Moreover, increased interest in financial matters will mean more jobs in financial journalism. In fact, all media will likely offer more financial advice and information.

Another jobs growth area is in the "middle office"—the new structural aspect of the securities business. The middle office handles the increasingly risky but lucrative derivative trading—futures, options, swaps—which technology is helping companies create. Middle offices provide data entry, trade processing and authorization, compliance control, risk management, revaluation of portfolios, and calculation of profit and loss for the derivative markets much the same way as the back office does for bonds and equities. With middle offices reporting directly to the derivative department, hedging, risk management, and global positioning can be built into products and trading operations right from the beginning. The trend toward the development of middle offices is part of a broader re-engineering aimed at streamlining operations and bringing the back and front offices closer together. Technology, such as the UNIX operating system, allows for work stations which are capable of running several programs simultaneously, thereby connecting many different aspects of the business. The middle office is a growth area because banks and security houses usually avoid such high-risk areas. To offer such services, however, one must account to regulators who want to see that the risk is being appropriately managed by a middle office. The major players adopting middle offices include Merrill Lynch Canada Inc., Goldman

BULLETIN BOARD

- **Job demand factors**: aging boomers preparing for retirement and wanting diverse financial planning services; growing mutual funds and RRSPs markets.
- **Job growth areas**: financial planners; mutual fund investors; media experts; middle office personnel specializing in derivative trading, and mergers and acquisitions.
- **Skills, abilities, qualities, education needed**: creativity, problem solving, decision making, risk assessment, and analytical skills; a diploma in finance essential.
- **Job reduction factors**: sophisticated investors demanding specialized information and trading services; investors able to trade stocks from any location; banks and insurance companies taking over many of the functions now delivered by stockbrokers and individual financial planners or small companies; the mutual fund market is extremely vulnerable to downturns which will scare many investors out of the equity markets and into the money markets.

CONTACTS
- Investment Dealers' Association of Canada
  33 Yonge Street, Suite 350
  Toronto, ON M5E 1G4 Tel. 416-354-6133 Fax: 416-364-0753

Sachs Canada, the Chase Manhattan Bank of Canada, and Japan's Nomura, Sumitomo, and Mitsubishi.

According to the Bank of International Settlements, trade in derivatives rose by 35 percent in 1992 with $4.5 trillion in outstanding contracts at the end of 1992. America's Federal Reserve monitored about $7 trillion in derivatives in the first quarter on 1993 alone. Tax and hedging strategies are encouraging the growth in derivatives. Thanks to outdated tax laws, investors enjoy many tax loopholes in this market. In addition, currency and interest-rate hedging accounts for the marked growth in this area, particularly in Europe where trading soared 66 percent in 1992 in response to concerns over Europe's Exchange Rate Mechanism—currency equalization among European Community countries. Uncertain economic times will continue to make the derivatives market an employment growth area.

Broker investment expertise will prevail in the mergers and acquisitions and the bond- and share-offering markets. Government debt and the privatization of many of its services will keep many dealers in business, as will the record merger and acquistion activity that began in 1993, with $19.3 billion in deals that had to be put together by security dealers and lawyers.

Although the Canadian brokerage industry's revenues increased 45 percent in the first half of 1993 over the same period in1992, the recent volume has strongly affected the processing side of the business. According to Ian Hendry, vice-president for human resources with Richardson Greenshields of Canada Limited, "Technological enhancements and organizational streamlining have enabled us to absorb the increase in business without affecting our employment numbers. There is a good deal of caution in the market due to the economic and political uncertainty which creates hesitancy to make capital expenditures that would generate jobs." Thus, employment figures for the industry are only up to an annualized 21,193 in 1993 over 19,666 in 1992—still significantly lower than the 27,000 employed in the brokerage industry in the pre-crash days of 1987.

Where the Jobs are in Real Estate

The real estate market will see hard times well into the future. The office building market has been crippled by the recession, downsizing, the trend toward home businesses, and the overbuilding of the expansionary late 1980s. The residential market has seen a declining number of potential new home buyers now that the youngest boomers are 30 years old. These trends, along with the lack of job security that influences all long-term purchases, undermine the profitability of the real estate industry.

Overbuilding in the 1980s and low inflation in the 1990s have altered the way real estate is valued and scared off the industry's traditional sources of financing. Pension funds, which currently invest about five percent of their assets in real estate, are buying on the basis of immediate annual returns of nine percent or more, depending upon the product type and market. According to a 1993 Royal LePage Real Estate

Consulting Services survey of 35 of Canada's largest pension funds, fund managers expect to increase their real estate holdings over the next ten years to eight percent of their assets. This means that several billion dollars will enter the market during the 1990s. Since investment targets are based on income generated by a property today, and not by the prospect of a capital gain, pension investors will devote 94 pecent of their real estate investment funds to existing buildings rather than participate in development projects. According to the survey, 13 of Canada's largest pension funds decided to avoid further investment in the real estate market in 1993, while the other 22 funds invested $1.5 billion in real estate and sold $121 million worth at the same time. Two-thirds of the funds plan to invest in real estate during the 1990s, but only three percent plan to reduce their holdings. Office buildings, which comprise 43 percent of the real estate held by fund managers, are targets for only 21 percent of the new investments since this market, which includes downtown and suburban office buildings and hotels, is not expected to recover until 1997-98. One-third of the 1993 acquisitions budgets were aimed at regional shopping centres which are expected to recover by 1995. Aside from industrial buildings (manufacturing) recovering in 1994, 64 percent of the fund managers felt that commercial real estate values would fall in 1994 and only seven percent would see a possible price increase. As pension funds usually adopt a long-term view of investment, 57 percent of the fund managers surveyed planned to retain their current real estate holdings for at least 20 years, with 73 percent planning to continue holding their assets for at least ten years.

In the short term, the greatest employment opportunities will be in the industrial building market. Since the residential market will only enjoy a small recovery, job seekers are not encouraged to pursue a career in this field. The cottage market, however, will pick up as boomers with young children purchase summer cottages for their families.

In 1996, many aging emptynesters will sell their homes and purchase condominiums. As more people retire and adopt a snowbird lifestyle, the condominium or townhouse market will expand even further, since owning a home is not practical under such circumstances. Real estate sales will enjoy a slight boost in the next few years when younger boomers with families purchase the homes of emptynesters who will have in turn heated up the condominium market. In 1991, about 54 percent of the households in Canada comprised only one or two individuals. Coupled with a rise in single-parent families—usually interested in modest housing—these families may wish to purchase the first houses owned by the young boomers now hoping to move into the emptynester homes.

Now that information technology is making it easier to advertise a property to a wide variety of potential purchasers, there is less need for a real estate agent to provide this service. Many boomers, confident of their negotiation and appraisal skills, will seek services that they can pay for à la carte so far as media listing, appraisal, and legal advice and services are concerned. Private selling will become the norm. The job growth area will be in providing services that facilitate the private sale market. RealtyBase, a Virginia firm, already allows prospective buyers and sellers to network with one another on a telephone-accessible computerized service, with the homeowners charged a one-time fee to list their property in the database.

The trend toward holding on to one's house for a longer period of time will also dampen the mid-boomer resale market somewhat. According to Greg Goy, manager of local market analysis at the Canada Mortgage and Housing Corporation, the 1990s will see homeowners staying in their homes longer since they want to avoid the disruption that moving inevitably causes, the cost and inconvenience, and the logistics involved in planning moves around dual-income careers. Paul Knowlton, a housing market analyst for The Corporate Research Group, sees mobility constrained by fewer job opportunities. Home-buying couples in their mid-30s are staying put for up to five years, according to Tammy Fait of Fortra Corporation. The situation is in great contrast to that of the 1980s when people seemed to be buying and selling homes as often as they were purchasing new cars. The changing economic picture around buying and selling homes accounts for some of the changes in consumer behaviour. According to Chris Taggart, vice-president of Tamarack Developments Corporation, "There are costs to selling a house and now there isn't the same capital appreciation as in the good old days when you could buy a house for $100,000 and sell it for $125,000 a few years later. Now it's more of a steady, long-term investment."

In the meantime, Royal LePage Real Estate Services Ltd. is closing 65 of its 265 branch offices, laying off over 100 employees and allowing its agents to negotiate commission fees now that some competitors are

BULLETIN BOARD

- **Job demand factors**: emptynesters moving into condo market, and younger boomer families taking over the larger homes being vacated; pension funds will increase real estate investment from five percent to eight percent of their portfolio, mostly in the already-built market.
- **Job growth areas**: long-term prospects in latter part of 1990s for property managers, home inspectors, commercial and residential appraisers, commercial and industrial sales positions, and residential sales positions in the condo, cottage, and larger home markets; service industry geared to facilitating the private home-selling market will emerge now that the technology exists to make this a cost-effective and less time-consuming way of buying and selling property.
- **Skills, abilities, qualities, education needed**: negotiating, selling, communicating, problem solving, analytical, and multimedia skills.
- **Job reduction areas**: commercial and residential sales jobs in the short term.
- **Growth limiting factors**: real estate fees will decline over the long term; office building market is oversupplied; fewer new-home buyers following on the heels of the boomer generation.

CONTACTS

☛ The Canadian Real Estate Association
Place de Ville, Tower A,
#2100, 320 Queen St.,
Ottawa, ON Tel. 613-234-3372 Fax: 613-234-2567

charging as little as three percent. To allay consumers' fears about making a major purchase during times of economic uncertainty, the real estate industry has also introduced mortgage insurance to protect homeowners from job loss.

Individuals contemplating a career in real estate should note that according to the Canadian Real Estate Association, "Eighty to 85 percent of the money earned in real estate is earned by 15 percent to 20 percent of those in the industry." Although 93,000 people were licensed to practise real estate in Canada in 1988, only about 82,000 are still working in the field.

Where the Jobs are in Business Services

Accounting

There are currently 53,000 professional chartered accountants (CAs) and 14,000 accounting students in Canada; 24,000 certified management accountants (CMAs); and 43,000 certified general accountants (CGAs). (CAs largely engage in auditing; CGAs and CMAs largely engage in industry.) One of the issues that currently concerns the accounting profession is the broadening of accounting responsibilities to all accounting designations. That is, accountants of some designations in one region of the country are permitted to perform functions that are not allowed accountants of similar designations in other regions—for example, the auditing function that can be performed by CGAs, CMAs, and CAs in British Columbia, but only by CAs in Ontario and Prince Edward Island. Ontario is now in the process of reforming the licensing system to allow CGAs and CMAs to prepare audits and validate financial statements, and the P.E.I. Supreme Court has ordered an end to restrictive licensing practices. As a result, many small firms will be able to offer a fuller range of services that will ultimately save companies money. In the past, a company might hire a small accounting firm to handle its day-to-day finances, but engage the services of a chartered accountant to prepare its taxes; the chartered accountant would then have to be apprised of all the company's financial dealings, something the small accounting firm has been acquainted with for some time. Companies working in more than one province will now be able to use the same small accounting firm in each province. This will simplify the accounting process for the company, saving it time and money.

Accounting firms have grown in size and scope of service to meet the global accounting needs of their clients. Many large full-service firms merged and consolidated in the1980s to create six large firms that dominate the accounting profession: Price Waterhouse, KPMG Peat Marwick Thorne, Coopers & Lybrand Limited, Arthur Anderson & Co., Ernst & Young, and Deloitte & Touche. As capital becomes more global—that is, people now invest around the clock worldwide—companies are trying to raise money in various countries. However, with accounting rules and procedures differing from country to country, complications in doing business globally arise. Establishing an international standard has become one of the accounting profession's abiding concerns.

Many companies have gone under as a result of the recession and many unhappy shareholders are now suing the accounting firms that gave ailing companies a clean fiscal bill of health. Even though errors made by auditors may have been small, the judgements against the accounting firms have been stiff simply because the firms have insurance and there may be no one else to sue. Insurance premiums are rising substantially, especially as accounting firms handle more global business, exposing them to billions or dollars in potential damages. Coopers & Lybrand is looking at over $500 million in lawsuits in 1993 in Canada, while in 1993 Ernst & Young agreed to pay a U.S. government agency $400 million (U.S.) over its audits of defunct savings and loans companies.

Although the accounting profession is trying to limit liability to a proportional blame level, partners in accounting firms face unlimited liability, standing to lose not only their jobs, but their investments and personal assets as well. According to Bill Broadhurst, the former chairperson of Price Waterhouse, "The coverage available in the insurance market is really limited. Deductibles have been increasing, coverage has been decreasing, and premiums going up tenfold." As a result of these changes, accounting firms assess their potential clients more carefully, educate clients on the limits of the accounting function, and have industry audit experts review the work of juniors as well as partners. And, to spread out the risk factor, there have been more mergers and consolidations amongst Canada's 20 major auditing firms. This has led to a ten percent reduction in staffing, especially among support staff and trainees as technology takes over their functions. Such reductions are encouraging many accountants to go directly into industry; whereas 4,823 students sat for their chartered accounting exams in 1991, only 3,700 did so in 1993.

Business fraud—some of the fallout of the recession and staff cutbacks—has resulted in more than $100 billion in business losses in North America. According to Lloyd Posno, forensic and litigation accounting specialist for Ernst & Young, forensic accounting "has grown extremely quickly in the past ten years...helped by the recession in the past three or four years." The recession has also increased demand for accounting managers who specialize in credit and collections. Obviously, accountants specializing in bankruptcies and receiverships do well during times of economic hardship and industry shakeouts. Money shortages are also increasing the need for financial managers and strategic planners in the

BULLETIN BOARD

- **Job demand factors**: growing need for financial information and financial management; environmental auditing; collection of accounts receivable; bankruptcies and receiverships; business fraud; globalization of competition.
- **Job growth areas**: environmental accounting; health and social services accounting; credit and collection accounting; budget analyst and financial management accounting; forensic accounting; bankruptcy and receivership accounting.
- **Skills, abilities, qualities, education needed**: consultancy, planning, computer, and system design skills in addition to traditional accounting skills; degree, diploma, certificate in accounting.
- **Growth limiting factors**: need for common accounting standards; economic growth; global competition; government regulations.

TIPS

➤ The official federal government forecast for 100,000 new jobs in accounting being created between 1989 and 1995 was revised downward in 1993 to 60,000.

CONTACTS

☛ Canadian Institute of Chartered Accountants
277 Wellington St. West,
Toronto, ON M5V 3H2 Tel. 416-977-3222 Fax: 416-977-8585

☛ The Society of Management Accountants of Canada
#850, 120 King St. West,
PO Box 176
Hamilton ON L8N 3C3 Tel 905-525-4100 Fax: 905-525-4533

☛ Certified General Accountants Association of Canada
#740-1176 West Georgia St.
Vancouver, BC V6E 4A2 Tel. 604-669-3555 Fax: 604-689-5845

areas of health and social services.

As public concerns over the environment mount, companies increasingly use the services of valuation experts, environmental damage assessment specialists, and accountants with regulatory experience. Large investors—pension funds, for example—will want to assess a company's environmental record before allocating equity funds. To meet these needs, accountants are showing companies how to integrate environmental procedures and reporting systems with their products. Many accounting firms also provide environmental audits.

Advances in technology, coupled with the broadening of accounting responsibilities to all accounting designations, is creating a greater trend toward in-house accounting. This is affecting many midsize and small accounting firms, which are trying to meet these changes by specializing in more areas and playing a greater consultancy role.

Although accounting is already a large field, it will likely grow even larger as the demand for financial information increases. New technology notwithstanding, there will always be a need for budget analysts, auditors, and credit/collection specialists, since these positions are necessary regardless of economic circumstances. The bigger firms offer the best opportunities and highest salaries, while smaller firms will likely merge in the long run to become full-service, consulting-oriented concerns in order to offset the shift to in-house accounting.

Legal Services

Statistics Canada reports that there was one lawyer for every 3,214 Canadians in 1967, but one for every 1,115 in 1992. Whereas there were 7,000 lawyers in Canada in the 1960s, there are now approximately 53,000. At the University of British Columbia, approximately 30 of its 230 graduates were without articling positions—triple the usual number. With many small- and medium-sized law firms still hurting from the recession, some graduates have had to accept unpaid positions instead of the usual $30,000 to $50,000 plus benefits. In order to deal with the current situation, some firms are coming up with novel arrangements such as sharing articling students or allowing articling outside the province, as Quebec is proposing. The Law Society of Upper Canada found that 42 percent completing their bar admissions course in 1993 had not obtained jobs, up from 25 percent in 1989. Increasingly, law firms are contracting out work to lawyers, especially since overhead takes up 52.5 percent of revenues nationally. A partner in a downtown Toronto firm costs between $150,000 and $250,000 for secretarial help, rent, and other overhead. Firms are also hiring fewer students because of the time, money, and energy required to train them. Instead, these firms are using law clerks or first-year lawyers who can do the work of several students.

Lawyers now face competition from independent paralegals who offer routine services to the public at lower fees than those of traditional law firms. Stiffer competition has meant that law firms now concentrate on aspects of the business that contribute most to the bottom line. Compensation is increasingly performance-based and includes a lawyer's bringing in new clients and training staff on the latest technology. Law firms are even using the services of market research companies to find how better to serve current and potential clients. Clients—more sophisticated legal consumers than their predecessors—often require that their lawyers furnish them with a cost/benefit analysis of various courses of action, along with a budget, and ongoing documentation and reassessment of the benefits or options during the litigation process.

As well as alternative dispute resolution gaining ground in many areas—aboriginal land claims, international trade agreements, and environmental disputes, for example—there is a trend toward "boutique firms" in which a network of specializations is created within a firm, each responsible for its own profitability.

Some legal specialties are growing, while others are in a serious slump. International law has become a growth area, with the globalization of trade and increased demand from multinationals for legal representation. Outsourcing has encouraged the growth of contract law. Environmental law, family law, wrongful dismissal litigation, and criminal law are other growth areas. Personal injury lawyers are suffering, with the advent of no-fault insurance. Since the real estate market is slowly picking up, business for real estate lawyers should increase over the next couple of years. Environmental and public relations law will become increasingly important as companies try to manage risk and damage control more effectively. With performance, hiring, and purchasing contracts becoming more complicated in the entertainment field—residual rights in connection with media merging and complicated marketing agreements, as well as product endorsements and television appearances, for example—celebrities will need lawyers as much as they need agents. Also in demand are lawyers who are conversant with the complexities of the high-tech computer world as software piracy, joint ventures, alliances, and information theft and copyright infringement increase. Immigration law will continue to grow, given the internationalization of trade, the presence of multination-

BULLETIN BOARD

- **Job demand factors**: globalization of trade; increasing rates of crime and divorce; rates of wrongful dismissal allegations.
- **Job growth areas**: international law; mergers and acquisitions law; criminal law; family law; labor law; bankruptcy law; environmental law; information and telecommunications law; public relations law; entertainment law; immigration law; medical, corporate, and accounting malpractice law; paralegal work; legal assistants.
- **Skills, abilities, qualities, education needed**: computer literacy, analytical, endurance, problem solving, communication, and stress management skills; two years of university, four years law school, one year articling, six months to bar exam.
- **Job reduction areas**: legal secretaries; court reporters.
- **Growth limiting factors**: market oversaturated with lawyers; alternative dispute mechanisms; excessive costs.

CONTACTS

- Canadian Bar Association
  #902, 50 O'Connor St.,
  Ottawa, ON K1P 6L2 Tel. 613-237-2925 Fax: 613-237-0185
  Toll free: 1-800-267-8860
- Canadian Association of Legal Assistants
  PO Box 967, Stn B,
  Montreal, PQ H3B 3K5
- Canadian Association of Legal Support Staff
  PO Box 3186,
  Winnipeg, MB R3C 4E7

al firms, the refugee claimant hearing process, and increasing worldwide migration of individuals from less developed countries to developed ones. Since malpractice is a growing area of concern, with doctors, accountants, corporate officers, and even lawyers themselves being sued, there will be more activity in this area of the law. And the long-term trend toward consolidation and mergers and acquisitions as part of a global competitive strategy, or as a consequence of industry shakeout, promises to make mergers and acquisitions law a job growth area.

Job security is in doubt as 64 percent of firms surveyed in 1993 by *Canadian Lawyer*—particularly the large firms—indicated that they planned to lay off lawyers or staff in 1993. Figures provided by the Law Society of Upper Canada indicated that 41 percent of the articling students in 1992 were retained, 17 percent found work elsewhere, and 42 percent were without work. In better times, 80 percent of the articling students are usually retained by the articling firms.

While it is difficult to get summer articling jobs, often with 500 to 600 law students vying for five or six positions, those who are hired can make up to $15,000 in a summer. According to *Canadian Lawyer's* 1992 national compensation survey, entry-level salary upon call to the bar fetches $38,000 nationally on average, and $50,000 for large firms.

The technology revolution has taken its toll on jobs for legal support staff. Software such as the Dragon-Dictate system used with Word Dancer allows lawyers to produce all correspondence, court documents, and memos without ever having to touch a keyboard or enlist the help of a secretary. Thus, it is now possible for four or five lawyers to share one secretary. Ontario will soon make a dent in the number of court reporters it hires by replacing many of them with video cameras and voice-recognition computers. The high-tech world is even entering the court appearance procedure, with many arraignments or meetings with public defenders or probation officers being conducted via videoconferencing. Clearly, these developments threaten employment for legal secretaries and court reporters.

Advertising and Public Relations Services

In the future, advertising and marketing will take a different approach to reaching its public as a response to the growth of the multimedia information age. The proliferation of television channels will lead to narrowcasting or niche marketing—special channels devoted to particular interests or markets so that target markets can be reached more efficiently. Data base marketing will become common: when a consumer purchases items electronically, a computer profile of that household's viewing and buying patterns will be generated and sold to interested manufacturers and retailers. Manufacturers will then contact the consumer directly about products that might interest him or her. And the consumer will be able to access product information electronically. The product can then be ordered by using a simple voice command.

Some consumers will hire purchasing agents who will carry out product analysis for them and document the consumer's past purchases and preferences. Products that may interest consumers will be brought to their attention so that they are not besieged by electronic junk mail. Purchasing agents will be paid by the consumer on a fee-for-service basis and agents will be forbidden from accepting any compensation from manufacturers. While advertisers will still be in the business of gathering and providing product information by selling an image, it will become harder to fool sophisticated consumers who have more ways of determining the quality or usefulness of a product through, for example, the purchasing agent.

An information-gathering function now in place is Compusearch, a leading micromarketer—that is, a company that engages in direct marketing to a focussed group in society. Compusearch has classified Canada's 644,000 postal codes according to 70 "lifestyle clusters." Each cluster is then coupled with spending estimates for 1,000 goods and service categories. The following is an example of Compusearch's "wealth-style" clusters: Canadian establishment (1.2 percent), aging urban sophisticates (2.3 percent), lifetime savers (2.7 percent), the materialists (6.5 pecent), armchair seniors (2.4 percent), country comfort (15.1 percent),

---

BUYING A BICYCLE ELECTRONICALLY

You wish to purchase a bicycle with certain features and in a specific price range. Once you enter this information into your computer, all available products meeting the specifications you have set out will be listed on screen. A local showroom will feature a wide array of bicycles for you to examine and test. The showroom will arrange for the bicycle you have chosen to be delivered to you within a short period of time. You will have a chance to examine the bicycle again and test-ride it. If you are not satisfied with the product, you will be allowed to return it as long as it is in pristine condition. If you are satisfied with the product and purchase it, the customer relations department and your purchasing agent will contact you from time to time to determine your level of satisfaction with the product. All recommendations will be noted and product improvements will be brought to your attention electronically.

middle Canada (15.4 percent), starting out (5.6 percent), mortgage slaves (16.1 percent), urban blue-collar (18.2 percent), rural working poor (9.6 percent), beyond their means (1.5 percent), and rough times (1.4 percent). The company produces a CD-ROM that provides on-screen access to a city intersection along with the number and type of business with the number of their employees, and a breakdown of the households in that neighborhood—all within any radius requested. Its "do-it-yourself" data is based on the 125,000 consumers who purchase saws and hammers; similarly, exact incomes, ages and languages of the 500,000 bargain hunters, 750,000 investors and 185,000 cottage owners are available. Another such company, Target Mail of Toronto, sells infor-mation on the products and brand names each household purchases to the package goods industry.

With superior manufacturing accessible even to smaller companies, the differences between products have decreased. The recession has helped make consumers aware of this, since many consumers, more con-scious of their personal bottom lines, began to purchase no-frills or store-label products and found that there was little difference between these products and the better known brands. This has focussed consumers on the price or value of items. Ironically, as products are becoming more similar, they are also becoming more numerous. In1992, 16,800 new products were introduced—a third more than in1987. Retailers took advantage of this increase by auctioning off shelf space and diverting advertising budgets into promotions, which focussed consumer attention on price. Currently, branding has shifted to the retailer, as Loblaw's Supermarket Limited's President's Choice products illustrate. In the U.S., the country's biggest retailer, Wal-Mart Stores Inc., launched its sec-ond own-label line called Great Value and is about to carry President's Choice products under a Wal-Mart label. Once entrenched in con-sumers' perceptions and purchasing outlook, the focus on price and value will be hard to dislodge, especially among aging boomers. As price becomes a crucial purchasing factor, advertising revenues will fall as advertising costs are sacrificed in order to reduce prices.

New technology such as full-colour digital copiers—that provide colour proofs for $2.50—and 3-D software is facilitating in-house advertis-ing and allowing the boutique or specialty advertising firms to better exploit the small business market. The trend toward narrowcasting also

BULLETIN BOARD

- **Job demand factors**: fragmentation of media into narrowcasting or niches; crisis management; new technology lowering imaging and printing costs.
- **Job growth areas**: freelancing; public relations; corporate communication; market research; specialty advertising.
- **Skills, abilities, qualities, education needed**: multimedia and computer literacy; problem solving; creativity; negotiation skills; image awareness; communication skills; college or university degree in advertising, corporate communications or marketing; M.B.A. highly desirable, and essential for public relations work.
- **Job reduction areas**: advertising generalists; permanent positions.
- **Growth limiting factors**: high advertising costs; shift to product promotion based on price or value; size of market niche.

CONTACTS

- Association of Canadian Advertisers, Inc.
  #803, 180 Bloor St. West,
  Toronto, ON M5S 2V6 Tel. 416-964-3805 Fax: 416-964-0771
- Canadian Association of Marketing Research Organizations
  #409, 1 Eva Rd.,
  Etobicoke, ON M9C 4Z5 Tel. 416-620-7420
- Canadian Automatic Merchandising Association
  #2008, 390 Bay St.,
  Toronto, ON M5H 2Y2 Tel. 416-368-0901 Fax: 416-864-0318
- The Canadian Public Relations Society
  #720, 220 Laurier Avenue West,
  Ottawa, ON K1P 5Z9 Tel. 613-232-1222 Fax: 613-232-0565

enhances the boutique or specialty advertising market. Small advertising companies are thus specializing in particular markets, such as the over-50 market or the foreign language programming market.

The 1980s saw many mergers in the advertising industry as agencies responded to the needs of national or multinational companies. Currently, medium-sized companies that lack a specific market focus or specialty are stuggling for survival. These companies will have to develop a niche market or join a network of specialized agencies if they expect to succeed.

Hiring freelancers has become a common practice in general advertising agencies as well as in direct mail agencies, particularly to pitch new accounts. The best place to get a start in the advertising industry—and perhaps the most exciting places to work—are in smaller agencies. What these lack in job security, they make up for in challenges and learning opportunities. Since individuals working in small advertising agencies may be called upon to perform a diverse number of jobs, this environment offers them the opportunity to learn many different aspects of the business.

Market research jobs will grow as collecting consumer information electronically increases in scope. Until some form of artificial intelligence is used, someone will have to process and analyze all that information. As the cost of launching a new product increases in a marketplace already crowded with new products, market research will become more essential in determining the risks involved in introducing a new product.

With the need to increase communication within an organization in order to stay focussed on pleasing the customer, anticipating market changes, and developing appropriate new products, corporate communication positions are a job growth area, as are public relations jobs. Crisis management—in such areas as environmental damage, product scandals, political blunders, questionable practices—the disappearance of the mass market, and the high cost of advertising all favour public relations as a means of reaching a target audience more cheaply and, in many instances, more effectively.

Architectural and Interior Design Services

Architects have been hard-hit by the recession. Architects specializing in industrial design, however, are beginning to feel more optimistic about the future. Many older buildings located in urban settings need modernization, and now that land values have dropped substantially, and the cost of money has declined, constructing a new building is becoming as cost-effective as renting an existing building. In addition, construction costs are down; suppliers have trimmed their profit margins to the point that materials are now 30 percent cheaper, despite the rise in the cost of lumber and the cost of hiring unionized labour. With the supply of preferred developed space diminishing, there is often no shortage of serviced land, with many municipalities having an eight-year reserve supply of unserviced land and potentially a 20-year reserve of unserviced land. Moreover, land prices may fall even further and many manufacturing companies are moving outside large cities to avoid punishing property taxes.

Typically, design-build projects are custom-built by a landowner or developer to specification for a future tenant at a prearranged price. Prospective tenants may include retailing operations such as discount retailers and medical, pharmaceutical, and high-tech companies that often need modern buildings with a combination of office, laboratory, testing, and shipping facilities. The oversupply in the office building market will persist for some time, particularly given the trend to office sharing and working at home or in work stations. Therefore, many units in office buildings may be converted to condominiums. Malls will be in for a shock, when the full potential of home shopping is realized. Once the economy recovers somewhat, there may be growth in the construction of monster malls that combine entertainment, shopping, and dining in innovative ways, such as the West Edmonton Mall.

Eventually, office and home design that incorporates the latest technology with emerging work, entertainment, landscaping, or recreation concepts will flourish. Furthermore, the trend toward working at home will encourage growth in the home renovation market. Since spending 50 percent to 100 percent more on construction and design can pay for itself in three to five years through increased productivity, any company in which salaries account for a substantial part of the company's cost are prime candidates for this kind of renovation or construction. Moreover, the trend towards growth in smaller companies will create a demand for the construction of smaller, more flexible office space.

While the residential market will likely remain relatively soft now that most boomers already own homes, the renovation industry will pick up as people customize their houses in response to the cocooning trend of the 1990s. As retiring boomers leave cities, more design opportunities will present themselves in both rural and urban areas. Eventually, more luxury condominiums will be built for snowbirds and retiring boomers no longer willing or able to bother with home maintenance.

The prefabricated or modular homes market has become a worldwide growth area. In the case of Ibor Canada, an architect designs and markets the homes but contracts out construction to factories in Ontario, Quebec, and the U.S. The units are assembled—except for brick and masonry—in the factory and transported to the location. The homes do not look any different than regular homes, but are better constructed in ideal factory conditions and are approximately 15 percent cheaper. Clearly, this will be an excellent area for architects to take advantage of.

An employment growth area for architects and builders is in the home inspection business. Although only ten to 20 percent of Canadian home buyers have a property inspected by an independent home inspector, the trend is growing, with an estimated 50 percent of the homes sold in Toronto inspected prior to sale for a fee of $300 to $400.

The imagination reels at the many architectural possibilities of the future. There will be many freelance, project-based opportunities with companies aggressively pursuing business in the Far East and Pacific Rim, where construction of all kinds is planned on a mammoth scale. For example, the proposed Australian-Japanese joint venture for building Multifunction Polis (MFP) is planned as a $10-billion urban development prototype that will set the standard for quality for the 21st century by combining elaborate resort facilities, telecommunications services, and high-tech programs designed to attract major companies worldwide: the City of Shanghai and the Chinese government are planning a massive redevelopment project involving an airport, container docks, tunnels, and bridges which will cost $10 billion and require the relocation of over a million people; the Phoenix World City is a cruise ship that will hold 5,000 passengers in its multistory apartment buildings, along with a 2,500-seat theater, a 100,000-volume library, nightclubs, cabaret, discos, a casino, a conference center, a marina for smaller craft within its hull, and a television and broadcast center; Aeropolis 2001 is a 500-storey high rise approximately five times as high as the World Trade Center in New York and costing an estimated $326 billion.

Now that new technology is capable of providing lighter fabric domes at lower costs, many projects that were formerly too costly are being reconsidered. The agribusiness is anticipating the construction of "bubble farms" in which thousands of acres are covered by dome units that protect seedlings and genetically engineered crops. The Japanese are proposing to alter the weather patterns of low-lying islands by enclosing them in tentlike structures, thereby making these islands more habitable.

BULLETIN BOARD

- **Job demand factors**: industrial design-build opportunities represent a better solution than renting older buildings; large multipurpose malls; ergonomic redesign of work and home environments to meet techno-logical innovations; retiring boomers moving out of cities; renovation, landscaping, and in-fill market—building new structure where older building was torn down—in existing residential locations of cocoon-ers; retiring boomers' desire for condo lifestyle.
- **Job growth areas**: industrial design; prefabricated or modular home market; home inspection; luxury condo market.
- **Skills, abilities, qualities, education needed**: proficiency in math, sci-ences, art, uban planning, ergonomics; five-year university program
- **Job reduction areas**: new-home market; office building market except for condo conversion; conventional malls.
- **Growth limiting factors**: the economy as a whole; saturated housing market; construction costs.

CONTACTS

- Interior Designers of Canada
  Ontario Design Centre,
  #506, 260 King St. East,
  Toronto, ON M5A 1K3 Tel. 416-594-9310 Fax: 416-594-9313
- Royal Architectural Institute of Canada
  #330, 55 Murray St.,
  Ottawa, ON K1N 5M3 Tel. 613/232-7165 Fax: 613/232-7559

They plan to use this approach on the ocean floor to redirect currents and create new fishing zones.

Architectural, interior design, and engineering firms now seldom hire full-time employees. In the late 1980s and early 1990s, most people employed in the design industries worked for large companies; now, how-ever, the majority are self-employed since firms cannot afford to retain staff when business is slow. Everyone in these industries has had to devel-op entrepreneurial and co-venturing skills, so as to successfully seek out projects. Indeed, it is essential that those interested in these fields expand their skills. Even interior designers are expected to have a thorough knowledge of computer assisted design since it can greatly reduce the time they spend on a project.

Jobs are not widely available in these industries. Only 33 percent of University of Waterloo's architecture students obtained summer work in architectural companies in 1993, compared to 85 percent in 1987. According to University of Waterloo co-op coordinator Bill Ungar, "The graduating class this year is not only looking at private firms, but at facilities management in institutions and corporations [and in] design fields like graphic design. They are branching [out] into urban planning and pursuing home-building companies."

Engineering Services

While technology such as computer assisted design and computer assisted manufacturing has reduced the need for engineers in some areas, there are critical shortages in many specialized areas. The Canadian Council of Professional Engineers (CCPE) projects a shortage of as many as 15,000 engineers in Canada by the year 2000. The CCPE reports that the demand for chemical engineers is expected to grow by 42 percent between 1990 and 2000 with most growth occurring during the latter half of the1990s. The number of chemical engineers is expected to grow by only 22 percent during this period, causing a significant shortage in this area. Similarly, the demand for electrical engineers, who often go into the computing and systems development field, is expected to grow by 44 percent with supply only increasing by 18 percent. For mechanical engineers, 70 percent of whom enter manufacturing while 30 percent work in mechanical engineering, a 45 percent increase in demand is anticipated versus an increase in supply by a scant six percent. For civil engineers, a 42 percent rise in demand will be accompanied by a supply increase of only11 percent. The demand for more engineers is expected to begin in earnest by 1995, though, clearly, economic circumstances will play an important role in dictating future demand, as will the immigration and emigration of engineers. Historically, the growth in the demand for engineers has closely corresponded with growth in the Canadian economy. However, since1971 there has been a gradual reduction in the relative percentage of engineers in relation to the growth in gross domestic product as a result of productivity improvements achieved by engineers already in the field.

The increase in demand for engineers will also vary according to industrial group, with agriculture and mining growing at a rate one-third less than most other groups. The demand for petroleum engineers is expected to show the highest growth rate—58 percent—thanks to projected energy investments. Proposed northern gas development—$4 billion—and environment and infrastructure improvement projects—$10 billion per year—will also generate a demand for more engineers.

Salaries for engineers typically plateau at the $65,000 level, beyond which engineers interested in higher salaries must move into management positions—a phenomenon which accounts for the significant representation of engineers in M.B.A. programs. The average life cycle of most engineering disciplines is less than 20 years as a result of engineers being promoted to management. In fact, many engineers become managers within ten years of entering the profession. The trend towards outsourcing, however, may decrease the need for engineer-managers, unless the managerial position is consultative.

In Ontario, 2.5 percent of the province's 52,000 engineers are currently unemployed; many of those are civil engineers who will benefit from infrastructure improvement projects, which are badly needed but have been delayed because of government deficits. Wayne Roth, director of Employment and Immigration Canada's Labour Market Outlook reports that in Ontario there is a shortage of design and development engineers, and electrical and electronic engineers. Gennum, a Burlington-based company that designs and manufactures silicon-integrated circuits, plans to increase its staff from 245 to 350 over the next five years with recruits who are able to work with analog circuits using bipolar transistor technology. But will Gennum be able to find engineers who are appropriately trained to take on this specialized work? Siemens Electric Ltd., the fifth largest electronics company in Canada, plans to expand its work force from 3,000 to 12,000 workers by the end of the 1990s. Although the company advertised 18 positions in its London, Ontario, automotive operation, only four of the 270 applicants were hired. The company has yet to find cooling systems engineers, development engineers, and product application engineers. Since companies such as these are not prepared to put years into training personnel, many are recruiting overseas, particularly in Asia.

The trend toward outsourcing, along with the growth of small busi-

BULLETIN BOARD

- **Job demand factors**: growth in telecommunications, information technology, and instrumentation engineering.
- **Job growth areas**: design, development, and electronic engineering.
- **Skills, abilities, qualities, education needed**: integrated manufacturing engineering program offered at University of Toronto is highly recommended.
- **Job reduction areas**: civil engineering—temporarily, until infrastructure improvements can be delayed no longer; possibly chemical engineering.
- **Growth limiting factors**: slow recovery of manufacturing industry; high cost of capital undermining expenditure in competitive high-tech industries.

CONTACTS

- Association of Consulting Engineers of Canada
  #616, 130 Albert St.,
  Ottawa, ON K1P 5G4 Tel. 613-236-0569 Fax: 613-236-6193
- Canadian Council of Professional Engineers
  #410, 116 Albert St.,
  Ottawa, ON K1P 5G3 Tel. 613-232-2474 Fax: 613-230-5759
- Federation of Engineering and Scientific Associations
  #206, 3199 Bathurst St.
  Toronto, ON M6A 2B2 Tel. 416-784-1285 Fax: 416-784-1366

nesses, will put engineers to work in smaller engineering firms specializing in outsource design work for many small manufacturing companies that cannot afford to retain full-time engineers. Even bigger companies such as General Motors are outsourcing auto parts design to suppliers who, in turn, seem to prefer to outsource on a contract basis. The brightest employment opportunities for engineers lie in the telecommunications, information technology, and instrumentation industries. Com-Dev of Cambridge, Ontario, Canada's largest exporter of communications satellite equipment, hopes to increase its work force from 530 to 800 by the year 2000. And Northern Telecom has announced its willingness to hire all of Canada's electronic engineering graduates by 1996.

Consultants and Small Professional Service Companies

Many executives have accepted early retirement in order to start up consulting careers, and many middle managers, especially those who are casualties of downsizing or re-engineering, have struck out on their own as consultants. This trend corresponds with companies moving toward project-based employment. There are abundant opportunities abroad for consultants who were formerly employed by a multinational and who are willing to relocate. Consultants thrive in the engineering and computing fields, as well as those in toxic and hazardous waste control, geotechnical engineering, and bridge design and rehabilitation.

In the past, consulting services focussed on large- and medium-sized companies; now, they will have to find innovative ways of serving smaller clients since most new businesses in the future will likely be small businesses. Since small businesses cannot afford to hire consultants, consultants may experience difficulty finding clients. They can get around this by setting charges on a contingency-fee basis. Expense Reduction Services, for example, does not charge a fee unless savings to the client company are forthcoming. The company's fee is 50 percent of the savings realized in the first year of implementing the consultant's recommendations. Consulting services will likely specialize in various aspects of small business growth and development—how the company can raise venture capital, for example. Consultants usually focus on savings areas small businesses tend to overlook—computer supplies, office supplies, courier services, maintenance and cleaning supplies, overhead, and material costs.

Larger companies often need consultants to implement new technologies, solve specific technology bottlenecks, help companies reorganize or re-engineer, provide training in working in teams as well as help companies save money in specific areas. With the widespread use of new information technology accompanied by corporate re-structuring, many companies require advice in the design, implementation, readjustment, and staff training fields. Previous job descriptions no longer apply, and managers, supervisors, and teams members must learn leadership skills such as coaching, mentoring, and delegating. For employees who are used to exercising authority, or conversely, being told what to do, such a change can be particularly painful, especially for older employees.

Now that more companies are outsourcing, small professional service

BULLETIN BOARD

- **Job demand factors**: new technology; incompatible technology; special applications; re-engineering; lack of team skills; outsourcing; growth in number of small businesses.
- **Job growth areas**: small service or consulting companies specializing in solving problems that are common to an industry; professional and operational services better outsourced.
- **Skills, abilities, qualities, education needed**: communication, creative problem solving, analytical,and business-specific skills; professional training and experience in area-specific fields.
- **Job reduction areas**: fields in which technology makes it easier to perform a function(s) in-house—printing or publishing on a small scale, for example.
- **Growth limiting factors**: the economy in general; the number of companies entering the business; standardizing of technology; expert systems and artificial intelligence that have built-in professional expertise.

CONTACTS

- Association of Independent Consultants
  #110, 2175 Sheppard Ave. East,
  Willowdale, ON M2J 1W8 Tel. 416-491-3556 Fax: 416-491-1670

firms that are geared to solving particular business, manufacturing, or technology problems find themselves very much in demand. Many companies realize that their new technology often require modification, since their hardware and software may be incompatible or inadequate. Small engineering and computer consulting companies can often provide quick-fix solutions or offer a total-service retainership. Larger companies are increasingly outsourcing infrastructure management functions. Typically, there are two kinds of infrastructure management functions that are now outsourced: the management of real estate assets—lease administration, negotiation, and management—and building operations— catering, landscaping, repairs and management, snow removal, cleaning and security; the second commonly outsourced function comprises business and facilities services—general services such as mail, courier, distribution, and reprographics or photocopying, fleet management, environmental control, day care, health services, clerical administration, and inventory administration. IBM's joint venture company, Triax Infrastructure Management Corp., for example, handles all of IBM's non-computer operations.

Competition will intensify in the consulting field, since there are few barriers to market entry. Today, there are consultants in almost every field—telecommunications, taxation, engineering, food services, broadcasting, and so on. Developing alliances with other professional and consulting agencies which offer complementary services as well as specializing in services most in demand or in areas where the cost saving to the consumer of the services are immediately visible will assure success and survival in this business.

Employment Agencies

Temporary help services that provide receptionists, keyboardists, word processors, bookkeepers, and data entry personnel will be in great demand in the future. Since 50 percent to 75 percent of all employees will either be working on contract or be hired on a more casual basis—just-in-time workers hired temporarily and let go as soon as their services are no longer needed—the demand for matching employers with employees will increase. While Canada Employment will continue to perform this function—perhaps on an on-line basis in the future—private agencies with more extensive prescreening facilities will be needed to service companies looking for individuals who can perform very specific tasks. KPMG Peat Marwick Stevenson & Kellogg, for example, has created a temporary executive agency as a response to the surplus of redundant middle managers looking for work. For the most part, its clients are midrange companies with annual sales of $200 million or more. Many of these companies found that they cut back too far when they downsized, and want to "try out" a new position before making it a permanent position. Given the growth of small businesses, which may not have the time or expertise to hire optimally, agencies that reliably and cost-effectively prescreen prospective employees will do well. Eventually, prescreening will go on-line, but individuals will still conduct preliminary interviews and reference checks as part of the prescreening process. As hiring becomes more scientific, companies will need to develop special areas of

BULLETIN BOARD

- **Job demand factors**: increasing trend toward hiring on a contract or casual basis; eventual shortages in high-tech areas; boomers retiring.
- **Job growth areas:** private agencies that can prescreen or recruit candidates cost-effectively.
- **Skills, abilities, qualities, education needed:** a solid understanding of the business environment; university degree in psychology, preferably at the master's level.
- **Job reduction areas**: traditional temporary employment services since eventually office and clerical workers will use electronic bulletin boards to advertise their services and will be working at home.
- **Growth limiting factors**: low barrier to market entry; government may try to assume the prescreening role to some extent; limited numbers of qualified people.

CONTACTS

- ACCIS - The Graduate Workforce Professionals
  #205, 1209 King St. West,
  Toronto, ON M6K 1G2 Tel. 416-535-8126 Fax: 416-532-0934
- Association of Professional Placement Agencies & Consultants
  #L-109, 114 Richmond St. East,
  Toronto, ON M5C 1P1 Tel. 416-362-0983 Fax: 416-360-5478
- Federation of Temporary Help Services
  #409, 1 Eva Rd.,
  Etobicoke, ON M9C 4C5 Tel. 416-626-7130 Fax: 416-630-5392

hiring expertise and will have to become more globally connected. Thus, to succeed in this area, small- or medium-sized companies will have to specialize, and large firms will have to include international headhunting as part of their mandate.

Headhunting firms will be vigourously seeking highly qualified candidates who are expected to be in short supply by the turn of the century. Since this shortage will be worldwide, headhunters will find themselves acting on behalf of foreign companies recruiting in Canada. Already the Japanese raid the University of Waterloo for its computer science graduates at the master's level. Hospitals in the U.S. often send recruiters to

Canada to lure doctors and nurses to warmer climates; given the wage changes likely to occur as a result of cost containment strategies in the health care field, these recruiters may be very successful in their future efforts. As technology becomes universally adopted, those countries expanding the most will experience shortages in high-tech personnel. Poorer countries whose populations always expand the fastest will lack suitably trained personnel even if they are able to import the technology. These shortages will become more acute as aging boomers begin to retire around 2001. Multinational headhunting firms will be the only ones remaining in the mature phase of this industry. Smaller companies will likely be out of business, merged, or acquired by the year 2000, except for the very specialized players. Medium-sized companies will have to specialize and cultivate international connections in order to survive.

DISTRIBUTION INDUSTRIES: TRANSPORTATION, COMMUNICATIONS, UTILITIES, AND THE WHOLESALE TRADE

Where the Jobs are in Transportation

• Trucking • Railways • Shipping • Air Transport
• Postal and Courier Transportation • Road Infrastructure

Transportation accounts for 3.5 percent of Canada's gross domestic product; 450,000 or 3.6 percent of the work force is employed in the transportation sector. Transportation workers also enjoy an average weekly salary of $650, which compares favourably with the national average of $550 in terms of domestic tonnes transported; trucking accounts for 36.5 percent; rail, 48.8 percent; and marine, 14.7 percent. Exports comprise 30 percent of Canada's gross domestic product, which puts the country seventh in the world in exporting, despite ranking 31st in population. With the increasing continentalization of trade as a result of the North American Free Trade Agreement (NAFTA), Canada is becoming one of three major players in a marketplace of 370 million people. The growing globalization of trade is increasing the amount of export business and thus shifting the traditional east-west movement of goods to a north-south, transborder orientation in competition with U.S. and Mexican transportation deliverers. The outcome of resulting competition in the transportation industry will in many ways determine the future of transportation in Canada.

In response to the need to streamline Canada's transportation system within the country and across borders, Advantage Canada was formed in 1992, its mandate to create a completely integrated transportation system. Its goals are to establish industry standards of quality, to foster alliances among intermodal carriers—for example, when cargo moves from ship to train to truck in one container which is transferred to the next mode of transport—so as to provide an efficient seamless flow of cargo, to reduce shipping costs by raising the volume of cargo shipped on Canadian routes, to implement a common standard for the electronic data exchange between the various carriers, and to work towards changing the taxation system so as to establish a level playing field with foreign competitors.

A logistics revolution is taking place in the way transportation is delivered. Because it no longer makes sense to have one plant in Mexico, another plant in the U.S., and a third plant in the U.S., production is being rationalized and transportation centralized. For example, it makes more sense to have one plant in the U.S. and transport the product to Canada and the U.S. Canada is at a particular disadvantage when it comes to logistics planning owing to our sparser population densities. Canadian companies pay five percent to ten percent more in distribution costs than American companies, reports James Ecker, a transportation consultant with KPMG Peat Marwick Stevenson & Kellogg. George Weston Limited finds that the logistics component for its bakery chain comprises 45 percent of its products' selling price, while Northern Telecom only pays a five percent premium in logistics costs. As might be expected, Canadian export companies are demanding lower transportation costs in order to survive in global markets. A multinational company whose Canadian transportation costs represented 11 percent of the plant's product cost strongly suggested to Canadian National (CN) that it reduce its transportation costs to eight percent or it would leave Canada. This, and other such demands have forced CN to cut 11,000 jobs from its North American operation.

Warehouse facilities, plant facilities, and distribution centres are being phased out in order to facilitate the just-in-time demands of customers. IBM Canada Ltd. closed 14 warehouses in Toronto and now stores its supplies to one warehouse in Markham, Ontario. As you might expect, all inventory is controlled by a local area network and extensive use is made of carousels and automated guided vehicles in its Sandrail high-density

BULLETIN BOARD

CONTACTS

- Chartered Institute of Transport in Canada
  Heritage Place,
  155 Queen St., 9th Fl.,
  Ottawa, ON K1P 6L1 Tel. 613-786-3111 Fax: 613-563-9596
- Transportation Association of Canada
  2323 St. Laurent Blvd.,
  Ottawa, ON K1G 4K6 Tel. 613-736-1350 Fax: 613-736-1395

storage system. IBM has reduced its product-moving times to better meet just-in-time manufacturing and retailing deadlines. And since paperwork has been eliminated as a result of the company's using electronic data interchange (EDI) to communicate with Canada Customs, border-crossing delays have been reduced by three days on average.

One way of reducing logistics problems is to outsource them to a company that specializes in logistics. Hewlett Packard (Canada) Ltd., for example, saved over $1 million in handling inventories by hiring J. D. Smith and Sons, which also provides a just-in-time delivery service for 3M. Unfortunately, according to a 1992 study by A. T. Kearney and the Canada Association of Logistics Management, Canadian companies are behind in warehousing, transportation or inventory management, with less than 15 percent of Canadian companies using the distribution requirement planning system which is essential for reducing inventories.

Transportation management positions now require a university degree since individuals in this profession must have a sophisticated understanding of technology as well as knowledge in such areas as logistics and total quality control. Currently working with six Canadian universities to build educational programs that meet the new high-tech requirements of the transportation industry, the Chartered Institute of Transport, an international organization with 20,000 members, continues to work at upgrading educational standards in the field.

BULLETIN BOARD

- **Job demand factors**: cost and efficiency in being able to provide just-in-time delivery; deregulation; international trade agreements.
- **Job growth areas**: information technology; quality control and logistics.
- **Job reduction areas**: fewer drivers will be needed, particularly of the private for-hire sort; warehousing jobs that are becoming increasingly automated.
- **Growth limiting factors**: competition in the U.S.; cabotage rights; customs duties and tariffs.

CONTACTS
- Canadian Trucking Association
  #300, 130 Albert St.,
  Ottawa, ON K1P 5G4 Tel. 613-236-9426 Fax: 613-563-2701

Trucking Industry

The overall expenditures of the trucking industry—the total amount spent annually for trucks, gas, employees— add up to approximately $20 billion and employs 200,000 individuals across Canada. This mature industry is in the midst of a trend toward deregulation. Twenty years ago, regulation guaranteed a profit to any carrier; but now that interprovincial authorizations are easy to obtain, common carriers are competing across the country. As a result of deregulation and the continentalization of trade, large operators have put small companies out of business or bought them up. The Private Motor Truck Council of Canada has lost 120 companies—one-third of its members since 1990.

Despite the move to larger trucking companies, the three largest Canadian companies are only one-quarter the size of American companies, as far as fleet size or revenue is concerned. U.S. carriers in the southern states enjoy lower costs than Canadian carriers and have cabotage rights advantages over their Canadian counterparts, given that customs rules favour their American competitors. Both U.S. and Canadian companies will be gearing up to compete for the enhanced opportunities which come into effect in1996, allowing Canadian and U.S. trucks to pick up and deliver in Mexico. After six years, they will be able to operate anywhere in Mexico.

Technology has entered the truck-driving field in the form of truck-top satellite dishes that can locate a truck within 100 yards anywhere in North America and enter this information into a central processing system for integration with other data. Instead of waiting for drivers to call in from checkpoints, messages are relayed instantly, and last-minute schedule changes can be made to improve delivery efficiency.

Despite the many changes that will increase the competitiveness of the trucking industry in Canada, there will likely be an industry shake-out, combined with many mergers and acquisitions. Job prospects are rather dismal for all except individuals involved in the information technology, quality control, and logistics side of the industry.

Railway Industry

The Canadian railway is the third largest in the world. Over $6 billion in annual revenue is generated by Canadian railways. It employs more than 60,000 people and it purchases $3 billion worth of goods and services annually. Unfortunately, Canada's large expanses of sparsely populated land does not provide the tax base necessary to support the railway on a competitive basis with the U.S.; Canadian railways pay 54 percent more tax than American railways. According to the *Financial Post*, "A train going from New York to Seattle pays $10,000 less in fuel taxes than one moving from Montreal to Vancouver." In terms of the overall cost of moving freight containers, Canadian railways pay 75 percent higher taxes per container-mile than American railways. Were market value assessment to proceed in Toronto, taxes would increase by $40 million.

This competitive disadvantage has resulted in countless layoffs in the industry and strong efforts to improve productivity. CN now moves three times as much freight as it did 30 years ago with 43,000 fewer freight cars, one-half the number of locomotives, and about one-third fewer employees. As the largest railway company in Canada, CN, without further cost cuts, will see its losses reach $1.5 billion by the end of the 1990s. Its employees—members of 14 different unions—earn an average annual salary of $44,000, uncompetitive with salaries offered in the U.S. Since the 1980s, CP Rail has also reduced its work force by one-third. The 23 different railways in the industry will likely be trimmed as well, with the formation of smaller networks as a result of the shutting down of unprof-

BULLETIN BOARD

- **Job demand factors**: an increasing export market.
- **Job growth areas**: information technology; finance and marketing.
- **Job reduction areas**: everywhere except in the information technology and quality control aspects of the industry.
- **Growth limiting factors**: uncompetitive cost structure in connection with taxes, wages, and geographical markets; automation.

CONTACTS

- Railway Association of Canada
  #1105, 800 Rene-Levesque Blvd. West,
  Montreal, PQ H3B 1X9 Tel. 514-879-8555 Fax: 514-879-1522

itable lines, the sharing of lines to compensate for excess capacity, and the purchasing of branch lines by independent operators. Plans are well underway—currently in the East—to privatize Canadian railways so that they can seek public as well as debt financing and perhaps undermine union wages.

The container industry, which dominates how freight is carried by rail and ship, is growing, with 5.8 million twenty-foot containers comprising the size of the world fleet. Intermodal transportation now allows containers to be carried by ship, truck, or rail as required. CP Rail's new RoadRailer uses hybrid freight-carrying trailers which have both rubber tires and steel wheels, so that the entire trailer can be switched from a highway to a train or vice versa. To enhance the freight handling capacities of cargo trains, steel containers are now stacked on top of one another, thereby doubling the amount of freight a train can carry.

The trend towards using high-speed trains may shift more business to the railway industry. While Bombardier Inc. has acquired the North American rights to France's TGV railway system, it is more likely that we will see Sweden's slightly slower X-2000 adopted in Canada, since it does not require an entirely new track infrastructure and is only half the price.

It is unlikely that the Canadian railway system will ever be competitive with its American counterpart. Employment will diminish over time as automation of all aspects of rail service becomes universal. Whereas CN employed 52,000 in the 1980s, it expects to reduce that figure to 22,000 by 1995. The company also plans to abandon 20 percent of its lines in central and eastern Canada by 1995 and sell an additional 30 percent of its unprofitable and underused lines to independent operators. An eastern line merger of CN and CP Rail would involve a co-production agreement aimed at reducing its work force by a third—10,000 workers—by 1995, spending $100 million in computer systems and forming agreements with trucking companies and U.S. railways.

Shipping

Of Canada's 15 ports, Vancouver is the largest, handling 63.3 million tonnes of the 182 million tonnes of cargo shipped Canada-wide. Vancouver is in the process of constructing a new general cargo and cruiseship terminal and a third container terminal to help meet the growing container market, which is likely to go from a throughput level (moving a container from one place to another) of 73.5 million containers to a worldwide level of 110.6 million containers by the year 2000. The new projects, planned for completion in 1995, will double Vancouver's container handling capacity. And as the Pacific Rim becomes a greater focus of trade, Vancouver's business should increase accordingly.

In Eastern Canada, however, the St. Lawrence Seaway is facing serious competitive difficulties. Although Montreal has spent $37 million over the past decade building container terminals, it must work harder to reduce Seaway charges. With shipping facing transportation challenges from Canadian and American rail networks, some ports may have to close and fleet sizes will diminish. With the Seaway not realizing a profit over the last decade, 15 percent of the staff have been laid off since 1990 and another 25 percent reduction is expected by the year 2000, leaving only 600 employees. Although dredging has increased load passage—that is, the weight a boat can carry before its hull hits the bottom in shallow waters—by up to an extra thousand tonnes for every foot dredged or $150,000 worth of extra cargo business on every voyage, Seaway charges cannot be reduced and the Western Grain Transportation Act provides subsidies for shipping grain from western ports which the East cannot compete against. Since the Seaway cannot survive much longer if present circumstances prevail, it is likely that the West Coast will increase its capacity at the expense of the East, and grain will be shipped to the rest of the world from Vancouver instead of from eastern ports.

BULLETIN BOARD

- **Job demand factors**: increasing Pacific Rim trade; increase in inter-modal transport.
- **Job growth areas**: the West Coast.
- **Job reduction areas**: St. Lawrence Seaway.
- **Growth limiting factors**: competition from Canadian and U.S. railways and U.S. ports.

CONTACTS

- Canadian Port and Harbour Association
  60 Harbour St.,
  Toronto, ON M5J 1B7 Tel. 416-863-2036 Fax: 416-863-4830
- Canadian Shippers' Council
  #250, 99 Bank St.,
  Ottawa, ON K1P 6B9 Tel. 613-238-8888 Fax: 613-563-9218
- Shipping Federation of Canada
  #326, 300 St-Sacrement St.,
  Montreal, PQ H2Y 1X4 Tel. 514-849-2325 Fax: 514-849-6992

Many of Canada's natural resources are shipped because of the bulk nature of the cargo. Thus, the shipping industry is very dependent on how well Canada's natural resources are selling abroad. While Canadian fruit, frozen meat, and seafood are sought after in the Far East, the grain market is more vulnerable to worldwide weather conditions, political subsidies, and protective tariffs.

Overall, the Ports Canada system has created more than 50,000 direct and spinoff jobs. Total revenues collected in 1991 was $5.7 billion. Any employment in the shipping industry will likely be on the West Coast, primarily in Vancouver.

Air Transport

The airline industry in North America has suffered very hard times. In the 1980s, deregulation enticed more competitors and resulted in too much capacity. Air Canada planned to have 7,000 fewer employees by the end of 1993 than in 1990, leaving 16,000 employees remaining . If the workers balk at the proposed five percent wage rollback, more workers

BULLETIN BOARD

- **Job demand factors**: emptynesters stimulating the air travel market.
- **Job growth areas**: the cargo charter market, but temporarily.
- **Job reduction areas**: everywhere else in the industry.
- **Growth limiting factors**: teleconferencing; oversupply of competitors; geographic and demographic considerations; larger, more cost-efficient U.S. airlines and carriers; declining importance of Canada Post.

CONTACTS

- Air Transport Association of Canada
  #747, 99 Bank St.,

will be cut from the work force. Every job category has been subject to cutbacks. Canadian Airline International Ltd.'s 1,800 employees have agreed to wage cuts over the next four years and are prepared to buy shares in the company to aid a $246 million investment by American Airlines Inc.

The technology explosion has not spared the air transport industry. Teleconferencing will reduce the need for business air travel, and once teleconferencing technology becomes affordable to the homeowner, individuals will be able to travel to the living room or office of anyone in the world. During the Gulf War, sales of British Telecommunications PLC videoconferencing equipment jumped 60 percent. Since then, business travel has diminished by 40 percent in Canada. Of course, not all business or social travel will disappear. Emptynesters and retired boomers will likely stimulate the industry in 1996 in the U.S. and in 1997 in Canada as the first wave begins to travel the world. It will, however, take a few years for the industry to reabsorb those already laid off once the shakeout process is complete.

Canada Post is the country's largest distribution company which uses transportation and is the airlines' biggest freight customer. Unfortunately, electronic mail, fax machines, and interactive computer networks are taking us closer to a paperless world at the expense of the airlines' best customer. Airlines may regain some business, however, when home shopping becomes more popular and there is greater demand for fast delivery from manufacturers.

The cargo charter market, which consists of planes flying within Canada for courier companies, is only a $50 million business. If transborder air regulations ever liberalize as promised and cabotage were no longer an issue, the Americans would likely take over this market, using their own systems and operators.

Postal and Courier Transportation

Although postal and courier companies are heavy users of other means of transportation, they still require their own transportation within each city. For example, Canada Post has its own fleet of 6,000 vehicles. To some extent, the survival of Canada Post will hinge on its ability to compete with courier companies to deliver or pick up items purchased through home shopping once home shopping becomes more popular. The mail order business will increase as a transition to home shopping.

As the world heads towards paperless communication, automatic billing, and a cashless society, 80 percent of the mail that business accounts for will diminish substantially. Canada Post has anticipated these developments through its purchase of Purolator Courier Ltd., a courier company hard hit by the recession, a heavy debt load, and stiff competition from Federal Express Canada Ltd. (Fedex) and United Parcel Service Ltd. (UPS). In 1990 in Canada, the courier business was worth $1.9 billion—6.3 percent of the transportation market— employed 26,480 people, and supported 2,433 companies—the 767 in Ontario accounting for $1.3 billion in revenue. Only 20 percent of the business is same-day delivery, with domestic deliveries accounting for 83 percent and commercial clients 79 percent of the overall business. For-hire truckers moved $149 million in express packages, and bus companies carried $89 million in rush consignments. The large courier companies, facing decreasing profits on express deliveries, are turning to business logistics—such as maximizing the speed versus cost tradeoffs— and other value-added services like preprinted mailing labels and small computer terminals that print waybills and simplify customs problems for small clients. Each of these courier companies is investing large sums in new technology with the hope of outdistancing its competition through improvements in efficiency.

DHL International Express of Mississauga, Ontario, manages 100 global accounts of multinationals that require comprehensive logistics services for warehousing and freight consolidation, air and road transportation, parts banking, and just-in-time deliveries. According to Ken Sternad of UPS, "Be it mail order, catalogue or TV merchandising, just-in-time retailing is already an important part of our business and should grow substantially in future years." With the price of overnight delivery dropping, thanks to lower air fares, more catalogue retailers are opting for this service.

Regional carriers have long since replaced taxis to deliver packages and envelopes locally. Companies such as Zipper Transportation Services Ltd., which handles 60 percent of the same-day deliveries in Winnipeg, Saskatoon, and Regina, are now only growing at a five percent annual rate compared with the 20 percent rate common in the mid-1980s. Fax machines and the recession have been responsible for slower growth. Successful regional carriers like Zipper have stood out from their competitors because they have come up with innovative ways to add value for its customers. Zipper is also a commercial dealer for Canada Post with computers networked to Priority Post. Typically, the company's drivers earn $20,000 annually.

According to the International Civil Aviation Organization, the Asia-Pacific region will experience as much as a ten percent rate of growth in freight traffic during the 1990s, making it the fastest growing market. Now that air express has become a regular part of doing business, both Fedex and DHL Worldwide Express have begun making inroads in the Asian market. It is anticipated that global contracts for distribution outsourcing is likely to be the battleground for the bigger integrated couriers. In 1992, Fedex obtained the first worldwide distribution contract, a ten-year $256.5 million contract for Laura Ashley Holdings PLC of Britain. In 1993, it secured a contract to deliver the high-tech products of National Semiconductors to customers anywhere in the world within two days. Airborne Freight of Seattle handles products from IBM, Eastman Kodak Company and Du Pont Canada Inc. globally. And UPS has a contract with General Motors Europe for just-in-time delivery of replacement auto parts. Since only five percent of North American transportation services involve outsourcing of distribution logistics compared with 25 percent to 30 percent in Europe, there should be a significant growth opportunity area in the courier business throughout the 1990s.

In the end, the large privately held courier companies—models of

BULLETIN BOARD

- **Job demand factors**: increasing importance of mail order; eventual revolution of television home shopping direct from the factory; just-in-time delivery; outsourcing of distribution logistics; global contracts; value-added services.
- **Job growth areas:** drivers involved in the pickup and delivery of mail order or home shopping items; intercompany delivery of parts and components.
- **Job reduction areas**: mail sorting and delivery; post office positions dealing with the public.
- **Growth limiting factors**: willingness of public to accept home shopping as alternative to shopping in person; fax machines and other forms of electronic communication; cost of air transportation; price of gas; potential for cross-subsidization between Purolator and Canada Post and preferred air rates.

CONTACTS

- Express Transport Association
  E-325, 2255 Sheppard Ave. East,
  PO Box 26,
  Willowdale, ON M2J 4Y1 Tel. 416-495-9611

efficiency in most cases—will likely triumph if an open-skies policy is adopted. The number of home- or office-delivery and manufacturing pick-up jobs will grow with consumers increasingly indulging in home shopping or taking advantage of mail order services. Fedex is already designing an interactive unit that shows customers how to send a package from a walkup kiosk. The trend toward working at home will also be a further boon to courier services.

Road Infrastructure

Although automobiles account for approximately 90 percent of passenger travel in Canada and the bulk of freight travel is conveyed by trucks, four out of every ten kilometres of Canada's highways are below minimum standards. A federal study released in1993 indicates that approximately 800 of the 3,534 bridges are below grade, 160 deaths are attributable annually to poor roads, and $20 million in property damage results from these accidents.

Roads have deteriorated because Ottawa has underfunded road infrastructure improvement projects. Whereas Washington assumes 23 percent of highway expenditures in the U.S., in the past Ottawa has only pitched in five percent for improvements to its highways. The Liberal government is now promising to put up $2 billion of the $6 billion needed for infrastructure improvement so long as the provinces come up with the remaining $4 billion. To bring back Canada's highways to minimum standard would require $14 billion over a ten-year period. In 1991, federal gas taxes brought in $6 billion, yet highway expenditures amounted to less than $200 million. In 1988, Canada spent $53,000 per kilometre on maintenance compared with $237,000 by Germany, $275,000 by France, $352,000 by the U.S., and $504,000 by Italy.

The Canadian highway system is worth $200 billion; however, it will likely cost three to five times the maintenance costs to replace them. The Fraser Institute estimates that repairing the roads would net the federal and provincial governments $350 million a year in savings from operating savings—the costs associated with clearing up accidents, plus the wear and tear on vehicles used to patrol highways, for example—reduced accident-related property damage, travel time savings, job creation, and reduced unemployment insurance payouts.

The province suffering the most is New Brunswick, which requires at least $2.2 billion to restore its 961 kilometres of highway. Fortunately, Ottawa signed a $300 million highway deal to improve that area of the Trans-Canada over the next four years, with the province chipping in an additional $300,000.

Canada's competitiveness depends, to a very great extent, on having an adequate infrastructure. Should Ottawa or the provinces not work hard to restore the country's highways, there will be costly long-term effects on all sectors of society. If, on the other hand, funds are made available for road restoration, there will be considerable employment opportunities for civil engineers and others involved in the various aspects of road repair and construction. Since most provincial budgets are slim, governments may well institute users fees that would help raise money for the recovery process. Unfortunately, this would only add to Canada's already prohibitive transportation costs.

BULLETIN BOARD

- **Job demand factors**: 40 percent of Canadian highways are below minimum standards.
- **Job growth areas**: civil engineers; road construction crew and jobs in road supply companies.
- **Growth limiting factors**: the previous federal government's refusal to pay for its fair share of highway improvement; limited provincial funds.

CONTACTS

☛ Canadian Society of Civil Engineering
EIC Building,
#700, 2050 Mansfield St.,
Montreal, PQ H3A 1Z2 Tel. 514-842-5663 Fax: 514-842-8123

According to former Minister of Transport, Jean Corbeil, the government's strategic capital investment will provide investment of more than $2 billion in transportation and communication infrastructure to 1998 and will generate from 4,000 to 5,000 jobs annually. In addition, the Liberal Party's promise to spend $2 billion on infrastructure—matched by the provinces' additional $4 billion—should guarantee many infrastructure improvements.

Where the Jobs are in the Communications Industries

Apple Computer predicts that a decade from now, the global business in multimedia will be worth $3.5 trillion. With this in mind, various modes of media delivery companies are intent upon grabbing as big a piece of the market as possible. Time Warner, the second largest U.S. cable television company and the world's largest media company, is one of the companies racing to control various media services. Even Canadian investors have placed their money on Time Warner as the potential winner of this big-stakes contest: the Bronfmans have bought a 5.7 percent share for $702 million and Paul Desmarais' Power Corporation of Canada is also taking a major share position in the company. Microsoft is providing the hardware and software necessary for television reception. Phone and cable companies will depend upon one another well into the 21st century because cable companies will be the largest deliverer of video transmission, but the phone companies are necessary for the delivery of video-on-demand to subscribers. Phone and cable companies are teaming up to compete against the new "deathstar" satellites capable of delivering 150 channels to its subscribers. Even Maclean Hunter Limited has been purchased by Rogers Communications Inc.—subject to approval by the Canadian Radio and Telecommunications Commission (CRTC)— in what is perhaps Canada's first foray into the merging multimedia field.

Computerized switching, controlled by phone companies, allows viewers to watch a program whenever they wish by simply pushing telephone buttons. Since it only takes five seconds to download a movie from an information warehouse, viewers can use their VCRs to control all aspects of watching the video, including rewinding, fast forwarding or freeze framing. With digitization becoming the standard, all information from any medium can be translated and manipulated. The digitization of the transmission signal will allow viewers to manipulate, edit, or store the video signals in any manner desired. Digitization also allows for compression of the signal with the result that more channels can be broadcast in a frequency range. Moreover, it improves channel reception.

The multimedia convergence war will be a clash of the titans. U. S. West, a Baby Bell phone company, has just invested $2.5 billion in Time Warner's multimedia unit in an effort to build a 28-city interactive cable television network, which would then compete with local telephone companies to provide enhanced telecommunications services such as computer data bases. In Canada, Videotron of Montreal has teamed up with BCE Inc., Bell's parent company, and CUC Broadcasting, an Ontario cable company, has formed a partnership with Telus Corp., owner of Alberta Government Telephones. In the U.S., AT&T is approaching Tele-Communications, the largest U.S. cable company, in order to take on Time Warner. AT&T has a global long-distance network, owns a computer company, makes customer terminals and computer chips and has the world's largest privately owned research and development facilities.

Even without optical fibre which would allow telephone companies to supplant cable companies, telephone companies can deliver two or three video-on-demand channels to the consumer's home over copper wire, thanks to frequency-boosting techniques. The British government has already granted licences to companies to experimentally send television

BULLETIN BOARD

- **Job demand factors**: telephone companies control the switching technology for video-on-demand and the enhanced telecommunications services.
- **Job growth areas**: telecommunications research and development; optical fibre installation.
- **Job reduction areas**: cable industry jobs in the long term.
- **Growth limiting factors**: rate of optical fibre installation; government regulation of the industry; ability of cable companies to entrench their share of the video and network market.

CONTACTS

- Canadian Independent Telephone Association
  #107, 2442 St. Joseph Blvd.,
  Orleans, ON K1C 1G1 Tel. 514-834-1177 Fax: 514-834-8806

signals over telephone lines. To ensure their eventual dominance in the delivery aspect of the multimedia format, Bell South is in the process of installing fibre optics to 130,000 customers, Deutsche Bundespost Telekom in Germany hopes to install 1.2 million fibre optic lines by 1995, and American Information Technologies in the U.S. is in the process of installing 2.5 million such lines at a cost of $1 billion by 1995.

The CRTC has yet to give telephone companies broadcast licence. However, since cable companies are providing some telephone services and hold shares in long-distance carriers, Bell is pushing for its share of the video transmission market. While it is unlikely that the issue will be resolved before the turn of the century, competition will likely emerge in the short term between telephone and cable companies for alarm services, data base access, voice messages, and electronic mail. In the long run, the multinational linkages and alliances are likely to play havoc with the attempts of individual governments to regulate electronic media effectively.

Jobs in the telecommunications industry will definitely get a boost from these developments. In the long run, telephone companies are likely to win, given the inherent superiority of optical fibre over other transmission mediums—using optical fibre, all information can be transmitted cost-effectively to every household by a single carrier. The computer and software industry will hire staff to develop this side of the technology. Despite eventual consolidation through mergers and acquisitions, most high-tech employees will be hired in this global growth industry for at least the next 20 years.

Radio, Television, and Cable

Every aspect of the broadcasting industry, from recording to editing and transmission, is being digitized. It will soon be possible, using "suitcase studios," to perform such functions as sound and video recording, and editing and transmission from the field. A documentary about Antarctica could be put together on location and the footage could be broadcast by satellite from the location over a network. This innovation will require field staff to develop the appopriate skills to perform these functions, if necessary, from a remote location.

Furthermore, since digital signals can be compressed to create more room in a frequency bandwidth, digital transmission will alter the number of channels or stations that can broadcast. It is now possible to have eight television channels in the frequency band used at the moment by a single channel. This will allow cable companies to increase the number of channels offered to subscribers before the introduction of optical fibre puts more stations on an individual's radio dial. The additional channels or stations will increase competition between stations for an audience, advertising dollars, and program material. The outcome is expected to be more narrowcasting—broadcasting to select audiences—such as jazz, rock, comedy, country, fashion, finance, age-specific programming, 24-hour news, nostalgia, real estate, sport-specific channels, classical music, and so on. More local coverage will appear in a station's attempt to come up with new material to fill additional air time. This will create more jobs for roving reporters, sportscasters, commentators, program producers, talk show hosts, and newscasters. Video- and/or sound-recording technicians will be needed to accompany broadcast journalists on their field trips, and technicians who can do on-site editing.

Many radio stations have chosen syndicated musical formatting, which narrows the role of the program director and the disc jockey to that of coordination and the bridging of material and information—that is, the commentary between songs. AM radio will likely make more aggressive moves into non-music narrowcasting with business news, consumer affairs shows, children's programming, religious programming, and seniors programming. Advertisers are insisting on narrowcasting to better reach the 25- to 54-year-old market.

Competition for musical programming from the U.S. is about to pick up in the radio broadcast area as the CRTC approved licences in 1993 for two services that will provide commercial-free, digital channels offering CD-quality music to cable subscribers. Over the next year, Digital Music Express, a U.S.-Canadian venture, will offer 33 different music channels to subscribers and Canadian Digital Radio will provide 38 additional channels.

The focus on community affairs will increase the importance of news reporting and sports coverage for both television and radio, especially for local cable companies. And since the greater number of channels will increase competition for advertising dollars, more advertising sales and promotion representatives will have to be hired. In order to reduce expenses, stations will share more resources and services with one another, including promotions, contests, and advertising options. There will be a conspicuous trend toward group ownership of or alliances between stations or channels so as to save on costs by sharing functions, equipment, and other resources. City TV, which owns MuchMusic and CHUM FM, illustrates such an alliance.

To reduce costs, stations are using the services of videojournalists rather than expensive television crews, both locally and abroad. Instead of sending out the unwieldy and costly unionized crews that most network stations employ, New York 1, a cable station that delivers local news 24 hours a day, employs 20 videojournalists—or veejays—equipped with compact HI8 cameras to film and report local events. According to Michael Rosenblum, a videojournalism consultant and lecturer at Columbia University in New York, "The traditional television crew is dying. The HI8 camera puts more people into the field and takes the news to places you can't afford to go with regular television crews." Once optical fibre is installed universally, veejays will be able to feed live from anywhere. A Canadian company, Patterson-Partington International TV Productions, already covers events live using satellite dishes mounted on trucks to send information to another truck for editing and graphic work; costs are thereby reduced by 80 percent. The British Broadcasting

Corporation (BBC) is using software written in-house to create a "virtual" studio that appears to be four times bigger than it actually is, and has replaced the need for three studios. The 13 camera operators that a traditional studio would have had to employ have been replaced by robotic cameras.

Competition between in-house production—broadcasters who do their own production rather than contracting it out—and syndicators will mean more jobs for producers and technicians in in-house production for the various networks and cable companies as each tries to develop its own profile. Independent production companies will form joint venture alliances with the networks as a way of outsourcing production functions which are not performed on a regular basis. There will be demand for more documentaries and news-based programming, two areas that appeal to aging boomers.

Competition will intensify everywhere in the industry. Cable companies have to worry not only about competition from other cable companies, but also from telephone companies entering the multimedia field. They are also competing with satellite dish companies, which offer consumers small-dish satellites that can send over 150 channels into their homes.

A temporary arrangement worked out with the CRTC regarding increased channel delivery requires that cable companies contribute $300 million to the Canadian production community in order to promote Canadian content in the face of competition from the many channels coming on stream. Rogers Communications is the first North American cable company to use digital compression, transmitting up to 500 channels via cable. In anticipation of future alliances with phone companies, Rogers has designed its network for future connection with telephone services. The purchase of Maclean Hunter by Rogers represents another step in Rogers' emerging multimedia ambitions.

Since the repeal of laws governing financial syndication in the U.S. gives networks more control over in-house production, networks will want to retain financial control over program ownership once a program is aired. The shift to in-house productions means more network-produced newsmagazine shows, more cheap-to-produce and easy-to-syndicate sitcoms and less serious drama, which are too expensive and ambitious for in-house production. News and information shows expanded

BULLETIN BOARD

- **Job demand factors**: proliferation of number of services, channels, or stations; need for original programming; globalization of information; Canada's lower production costs compared with those in the U.S.
- **Job growth areas**: newscasters; sportscasters; talk-show hosts; community information and documentary hosts; on-the-scene reporters; producers; technical support staff; advertising and promotion representatives; videojournalists.
- **Skills, abilities, qualities, education needed:** creativity; versatility; technical or area-specific expertise; flexibility; ability to use the various portable technologies; college diploma is minimum requirement.
- **Job reduction areas**: potentially all areas depending on how the multimedia competition unfolds; television crews.
- **Growth limiting factors**: intense competition from other broadcasters and from other broadcast, information, and entertainment media.

CONTACTS

- Alliance of Canadian Cinema, Television & Radio Artists
  2239 Yonge St.,
  Toronto, ON M4S 2B5 Tel. 416-489-1311 Fax: 416-489-1435
- Association for the Study of Canadian Radio & Television
  c/o Centre for Broadcasting Studies, Concordia University,
  1455 de Maisonneuve Blvd. West,
  Montreal, PQ H3G 1M8 Tel. 514-848-2385
- Canadian Association of Broadcasters
  350 Sparks Street, P.O. Box 627, Station B
  Ottawa, ON K1P 5S2 Tel.613-233-4035 Fax: 613-233-6961
- Canadian Association of Broadcast Consultants
  c/o Rogers Broadcasting, 25 Adelaide St. East, 12th Fl.,
  Toronto, ON M5C 1H3
- Canadian Association of Broadcast Representatives Inc.
  c/o CanVideo TV Sales,
  #310, 2200 Yonge St.,
  Toronto, ON M4S 2C6 Tel. 416-482-6200
- Canadian Film & Television Production Association
  #404, 663 Yonge St.,
  Toronto, ON M4Y 2A4 Tel. 416-927-8942 Fax: 416-922-4038

two percent in 1993 to 15 percent of prime-time scheduling and come-
dies expanded from one percent to 37 percent of prime-time scheduling.
In the future, networks will bring advertisers in early in the development
phase, in order to reduce the financial risk of launching new programs.

According to J. Max Robins, TV editor of *Variety Magazine*, there will be
more family programming and closer financial and creative ties between
commercial networks and advertisers. Speaking at the 1993 Broadcast
Research Council Annual Fall TV Preview, he noted that because of their
fear of losing advertising dollars, networks are becoming more conservative and are emphasizing family programming. With little or no advertising revenue growth projected, experimentation in programming has
become too risky.

Europe and Eastern Europe with its 400 million potential viewers is a
growing market. Southeast Asia and Japan combined are even bigger
markets and growing just as quickly as the European and Eastern
European markets. By the year 2000, approximately 900 million households worldwide will own television sets and will want specialized programming. In the short term, satellite delivery will have a more impressive effect on programming once home viewers are receiving 150 to 200
channels. Alliance Communications Corporation, which distributes television and feature films domestically and internationally, and holds exclu-
sive distribution rights to many foreign films, is proof that even Canadian
independents can survive in these international markets.

Writing and Journalism

Individuals contemplating a writing career must look at this field in the
context of the information and multimedia revolution. The best-paid
writing jobs will be in speech writing, public relations writing, and technical writing. The market for copywriters and freelancers will become
increasingly fragmented and unpredictable. Technical writers will prosper since documentation for computers, software, instrumentation,
home entertainment, and other gadgetry must be written. Eventually, all
technical material will be presented and explained interactively, with
video demonstrations built in as required.

With the broadening of news and business coverage putting corporate and government leaders in the media spotlight more often, there is
a move towards presenting carefully crafted policy position statements.

Public relations writers will be hired to present the growing number of corporate and public positions on issues that are publicly scrutinized and debated. As the world becomes more complicated, the need for specialization within this field increases—public relation experts in the areas of law and the environment, for example.

Speechwriters often train in corporate or government public relations before taking up this rather risky profession—risky because if the speech fails, the speechwriter may lose credibility and opportunities for future employment. Speechwriters are responsible for writing "scripts" for executives and politicians, and editorials for others, as well as helping the speech givers with their delivery style. In order to control the message going out from Ottawa, the federal government spends about $2 million a month hiring speechwriters.

Copywriters are very often hired on a freelance basis, given the variability in advertising revenues and accounts. This field encompasses direct mail, magazines, newspapers, and radio and television. In the past, the best paid copywriters worked in television because of the medium's market reach. With the advent of multimedia home shopping and narrowcasting, copywriters will have to focus on the objective details of a product—price, for example—and be less concerned about promoting a product's image or the image a product will give the consumer. And as more consumer shopping agents and product reviewers appear on the scene, copywriting will become increasingly less relevant as consumers demand straightforward information for comparative purposes.

Freelance writing is an extremely competitive field which is most lucratively taken up by individuals who have previously written full-time for a print medium. Freelance writers cannot survive in this field unless their articles are frequently published in magazines. In the long run, however, magazines will be replaced by specialty television channels that provide the same information as a magazine but in a context that gives viewers greater control over the message. For example, viewers will be able to pursue information to their desired level of interest and in a preferred format. This approach to presenting information will require the talents of freelance writers who can adapt to the multimedia demands of a project.

Competition for writing jobs will continue to be stiff since the print medium as a whole is suffering staff cutbacks. With television becoming the primary delivery mode of all information, the most lucrative writing

BULLETIN BOARD

- **Job demand factors**: an electronically wired world makes multimedia communication inevitable; declining literacy rates at the high end; need to consume large amounts of information of all kinds easily; importance of image in a high-profile world.
- **Job growth areas**: technical writers; public relations writers; speech-writers; TV journalists.
- **Job reduction areas**: all forms of print journalism.
- **Growth limiting factors:** size of narrowcast market and its purchasing power.

CONTACTS

- Canadian Association of Journalists
  St. Patrick's Building, Carleton University,
  1125 Colonel By Dr.,
  Ottawa ON K1S 5B6 Tel. 613-788-7424 Fax: 613-788-5604
- Freelance Editors' Association of Canada
  35 Spadina Rd.,
  Toronto, ON M5R 2S9 Tel. 416-975-1379 Fax: 416-975-1839
- Media Club of Canada
  PO Box 204, Stn B,
  Ottawa, ON K1P 6C4 Tel. 613-236-3325
- Periodical Writers Association of Canada
  The Writers Centre,
  24 Ryerson Ave., 2nd Fl.
  Toronto, ON M5T 2P3 Tel. 416-868-6913 Fax: 416-363-6691
- Radio Television News Directors' Association
  #110, 2175 Sheppard Ave. East,
  Willowdale, ON M2J 1W8 Tel. 416-756-2213 Fax: 416-491-1670
- The Writers Union of Canada
  24 Ryerson Ave.,
  Toronto, ON M5T 2P3 Tel. 416-868-6914 Fax: 416-860-0826

jobs will be in television journalism. To be effective in this field, performance skills and familiarity with the workings of a newsroom are important, as is expertise in a variety of information-related areas. Although news and sports broadcasts are becoming more popular, the syndication of many information, sports, and news functions may result in networks keeping a small core of staff and hiring freelancers on a demand basis in an effort to reduce costs.

Where the Jobs are in Utilities

The recession has taken its toll on these extremely mature industries. Consequently, the utilities have suffered staff cutbacks and hiring freezes. This is expected to be the case for some time to come. Ironically, the utilities which were so aggressively promoting energy conservation have become victims of their own success in this endeavour. Now that consumers—both companies and individuals—are more conscious of ways to save their utilities dollars, the demand for many utilities such as hydro has diminished. Even once the demand for utilities increases, automation of many of the management information systems will curtail employment. Before long, for example, meter readers will go on the endangered jobs list as the kind of information they collect goes on-line, along with other information such as water usage and sewage levels.

Ontario Hydro is trying to make itself more accountable by providing various services including energy management, and more market-oriented by incorporating activities that add value and produce profit, such as selling its expertise to foreign markets and developing green, industrial technology-related opportunities. In addition to this, Ontario Hydro spends $300 million annually on research and development in such areas as fuel cells and power systems. Ontario Hydro's joint projects with battery manufacturers and the auto industry may lead to the development of a commercially viable vehicle which would recharge itself at night when Ontario Hydro's capacity is unused. This innovation would open

---

POWER FAILURE ...

In 1993, Ontario Hydro laid off 10,500 of its 22,000 employees, including 20 division heads, and 200 of the 700 managers on staff. Executives have been told to reapply for their own jobs which they have done for ten or more years in many cases, with as many as 70 managers applying for a single position. Of the 65 senior managers who were expected to lose their jobs in 1993, only 46 were rehired. Absenteeism is on the rise as people take days off to look for other jobs.

BULLETIN BOARD

- **Job demand factors**: high price of electrical energy; public's desire for environmentally friendly energy sources.
- **Job growth areas:** electrical engineers and lawyers; water purification and sewage treatment jobs for engineers in the long term.
- **Job reduction areas**: Hydro employees.
- **Growth limiting factors:** government intervention on behalf of Hydro.

CONTACTS

- Canadian Council of Electrical Leagues
  #1000, 2 Lansing Sq.,
  North York, ON M2J 4P8 Tel. 416-495-0052 Fax: 416-495-1804
- Canadian Public Works Association (Inc.)
  67 Kingsway,
  Winnipeg, MB R3M OG2 Tel. 204-475-5656 Fax: 204-477-5643

up many employment opportunities at Ontario Hydro for individuals with the appropriate expertise.

The latest area of interest is co-generation—a process that uses industrially produced steam to generate electricity in an environmentally friendly way and at a significantly lower cost than what Ontario Hydro offers. Provincially, hydro companies have resisted the move toward privately owned and operated co-generation because it effectively steals their business. Nonetheless,with the many legal issues surrounding energy and the environment, along with the eventual privatization of some energy sources, this is an area to get into as a lawyer or engineer interested in the electrical energy field. Indeed, with all nuclear-generating station plans on hold, and most utilities not hiring, co-generation presents a potential growth area for employment, as long as government regulation does not impede its growth.

Improvements in electrical cars and battery technology are proceeding steadily, but it will be some time before research creates a viable option to traditional modes of transportation. Future concerns about water purification and sewage treatment will lead to employment in these and other environment-related areas when governments and municipalities address these issues, budget constraints notwithstanding.

BULLETIN BOARD

- **Job demand factors**: disappearing with home shopping and just-in-time inventory replenishment information technology replacing the need for wholesaling; small business will still need some warehousing.
  CONTACTS
- ☞ Canadian Association of Wholesale Sales Representatives
  #336, 370 King St. West, PO Box 2,
  Toronto, ON M5V 1J9 Tel. 416-593-6500 Fax: 416-593-5145

Where the Jobs are in the Wholesale Trade

Can you imagine a world in which "I can get it for you wholesale" falls on deaf ears? Although wholesaling will not disappear entirely since small businesses will continue to require some warehousing, it will shrink in importance and the jobs associated with it will disappear. The wholesale trade will be replaced by information technology—just-in-time inventory replenishment—designed to integrate all raw material suppliers, manufacturers, and sellers. Direct delivery of goods from factory to consumer as home shopping becomes more popular will also obviate the need for wholesalers.

Ironically, the wholesale trade has helped keep the prices of goods higher in Canada than in the U.S. In the U.S., where there are far fewer wholesalers as most manufacturers ship directly to retailers. In a cost crunch, the middle person always ends up disappearing. In an age of global competition, Canada will not be able to afford a wholesale trade that effectively adds no value other than for unnecessary warehousing.

Traditional Services: Retail Trade, Hospitality, Culture and Recreation, Personal Services

Because traditional services are usually directed towards meeting the local or national needs of consumers, they are often not subject to as much global competition as the dynamic services industries. The lower value-added nature of service products also makes them less vulnerable to the kinds of productivity growth and technological change that characterizes the dynamic services.

Where the Jobs are in the Retail Trade
- Discounting • Department Stores • Malls
- Furniture • Food Retailing • Clothing Stores
- Cosmetics Industry • Pharmacy Market • Car Dealerships

In 1992, in an industry that sells Canadians $425 billion in consumer goods, 3,200 retailers went bankrupt owing $1 billion. Changes in consumer spending are revealing. Since 1991, spending per person represented 39 percent of after-tax income, compared with 45 percent in the late 1980s, 50 percent in the early 1970s, and 41 percent during the 1981 recession. From 1981 to 1992, total after-tax income doubled, prices rose by 78 percent and the economy grew by 90 percent. Thus, although the population grew, personal income spending after taxes did increase by $7,500 per person, but of that amount, retail spending accounted for only $2,500. The increase in personal spending, coupled with a decline in retail sales, reflects a tendency on the part of consumers to purchase other services such as investment, health care, and RRSPs.

Overall, services accounted for 52 percent of consumer spending in

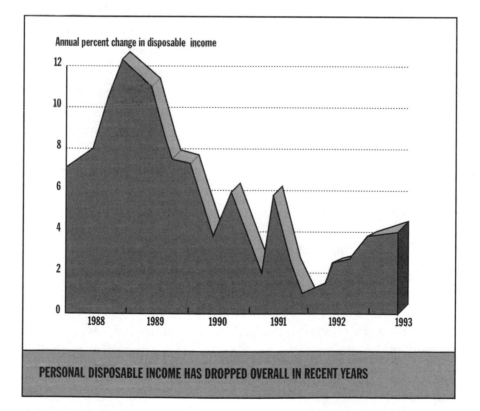

PERSONAL DISPOSABLE INCOME HAS DROPPED OVERALL IN RECENT YEARS

1992, compared with 44 percent in 1981. Non-retail spending rose twice as fast between1981 and1992 than retail spending during the same period. Along with increased taxation reducing the purchasing power of Canadians, these trends have hurt the retail industry as a whole.

According to retail analyst Joe Williams, the recession is over as far as retailing is concerned and factors that are influencing shoppers today will continue to the end of the 1990s. Aging boomers traditionally spend less in retail stores and shop at fewer stores. The 24- to 34-year-old age group is typically the biggest retail spending group, since they are engaged in setting up a home and having children. Unfortunately, its numbers will drop by 20 percent between 1991 and 2001.

The Category-Killers

Shoppers demanding better value has given rise to the category-killers or low-price, high-volume companies such as Toys "R" Us (Canada), Costco Wholesale Corporation, Price Club Canada Inc., Business Depot and Aikenhead's Home Improvement Warehouse Inc. In 1993, discounters and warehouse clubs rang up $9.5 billion in sales in general merchandise, not including food, in contrast with traditional department stores that had $9.1 billion in sales in the same year. The category-killers succeed because they offered a large selection of items which they sell at reduced profit margins—11 percent on average versus 40 percent for a full-line department store. Unlike traditional stores, they are not burdened by high overheads and inventory investments that constrain their ability to reduce their profit margins or prices. Warehouse chains have their goods shipped directly from the manufacturer to the store, thereby sidestepping wholesale and inventory warehousing costs. Fast turnover of merchandise because of low prices and just-in-time inventory systems eliminates the need for separate warehousing. The formidable presence of category-killers is best illustrated by the recently merged Price/Costco, which will operate 195 warehouse stores in Canada, U.S., and Mexico, with annual sales of approximately $16 billion (U.S.). According to Doug Tigert, retail and marketing professor at Babson College in Massachusetts, "Virtually every city in Canada that has 100,000 people in the trading radius will get a warehouse club." He forecasts that approximately 75 to 100 "warehouse clubs" will be operating in Canada by the end of the 1990s, with the invasion coming largely from the U.S. Tigert predicts that market penetration will reach 45 percent to 50 percent in Toronto and other major cities. Vancouver and Montreal warehouse clubs have already reached penetration levels of 22 percent and 21 percent, though Toronto is still only at the five percent level.

The last upsurge in spending on homes and the accompanying purchase of high-ticket items like washers, dryers, refrigerators, stoves, televisions, and furniture occurred during the 1980s as the last baby boomers reached their peak family-forming years. Demographic trends indicate reduced consumer spending in the 1990s on footwear, clothing, and household items by 15 percent as a percentage of disposable income. Consumers are currently more conservative and pragmatic in their spending since they can no longer count on a growth in personal income. A drop in real income is one of the reasons for the current low inflation rate.

The retailers who will likely succeed in the immediate future will be the Aikenhead Home Improvement Warehouse or Toys "R" Us style of discount store, since they focus on a specialty market and offer a wide selection of goods. In the future, the only viable alternative to home shopping will be to visit an outlet that allows a consumer to view merchandise in a particular category, and choose and purchase an item at a cost slightly above the home shopping price. Retail outlets will act as convenience stores when consumers need a product immediately. Lower-priced items will fare best in this purchasing environment since, in most cases, the savings from home shopping for more expensive items will outweigh the premium the consumer would have to pay for convenience. For example, the consumer in the market for a refrigerator would visit an outlet that displays a selection of these items. The consumer would then order the appliance electronically from the manufacturer. Since on any given day the manufacturer would have a large number of orders from the city in which the consumer lives, shipments of manufactured items would be delivered to that city daily. Purchasing directly from the factory allows the factory to get a sense of what is selling and in what quantity. With everyone in the supply, production, and delivery chain interconnected electronically, no one in the value-adding process is carrying much in the way of inventory, which means prices can be kept low.

One of the weaknesses of the category-killer strategy is their often-remote locations. In order to stock and display a wide selection of products, discounters must use large tracts of land. To avoid the exorbitant taxes that they would have to pay if their outlets were in large cities, most discounters locate their stores in industrial areas or just outside the city limits where taxes are lower. So, it is often inconvenient for consumers to get to a discount location. Savings-conscious consumers will make the long trek to a discount warehouse or mall but once they can have a product delivered to them straight from the factory, the tide will shift to the home shopping market for all major purchases.

Although in the future consumers will be able to rotate or zoom in on any product and have all questions answered interactively on his or her television screen, the desire to personally examine products will not disappear, and will create a demand for display outlets that feature a sample of each product from a number of manufacturers who rent space at the display outlet. The consumer will come to the display outlet—which will be conveniently located—and examine the product he or she is interested in and will order the item from the manufacturer represented at the outlet. In every large urban centre, this kind of ongoing trade show will exist for each category of items. Large discounters will have to narrow their market to lower-priced, low-involvement products requiring minimal floor staff, so as to keep prices competitive with the home shopping market. However, there will always be a demand for face-to-face customer service since not all consumers are sophisticated enough to trust their own judgement. Moreover, just as not everyone subscribes to or takes the advice of consumer report magazines, some individuals will balk at the idea of hiring a consumer purchasing agent for assistance.

Department Stores

Department stores such as Eatons, Sears, Woodwards, and The Bay will run into serious trouble trying to hold on to their customers. In the long run, these stores will not survive, at least not in their present form. Even Canada's largest discount department store—Zellers—is broadening its merchandise selection in preparation for the possibility that Wal-Mart, the U.S. discount giant, will expand into Canada; Wal-Mart carries about 75,000 items compared with Zellers' 56,000 and is already in the process of buying land for its planned stores in Canada. Zellers also plans to open 20 to 25 new stores in Canada annually from between 1993 and 1997 and to expand its innovative Club Z business-member list by at least ten companies. With profit margins being squeezed by falling prices, staff at all levels are rewarded by profit sharing if they help reduce costs. Even part-time employees can earn up to $1,000 annually through profit sharing.

In 1992, Japan's department store sales were also down by 5.7 per-cent—the first fall in their sales since 1965. Although the Japanese are not used to discount stores, big discount companies such as Bic Camera are growing so rapidly that, for some of Bic's specials, up to 6,000 shop-pers line up to get in to the stores. Using the same point-of-sale inventory control technology as the Price Club, Japanese discount retailers are will-ing to give up the right to return merchandise to suppliers in favour of lower prices. The regular retailers have had to resort to bypassing whole-salers altogether by buying directly from the manufacturers so as to keep prices down. The bigger companies like Bic grow, the more cost-cutting measures they can demand from manufacturers and wholesalers. As in North America, the shift in power from suppliers to discount retailers is reducing prices dramatically. When interactive shopping arrives, howev-er, discounters will be out of business once items can be bought directly from the manufacturer via a consumer's television screen. In the U.S., department stores have begun to offer shopping channels for their stores—Macy's and Lindstrom's, for example—so that customers can browse at home first. Department store CD-ROMs are also replacing cata-logues in the first step towards interactive shopping. This device allows consumers to roam the aisles visually and choose and order items elec-tronically.

Malls

To succeed in the future, malls will have to come up with a compelling mix of retail stores and services. Some malls will focus on a common theme, such as kitchen and bathroom items. The most successful malls will carry select specialty merchandise. Besides staying on top of trends and providing excellent customer service, an innovative approach will be crucial to survival. For example, more and more malls are growing up around large discounters in order to take advantage of complementary shopping potential. Eventually, large related specialty discounters will locate their stores close to one another in order to increase their con-sumer drawing power. These coordinated discounter developments will become the true discount malls of the future. But no matter how a mall is configured, all Canadian mall retailers will have to deal with fierce competition from the large U.S. retail chains following in the wake of The Gap, Toys "R" Us and Price Co. which have huge supplier networks in place in the U.S. Since these U.S. chains are typically better managed and financed, they will use price and aggressive advertising as a means of stealing market share and driving competitors out of business.

The Furniture Market

The furniture market has been beset by a record number of bankruptcies, and will likely continue to suffer since demographics do not favour this market. There are fewer first-time home buyers needing to furnish a home and prepare for a family. The furniture market has shifted to the home office market, which is expected to account for 40 percent of all work done by the year 2000. While many furniture stores are going under, the Business Depot is expanding in the office supply markets thanks to the boom in home offices. Many computer companies are teaming up with retailers to focus on this growing market: Compaq Computer has moved into Multitech, Business Depot, and Compucentres; Dell Computer Corporation is teaming up with Price Club, Business Depot, and Consumers Distributing; AST has partnered with Majestic Warehouse, Aventure in Quebec, London Drugs in the West and Sears; Apple Canada now distributes its products through Majestic, Multitech, and Future Shop Discount Superstores, which led in the campaign for the home office market. In 1992, the discounter sold $350 million in office equipment by guaranteeing low prices by purchasing in volume. Job growth will keep pace with the growth in the home office market, either in furniture or equipment. Corporate cost cutting and the recession have opened the markets for rented or leased furniture and recycled furniture. In addition, new technology makes it possible to remanufacture and reassemble used furniture at a fraction of its original cost.

Food Retailing

In food retailing, discounters such as the Price Club succeed because 92 percent of its shoppers buy bulk food at discount prices, and there is a smorgasbord of items selling at a discount that browsers buy on impulse since they know the price will be reasonable. Floor staff is kept to a minimum to reduce costs. As grocery stores begin to offer bulk discount food at prices close to those found at the Price Club—as Loblaws has already begun to do—the reason for making a long trip to a warehouse—20 kilometres on average as opposed to two to three kilometres to traditional supermarkets—will diminish, given the limited selection in the non-food categories. As other retailers move to the warehouse approach, consumers will head to the appropriate specialty discounter's warehouse.

Further intense competition in food retailing is expected to force at least one major supermarket chain out of business. A 1993 report by Ernst & Young suggests that North American supermarket chains will have dwindled from 30 to ten by the year 2000. The food retailing industry has seen more changes in the past three years than in the past 30. Consumers have spent less on staples than they did 20 or 30 years ago, and most consumers are purchasing fewer higher-priced or impulse items. As a result, stores have cut prices on all items. Not surprisingly, then, Coca-Cola Beverages Ltd. share prices have dropped by over 25 percent below their 1989 high, while Cott Beverages Inc. and its house-

---

THE ELECTRONIC SUPERMARKET

It has been predicted that by the year 2001, 20 percent of American households spending $24 billion annually will do their food shopping electronically. Demographics indicate that electronic shopping will be adopted in Canada once it can be done interactively. In Quebec, Videotron's customer services are added to the cost of cable services. Computer software marketed by Chicago's Peapod Delivery Systems allow IBM or Mac users to access an electronic supermarket stocked with 15,000 grocery items. Payment of the purchasing fee—the cost of buying goods electronically—representing five percent of grocery tab plus a $4.95 delivery fee can be made electronically or on delivery. U.S. Order permits shoppers in the Washington and Detroit areas to order from a catalogue of 6,500 items using a ScanFone equipped with a credit card scanner and a light wand for scanning bar codes. Consumers have the option of avoiding delivery fees by picking up the food themselves. For those who prefer to shop in person, Anderson Consulting and Videocart have devised a shopping cart that allows shoppers to scan their groceries and pay with a debit or credit card without having to go through a checkout counter.

brand soft drinks beat its 1989 high by 2000 percent. The shift has been to running low-cost, low-price operations with everyday low prices. These changes will have a profound effect on suppliers who will have to cut prices even more. This will not be a good job growth area.

According to Glen Terbeek, director of Smart Store, "Consumers have more demands on their time than ever before. They have little time to shop and prepare meals. If it makes sense for consumers to buy staples at home, retailers are going to have to be offering more specialty goods and services to attract people to their stores." This trend, along with an increase in the number of meals eaten at home but pre-prepared elsewhere, should take hold in 1996, as emptynesters in record numbers begin to embrace such conveniences.

Clothing Stores

Clothing stores have been hard hit not only by the recession but also by a preference on the part of the consumer to purchase casual clothes. Since these are far less expensive than the more traditional office "uniform," clothing retailers are feeling the crunch in no small measure.

Demographics—such factors as the aging population, the growing wealthy retiree market, two-income families, and the increase in the number of children—will dictate future areas of job growth in the clothing industry. Less expensive designer lines aimed at the affluent baby boomers have done well. Similarly, the mini baby boom will lead to more

---

DRESSING FOR SUCCESS ...?

Companies like General Motors and IBM are questioning their dress codes as well as their corporate structures. The president of General Motors now allows executives to dress casually if they are planning to work in their offices. Likewise, IBM—originally called Big Blue after its former blue-suited executives—is trying to alter its stiff image and mind-set. Even its Canadian president has been known to wear sports shirts and casual slacks to work. Between 1985 and 1992, the number of suits sold in the U.S. fell by 34 percent, and in Canada, suit sales fell by 25 percent between 1990 and 1991. A Mediamark Research report shows that during 1992, 41 percent of men in the U.S. purchased jeans, 14 percent bought suits and 13 percent acquired sports jackets.

designing for the upscale children's market and the maternity outfit market. Greater emphasis will be placed on meeting the clothing demands of emptynesters and the growing number of retirees. The increase in weddings has sparked more interest in this area of retail clothing as well. Even upscale designers are successfully segmenting their lines to reach different markets. In Canada, for example, there are six Ralph Lauren marketing salespersons who earn over $600,000 each annually by marketing the various lines to different target markets.

The clothing retail market is undergoing a change structurally. Increasingly, designers and manufacturers are bypassing traditional retailers by setting up shop themselves, particularly in the high-end where there is a narrower market and where they can avoid the shakeout taking place among the department stores. Outlets operated by manufacturers and designers are replacing jobbers or discount stores. Even with department stores, the trend is toward boutiques run by manufacturers and designers who are responsible for staffing and displays. In the stores themselves, a computerized point-of-sale network called Quick Response links manufacturers, suppliers, and retailers so as to prevent overruns and to reduce order delivery time of goods. Benetton takes the guesswork out of consumer purchasing habits by using Pinpoint Retail Systems which identifies what customers are buying, including size, colour, and style of item. These strategies help designers and manufacturers determine what is selling and what is not, thereby allowing them to test-market merchandise and avoid costly overruns.

Another smaller but growing market is the knock-off fashion market. Within three weeks or less of the haute couture or expensive ready-to-wear lines hitting the runways, companies specializing in credible imitations at deeply reduced prices have copied the big-name designers. This market has done exceptionally well. Many designers have tried to preempt this business by offering their own less expensive ready-to-wear lines.

If you are interested in pursuing a career in this field, your safest bet is to stick with the demographic-oriented markets. The trend toward centralized—head-office controlled—marketing in the U.S. has created a demand for product managers employed by apparel companies to help retailers decide their clothing design needs and then arrange for producers—typically foreign—to provide the requested items.

The Cosmetics Industry

The $16.8 billion (U.S.) American cosmetics industry has weathered the recession well as it experienced a five percent annual increase in sales. Sales for specialty products that protect the skin from sun damage have grown by seven percent a year; men account for 27 percent of the sales from skin care products; and makeup sales are expected to increase by ten percent annually, given an increase in demand from the aging boomer population. Job prospects in this industry are good.

The Pharmacy Market

Currently, the pharmacy market is trying to cut costs in any way it can. Mail-order drugstores such as Meditrust Pharmacy Inc. takes orders by phone, fax, and mail, then ships drugs by courier or Priority Post within 24 hours. By charging $5 per prescription as opposed to the usual $9 to $12, and shipping three-months supplies at once, individuals and companies can cut their drug plan bill by 25 percent. In the U.S., mail order has become widely accepted, with the biggest supplier, Medco Containment Services Inc., enjoying a revenue of $2 billion annually. Similar services have captured six percent of the pharmacy market. With drug prices often jumping 15 percent to 20 percent a year and the boomer population aging, an increased use of expensive pharmaceuticals will force company drug plans and governments subsidizing drugs for seniors to shift their business to the mail-order market. With drug plans expected to cost employers as much as pension plans by the year 2000, mail-order delivery is expected to grow from 17 percent to 20 percent of the market. Long-term drugs such as those for allergies, birth control, diabetes, and heart disease will end up in the mail order market. Fortunately for local pharmacies, the aging boomer market will likely ensure a dependable cash flow well into the future. The trend toward ambulatory out-patient care favours the increased use of pharmaceuticals, which will benefit all pharmacies. With an already saturated market, the pharmacy industry does not offer many future employment opportunities except in the mail-order area.

Car Dealerships

According to automobile industry analyst Dennis DesRosiers, the industry has twice as many dealerships as it needs and will consequently suffer an unavoidable shakeout and change in management style. Industry sales

BULLETIN BOARD

- **Job demand factors**: value for consumer's money; wide selection; lowest price; customer service; convenience; low inflation which lowers savings levels; low interest rates which lowers household mortgage payments and other debt payments.
- **Job growth areas**: large discount stores; specialty stores offering wide selection; mail-order pharmacies; home office businesses; aging boomer fashion market; casual wear; high-tech car mechanics.
- **Skills, abilities, qualities, education needed**: computer literacy; marketing and communication skills.
- **Job reduction areas**: department stores; supermarkets; furniture stores; clothing stores; car dealerships.
- **Growth limiting factors:** the economy; home shopping technology; competition; demographics; inflation; high interest rates.

CONTACTS

- Retail Council of Canada
  #600, 210 Dundas St. West,
  Toronto, Ont., M4G 2E8
  Tel. 416-598-4684 Fax: 416-598-3707
- Retail Merchants Association of Canada
  1780 Birchmount Rd.,
  Scarborough, ON M1P 2H8 Tel. 416-291-7903 Fax: 416-291-5635

have declined for four consecutive years and revenues from the service end of the business have been dismal. The industry will place greater emphasis on lowering inventories, attracting more repair and service work, and on keeping overheads low. The casualties will likely be the big dealerships with their bloated inventories and large lots. In Canada, the average after-tax price rose to 49 percent of the average family's annual income in 1993 compared to 37 percent in the early 1980s. Inflation, more sophisticated automotive components, taxes, the move from small cars to minivans and four-wheel-drive vehicles, and the desire for more loaded vehicles account for the lag in sales as consumers cannot afford the more expensive transportation they now prefer. Although car sales are expected to rise in 1994 by seven to eight percent as many cars become too expensive to repair, affordability will become a key factor as long as economic uncertainty prevails. In 1993, the 16 percent decline in the sale of Japanese cars reflects the closing gap between Japanese and North American cars with respect to quality.

Small reputable specialty garages will survive, since economic uncertainty makes consumers hang on to their cars longer. Now that people are driving their cars longer before trade-in and do-it-yourselfers are having trouble fixing cars that are equipped with modern technology, the automotive repair business is bound to improve for dealers who can afford all the required technology. It is predicted that the repair market will grow from 25 percent to 27 percent of dealership business by 1997, translating into a $200 million increase. The cost of repairing old vehicles has improved slightly as a result of the free trade deal, which has kept auto parts prices competitively low, as has the selling of parts through such outlets as Price/Costco warehouses. Mechanics specializing in the newer technologies as they relate to luxury cars will be in demand as the luxury car market improves later in the decade.

Where the Jobs are in the Hospitality Industry
Travel

The Canadian travel industry represents a $26 billion business, which employs 615,000 people and attracts $7.4 billion a year from foreigners. The decline in the dollar's value has curtailed travel plans by Canadians outside Canada, but should make Canada more attractive to foreigners looking for travel bargains. The exception might be visitors from the Pacific Rim who do not come for Canada's lower dollar since travel has always been inexpensive for them. In 1993, only 59 percent of Canadians planned to travel, this representing a five-year low. Sixty-three percent of those who book a holiday, will travel within Canada compared with 58 percent in 1992, when the dollar was higher.

Tourism is a fundamental part of many provincial and regional economies. Climate often plays a large role in determining where the vacationer will choose to go. For example, the West Coast with its milder weather was favoured in 1992-93; this hurt travel to the East Coast during that period. Provinces that are aiming at the 45-plus age group, such as Prince Edward Island, will likely experience substantial growth in travel. By 1996, travel undertaken by aging emptynesters should pick up considerably. Vacations aboard one of the many cruise ships that sail the Inside Passage to Alaska will likely find favour with this crowd, as will adventure trips, health-related tourism, cross-border shopping trips, and ecotourism or low-environmental-impact travel. In Ontario in 1991, travel generated $17 billion which was more revenue than forestry, agriculture, and mining combined, and accounted for 6.6 percent of Ontario's work force. Losing seven percent of the U.S. and overseas market from 1986-91 is cause for concern, considering the travel industry is the fourth biggest industry in Ontario and represents the fourth biggest area of exporting. Canada's poor road infrastructure, with 40 percent of its roads sub-standard, will take its toll on tourism as Americans travelling by car make up 78 percent of Canada's foreign tourism market. Since 1986, 17 percent fewer Americans have travelled to Canada, yet the number of Canadians travelling to the U.S. during that period doubled. The demographic shift of Americans to the South hasn't done the Canadian travel industry any good, either. Aggressive marketing is necessary to impress upon Americans that travel bargains are to be had in Canada. According to a 1993 report by the Conference Board of Canada, the volume of pleasure trips Americans take in Canada is not expected to hit prerecession levels until 1996.

Prospects for the business travel market are not bright. The Conference Board of Canada reports that 40 percent of Canadian companies planned to cut back on business trips during the last half of 1993 compared with 23 percent in a similar survey in 1992. When corporate restructuring removed middle managers, it also removed the group most likely to travel. In addition, 25 percent of the companies surveyed planned to reduce travel in 1994 by using teleconferencing and fax machines. No growth in this sector of the travel business is expected for the rest of the 1990s, and many jobs will likely be lost in the hotel industry as a result.

Cruise lines, airlines, resorts, and hotels will compete with one another in selling travel services themselves to avoid paying travel commissions to agencies. On-line services such as American Sabre reservation system make this easy since consumers can use their home computers to reserve directly. There will have to be a consolidation of travel agencies in the emerging shakeout. According to *Travel Weekly*, the small- or medium-sized agencies which survive will do so by targeting small- and medi-

BULLETIN BOARD

- **Job demand factors**: low dollar; aging boomer market; eventual economic growth.
- **Job growth areas**: companies focusing on the 45-plus boomer market; ecotourism; adventure trips; corporate incentive travel; computer travel systems experts.
- **Skills, abilities, qualities, education needed**: computer literacy; communication, problem solving and marketing skills.
- **Job reduction areas**: companies restructuring, merging, or going out of business.
- **Growth limiting factors**: teleconferencing and fax machines; disappearance of middle management; the weather; road infrastructure; the Canadian dollar; international competition for tourists.

CONTACTS

- Alliance of Canadian Travel Associations
  #1106, 75 Albert Street,
  Ottawa, ON K1P 5E7 Tel. 613-238-1361 Fax: 613-238-8949
- Tourism Industry Association of Canada
  #1016, 130 Albert Street,
  Ottawa, ON K1P 5G4 Tel. 613-238-3883 Fax: 613-238-3878

um-sized corporations, often in the sales incentive market, which rewards top sales staff by giving them trips. Specialization and niche marketing will become the key to survival, especially for small travel companies, and consortiums of independent, non-chain agencies will have to form networks to match the purchasing and marketing power of chains and franchise operations.

Automation is expected to increase in the industry as more agencies complement their on-line reservation systems with computerized management systems that track suppliers and customers. Worldwide travel computer standardization is slowly taking shape and will require the hiring of corporate travel professionals or managers with appropriate computer skills for multinational companies.

According to the report "Travel & Tourism: The World's Largest Industry," gross sales of travel and tourism are expected to account for

$3.5 trillion of gross domestic product in1993 (six percent of world total, seven percent of global capital spending, 13 percent of worldwide consumer spending and 127 million jobs or one out of every 15 workers). Although world economic growth is expected to be sluggish until the mid-1990s, expenditures on travel and tourism are expected to rise from $1.8 trillion in 1990 to $5.8 trillion in 2005 or a compounded growth rate of 3.9 percent annually. Despite further worldwide political fragmentation and tension in such countries as Germany, and Russia, and the former Yugoslavia, the 1990s are viewed as more promising than the 1980s with respect to the travel industry.

Accommodation

The hotel business will be adversely affected by the decline in business travel. The construction boom of the 1980s led to an oversupply of hotel rooms similar to the overbuilding that characterized the office supply market. The ensuing intense competition in the 1990s is likely to bring about industry segmentation with two types of hotels emerging: the high-quality luxury hotels catering to the older, affluent traveler, and the limited-service hotel geared to the economy market. As with the travel agency market, consolidations of hotels is likely to continue, given that half of the rooms worldwide are already controlled by the top 25 chains. If independent hotels are to survive, they will have to join chains, or form consortiums to gain the financial and marketing competitiveness of the larger chains.

To capture the business travel market, hotels will have to offer guests rooms that include fax and answering machines, computers, modems, and other office equipment. Other services— meeting rooms, sports and health facilities—will need to be first-rate. The economy business travel market will likely offer business facilities centrally located, and the rooms will operate on a self-serve basis, with food vending machines and built-in bars.

Hotels are becoming internationalized as trade becomes more global. They must now offer foreign guests the services and cuisine they are accustomed to in their own countries. Hotels interested in capturing this end of the market must hire multilingual staff, offer cosmopolitan menus, and provide multilingual directories, brochures, and pamphlets. Moreover, staff must be willing and able to offer a variety of information

BULLETIN BOARD

- **Job demand factors**: aging boomer market; globalization of trade; hotel rooms need to substitute for offices; growing market of economizers who cannot afford luxury travel.
- **Job growth areas:** multilingual staff for international hotels; marketing personnel; luxury hotels aimed at older wealthy patrons; market-focused budget accommodation.
- **Skills needed**: communication; knowledge of foreign languages; computer, problem solving, and marketing skills.
- **Job reduction areas**: medium-level hotels which are neither budget- nor luxury-oriented; hotel jobs which are being automated.
- **Growth limiting factors**: telecommunications technology replacing business travel and eventually personal travel to some extent; international competition.

CONTACTS

- Hotel Association of Canada
  #1016, 130 Albert St.,
  Ottawa, ON K1A OL6 Tel. 613-237-7149 Fax: 613-238-3978

and assistance to foreigners confused by Canadian customs.

The hotel industry is shifting from operations-based management to a marketing focus. Hotels are working harder to bring in business by catering to the particular needs of a market segment. Hotels will, for example, begin to offer special services directed to an aging population, such as nursing care and geriatric health care while the individual is a guest of the hotel. Eventually, the hotel industry may even enter the senior citizen housing market by renting rooms to seniors on a monthly or yearly basis, and by providing appropriate support services such as health care.

Technology and automation are facilitating the reservation and service aspects of operating a hotel—remote check-in, in-room check-out, robotic cleaning, and smart cards that serve as keys—but will reduce the numbers of check-in, cleaning, and reservations staff. Motels, resorts, and bed and breakfast accommodation geared to the needs of aging boomers will grow in those areas or locations most likely to appeal to the travel and sightseeing wishes of this market segment.

Restaurants, Food Shops, and Catering

Restaurants must keep a close eye on their bottom lines, or they will very quickly go out of business. To a great extent, the prima donna chefs and extravagant restaurants of the 1980s have been replaced by restaurants serving simpler foods in generous portions. The emphasis has shifted to value and comfort foods.

The risk associated with seeking employment in trend-oriented restaurants lies in the restaurant's timing in taking up one trend or moving on to the next. Following trends usually implies frequent renovations, expensive chefs, fickle public tastes, and lots of competition. Complicating matters further, consumers are increasingly patronizing take-out gourmet shops, the precooked food departments of supermarkets, delis, drive-thrus, and food delivery companies. As a result, the restaurant market is shrinking and will continue to do so, at least until emptynesters grow in numbers and begin to repatronize restaurants. Since many older people often prefer blander, healthier foods, it is likely the neighbourhood restaurant that offers excellent customer service, a healthier menu, value for money, and take-out and delivery will do well. The shift to cocooning and the emphasis on family values has also created a shift to convenience foods. Parents who would rather spend quality time with their children rather than hours preparing meals from scratch are opting for convenience foods. A survey conducted by the Canadian Restaurant and Foodservice Association, indicated that consumers were moving away from better quality food, which saw an eight percent drop from 1991-92, toward better value, which increased by 11 percent over the same period.

As the closing of a number of Olive Garden restaurants and 13 Red Lobster's 70 full-service, sit-down restaurants indicates, Canadians do not like the concept of dining uniformity in the medium-priced restaurant market. Unlike in the U.S. where Red Lobster had more than $1.5 billion (U.S.) in sales in 1992 and over a 25 percent share of this particular food market, the cost of doing business in Canada—high overhead, the Goods and Services Tax (GST), taxes, minimum wage—precludes success unless the volume is extremely high. In the U.S., Olive Garden and Red Lobster restaurants account for 33 percent of sales for General Mills Inc., which plans to open 50 more restaurants in the U.S. Taco Bell Corp., on the other hand, is enjoying a phenomenal success in Canada. Pursuing a no-

BULLETIN BOARD

- **Job demand factors**: aging population wishing convenience foods and healthy light foods; weak economy reinforces value as a priority; cocooners or families preferring to eat at home.
- **Job growth areas**: take-out; delis; supermarket-prepared foods; home delivery; catering to the elderly.
- **Job reduction areas**: expensive restaurants which do not give value for money.
- **Growth limiting factors**: public tastes; economy; competition; demographics.

CONTACTS

- Canadian Restaurant and Foodservices Association
  #1201, 80 Bloor St. West,
  Toronto, ON M5S 2V1 Tel. 416-923-8416 Fax: 416-923-1450
  Toll free: 1-800-387-5649

frills fast-food approach, the chain was able to drop its prices by 25 percent over the past five years. Half the items on its menu sell for under a dollar. Their expansion into the public gathering place market—airports, schools, and movie theaters— via portable carts and kiosks, has been a stunning success. The convenience and value that are the winning combination here, will also boost sales in the food vending machine business. Customers are now able to purchase a cappuccino from a machine for as little as 70 cents. Items such as pizza, piroshki, and french fries are also available in vending machines.

Value-oriented catering companies will do well in the 1990s once the economy shows a modest improvement. Catering, chain, or contract firms that target day-care centres, nursing homes, continuing care communities, and facilities for the elderly of any other kind are likely to prosper over the long term.

Where the Jobs are in Culture and Recreation
Culture

Approximately 430,000 Canadians work in the cultural sector. Canadians spend $29 billion on the arts and cultural goods and services annually.

This represents a 63 percent increase from 1982 and is surpassed only by the amount of spending on shelter, food, and transportation. The Conference of the Arts reports that in 1989 Canadians made approximately 14 million visits to performing arts events and 24.5 million visits to museums. The overall economic output of the cultural sector in 1991 was $17 billion or 2.5 percent of the country's gross domestic product. Cultural exports reached $1.3 billion in 1990, which represents a 44 percent increase over 1982.

Although the federal arts policies of the 1970s and 1980s led to a cultural labour force growth rate of 122 percent over the last ten years — twice the growth rate of the labour market as a whole—there has recently been a ten percent reduction in Canada Council grants, $13 million cut from the Canadian Film Development Corporation and a $20 million reduction in the CBC budget. Total direct and indirect federal arts spending has declined from approximately $2.93 billion in 1989-90 to $1.84 billion in 1992-93. The GST has reduced book sales from ten percent to 15 percent; magazine circulation has declined by 5.7 percent and their newstand sales are down 30 percent. The postal subsidy to book and magazine publishers has been reduced by 50 percent, with further cuts pending. Canadian film production capital cost allowances have dropped from 100 percent to 30 percent, and legislation to give Canada more control over film distribution was abandoned in the wake of the Free Trade Agreement. These reductions have lowered employment in many areas and shortened the season for performing arts groups. Thus, although "the cultural industries...in the 1980s ranked fifth in employment, fourth in wages and salaries, and ninth in revenues among Canada's manufacturing sectors," according to a Film and Television Council of Canada report, those looking for jobs in the cultural sectors should be aware of government cutbacks in funding and the likely impact of this on the future of employment in this sector.

The NAFTA, which militates against Canada's strengthening its cultural sectors, will pose a serious challenge to Canadian cultural industries. Consider the following statistics: Canadian books account for only 20 percent of the Canadian market; Canadian sound recordings, 11 percent; Canadian magazines, ten percent; Canadian-made English language television drama, eight percent; and Canadian films, four percent of the movie market and five percent of the home video market. Perhaps

BULLETIN BOARD

CONTACTS
- Canadian Conference of the Arts
  189 Laurier Ave. West,
  Ottawa, ON K1N 6P1 Tel. 613-238-3561 Fax: 613-238-4849
- Council for Business & the Arts in Canada
  #1507, 401 Bay St.,
  Toronto, ON M5H 2Y4 Tel. 416-869-3016 Fax: 416-869-0435

the Liberal government's job creation plan will target the cultural sector in a way that does not broach the NAFTA since it only takes $20,000 to create a job in this sector, versus $100,000 in light industry and $200,000 in heavy industry.

Publishing

The publishing industry represents a $1.5 billion market which is headed for difficult times. Costs are killing the industry as the GST, plus shipping, mailing, and paper and production costs reduce profit margins to less than one percent in some cases. Competition in the form of electronic books will pose a new challenge to the industry. At the 1993 American Booksellers Association conference in Miami, The Voyageur Co. showed a compact disc that provides both text and a video performance of *Macbeth* on the same monitor. At the 1993 Frankfurt Book Fair, 170 companies filled a hall under a banner that read, "Frankfurt Goes Electronic" and displayed electronic gadgetry that sang, spoke, and moved. Klaus Sauer of the German Booksellers and Publishers Association tries to put these changes in perspective by saying, "The function of the publisher does not consist of trading paper. [It is] the task of communicating the intellectual product of the author to the end-user by the best means possible." Some industry experts predict that by the year 2000, roughly 40 percent of the publishing business will be electronically based. Will this new technology kill the printed book? Florian Langenscheidt, whose family owns one of Europe's biggest language and reference publishers answers the question cryptically, "Neither the bicycle nor walking were killed off by the car."

Given the uncertainty of its future, it might be wise to avoid looking to publishing for employment. According to the Don't Tax Reading Coalition, book sales have fallen by five percent to 15 percent, with mass-market paperbacks and textbooks suffering the most. A number of major booksellers have already succumbed to the drop in book sales.

Textbook publishers are not immune to the impact of new technology, either. McMaster University is the first Canadian institution to use Xerox's Docutech machine to print books and course materials on demand, allowing revision of the latter on an ongoing basis. These custom textbooks can be produced for $12, including royalties, as opposed to the $35 for the average publisher-produced university textbook. Docutech can reproduce an entire book, including binding and cover, within a minute!

Typically, the success of a magazine depends on the economic prosperity surrounding the industry upon which it focusses. The $850 million Canadian magazine industry is currently threatened by split-run publications of American magazines which have American content but Canadian advertising—*Sports Illustrated, Bodyshop Business Canada,* for example. In 1993, Time Canada announced plans to print six Canadian editions of magazines in addition to *Sports Illustrated.* Since the magazines are printed in Canada, Revenue Canada cannot interfere with this practice. The federal government has announced, however, that future split-run editions of magazines will have to meet with the approval of Investment Canada. When the GST came into effect, subscription renewals fell by 40 percent, though the average industry circulation is down by only six percent, most likely because of the buffering effect of artificial free distribution—in which a region is blanketed with free copies—used to sustain advertising revenues. The Canadian Magazine Publishers Association claims that roughly 50 million copies of foreign magazines are imported into Canada each year without having to pay the GST. The Canadian magazine industry will suffer considerably from these tax and competitive disadvantages.

In the long term, magazines and newspapers will be replaced by the multimedia format, which is where their advertisers will probably migrate. The increasing trend toward narrowcasting and news/magazine/information television programming will overtake the magazine

BULLETIN BOARD

- **Job growth areas**: researchers; scriptwriters for broadcast journalism.
- **Growth limiting factors**: electronic books; other media; trend toward multimedia presentation of information and fiction; U.S. split-run magazine publications.

CONTACTS

- ☛ Association of Canadian Publishers
  260 King St. East,
  Toronto, ON M5A 1K3 Tel. 416-361-1408 Fax: 416- 361-0643
- ☛ Canadian Book Information Centre
  260 King St. E., 2nd Fl.,
  Toronto, ON M5A 1K3 Tel. 416-362-6555 Fax: 416-361-0643
- ☛ Canadian Book Publishers' Council
  #203, 250 Merton St.,
  Toronto, ON M4S 1B1 Tel. 416-322-7011 Fax: 416-322-6999
- ☛ Canadian Booksellers Association
  301 Donlands Ave.,
  Toronto, ON M4J 3R8 Tel. 416-467-7883 Fax: 416-467-7886
- ☛ Canadian Daily Newspaper Publishers Association
  #1100, 890 Yonge St.,
  Toronto, ON M4W 3P4 Tel. 416-923-3567 Fax: 416-923-7206
- ☛ Canadian Magazine Publishers Association
  2 Stewart St.
  Toronto, Ont. M5V 1H6
  416-362-2546 Fax: 416-362-2547
- ☛ The Don't Tax Reading Coalition
  260 King St. East,
  Toronto, ON M5A 1K3 Tel. 416-467-7904 Fax: 416-361-0643

and newspaper industry once television becomes fully interactive. In the not too distant future, viewers will be able to ask their "channel box"— VCRs will disappear since VCR-type information can be computer-stored—to scan all programs that cover certain topics and anthologize the material for later viewing. Using Compuserve, a computer information service, viewers can ask their computers to search for news stories on any topic from the various wire services and store them. "Journalist" by

PED Software will customize a consumer's online newspaper by gathering news items of interest from the various news services and placing them in prearranged columns. Some magazines now appear first in Compuserve, America On-line or Prodigy before they appear on the stands. Over 25 magazines such as *The New Yorker* and *The Economist* are now available via the electronic newstand found on Internet. Recently, *Time* magazine and Kiplinger's *Personal Finance* magazine allowed subscribers to view text, ask questions, and comment on articles through these networks, and *Newsweek* introduced a quarterly CD-ROM. Within three weeks of its introduction, *Time* found that its subscribers used the service 126,563 times.

Motion Picture, Audio and Video Production and Distribution

In 1992, films and television projects generated $300 million in revenue for Canada, with local network programs, commercials, and in-house corporate film bringing the total close to $1 billion. Between 1983 and 1988, the independent Canadian film and television industry personnel roster grew from 6,400 to 29,000. And in 1992, the movie industry generated 20,000 jobs in Ontario. In 1993, the film industry brought Ontario an estimated revenue of $338 million in 1993; film and television production in B.C. brought the province $286 million in the same year. For Ontario, the center of activity was Toronto; for B.C., it was in Vancouver.

Ninety-five percent of Canada's $1 billion film industry is concentrated in the Greater Toronto Area. More than 500 films have been shot in Toronto in the past decade. Toronto is the third-largest film-making centre in North America. Several factors contribute to the industry's growth in Toronto: high-quality, low-cost equipment, talent, and film crews are available in Toronto—$75,000 per day to film a television show in New York, $35,000 in Toronto; Toronto's post-production facilities offset the need to fly to Los Angeles or New York for editing; American production companies have found that Canadian unions are more flexible than their U.S. counterparts; Toronto is the broadcast capital of Canada with the head offices of the Canadian Broadcasting Corporation (CBC), CTV, and Global located there. Since 1990, the Ontario government has spent $14 million annually on rebates to investors in Ontario film and television productions stimulating $400 million in production rebates.

Vancouver is equally attractive for television and film production, with its excellent locations, a climate that allows year-round shooting, and

North America's largest sound stage—The Bridge Studios—located them. Moreover, it takes only two hours and 15 minutes to commute between L.A. and Vancouver. In 1978, B.C.'s film industry was worth only $12 million; today, it's worth $286 million! Every dollar spent in film and production in Canada generates several more in spinoff businesses, with real estate companies, car rental companies, cleaners, hotels, caterers, restaurants among those benefitting.

The recession has led some Canadian broadcasters such as CTV, the country's largest, to decrease its commitment to Canadian programming by 37 percent. Since it only costs approximately $65,000 per hour to air an American sitcom versus spending ten to 20 times that amount producing the Canadian equivalent, the difference in the profits a company can realize has created considerable tension in the industry.

The Directors Guild of Canada would like to see more of the $1.5 billion in annual film and video revenues stay in Canada instead of flow back to Hollywood companies. The 1,200-member association, which represents directors, production and location managers, designers, art directors, editors, and others in the film and television production industry, hope to press legislation that will allow Canadians the right to bid on distribution rights. Since culture is exempt from the Free Trade Agreement, it is hoped that such legislation could be passed without protest, thereby strengthening Canada's ownership in film distribution. This, in turn, would create a source of funds for more and better Canadian productions.

The technological innovations leading to large-screen television and video-on-demand will likely undermine the movie theater industry as more cocooners opt for watching movies at home. Theaters which specialize in large-screen formats for Imax-style films will continue to attract an audience, but in the long run, 3-D or virtual reality movies will supplant the spectacular effects of the larger screens. By the year 2000, all movie theaters will receive their films for projection via satellite. Obviously, this will eliminate many jobs in the film distribution industry.

Many special effects companies have grown up around the film industry. Animation and morphing software companies have flourished in Canada, with Alias Research producing the software for such movies as *Aliens, Terminator 2* and *Jurassic Park*. Other fringe companies focus on small market niches. Pyrotek Special Effects, for example, specializes

BULLETIN BOARD

- **Job demand factors**: inexpensive production facilities and flexible unions; high-quality facilities, technical staff and talent pool; need for more programming in a 500-channel world.
- **Job growth areas**: all aspects of film and television production; post-production; special effects; video production.
- **Skills, abilities, qualities, education needed**: communication, visual, auditory, analytical, creative and problem-solving skills.
- **Job reduction areas**: film distribution industry.
- **Growth limiting factors**: legislation surrounding distribution rights; government incentives; cost advantages of filming in Canada.

CONTACTS

- Academy of Canadian Cinema & Television
  158 Pearl St.,
  Toronto, ON M5H 1L3 Tel. 416-591-2040
- Alliance of Canadian Cinema, Television and Radio Artists
  2239 Yonge St.,
  Toronto, ON M4S 2B5 Tel. 416-489-1311 Fax: 416-489-1435
- Association of Canadian Film Craftspeople (Ind.)
  #105, 65 Heward Ave.,
  Toronto, ON M4M 2T5 Tel. 416-462-0211 Fax: 416-462-3248
  Canadian Film & Television Production Association
- Canadian Alliance of Video Professionals
  #400, 407 St-Laurent, Montreal, PQ H2Y 2Y5
- Canadian Film and Television Production Association
  #404, 663 Yonge St.,
  Toronto, ON M4Y 2A4 Tel. 416-927-8942 Fax: 416-922-4038
- Canadian Motion Picture Distributors' Association
  #1603, 22 St. Clair Ave. East,
  Toronto, ON M4T 2S3 Tel. 416-961-1888 Fax: 416-968-1016
  - Directors' Guild of Canada
    #401, 387 Bloor St. East,
    Toronto, ON M4W 1H7 Tel. 416-972-0098 Fax: 416-972-6058
- Independent Film & Video Alliance
  PO Box 545, Succ. Desjardins,
  Montreal, PQ H5B 1B6 Tel. 514-277-0328 Fax: 514-272-1797

in creating indoor pyrotechnics as well as creating the stunning effects of devastation and destruction in movies such as *Prom Night IV* and *Blown Away*.

The video industry has grown to meet the need for training, corporate, and educational videos. On a smaller scale, freelancers will continue to find work shooting videos for such special events such as bar mitzvahs, weddings, birthdays, and ribbon-cutting ceremonies.

Sports and Recreation Clubs and Services

The five major markets in the recreational services field are: the elderly; aging boomers; boomers in their thirties; children of boomers in their thirties; and children of boomers in their forties. Recreational services that combine the interests of more than one wealthy market segment and change as the interests of that market change will survive and even do well. Many will remember how Club Med went from being a singles haven to a family-oriented holiday club; both market focusses mirrored the needs of early boomers at two different stages in life. The aging boomer market is beginning to give up vigorous sports like squash or hockey, and even tennis to some extent, in favour of swimming, golf, and fishing. For that market segment, cross-country skiing is gaining on downhill skiing, and power boating has completely bypassed sailing as an interest.

The children of the aging boomers, on the other hand, are interested in weight lifting, rugby, baseball, hockey, tennis and squash, but are not yet wealthy enough to support expensive club memberships. Chances are these baby busters are students, underemployed or unemployed at the moment.

The young-to-middle-aged boomers are in their early to mid-thirties and have started a family. These individuals typically join ski clubs, and go to cottages and other recreation areas that the whole family can enjoy. In about seven years or so, their children and the children of aging boomers, will be interested in playing hockey, tennis, baseball, and football. In the meantime, many of these children will spend their summers at sports camps.

As for the the elderly, this market segment is taking up lawn bowling, bowling, swimming, card games, curling and boat cruises.

In pursuing a career in sports and recreation, the job seeker is advised to follow the sporting interests of the aging boomers, the better-off family

---

BULLETIN BOARD

- **Job demand factors**: demographics
- **Job growth areas**: sports facilities for affluent retirees, aging boomers, young to middle-aged boomers and their children.
- **Job reduction areas**: vigorous sports
- **Growth limiting factors**: just as demographics is a demand factor, it is also a growth-limiting factor; the economy; competition.

CONTACTS

- Canadian Resort Development Association
  48 Hayden St.,
  Toronto, ON M4Y 1V8 Tel. 416-960-4930 Fax: 416-923-8348
- Canadian Sports & Fitness Administration Centre
  Place R. Tait McKenzie, 1600 James Naismith Dr.,
  Gloucester, ON K1B 5N4 Tel. 613-746-0060 Fax: 613-748-5706

---

boomers in their thirties, or the wealthy retirees market. Sports and recreation facilities geared to a kinder, gentler and wealthier clientele will meet with success as the emptynesters arrive in full force in 1996.

Hobbies and Crafts

Service industries tied to emerging boomer hobbies are flourishing and will continue to do so though competition will intensify. Crafts such as fabric painting, knitting and jewelry making have become more popular. In 1992, 82 percent of all American households had at least one or more persons who practised crafts, a 17 percent increase over 1988. Since craft and hobby participants tend to have lower household incomes than non-participants, the recession has helped spur the industry. The trend toward an appreciation of quality and creativity has increased the appreciation of finely crafted, one-of-a-kind items. Developing countries in South America and the Pacific Rim are already taking advantage of the growing trend. Moreover, aging boomers are enjoying quieter, more introspective pastimes, which accounts for the increasing interest in bird watching, nature walks and hiking, photography, fishing, gardening, visits to historical sites and stamp collecting. Companies taking advantage of these trends will do well.

BULLETIN BOARD

- **Job demand factors**: the recession; trend toward quality and creative self-expression.
- **Job growth areas:** craft supplies; artisans; photography; gardening supplies and design; nature stores; historical preservation and exhibition.
- **Growth limiting factors**: increasing competition from developing countries supplying craft items.

CONTACTS

- Canadian Craft and Hobby Association
  4404 - 12 St. NE, PO Box 44,
  Calgary AB T2E 6K9 Tel. 403-291-0559 Fax: 403-291-0675

Where the Jobs are in Personal Services

As the boomer population ages, there will be a greater demand for convenience services of all kinds. Such areas as hairdressing, barbering, cleaning, laundering, and burial services comprise the personal services. Franchising services is growing as a means of standardizing services, cutting costs, and delivering a better standard of personal service.

Since it is relatively easy to enter the personal services field, competition for jobs is heavy, which is one of the reasons that franchises will likely take over this field. Magicuts, for example is a no-frills hair-cutting business that uses technology to cut costs and offer better customer service. Each outlet tracks inventory, total sales, sales patterns, and customer preferences on computer. As a result, inventory costs have been reduced, paperwork largely eliminated, scheduling of employees, and direct marketing campaigns made more effective, customers impressed by stylists who remember preferences as well as general personal information and customer waiting times minimized.

For most personal service companies, franchises are usually the only outlets financially equipped to take advantage of technology. Heavy competition in personal services keeps profit margins to a minimum and therefore gives the competitive edge to the business that can cut costs without reducing customer service. As Magicuts reveals, it is possible to cut costs and still improve customer service. In any business, that is a winning strategy.

BULLETIN BOARD

- **Job demand factors**: aging boomers seeking convenience, value, and personal attention; the recession.
- **Job growth areas**: franchises; funeral services.
- **Growth limiting factors**: population size; demographics; easy entry into personal services field increasing competition for jobs.

CONTACTS

- Funeral Association of Canada
  177 Bartley Bull Pkwy.,
  Brampton, ON
  L6W 2K1
  Tel: 416-459-5383 Fax 416-452-8197
- Canadian Cosmetics Careers Association Inc.
  26 Ferrah St.,
  Unionville, ON
  L3R 1N5
  Tel: 416-470-1966
- Dry Cleaners & Launderers Institute
  One Eva Rd.,
  Etobicoke, ON
  M9C 4Z5
  Tel: 416-620-5683 Fax: 416-620-5392

Non-Market Services: Educational Services, Social Services, Public Administration, Health Services

While competition has not been a major factor in determining the survival of non-market services, the services themselves have always been vital to the country's economic competitiveness. In a global economy which demands international competitiveness and at a time when governments are burdened by debt, more is being expected by these services at a lower cost. This may well result in the deregulation and privatization of many non-market services. Productivity growth, new approaches to management and technological change are transforming the ways in which these services are being delivered. In the case of education and health services, costs and demographics are providing the impetus for change, cost accountability, and outcome-based evaluation procedures.

With respect to government hiring practices, only 1,360 university graduates were hired for federal officer-level positions in 1992, yet only 150-160 such positions were available in 1993. Altogether, 13,000 new public service employees were hired in 1992. Recent hiring freezes are likely to affect most non-market service areas.

Where the Jobs are in Educational Services
• Schools • Colleges • Universities • Private Sector Training

The education industry in Canada is larger than the beverage, food, forestry, clothing, plastics and rubber industries combined. In British Columbia, for example, there are more university professors than forestry workers. In fact, one out of every ten Canadians is employed in the education industry. Ottawa spends roughly $13 billion on education, including $4 billion in transfer payments to the provinces; adding the amount spent by the provinces, Canada spends about $55 billion a year on education or approximately six percent of the gross domestic product. Once the idea and practice of lifelong learning is universally adopted, these figures will rise; that is, if the governments can afford to pay for these programs.

The large amount spent on education coupled with declining sources of revenue has led to an examination of how appropriately or efficiently the money is being spent. Between 1980 and 1990, educational bureaucracies grew disproportionately. In secondary school boards in Ontario, the number of consultants grew by 80 percent and the number of teachers removed from classroom and performing other roles in the education system—administrative, for example—increased by 128 percent, yet the student population increased by only six percent. To meet the costs of additional services, the Ontario school budget has grown 143 percent with 55 cents of every dollar ending up in the classroom. What are these "additional services"? Some new programs include heritage language instruction, hot lunches, wide-scale bussing, special education, French immersion, career counselling, AIDS education, gifted programs, elite sports training, and English as a Second Language (ESL).

The Ontario and B.C. governments have ruled that all public service workers, teachers included, comply with a social contract aimed at eliminating jobs or reducing incomes by significant amounts—$2 billion in Ontario. Legislation giving school boards or employers the power to revoke collective agreements and impose their own fiscal solutions is used as the big stick to ensure employees' compliance and cooperation. Cuts in education spending will likely result in cuts in additional services and will encourage hiring in private industry to teach in certain areas. Rather than use teachers as librarians, boards will hire library assistants to assist a librarian who is not a teacher. Technical courses will be taught by non-teachers from industry, often in an industry setting. Other subject areas on the potential substitution hit list are guidance, art, music, drama, ESL, and physical education.

In the long run, not even administrators will be immune, with cost-benefit analyses showing that fewer are needed. In Washington, D.C., the public school system had 53 students for every bureaucratic staff member, whereas the Catholic school system which did not receive government funding had a ratio of 2,941 to one. In Ontario, there are ten students for every bureaucratic staff member. Using the results of scholastic achievement tests, graduation rates, and other formal indices of educational success, finance professor Bruce Cooper of Fordham University College of Business Administration, New York, showed that boards which spent more of their budget in the classroom had higher rates of success. It is very possible provincial governments intent on streamlining the public school system will restructure school boards. Trustees' jobs may be eliminated entirely since these roles will likely be subsumed by provincial ministries of education.

The growing integration of education and business in providing education and training is affecting education at all levels. In an attempt to bridge the worlds of education and work, many school boards, colleges, and universities have added co-op placements to their diploma or degree courses so that students experience what they are training for and so that schools will develop a rapport with the business community. In fact, many schools have formed partnerships with local businesses. The London Investment in Education Council, for example, was established in 1990 by representatives from labor, business, school boards, social organizations, cultural groups, and schools in an effort to promote and facilitate lifelong learning in the community. In Winnipeg, Birds Hill Elementary School has enlisted local businesses to provide plant tours, workshops, and after-four classes; it is not unusual for sixth-graders to spend a day at Northern Telecom installing computer chips onto integrated circuit boards they themselves designed, then test the board's functioning ability. Other programs offered at the Birds Hill Elementary include: Engineering After School in which students work with civil, mechanical, and electrical engineers who volunteer their time; Science Moms meetings that encourage girls to pursue careers in science; and the Parent Technology Group in which parents organize and participate in tours to local high-tech sites and offer technology workshops. In New Brunswick, colleges collaborate with industry to develop courses that meet specific job needs such as telemarketing—now a two-year option in Moncton College's business technology program. Increasingly, colleges and universities are establishing articulation programs with one another, with apprenticeship programs, and with public schools.

Once the transitions between all deliverers of education and training are smoother—public, private, and on the job—students and workers can go from school to school, from school to work, from work back to school, and from retraining back to work in an ongoing lifelong cycle. We must build a lifelong learning society. Our competitive ability, which underpins our standard of living, depends on it.

Most jobs in education will be in adult retraining. At the moment, there are 4.8 million adults enroled in continuing education and training courses in Canada—twice as many as ten years ago. While demographics would have dictated a decline in college and university enrolments over the past decade, enrolments and applications have actually increased as older people come to recognize the importance of higher levels of training or education. Twenty years ago, the average college student was 18, 19, or 20 years old; in 1992, only 31 percent were 19 or under and 24 percent were 25 or older. Only 36 percent had been attending high school the previous year. In the short term, our competitive survival as a nation does not depend on our graduating superior younger students from our school system, but on our ability to retrain existing workers.

Currently, the regular school system sends young graduates into the work force who end up becoming 1.5 percent of the work force. In the 1970s, the work force grew annually by 3.6 percent. By 1996, however, it will likely grow by only 1.3 percent. In other words, all the graduates between 1993 and 2005 will represent less than 15 percent of the work force, while two-thirds of those who will be in the labour force in the year 2005 are already part of the labour force.

Only 31 percent of Canadian companies offer training, and those that do—large companies that can afford it—provide only a few days of training on average, with most of the training offered to managers, not to frontline workers. Worker training often consists of compulsory safety training mandated by the government or by a union contract. Unfortunately, small companies are least able to afford training, yet virtually all job creation will come from the growth of small companies. This structural shortcoming will compel governments to alter their tax, unemployment, and educational spending policies to help businesses in general—and small businesses in particular—increase the training component of their operations. The federal government is already planning to reallocate unemployment insurance funds to training allowances; Ontario has established the Ontario Training and Adjustment Board which brings together representatives from business, labour, education, and minority or disadvantaged groups to oversee the spending of $400 to $500 million dollars on training at a local and regional level. As a result of these initiatives, many training/upgrading jobs will be created. It is yet to be determined how these grants will be dispersed. Although many private training organizations can offer training at a lower cost than established learning institutions, many workers are not even at a level where they are trainable. According to the Economic Council of Canada, one million young people will leave school in the next decade unable to read or balance a chequebook; 28.5 percent of peoples aged 16 to 24 are unable to read a newspaper article, and 44.5 percent have trouble working with numbers. When one considers that the dropout rate was 69.7 percent in the early 1950s, it should be obvious that an even larger percentage of today's work force is functionally illiterate.

It is estimated that illiteracy costs Canada $4 billion in lost productivity, not to mention invisible costs in the anguish and low self-esteem of the individuals affected. For this reason, companies will ask governments to offer literacy and numeracy programs to the company's workers, or tax incentives to get workers to the point where they are at least trainable.

Despite the undeniable benefits to a company of upgrading its work force, many companies will not train workers because of the "freerider" problem; that is, companies are afraid to invest in employee training because other companies that do not provide these programs will offer these trained employees higher wages since they have not incurred training costs and can therefore afford to offer more attractive salaries. According to the report entitled "People and Skills in the New Global Economy," 58 percent of high-tech firms reported experiencing freerider problems. Until government tax and training policies favour company training, few companies will likely pursue worker training and upgrading as a way to improve competitiveness. Instead, they will most likely hire employees who already possess the appropriate skills.

The demand for computer literacy has spawned training courses virtually everywhere. This market will expand as the price of computers and software fall and as computers become more powerful, versatile, and user-friendly.

In determining where the training jobs will be, bear in mind that governments have cut back transfer payments to school boards, colleges, and universities, which has led to substantial increases in fees and the closing of many programs. Applications to post-secondary institutes, however, are at a record high, with the result that the majority of well-qualified applicants are rejected; there are just not enough places in the programs to accommodate the large numbers that apply. Part-time enrolment has burgeoned to make up for the full-time program shortage. The British Columbia Institute of Technology in Burnaby has seen its part-time enrolment grow from 30,000 in 1985 to 43,000 in 1993, while full-time enrolment has remained at 10,000 because of limits on government spending. Between 1985 and 1990, increased college enrolment of 6,500 in Ontario resulted from students aged 25 or older applying, many of whom went to make up the 800,000 part-time students who outnumber the full-time students six to one. Undoubtedly, many of the part-time students would enrol in private institutes full-time if they felt the added cost would lead to a desirable job.

With the heavy emphasis on cost containment, it is unlikely that public learning institutes will be able to afford to purchase the continually improving technology on an ongoing basis. Private training deliverers with closer links to industry are more likely to arrange mutually beneficial agreements regarding on-site training, the sharing of technology, and co-op placements. Governments may well use this as an opportunity to privatize much of the education process so as to cut costs and improve efficiency. Already, revenue from Ottawa to finance college-based training programs has fallen to $75 million in 1993, a significant drop from the $170 million spent in 1986; the private sector has been getting the training money instead. Unless the public education system becomes more responsive to the competitive job market and the disgruntled taxpayer, other private deliverers of education and training will continue to flourish.

In 1991, Ontario colleges spent $30 million on full-time ESL classes, while Toronto taxpayers spent $83 million for these programs for public school children and $47 million for adult ESL. The financial strain created by the growing demand for these services has made many school boards cut back on English as a Second Language since there is only partial federal funding for adult ESL and none for schoolchildren. The demand for this training is so great that classes have sprung up in church basements, community centers, libraries, and other areas where volunteers are available.

Immigration rates will play a major role in determining future English-language training needs. Although immigration rates are likely to fall to 150,000 immigrants annually from the 250,000 annual rate during the Mulroney years, it will be politically difficult to tamper with the family class application process which brings countless numbers of illiterate and unskilled foreign language immigrants into Canada annually, according to an immigration study by the Atkinson Fellowship in Public Policy.

In colleges, after nursing courses, ESL and basic skills programs require the greatest expenditure. Despite all of the upgrading efforts of colleges, however, a 1991 survey by the Canadian Federation of Independent Business found that less than 50 percent of small business owners were pleased with college graduates. Along with high school graduates, college graduates were characterized as incapable of reading manuals, unable to express themselves verbally or in writing, and incompetent in math. Indeed, literacy problems affect the day-to-day operation of 70 percent of Canadian companies. Since these workers will require skills upgrading, there will be substantial job growth in providing such training at all levels. In 1992, $1.6 billion from the unemployment insurance fund went towards training, up 47 percent from 1991 and 81 percent over 1990. This trend will have to continue if Canada is to become competitive.

Job seekers interested in acquiring teaching positions in elementary schools, secondary schools, or post-secondary institutes may have some difficulty as a result of cutbacks in education spending. Even though application rates are at record levels for positions in post-secondary institutes, programs are being cut. The largest job growth area is in teaching part-time students. All levels of education will see over 50 percent of their staff retiring early in the next century as the boomers begin to retire. Since birth rates have been rising of late, some additional hiring will be required as these baby boom "echo" students make their way through the education system, unless the electronic classroom has replaced traditional education by then.

Burnaby South 2000 is just the beginning of a technological revolution in education. The structure of education at all levels will change drastically once information technology is firmly embedded in the learning process. Computers are becoming more and more "personal" in determining how a student learns, with computerized testing now able to accurately measure a student's abilities. Not only can computers determine what cognitive processes the student used in solving a problem, they can also identify and help the student work on refining their thought processes.

In the future, education and training will be available through learning packages that students or employees can use on their own, ideally at

---

THE ELECTRONIC CLASSROOM

The future of teaching becomes uncertain as technology transforms both the teaching and learning process. Burnaby South 2000 is a secondary school which is blending state-of-the-art audio-video technology and education. All classrooms are wired with optical fibre and the school has access to laser discs, compact-disc television readers, computer cameras, high-tech slide and movie projectors, local television stations, VCRs, worldwide wire services, computers, satellite feeds, and a high-tech industrial education laboratory. IBM, B.C. TEL, MPR Teletech Ltd., Dynacom Communications, Franklin Hill & Associates, and Creative Learning International are actively involved with the school. Video monitors, modems, microwave signals, and satellites allow the school to broadcast school news and interact with people all over Canada and worldwide. Free educational broadcast packages are received from overnight feeds and an organization of teachers in Colorado provides accompanying lesson plans.

BULLETIN BOARD

- **Job demand factors**: unaffordability and ineffectiveness of current education system; need to address learning deficiencies of individual learners; requirements of business world; ever-increasing educational potential of technology; immigration; functional illiteracy and innumeracy; upgrading needs of unemployed and employed adults.
- **Job growth areas**: ESL; adult education at the primary and secondary levels; part-time positions at colleges and universities; private learning institutes; electronic educational broadcasting; co-op education programs; specialized business areas.
- **Job reduction areas**: jobs in public schools.
- **Growth limiting factors**: increasing government and municipal debts; tax revolts; public's and business's perception of education system; business's capacity to afford training; educational or training tax incentives; freerider problem; demographics; population size; immigration policies.

home. The savings that companies and educational institutions will realize as a result will more than compensate them for any upfront expenditures in technology and software. In this sense, most learning will be distance learning. Once all courses can be accessed at home by interactive television technology, the notion of school, training, libraries, art galleries, and museums, will be transformed into a virtual reality that individuals can fashion to their needs. Although interactive electronic education will likely require fewer teachers, there will still be "real" classrooms. However, they will be less important and more infrequently used except at the elementary level. Education will be driven by the individual needs of each learner who can consult with a teacher or mentor by using videoconferencing as the need arises; group work assignments can be completed by videoconferencing at prearranged times.

The development of the electronic classroom will be spurred by the unaffordability and ineffectiveness of the current educational system, the growth of private and alternative schools, the deterioration of public schools, and the use of technology in all aspects of life. The most prolific job growth areas will be in technology design and implementation.

BULLETIN BOARD

CONTACTS

- Canadian Education Association
  #8-200, 252 Bloor St. West,
  Toronto, Ont. M5S 1T8
  Tel 416-924-7721 Fax 416-924-3188
- Acces for New Canadians
  431 Roncesvalle Ave.,
  Toronto, ON M6R 2N3
  Tel. 416-530-1455
- Canadian Association for Adult Education
  29 Prince Arthur Ave.,
  Toronto, ON M5R 1B2
  Tel. 416-964-0559
- Canadian Association for Co-operative Education
  #203, 1209 King St. West,
  Toronto, ON M6K 1G2 Tel. 416-535-6993 Fax: 416-535-3994
- Canadian Association for University Continuing Education
  #1001, 151 Slater St.,
  Ottawa, ON K1P 5N1 Tel. 613-563-1236 Fax: 613-563-7739
- Cooperative Career & Work Education Association of Canada
  295 Fennell Ave. West,
  Hamilton, ON L9C 5R7
  Tel. 905-575-2351 Fax: 905-575-2202
- Canadian Association of School Administrators
  #8-200, 252 Bloor St. West,
  Toronto, ON M5S 1V5 Tel. 416-922-6570 Fax: 416-924-3188
- Professional Development Institute Inc.
  1206 Bank St.,
  Ottawa ON K1S 3Y1 Tel. 613-523-3333 Fax: 613-235-1115
- TESL Canada Federation
  755 Queen St. West,
  Toronto, ON M5J 1G1 Tel. 416-351-0512

Organizations that specialize in the continuous "recycling" of adult learn-ers to meet the needs of employers will always be hiring more program facilitators and developers. To survive and flourish as a teacher/trainer, job seekers must keep pace with changes in technology and learning, and know how to provide training services cost-effectively.

Libraries, Museums, Archives, and Research Information

No aspect of contemporary life has escaped the dramatic impact of the information revolution, with libraries, museums, and archives no exception. Everything is moving on-line. As mentioned earlier, there will soon be virtual reality versions of art galleries, museums, science centres, world expositions, zoos, encyclopedias, theme parks, instructional material and fiction, and historical events. The digital imaging of documents will replace the need for physical access to primary sources or even microfiche libraries.

For a minimal charge, on-line information services such as America On-line, Prodigy, Internet, and Compuserve provide unlimited amounts of information and topic-based forum-type discussions. Computer users can conduct information searches in the on-line libraries, scour press services for specific stories, browse through "electronic" encyclopedias, read magazines on-line before they appear in print, and collect newspaper articles by scanning online or home CD-ROMs.

For individuals interested in scientific and industrial research, a new library service has emerged called Teltech Resource Network Corporation of Minneapolis. Researchers and scientists spend a frustrating amount of time learning how to use computer commands so that they can access databases in search of published research material. Teltech offers an exciting alternative. The company hires scientific analysts under contract to provide answers to research questions within 24 hours. Each analyst is familiar with the more than 1,600 databases Teltech has at its disposal. After the expert provides clients with answers to their queries, Teltech canvasses the clients to ensure that they are satisfied. The company reports that over 90 percent of its clientele is satisfied, and for those who are not, other analysts are provided gratis. Moreover, Teltech is willing to contact agencies or suppliers of products that clients may need in the course of their research. An independent study of 20 randomly chosen Teltech customers revealed that 13 felt that the profit they accrued from using the service was approximately16 times greater than its cost. Since this service is expected to add $6 billion annually to the U.S. economy, state subsidies

BULLETIN BOARD

- **Job demand factors**: need for compiled information from different sources; ability to sort through increasing volume of information rapidly; need for easy access to information worldwide.
- **Job growth areas**: services which compile and sort through a variety of databases.
- **Job reduction areas**: traditional lending libraries.
- **Growth limiting factors**: diffusion of technological innovation throughout society; government's willingness to subsidize various services; speed of technological developments.

CONTACTS

- Canadian Association for Graduate Education in Library, Archival, & Information Studies
  c/o School of Library & Informational Studies,
  Dalhousie University,
  Halifax, NS B3H 4H8 Tel. 902-494-3656 Fax: 902-494-2451
- Canadian Association for Information Science
  University of Toronto,
  Faculty of Library and Information Science,
  140 St. George St.,
  Toronto, ON M5S 1A1 Tel. 416-978-7111 Fax: 416-971-1399
- Canadian Association of Research Libraries
  Morisset Hall, University of Ottawa
  #602, 65 University St.,
  Ottawa, ON K1N 9A5 613-564-5864 Fax: 613-564-5871
- Canadian Library Association
  #602, 200 Elgin St.,
  Ottawa, K2P 1L5 Tel. 613-232-9625 Fax: 613-563-9895
  Toll free: 1-800-267-6566
- Canadian Museums Association
  306 Metcalfe St.,
  Ottawa, K2P 1S2 Tel. 613-567-0099 Fax: 613-233-5438

are making this service available to small businesses

The Teltech example illustrates the direction libraries and other information storage systems are heading. Once the portable electronic book and CD-ROM—which will even read the book to the user—becomes commonplace, there will be little need for "physical" libraries. As government debt continues to mount and books get more expensive to publish, libraries will likely see their budgets cut severely. Having already eliminated the Economic Conference Board of Canada and the Science and Technology Board, and curtailed the CBC's budget, the government is unlikely to spare libraries from the ravages of downsizing, cost rationalization, or re-engineering. The ability of modern technology to provide the same information in a more widely available format will supersede the need to have access to the hard copy version of texts, and those who insist on using the older format will likely pay a premium for a courier-based lending library.

Where the Jobs are in Social Services
Daycare

The daycare field is expected to be an employment growth area as the number of preschool children is expected to rise between 1993 and 2005. More parents are making use of daycare services, especially as more and more women enter the work force. The dual-income family is now the norm rather than the exception. Women are returning to work sooner after childbirth, which also contributes to the rising labour-force participation rate among women ages 16 to 44. Moreover, as daycares increasingly gain the reputation of being structured and dynamic learning environments, many parents will choose this option for their preschoolers over the unprofessional services of a nanny, live-in worker, babysitter, or relative.

This field is not known for its high salaries. Job seekers who choose to pursue a career in this area are clearly committed to the non-monetary rewards of the profession. The low pay, however, encourages high turnover, which further increases employment opportunities.

If the federal or provincial governments were to choose subsidized daycare as an alternative to single parent welfare, the need for daycare workers would escalate dramatically. The supply of daycare centres is nowhere near the actual demand for such services, reports a Vanier Institute of the Family study, with one licensed daycare space for every ten working mothers in Canada. Fortunately, the Liberal government has promised to create 50,000 daycare spaces, up to a total of 150,000 for each year the economy grows by three percent.

BULLETIN BOARD

CONTACTS

☛ Canadian Child Care Federation
#401, 120 Holland Ave.,
Ottawa, ON K1Y 0X6 Tel. 613-729-5289 Fax: 613-729-3159

☛ Canadian Day Care Advocacy Association
323 Chapel St.,
Ottawa, ON K1N 7Z2 Tel. 613-594-3196 Fax: 613-594-9375

Psychologists, Psychiatrists, Social Workers, and Other Mental Health Workers

An estimated 25 percent of the population suffers from mild depression, which ends up being treated by drugs or counselling, while ten percent become dependent upon long-term anti-depressants or are hospitalized. According to one British study, mental illnesses increase during times of change. In Canada, the recession and uncertainty about the future have caused individuals considerable anguish. In 1992, a national study of stress and depression by the Canadian Mental Health Association and the Canadian Psychiatric Association revealed that 47 percent of Canadians feel "really stressed" at least a few times a week and in some cases all the time. Work and financial pressures accounted for the highest levels of stress experienced by people 25 to 54 years old.

In a national health survey conducted biannually by economist Earl Berger and Price Waterhouse, the number of individuals expecting to develop health problems as a result of work-related stress doubled since 1989, with six out of ten workers cited on-the-job stress as having already caused them health problems. Thirty percent to 50 percent more women than men feel they will likely fall victim to stress-induced health problems. By profession, 28 percent of professional, administrative, and managerial employees versus 18 percent of skilled, semi-skilled, and service workers felt susceptible to health problems brought on by stress at work. The Canadian Mental Health Association estimates that employers are paying $1 billion annually in costs associated with job stress. U.S. studies estimate the cost of depression anywhere between $27 and $100 billion annually through lost productivity, higher susceptibility to illness and loss of life through suicide. The annual U.S. market for anti-depressants alone is worth a hefty $1.1 billion.

It was found that the major cause of stress was reorganization of the workplace. Many also suffer from stress because they are staying in jobs they hate for fear of not being able to find jobs if they quit. As casual and contract work becomes a reality for many individuals, stress-related illnesses will become even more widespread. Not surprisingly, relaxation clinics have seen their clientele double since 1993, and business for massage therapists has increased substantially as well. Anxiety and panic disorder clinics are trying to cope with a growing clientele. In 1992, between 20 percent and 25 percent of Canadians suffered panic attacks. Dr. Mel Goodman, past president of the General Practice Psychotherapy Association, reports, "Fifty percent of visits to family doctors involve nonorganic [mental] problems." The aging population will also increase the demand for the services of therapists, psychologists, and psychiatrists. There is and there will continue to be a shortage of psychotherapists and psychologists. In fact, most of Canada's 12,000 psychologists and 3,500 psychiatrists are fully booked. Generally speaking, if you live in a large urban center and need to visit a psychiatrist, you have a long wait ahead of you, or more frustrating, you may find that you can't even get on a psychiatrist's waiting list.

Many companies and unions, recognizing the need for employee counselling, provide access to counselling as part of the work contract. Warren Shepell Consultants Corp. of Toronto earned $8 million in 1992 by offering counselling services to the employees of large corporations such as American Express Canada Inc., Du Pont Canada Inc., General Electric, IBM, Molson Companies Ltd., and Northern Telecom. The company makes its counsellors available 24 hours a day year-round, and estimates that it saves employers $7 for every $1 invested in its employee assistance programs.

Studies have shown that individuals in a high-income bracket are more prone to anxiety, while low-income individuals are more susceptible to depression. We might argue, therefore, that since the number of low-income earners will increase as the trend to part-time, contract, and casual hiring becomes more firmly entrenched, so will the number of people suffering from depression. Furthermore, the trend towards eradicating middle management will create a very large group of displaced managers who will likely experience bouts of anxiety. With individuals almost universally uncertain about future employment in a changing economy, there will be an increased need for social workers, community workers, welfare workers, psychiatric nurses, and addiction or human services counsellors. The doubling of violent crimes by adolescents in the past decade will likely escalate as family stress levels continue to rise. More child- and youth-care workers will be needed to assist families in dealing with young offenders. In Canada, 60 percent of the female-led single parent families live below the poverty line with 45 percent of all Canadian children likely to experience life in a single-parent family before the age of 18. The devastating effect of divorce on children, as described in an *Atlantic Monthly* article entitled "Dan Qualye Was Right," suggests that the social and psychological repercussions of life in a single-parent family will be profound and will be exacerbated by the long-term effects of unemployment. According to Dr. Paul Steinhauer, senior psychiatrist at Toronto's Hospital for Sick Children, the incidence of reported child abuse has doubled in the past five years, and one in five children or adolescents has at least one psychiatric disorder.

In 1981, only four percent of Ontarians received welfare. There has been a substantial jump, with 17 percent of the population in Ontario under 60 receiving some form of social assistance. The current $10 billion in welfare expenditures in Ontario represents a tripling of cost within the last few years. Besides increasing the need for welfare workers, this huge jump also portends a need for more health, social, and psychological services.

The trend toward integrating special needs individuals—the mentally or physically challenged—into the community will create a demand for trained social service personnel who can facilitate this transition. And the trend towards moving the elderly out of institutional settings and into the home will require the services of community-based gerontology specialists.

Psychologists have moved into all aspects of the business world as human resources, leadership, teamwork, non-monetary motivation, and user-friendliness become more vital to corporate competitiveness. Cognitive psychologists are even involved in the design of software, to make sure that programs works in a user-friendly manner and that instruction manuals are easily understood. As hiring and training become more "scientific," psychologists will play a greater role in career

BULLETIN BOARD

- **Job demand factors**: the recession; corporate reorganization; uncertainty about the economic future; staying in undesirable jobs out of fear; aging population.
- **Job growth areas**: psychologists; psychiatrists; psychotherapists; social workers; community workers; child- and youth-care workers; massage and relaxation therapists; correctional workers; welfare workers; psychiatric nurses; gerontology specialists or activation coordinators;
- **Skills, abilities, qualities, education needed**: at least a master's degree is required of those interested in aspiring to supervisory or executive positions.
- **Growth limiting factors**: ability and willingness of governments, corporations and individuals to pay for psychological services; the economy

CONTACTS

- Canadian Association of Social Workers
  55 Parkdale Ave.,
  Ottawa, ON K1Y 1E5 Tel. 613-729-6668
- Canadian Mental Health Association
  2160 Yonge St., 3rd Fl.,
  Toronto, ON M4S 2Z3 Tel. 416-484-7750 Fax: 416-484-4617
- Canadian Psychiatric Association
  #200, 237 Argyle,
  Ottawa, ON K2P 1B8 Tel. 613-234-2815 Fax: 613-234-9857
- Canadian Psychological Association
  Vincent Rd.,
  Old Chelsea, PQ J0X 2N0 Tel. 819-827-3927 Fax: 819-827-4639
- Canadian Public Health Association
  #400, 1565 Carling Ave.,
  Ottawa, ON K1Z 8R1 Tel. 613-725-3769 Fax: 613-725-9826
- Family Service Canada
  55 Parkdale Avenue
  Box 3505, Stn C,
  Ottawa, ON K1Y 4G1 Tel. 613-728-1865 Fax: 613-728-9387
- Social Science Federation of Canada
  #415, 151 Slater St.,
  Ottawa, ON K1P 5H3 Tel. 613-238-6112 Fax: 613-238-6114

BULLETIN BOARD

- **Job demand factors**: rising crime rates and expanding population; aging population's preoccupation with security and safety.
- **Job growth areas**: private security firms; opportunities for women and minority groups in police and firefighting professions.
- **Growth limiting factors**: municipal budgets and tax revolts.

CONTACTS

☞ Canadian Association of Fire Fighters
2 Gamron Ave., RR#4,
Uxbridge, ON L9P 1R4 Tel. 905-649-1586 Fax: 905-649-1587

☞ Canadian Guard Association (Ind.)
#305, 2841 Riverside Dr.,
Ottawa, ON K1V 8X7 Tel. 613-737-4417

☞ Canadian Police Association
141 Catherine St.,
Ottawa, ON K2P 1C3 Tel. 613-231-4168

☞ Federal Association of Security Officials
#505, 88 Metcalfe St.,
Ottawa, ON K1P 5L7

counselling, testing, skills and personality assessment. Their role in industrial organizations is continually expanding, with many acting as consultants as companies restructure.

Where the Jobs are in Police and Firefighting Services

Firefighting and police services normally enjoy substantial employment growth. In the past, these occupations would grow as the population grew. Today, however, municipalities have cut all expenditures as a result of eroding tax bases and tax defaults and are not hiring in these areas. Taxpayers are at their limit of fiscal tolerance and are unlikely to support further increases in the mill rate—the taxation rate as a percentage of the value of their homes. However, with crime rates escalating at over double the rate of population expansion, the need for increased protection has become an important civic issue.

Firefighters and police departments are involved in quota hiring systems which will benefit minority groups, including women, who seek employment in these areas. Since hiring practices will not rise fast enough to meet the security needs of the population at large, there will be a rapid increase in employment among private security firms. An aging population will be very security-conscious and will be willing to pay whatever price is necessary to ensure their safety.

Although the transition to a cashless society will lower the rate of mugging, thieves will still be interested in stealing personal possessions. Eventually, everyone will be fingerprinted in some sense and will own personal alarm systems. Forensic science and satellite surveillance will improve to such an extent that criminals will find it harder to avoid getting caught. Eventually, therefore, jobs will be in the high end of policework.

WHERE THE JOBS ARE IN MANUFACTURING

A survey of ten countries—Canada, Japan, Australia, U.S., Germany, France, Sweden, Britain, Italy and the Netherlands—showed that over the past three decades employment in manfacturing fell from 27 percent to 21 percent. In Canada and the U.S., manufacturing jobs grew between 1960 and 1989 but have fallen off since. Manufacturing soared more than 30 percent between1983 and1989 and from1970 to1974, leading the economy in both instances. In 1976, there were 3.4 million goods-producing jobs and 6.1 million service jobs in Canada. By 1992, 3.3 million jobs were in the goods-producing sector and 8.9 million were in the services. According to futurist John Kettle, if these trends continue, there will be 3.6 million goods-producing jobs and 11.9 million service jobs by 2003.

For the last 20 years, the contribution Canadian manufacturing has made to the country's gross domestic product has remained the same, and when compared with the U.S. or the G-7 industrial nations. The economic gains that manufacturing has enjoyed as a result of new products, new processes, and automation has been at the expense of the manufacturing work force, which has fallen from 23.5 percent of the overall work force in the 1960s to 15.2 percent in 1993. Stiff competition has kept prices down and profit margins at 1.5 percent of sales despite growing sales. Productivity improvements have resulted from cutting costs—that is, through laying off workers. According to Stephen Van Houten, president of the Canadian Manufacturers Association, manufacturing will change more in the next seven to ten years than in the past 50 years as companies install advanced technology and reorganize factories to make a variety of goods. Van Houten maintains that unions will not be able to stop thousands of workers from selling their skills to employment agencies that will farm out them out to companies on a continual basis.

Even the Japanese are expected to lay off 2 million workers in 1993, with workers in the manufacturing sector accounting for two out of every three laid off. During the 1980s, Southeast Asian countries which became rapidly industrialized, increased their portion of the manufactured-goods trade from 4.2 percent to 8.5 percent, taking market share away from all the industrialized countries, including Japan. Such a transfer of manufacturing to developing countries is a normal part of economic evolution, and has been facilitated by inexpensive transportation and new manufacturing techniques.

Competitive pressures have led to the universal adoption of the ISO 9000 quality assurance programs, which are set by the International Standards Organization (ISO) and which are recognized in 89 countries. Qualification requires that a company document its procedures and upgrade them where necessary before verification by an independent agency, which also returns periodically for partial audits. Toronto Plastics, for example, implementing ISO quality initiatives, reduced its defects from 150,000 per million parts to 15,000 with the hopes of eventually reaching the world-class level of 1,000. Northern Telecom aims to have all 55 of its worldwide plants certified in the near future. And in the U.S., General Electric's plastics division ordered its suppliers to meet ISO standards.

Given the interdependency between the goods and services sectors, improving efficiency in the services supplied to manufacturers would strongly improve the latter's competitiveness. According to the *Economist,* "GM's biggest supplier is not a steel or glass firm, but a health-care provider, Blue Cross-Blue Shield. In terms of output, one of GM's biggest 'products' is financial and insurance services, which together with EDS, its computing-services arm, account for a fifth of total revenue.... At Sony, as much as a fifth of its revenues now come from its film and music businesses. Add in design, marketing, finance, and after-sales support, and service activities account for at least half of Sony's business." Even many manufacturing-related services such as design and engineering are now being contracted out to independent companies.

Most important in determining success in the manufacturing industry is the state of the economy as a whole. As Peter Cook, economics editor of the *Globe & Mail,* asserts, "The main determinant is not whether tariffs are cut by a minor amount in a free-trade agreement. It is how successful Canada is in keeping internal costs under control. The patterns of the past show that when the business climate deteriorates—because of an overvalued currency, a bout of wage inflation or government intervention to raise taxes, impede investment or increase regulation—Canada puts its manufacturing base at risk." The drop in value of the Canadian dollar coupled with the low inflation rate have boosted manufacturing exports to begin to lead Canada out of its current recession. Though it accounts for less than 20 percent of the economy, manufacturing has been responsible for over 50 percent of Canada's economic growth since the summer of 1992, reaching roughly 90 percent of its 1989 peak. Despite having risen nine percent since the summer of 1992, there has been no employment growth until 1994 which has finally seen some job recovery.

By the end of 1994, Canadian manufacturers will have closed the cost-productivity gap with the U.S. as the declining Canadian dollar, slower wage gains, and lower health costs begin to level the playing field. Although Canadian manufacturers have made strides in the productivity of their operations by using new technology, Canada still trails the U.S., with only 58 percent of Canadian manufacturers using advanced technology compared with 74 percent of their American counterparts. According to the *World Competitiveness Report,* Canada ranked 15th in the quality of production technology its manufacturers used. The high cost of Canadian capital in a capital-intensive industry makes it impossible for many mature companies to afford the newer technologies given the rate of return on the cost of capital in industries where competition is based on low prices and thin margins. However, if these companies do not invest in technology, they will not survive.

Employment opportunities in manufacturing will not increase dramatically over the next ten years. Individuals with expertise in high-tech areas will comprise the majority of hirees. Outsourcing will spur growth in many small design and engineering services. Supplier services will play an important competitive role in manufacturing and many jobs will be

BULLETIN BOARD

- **Job demand factors**: the need to reduce costs and improve production efficiency.
- **Job growth areas**: quality assurance personnel; numerical control technologists; automation design, manufacturing, maintenance, and sales personnel; independent design and engineering services; other supplier service areas.
- **Job reduction areas**: all low-skilled and some medium-skilled jobs.
- **Growth limiting factors**: government policies; multinational manufacturing decisions; competitiveness of supplier services; wages; inflation; currency's comparative value; government debt and the resulting interest rates; rate of technological innovation and its adoption.

CONTACTS

☛ Canadian Manufacturers' Association
75 International Blvd., 4th Fl.,
Toronto, ON M9W 6L9 Tel. 416-798-8000 Fax: 416-798-8050

created in this area as manufacturers become more global or export-oriented. Government policies will likely be most significant in determining the industry's future. With 3.3 million Canadians currently working in manufacturing, the livelihoods of scores of people will depend on how these factors play themselves out.

Construction Industry

Between 1984 and 1990, construction spending in Canada rose from just under $57 billion to over $102 billion. In 1992, however, the industry experienced a ten percent decline to $92 billion. This pattern is typical of the construction industry which grows faster than the economy during a boom and contracts during a downturn in the economy. Private construction, which represents two-thirds of all construction spending, comprises the construction of houses, factories, office buildings, stores, oil and gas wells, pipelines, refineries, railways and telephone and cable-television lines. Between 1982 and 1990, private construction increased by 106 percent to $74 billion, but fell by 16 percent to $62 billion during 1991 and 1992. Between 1982 and 1990, spending on residential housing tripled to $41 billion while commercial space construction rose by 135 percent to $16.6 billion and factory construction increased by 43 percent to $4.3 billion. Between 1990 and 1992, however, housing fell by nine percent and commercial and industrial spending by 35 percent. The surplus of office towers, shopping malls, and industrial parks will dampen recovery in these sectors. Industrial design building, however, is on the increase. Home offices, office sharing, and home shopping may eventually have a profound dampening effect on the commercial and retail markets. In 1993, the construction of single detached homes was growing at a 15 percent rate, thanks to lower interest rates, declining house prices, and the demand of the tail end of the baby boom.

Public sector construction—projects that focus on schools, hospitals, sewage systems, waterworks, electric-power plants, and transmission lines—grew by 45 percent to $21 billion from 1982 to 1990. Between the 1990 to 1992 recession years, however, public construction expanded an additional nine percent to $23 billion. One reason for this growth is the steady increase in the population, which leads to a demand for the construction of schools, hospitals, roads, and water systems. Another reason is construction work on megaprojects such as Ontario's Darlington nuclear plant and Manitoba's Limestone hydro dam—projects that take so long to complete and, once started, are usually impervious to most

---

HARD-HAT ROBOTS

In the future, robotics will have a dramatic impact on the construction industry. The Obayashi Corporation already has workers using television to monitor the progress of robots. On top of an emerging building, a box-like construction factory moves up along with the construction of the building. Inside, the components are moved by automatic lifts as giant vacuum suckers grab the floor and lift them to the appropriate places. Welding robots seal beam sections while moving on circular tracks. Only one-sixth the number of workers are required. The Tansie Corporation utilizes a covered platform resting on the building's central core which is raised via a powerful jack. With crane operators now able to build outer sections of a building six floors below it, floors can be built in three days, as opposed to the customary five or six. In these roof-covered systems, work can continue regardless of the weather.

BULLETIN BOARD

- **Job demand factors**: population growth; better-designed industrial buildings which efficiently incorporate information technology and work flow.
- **Job growth areas**: public construction, particularly road infrastructure; industrial design buildings; small single-family dwellings; building and exporting prefabricated houses; renovation and repair once the economy improves; cottage winterization and construction of country estates; black market renovation; companies with contracts abroad; condos for retirees moving to British Columbia.
- **Job reduction areas**: Office, mall, and other commercial construction in the short term and possibly in the long run.
- **Growth limiting factors**: population; government funds available; home offices; home shopping; economy; labour and raw material costs.

CONTACTS

- Canada Construction Skills Association
  2395 Speakman Dr.,
  Mississauga, ON L5K 1B3
- Canadian Construction Association
  85 Albert St., 10th Fl.,
  Ottawa, ON K1P 6A4 Tel. 613-224-4471 Fax: 613-236-9526
- Canadian Home Builders Association
  #502, 200 Elgin St.,
  Ottawa, ON K2P 1L5 Tel. 613-230-3060 Fax: 613-232-8214

economic circumstances. A major project that will stimulate employment is the construction of the bridge between New Brunswick and Prince Edward Island. Many companies are finding work in Asia, and, for the foreseeable future, there will be many opportunities for larger construction companies to obtain work in the Far East.

Clearly, while boom times tend to favour the private construction industry, job security is to be found in the public construction sector, especially during a recession. Although construction was expected to rise by 3.5 percent in 1993 and by only one percent in 1994—not including potential government projects—it will not match the 1991 level. Therefore, it will be some time before the 120,000 workers laid off since 1989 get their jobs back.

For those new to the industry, the best jobs are in the industrial design and public construction areas, and even then, many will have to wait for workers to retire later in the decade. The home repair and renovation market will likely pick up once the economy improves. Although there was a 21.4 percent drop in the amount spent on home repairs between 1989 and 1991, there was only a 2.3 percent drop in the number of households spending at least some money on home repairs. Eventually, retirees will consider winterizing their cottages or purchasing country estates as an alternative to home ownership once they become snowbirds and urban crime rates escalate.

Some specialty markets are doing well, such as the prefabrication or modular homes markets, offices or cottages, which are cheaper to build, better constructed, and can be added on to at a later date. Both the domestic and export markets have been favourable for these products and will likely continue to be, as long as the virtues of price and quality remain a competitive edge.

Black market renovation makes it difficult to accurately report on residential construction activity. According to an estimate by the Canadian Home Builders Association, it is believed that 55 percent of all renovations in Canada involve non-recorded cash payments. Such a significant amount of undisclosed renovation activity represents a substantial increase over the 30 percent level of black market renovations prior to the introduction of the GST.

Automobile and Automotive Parts Industry

The significant improvements in productivity since 1990 has created a cost advantage in building cars in Canada instead of the U.S. Industry, Science and Technology Canada reports that in 1989, it cost $1,297.22 to produce a car in the U.S. as opposed to $1016.28 in Canada. In 1992, a U.S. car cost $1,444.56 to produce, and to produce a Canadian automobile, $1,096.38. From 1989 to 1992, cost savings improved from $280.94 to $348.18, the cost improvement partly a result of the lower Canadian dollar. The *Harbor Report* on North American automotive industry competitiveness between 1986 and 1992 found that three Ontario plants were in the top ten of the 31 Big Three—the General Motors Corporation, Ford Motor Company, and Chrysler Ltd.—passenger car assembly plants, and two Ontario truck assembly plants placed in the top ten out of 27 such plants. Morever, a 1993 Canadian Automobile Association survey indicates that 75 percent of the car owners—a record percentage—were very satisfied with their cars. In addition, 35 percent of Ontario autoworkers had some post-secondary education compared with less than 30 percent in Georgia and less than 25 percent in Tennessee. While these improvements may generate optimism about the future of the automobile manufacturing industry, storm clouds are gathering on the horizon nonetheless.

Only 11 percent of Ontario autoworkers are knowledge workers with engineering or technology degrees or diplomas. This figure represents the same proportion as 12 years ago. But in the U.S., since 1981, the proportion of knowledge workers in Michigan grew to 25 percent from 16 percent, and from 11 percent to 26 percent in Tennessee. These changes reflect the concentration of research, engineering, and design facilities located in the U.S. Ontario is still using the straight assembly-line-type operation and must therefore compete with the new automotive belt of Tennessee, Georgia, Kentucky, and North and South Carolina based largely on salary, tax holidays, role of unions, financing costs, and level of government regulation. At the moment, Canadian autoworkers enjoy the benefits of a low dollar and less expensive health-care costs, factors that have created a $5.40(U.S.) an hour competitive advantage over their American counterparts, $4.01 an hour over Japanese autoworkers, and $10 an hour over German autoworkers.

None of the major automakers anticipated a simultaneous weakness in the North American, European, and Japanese auto markets. With worldwide excess production capacity totaling 8.2 million cars and trucks annually—enough production to keep more assembly plants busy than General Motors has in all of North America—a major industry shakeout is unavoidable. In an effort to grab more market share, the Japanese auto industry kept building production capacity so as to keep volumes high and costs low. Such excess capacity has led Nissan Motor Corporation to post its first loss since 1946. Between1982 and 1992, automakers worldwide built 25 new assembly plants. With Chrysler's debt ratings tied to junk bond levels and Ford's European operation temporarily putting the company in the red, despite laying off approximately12,000 workers, unemployment will loom large as a prospect for many companies eventually.

To make matters worse, the U.S. has arbitrarily raised the country-of-origin rules governing Canadian exports to the U.S. to 60 percent and 62.5 percent from 50 percent, depending on the vehicle. Such a high level may encourage Japanese auto makers to make more use of their U.S. plants to serve the American market. With 75 percent of all autos manufactured in Canada normally destined for sale in the U.S., the Canadian industry is particularly vulnerable.

To improve the educational level of its Canadian work force, General Motors is willing to spend $1 million on skills upgrading. Such a strategy represents an attempt to attract more higher-value-added contracts to Canadian plants. General Motors is seeking a 500 percent increase in the number of workers who will be upgrading their skills. All 14,000 Oshawa-area General Motors employees are eligible for counselling in order to establish a learning plan best suited to their skills. With robotics increasingly becoming a presence in the auto industry, the only jobs that will survive in the long run—aside from administration—will be in the robotics maintenance, numerical control, and research and design ends of the industry.

In an effort to save the industry, the Big Three and other major automakers have formed ten research and development consortiums to explore such areas as materials, fuels, environment, batteries, recycling, computer assisted design, emissions, and safety. Development is restricted to the predevelopment stage so as to avoid antitrust concerns. Toyota, somewhat pessimistic about the future of the auto industry, has begun to diversify into aviation technology, airport construction, prefabricated housing, and financial services. While only two percent of the company's $81.3 billion (U.S.) annually revenue is in the non-auto sector, Toyota hopes to increase it to ten percent before too long. It would be wise for all Canadian assembly-line autoworkers to also consider diversifying out of the auto industry since, in the long run, the entire auto assembly operation will be automated. In the short term, the popularity of certain vehicles, such as minivans or all-terrain vehicles, may determine which plants close and which stay open.

The auto parts industry has been prospering of late thanks to the

Free Trade Agreement, the GST, and the lower dollar. These factors have helped lower prices for auto parts and made the Canadian parts industry more competitive. According to "The Automotive Aftermarket Industry Outlook Study," duties of 9.2 percent on parts crossing the Canada-U.S. border have been gradually eliminated since 1989. Replacing the old 13.5 percent manufacturers sales tax with the seven percent lower GST reduced the price of parts but raised labour costs. The study estimated the net effect of the GST to be a 3.3 percent reduction on parts and labour costs to consumers. Since any value of the Canadian dollar at the 82-cent level or lower is the rule of thumb for making money among parts suppliers, so the current 73-cent dollar has been a boon to the industry. These factors explain why the prices on parts ranging from batteries to tires and spark plugs only rose by 1.5 percent a year since 1986, versus the 4.2 percent annual increase for all other consumer goods.

The recession, along with the decision by the Big Three to give more business to fewer parts sources, led to the closing of 54 Canadian auto parts plants, leaving 580 parts plants in the country. In the meantime, the Big Three's vehicle sales have gradually picked up at a faster rate than imported sales, leading to a demand for more North American parts. Japanese plants in North America are purchasing more Canadian parts to help lower Japan's auto trade surplus with the U.S. and to lower their own costs. General Motors' decision to outsource more of its parts rather than produce them in-house, has led to 172 Canadian companies winning $725 million worth of new work annually from General Motors. The bigger suppliers—for example, Canada's Magna International Inc., which is the fourth largest auto parts company in North America with 68 plants and $2.5 billion in annual sales—has been asked to assume more product design and engineering responsiblities, and to develop and pay for the tooling of components that was previously done in-house. Unless government assistance is forthcoming, smaller companies are at a distinct disadvantage in raising financing for the tooling costs and will have to become more specialized.

From an employment perspective, the Canadian industry's job count peaked at 90,000 in 1989 and declined by six percent in 1990, 14.5 percent in 1991, and five percent in the first half of 1992. Productivity gains of 21 percent since 1990 have left plants operating at only 70 percent to 80 percent capacity, despite the increase in business. In a soft global mar-

BULLETIN BOARD

- **Job demand factors**: the low Canadian dollar and lower health care costs; outsourcing of parts design, engineering, and manufacturing.
- **Job growth areas**: large auto parts suppliers; automation and quality control specialists; parts design and engineering.
- **Job reduction areas**: all low-skilled areas.
- **Growth limiting factors**: taxes; workmen's compensation; cost of electricity; social legislation such as pay equity and unemployment benefits; trainability of employees; trade agreements; origin of content rules; popularity of types of vehicles made in Canada; government's willingness to assist in training or financing.

CONTACTS

☞ Canadian Automobile Association
1775 Courtwood Cres.
Ottawa, Ont. K2C 3J2
Tel. 613-226-7631 Fax: 613-225-7383

☞ Automobile Industries Association of Canada
1272 Wellington St.,
Ottawa, ON K1Y 3A7 Tel. 613-728-5821 Fax: 613-728-6021

☞ Automotive Parts Manufacturers' Association
#516, 195 The West Mall.,
Etobicoke, ON M9C 5K1 Tel. 416-620-4220 Fax: 416-620-9730

☞ Automotive Parts Sectoral Training Council
#203, 140 Renfrew Dr.,
Markham, ON L3R 6B3

ket, auto assemblers are forced into price-based competition, which has in turn forced them to insist on productivity gains among suppliers in contracts that include component price decreases over time. General Motors requires that component prices drop by 60 percent if suppliers hope to continue their relationship with the company. Combined with price decreases, suppliers are also expected to meet tougher quality and delivery standards. Fortunately, Canadian parts manufacturers have long perfected the ability to produce small batches, which will be an advantage as auto assemblers shorten product development time frames and set more modest sales goals for some vehicles.

The need for ongoing productivity improvements has led companies to adopt a team-based approach and to foster continuous learning environments. Under a three-year massive training plan supported by $20 million in funding from industry and government sources, 40,000-50,000 auto parts workers will be trained in three areas: changes in the industry under global restructuring; modern technology including work organization, applied mathematics, computers and robotics; and workplace communication and involvement.

Aerospace, Defence, and Other Transportation Manufacturing

The Canadian aerospace and defence sector is a $9 billion production industry, the sixth largest in the world, and a vital source of foreign currency for Canada—70 percent is exported with 50 percent going to the U.S. A study of the defence and aerospace industries by Ernst & Young surveyed 29 leading CEOs who oversee companies with sales in excess of $300 billion U.S. and employ two million people. The report concluded that Canadian companies in these industries must diversify operations, market new technologies, and develop strategic alliances with former competitors if they are to survive the restructuring taking place in the industry. Since North American companies lack the strategic alliances commonly found in their European counterparts, they may lose market share much the same way the automobile and steel industries have in the past.

The lack of megaprojects in these industries will lead to considerable downsizing and diversification worldwide. President Clinton's decision to scale down the U.S. space station Freedom may mean that the proposed robotic arm, which was to be designed for the project by Spar Aerospace, may be scrapped—something which underscores the need for diversification. Canada's opportunity lies in forming specialized sector companies which can recruit some of the highly talented surplus staff from companies that are downsizing. Small companies with high-tech expertise will be subcontracted by the larger ones to handle specialized areas of the $10 million to $20 million contracts, which are the current industry norm. An example of the diversification process in Canada is Spar Aerospace's decision to transform itself from an aerospace company into a global telecommunications operation. Although 60 percent of its revenue comes from its space operations, the company hopes that 50 percent of its revenue will be coming from software and communication by 1996.

The defence industry is currently in retreat. General Electric's jet engine division plans to eliminate1,600 jobs in 1994 because of a reduced defence budget and faltering orders from commercial airlines.

In many ways, Bombardier represents the non-road transportation industry in Canada. In the aircraft industry, it owns both Canadair and de Havilland Inc. Unfortunately, the worldwide commercial aeropace industry is in retrenchment with a glut of new planes parked in desert shelters waiting to be purchased. Airlines will be unable to afford new large airplanes to replace existing fleets during the 1990s without government assistance or manufacturers taking on the burden of financing new orders since private investors and banks have fled the market. Boeing, Airbus, and McDonnell Douglas increased their exposure to financing customer sales by about 30 percent to $8.3 billion, a figure which is expected to grow to $20 billion by the year 2000. In the boom years of the late 1980s, growing passenger counts encouraged airlines and aircraft leasing companies to go on a buying binge until the recession came along and options on new planes were dropped, firm orders were delayed, and many existing ones cancelled. In the summer of 1993, de Havilland had to shut down its plant. On the positive side, 400 new jobs have been created in 1994 at Dorval, St. Laurent, and de Havilland as Canadair has begun to receive orders for its Regional Jet, a 50-seat aircraft that Canadair spent $275 million to develop between 1989 and 1992. A Stanford University study commissioned by Bombardier forecasts a demand between 1993 and 2010 for 7,000 aircraft in the 20-90-seat category, including its own business jets. This projection is based on the growth of smaller, regional airlines in the U.S. which are more profitable and more likely to grow faster than the ailing larger-plane market. Currently, Bombardier has orders worth $3.3 billion in its aerospace division and its decision to produce its new global express long-range corporate jet will add 2,000 new jobs between 1993 and 1998, mostly at its de Havilland plant.

Boeing optimistically forecasts that 5,500 new jet aircraft will be needed between 1993 and 2000—70 percent for growth and the rest for replacement. To purchase this number of planes, airlines would need to raise $45 billion annually at 1992 prices. Airbus optimistically projects that it could raise half that money. Even if manufacturers were to spring

BULLETIN BOARD

- **Job demand factors**: small high-tech specialized aerospace firms; small regional airline planes eventually; subway and rail car replacement or refurbishing; watercraft market.
- **Job growth areas**: subway and rail car plants.
- **Job reduction areas**: aerospace generally.
- **Growth limiting factors**: willingness of governments to subsidize various transportation markets; peace; troubles in the airline industry; decisions to refurbish as opposed to replace; popularity of water and winter sports which are demographically determined; decline of business travel.

CONTACTS

- Aerospace Industries Association of Canada
  #1200, 60 Queen St.,
  Ottawa, ON K1P 5Y7
  Tel. 613-232-4297 Fax: 613-232-1142
- Canadian Industrial Transportation League
  #706, 480 University Ave.,
  Toronto, ON M5G 1V2
  Tel. 416-596-7833 Fax: 416-596-1272

for the rest, chances are there would be a credit crunch affecting both the manufacturers and the airlines as investors and banks get increasingly nervous. With business travel down 40 percent and travel in the latter half of the decade largely consisting of leisure travel as aging boomers take to the skies, it is possible that North American and Western European markets might stop growing altogether. Despite the short-term difficulties, the industry is expected to pick up after the year 2000, once the dust settles from the industry consolidation process. By then, however, the Pacific Rim will have broadened its aerospace manufacturing capacity.

Between 1988 and 1993, Bombardier's sales have grown from $1.4 billion to $4.4 billion, representing a 26 percent annual compound rate of growth—quite an accomplishment through a recession. However, the company may run into trouble with its proposed fast-rail plans. Having acquired the rights to France's TGV fast-rail system, it is trying to sell Canadian and American politicians on the idea of investing in high-speed rail systems, without much success. Its competitor, the Swiss-Swedish X-2000, will likely win out since it is half the cost and does not require the investment of public funds.`

Bombardier has met with success in the new rail and subway car market which is expected to exceed 4,000 cars in North America by the end of the 1990s, not counting the hundreds which will need refurbishing. A $41 million upgrade is expected to create more than 500 jobs at its subway car plant in Thunder Bay, Ontario, by 1996. This amounts to a doubling of its work force there. Bombardier has expanded into Mexico, where it has a three-year contract to refurbish 234 subway cars at its Concarril division with half of the contract benefitting the Kingston, Ontario, division of UTDC Inc.

Aside from its well-established mature skidoo market, Bombardier is fighting the Japanese for the fast-growing watercraft market with products such as Sea-Doo—the equivalent to Japan's Jet Ski. By covering both winter- and summer-season sports, the company manages to employ its workers year-round. So far, its success includes grabbing 11 percent of the Japanese sit-down personal watercraft market.

Food and Beverage Processing Industry

The $44 billion grocery products manufacturing industry, which is the second largest industry in Canada after forestry, has seen 25,000 jobs disappear since 1988. Meat and poultry products accounted for 44,000 jobs with the meat products market peaking in 1977, though the poultry market has yet to peak. Fish products account for 27,700 jobs and this sector is on job endangered list as far as its future is concerned. The dairy product industry, which peaked in 1979, employs 21,200 workers. The feed sector, which employs 15,500 workers, reached it peak in 1986. Bread and bakery products account for 28,500 jobs, but the sector peaked in 1973. Other food products markets, when combined, peaked in 1985 and employ 26,000 workers.

A study conducted by the University of Guelph's George Morris Centre that compared Canadian food processors to their American counterparts, found that the Canadian processors were less competitive in 15 out of 19 processing areas including poultry, frozen fruit and vegetables,

---

BULLETIN BOARD

- **Job demand factors**: quality; value; specialty needs or preferences; health concerns of aging boomers.
- **Job growth areas**: specialty markets including ethnic markets; private label processors; bottled water; nutri-ceutical market.
- **Job reduction areas**: all other areas.
- **Growth limiting factors**: U.S. food processors; trade agreements; inter-provincial trade barriers; consumer preferences.

CONTACTS

- Canadian Association of Specialty Foods
  #409, 1 Eva Rd.,
  Etobicoke, ON M9C 4Z5 Tel. 416-626-6239 Fax: 416-620-5392
- Canadian Bottled Water Association
  #7, 30 West Beaver Creek Rd.,
  Richmond Hill, ON L4B 3K1 Tel. 416-886-6928 Fax: 886-5872
- Food Institute of Canada
  #415, 1600 Scott St.,
  Ottawa, ON K1Y 4N7 Tel. 613-722-1000 Fax: 613-722-1404
- Grocery Products Manufacturers of Canada
  #301, 885 Don Mills Rd.,
  Don Mills, Ont. M3C 1V9
  Tel. 416-510-8024 Fax: 416-510-8043

---

soft drinks, and pasta. However, Canadian food processors excelled in red meat, sugar, breakfast foods, and flour mix. Canada's total net agriculture and food trade balance grew from less than $1.5 billion in 1989 to $3.5 billion in 1992.

Companies that are prospering despite the recession are involved in niche markets, make productive use of technology innovations, employ mass customization, or sell specialty products. For example, Clearly Canadian Beverage Corporation is hoping to cash in on the aging boomer "nutri-ceuticals" market which consists of beverages containing "healthy" ingredients. In Ontario, the retail bottled water market grew by 25 percent over a 52-week period now that 40 percent of Ontarians use bottled water as a healthier alternative to tap water. Store brands or private-label brands such as President's Choice have benefitted from consumers abandoning the high prices associated with brand-name products. Store-brand products accounted for 24.3 percent of the Canadian supermarket products purchased over 1993 versus 18 percent in the U.S. The increase in the number of television channels has splintered the consumer market, making it harder or more expensive to reach all consumers in order to establish brand identity. With a reduction in the quality differences between products and consumers becoming more educated and adventurous in their food choices, most consumers are willing to comparison-shop. Unless the quality is clear to the consumer or unless the product is unique, consumers are unwilling to pay a price premium for image. Loblaws currently spends $25 million annually developing products that will capture the specialty or gourmet market. It has agreed to produce 350 private-label products for Wal-Mart in the U.S.

Accompanying this trend is the large number of layoffs and reduced advertising expenditures announced by Proctor & Gamble Inc. Cereal manufacturers can no longer raise their prices the customary annual eight percent to ten percent on household brands. Kelloggs, for example, raised the price on its cornflakes by only one cent in 1993, perhaps in response to the fact that President's Choice cornflakes sells for $1.99 compared to Kelloggs Canada Inc.'s $2.75 for an equivalent box. The best employment opportunities will be in companies such as Loblaws or in specialty companies which understand their customers' needs and can anticipate market trends or opportunities.

Chemical Industry

Canada's chemical industry is bigger than its pulp and paper industry and employs 84,000 individuals, 60 percent of whom live in Ontario. From June 1989 to October 1991, 15.2 percent of jobs in the industry were lost in Canada, compared with only 0.6 percent in the U.S; rubber and plastics were down 26.9 percent, compared with 2.2 percent in the U.S.; and petroleum and coal sectors lost 10.3 percent of their jobs, versus 2.6 percent in the U.S.

Although Gerald Finn, vice-president of the Calgary-based multinational, Novacor Chemicals (Canada) Ltd., believes that greater access to Mexico will create more petrochemical jobs in Canada as the industry increases production, the forecast for this traditional industry is not terribly optimistic. Western chemical companies used to look to the Far East

BULLETIN BOARD

- **Job demand factors**: growing Latin American and Asian economies; need for environmentally friendly product substitutes.
- **Growth limiting factors**: trade agreements or barriers; environmental regulations; overcapacity.

CONTACTS

- The Chemical Institute of Canada
  #550, 130 Slater St.,
  Ottawa, ON K1P 6E1
  Tel. 613-232-6252 Fax: 613-232-5862
- Canadian Association of Chemical Distributors
  #101, 505 Consumers Rd.,
  Willowdale, ON M2J 4V8 Tel. 416-502-1166 Fax: 416-502-1784
- Canadian Chemical Producers' Association
  #805, 350 Sparks St.,
  Ottawa, ON K1R 7S8 Tel. 613-237-6215 Fax: 613-237-4061
- Canadian Manufacturers of Chemical Specialities
  #702, 56 Sparks St.,
  Ottawa, ON K1P 5A9 Tel. 613-232-6616 Fax: 613-233-6350

to absorb much of its supply, but that was before there was such stiff competition from Asian countries. Although Asia's non-communist Pacific Rim— Japan, South Korea, Taiwan, Hong Kong, Australia, and the six ASEAN countries—account for one-third of the world's demand and are expected to consume 40 percent by the year 2000, China and Japan are expected to be net exporters of chemicals, instead of running their current annual trade deficit of $14 billion. Other Asian countries are also hoping to export chemicals at prices western chemical multinationals are going to have difficulty matching. Excess capacity will likely be created as more Asian producers emerge. An industry shakeout at the turn of the century is unavoidable, with western companies very possibly the big losers. Regulations among western countries have reduced profit margins and made these companies vulnerable to even more price wars.

The International Joint Commission, the watchdog on Great Lakes pollution, has recommended the phasing out of chlorinated chemicals which are used in a wide range of products including pesticides, plastics, and pharmaceuticals. A report prepared for the Chlorine Institute concluded that finding substitutes for chlorinated chemicals, which comprise 50 percent of the substances produced by the industry, would cost the Canadian and U.S. economies $100 billion. The report suggests that one million jobs would be threatened in the U.S and 84,000 jobs in Canada.

Nuala Beck identifies the new economy sectors of the chemical industry as industrial chemicals, plastics and synthetics, pharmaceuticals, and paint and varnish; and old economy sectors as toilet preparations and soap and cleaning products. Beck sees 72 percent of the industry's activity taking place in the new economy. The future for this industry is not favourable. Most Canadian chemical firms are in the lower end of the value-adding scale and are therefore the most vulnerable to price competition. Job security will lie in the pharmaceutical and specialty chemical markets.

Steel Industry

Although there has been a modest turnaround in the struggling steel industry as demand has picked up for steel in the U.S., the industry is not in good shape. Between 1987 and 1993, Stelco Inc.'s work force dropped by 40 percent to 11,600 and Dofasco Inc.'s plunged 34 percent to 8,200. Labour-saving technologies, imports from overseas, slow economic growth, competition from substitute materials such as plastics, trumped-up dumping violations, and superefficient producers in other countries have crippled the industry.

The U.S. commerce department recently found 19 countries guilty of dumping, and its subsequently imposed anti-dumping duties of up to 109.22 percent have effectively closed the U.S. market to most foreign producers. Since the commerce department routinely finds 97 percent of foreign companies it investigates guilty of dumping, the $100 million spent on the first round of legal defense against these steel dumping charges is largely wasted money. Ironically, the U.S. claims that Canadian steel producers accepted $30 billion (U.S.) in subsidies over the past two decades, yet the U.S. subsidizes each steelworker's job at an annual cost of $750,000 per worker. The situation is a classic Catch-22. Any foreign company that is more efficient than U.S. companies is automatically guilty of dumping, because any company selling its steel products at less than 0.5 percent lower than the normal U.S. producer price is deemed guilty of dumping. Although in 1993 Canadian steel exporters won the first part of the dispute, as far as hot- and cold-rolled steel is concerned, an appeal is pending regarding charges that Canadians were dumping steel in the U.S. Recent GATT negotiations have at least attempted to raise the anti-dumping level to two percent, instead of 0.5 percent.

To avoid anti-dumping charges, Dofasco will close more Canadian plants, but build mini-mill plants such as Nucor Corp. in the U.S. Nucor uses German technology and its work force is non-unionized. Wages are $8.78/hour versus $17.98/hour in Canada. Workers are paid under a bonus system and a profit-sharing plan. However, there is no pension or retiree medical plan. As a result of the plant's efficiency—it only requires 0.8 worker-hours per ton versus the normal three to four worker hours per ton—the steel workers earn an annual salary of $40,000 to $45,000. Co-Steel Inc., which has a plant in Whitby, Ontario, is another mini-mill plant that enjoys the same success as Nucor in the U.S. Dofasco and Co-Steel have entered a joint venture to build a $300 million mini-mill in Kentucky. Mini-mills, which use ever-abundant scrap as a raw material— 80 percent versus 20 percent to 30 percent for integrated mills—are hoping to move beyond producing low-grade steel by adding higher quality iron and improving production methods.

Six Canadian steel companies, including Stelco and Dofasco, are pinning their hopes on Project Bessemer, a research project being conducted under the aegis of the National Research Council of Canada. The project involves studying the feasibility of direct strip casting as a replacement for the extremely expensive whole hot-rolling process. If successful, direct strip casting would replace the scrap steel process and would only cost $30 million, versus the hundreds of millions needed for a new mill. Industrial application is at least five years away, but Canada's steel mills could then be remodeled without compromising quality.

The steel industry's future in the steel pipe and tube area (natural gas pipe; castings for dental and surgical instruments, aircraft parts, and plastics) and wire (fine steel wire used to diffuse the explosive charge of car airbags) looks good. However, there is cause for concern in the areas of cold-rolled steel, hot-rolled steel, iron and steel foundries, and electro-metallurgical products.

Unless you are involved in the design, operation, and maintenance of

BULLETIN BOARD

- **Job growth areas**: product- or process-improvement research and development.
- **Job reduction areas**: steelworkers
- **Growth limiting factors**: labour-saving technologies; imports from overseas; competition from substitute materials; superefficient producers in the U.S.; high cost of capital; discriminatory U.S. anti-dumping rules.

CONTACTS

- Canadian Steel Construction Council
  #300, 201 Consumer Rd.
  Willowdale, Ont. M2J 4G8
  Tel. 416-491-9898
- Canadian Steel Producers Association
  #1425, 50 O'Connor St.,
  Ottawa, ON K1P 6L2
  Tel. 613-238-6049 Fax: 613-238-1832
  (Note: also location of Canadian Steel Industry Research Association)
- Canadian Steel Service Centre Institute
  #501, 345 Lakeshore Rd. East
  Oakville, Ont. L6J 1J5
  Tel. 416-842-1861 Fax: 416-842-5836
- Canadian Steel Trade & Employment Congress
  #803, 234 Eglinton Ave. East
  Toronto, Ont. M4P 1K5
  Tel. 416-480-1797 Fax: 416-480-2986
- Reinforcing Steel Institute of Canada
  1 Sparks Ave.,
  Willowdale, ON M2H 2W1 Tel. 416-499-4000 Fax: 416-497-4143

steel labour-saving technology or a specialty application in a growing area, it would be wise to look for work in another field. Companies that solve problems for steel mills will have obvious hiring potential. Blast Cleaning Products Ltd. of Oakville, Ontario, for example, which designs, manufactures, and installs sandblast units for steel products, has prospered in such processes as eliminating scale from girders in the cooling-down process of making steel, cleaning railway cars of rust, paint, and scale- and blast-cleaning steel farm equipment. The company exports 90 percent of its products. China, for example, has purchased a dozen sand-blast units at about $250,000 each for its steel makers.

Most steel companies worldwide now spend their research and development funds on developing new materials and new products, given the growing competition from plastics, fibres, composites, and other innovative materials, as manufacturers are increasingly demanding higher quality or more specialized metals. Unless the Canadian steel industry shifts from research on how to reduce costs on commodity steel to developing higher value-added products, they will not survive. Diversification into other areas—such as construction—will also be essential. For example, Lido Wall Systems of Mississauga, Ontario, has shown that studs, trusses, and basement beams can be replaced by steel—in a prefabricated manner—so as to deliver a house with perfectly straight walls within two weeks.

WHERE THE JOBS ARE IN THE NATURAL RESOURCES INDUSTRIES

The prognosis for Canada's natural resources industries is poor, with Canada no longer very competitive in this area. Unfortunately, Canada has exhausted its supply of easily extractable resources. The forests that remain are harder to get to—further inland or on remote islands, in the case of B.C., for example—the major mineral motherlodes have been mined out, drilling for oil is no longer easy now that the large, easily drilled deposits have been fully exploited, fishing is an exercise in diminishing returns, and most hydro dams have already been built in the most practical locations. Other countries, particularly developing countries, can often extract natural resources more cheaply, because their labor costs are lower and the easy-to-extract resources have not been fully exploited. Since most purchasers are concerned with price, these are the markets they will patronize. Moreover, the Commonwealth of Independent States (CIS) has a wealth of natural resources waiting to be exploited. There is as much oil in the Russian states as there is in Saudi Arabia. Because of its political and economic difficulties, Russian states have been unloading natural resources onto world markets in order to get their hands on as much hard currency—U.S. dollars—as they can. This has driven down the price of aluminum.

Compounding the problem is that the many improvements in efficiency means that less material is required to construct or operate many manufactured items—fuel-efficient lightweight cars, for example. And new synthetic substances are replacing natural ones because they may be cheaper to make and more durable or functional purposes—fiberglass car bodies replacing metal, plastic replacing wood, and ceramics replacing steel.

While it is possible that modern technology could substantially improve the extraction and fabrication aspects of the natural resources industries, few Canadian companies have shown interest in doing so until quite recently. In fact, 60 percent of Canada's pulp and paper industry has been using technology that dates back to the 1930s! When times were good—profits up and currency low—virtually all of Canada's competitors upgraded their production facilities. With few exceptions, however, Canadian companies passed up every opportunity of this kind. Economists have decried this fact repeatedly, but their protests were to no avail. For example, our pulp and paper industry spent 0.3 percent of its 1988 revenues on research and development as opposed to 0.8 percent to one percent spent by Sweden, Japan, and Finland. Historically, the pulp and paper industry in Ontario has not invested in technological improvements, choosing to rely on inexpensive wood and a low Canadian dollar instead. Economists have also urged companies in this sector to add value to the natural resources by processing them further into finished products, where the profits are higher and the long-range economic prospects better. Unfortunately, these companies did not pay attention. Over 40 years of complacency are now having the anticipated effect. Canada's low value-added strategy contrasts sharply with Sweden's pulp and paper industry which, when the kroner was devalued in 1982, used the increased profits to expand into higher-value production areas, unlike Canadian producers who did nothing to take advantage of a lowering of the Canadian dollar. The same situation pertains to Canada's chemical industry, where the country's trade deficit tripled between 1983 and 1986 as a result of our concentration on lower value-added products instead of the growing, more profitable, higher value-added specialty chemical markets.

Some companies are waking up to the current economic reality, but the prognosis is not promising: at least 50 percent of those employed in

BULLETIN BOARD

- **Growth limiting factors**: Canada's resource industries have pursued a low-value-added, cost-based strategy that will prove their undoing now that developing countries can grow or extract natural resources at lower cost and in higher volumes; many countries which used to be importers of natural resources are now or will be large exporters of resources; most of the other major industrialized countries have much superior technology in their resource industries and a lower cost of capital allowing them to acquire newer technology as needed; greater efficiency and resource material substitution.

the natural resource industries will likely lose their jobs, and now that the relative cost of capital is high and prices of commodities low, many companies cannot afford to borrow the large sums of money necessary to upgrade their technology.

Natural resources will play an ever-diminishing role in the Canadian economy, and only the downsized lean and technologically mean will survive. The one advantage Canada has is that, in the long term, there will be a shortage of natural resources as the developing countries continue to consume a larger share of the world's resources. With the world's population doubling every 40 years or so, there is only so much to go around.

Forestry

A Price Waterhouse survey of the world's 50 largest forestry companies ranks Canada's major forest companies as the industry's worst financial performers in 1991. The industry lost $1.38 billion in 1992, which was an improvement on the $2.5 billion lost in 1991. In 1993, expected losses should approach $750 million, before turning into the black in 1994. A lower dollar plus rising prices for lumber and panelwood offset the 1991 losses in 1992. A glut of production capacity around the world drove down prices in many pulp and paper markets.

Canada has lost much of its traditional competitive advantage now that power is no longer inexpensive and the low-cost wood supply has been depleted. Its competition comes largely from efficient operations in the southern U.S., South America, and Scandinavia. Canadian industry labour costs continue to be higher than in these competitor countries. Its debt-to-equity ratio is far above the industry 50 percent norm with $17.4 billion in debt and $18.5 billion in equity, with industry cash flows not sufficient to support these capital expenditures. Canadian taxes, fees, reduced annual cutting rights, and other restrictions have curtailed the industry's global competitiveness. Since every 1,000 cubic metres of timber generates 5.8 jobs across Canada, British Columbia's decision in 1992 to remove two million cubic metres of timber available for cutting will reduce job creation by 12,000 jobs over the long run.

As many European countries move toward eco-labeling of forest products, companies who engage in clear-cut logging or whose pulp is bleached with chlorine will likely be accused of contravening sustainable forestry practices. This has encouraged a forestry companies to redouble their public relations efforts by spending $2 million annually on demonstrating how they are taking "greener" approaches to forestry.

Canadian Forest Products Ltd. has become the first Canadian company to certify its pulp mills according to ISO standards and to allow independent inspectors to audit its sustainable forestry practices. Despite the noble efforts of these companies, lumber now faces a ban in Europe over sawyer beetle larvae found in two shipments of non-pine wood to Europe. Heat treating the wood to eliminate the problem would add two percent to 15 percent to Canadian exporters' costs for certain grades of lumber. The untreated wood market in Europe represents about $500 million per year with non-pine wood accounting for 40 percent. With the European market depressed at the moment, most shipments are headed to the U.S. or Asia. Many of these changes are inevitable since the British Columbia government introduced legislation requiring smaller clear cuts, better access roads to prevent slides into fish spawning beds, and stiff fines to back up its demands.

The newsprint sector lost $929 million in 1992—50 percent higher than its 1991 loss. With newsprint capacity the same as before the recession, but prices collapsing, a shakeout in this sector is inevitable. With the newsprint market depressed, Abitibi-Price Inc. has decided to broaden its product line into the specialty paper markets such as construction paper, file folders, index dividers, bag stock, and target paper. The company also hopes to enter the food packaging, automotive painting and specialty bag markets. Such diversification is essential for survival in this industry. In the long run, the trend towards a paperless, electronic world will undermine newsprint sales; in the short term, the phasing-out of tariffs on paper products and lumber as a result of the GATT will help the foresty industry export more.

In 1992, the forest industry contributed approximately $23 billion to Canada's foreign exchange earnings and accounted for close to one million jobs. Forestry generates more revenue than fishing, farming and mining combined. Unfortunately, since seedling replanting is below the sustainable cutting level, there will be an eventual decline in the industry as dramatized by the shift to engineered wood—wood composites which are lighter and stronger, but more expensive and can only be used indoors—now that 90 percent of the Douglas fir have been logged in the Pacific Northwest. Ironically, as modern technology makes each logging industry worker more productive, it also accelerates the exhaustion of forest resources. Moreover, low-cost, high-quality, plantation-grown fibres produced in the Pacific Rim and Latin America which have shorter replacement periods of seven to ten years versus Canada's 50 to 70 years pose an additional threat to the industry. With Indonesia emerging as one of the world's fastest-growing pulp and paper producers, Canadian companies, headed by the leading pulp mill engineering consultant, H. A. Simons of Vancouver, have managed to acquire $200 million of an estimated $800 million project in that country. With workers in Indonesia earning $2 a day and transportation costs lower than for the British Columbia interior or Alberta producers, Indonesia's hardwood plantations, which replenish themselves in seven years, are capable of producing pulp at a considerable profit for $400 (U.S.) a tonne, compared to $600 for B.C. producers and $500 for low-cost producers in the southern U.S. Job seekers interested in working in the forestry industry should consider obtaining jobs with companies working abroad, such as Sandwell of Vancouver, which has bid on a billion-dollar world-scale pulp mill proposed for Sumatra. With environmental experts, such as Hatfield Consultants of North Vancouver, handling over $1 million in environmental assessment related to the Simons' project, jobs with companies assessing environmental concerns at home and abroad are another avenue worth exploring.

Without a doubt, Canadian forestry companies are eyeing the forests of the CIS since it contains 25 percent of the world's wood reserves,

BULLETIN BOARD

- **Job demand factors**: lumber and paneling are currently needed.
- Job growth areas: environmental assessment; Far East, Latin America, and perhaps Russia eventually.
- **Job reduction areas**: almost everywhere, but particularly in the newsprint markets.
- **Growth limiting factors**: taxes; fees; cutting rights curtailments; labour costs; environmental concerns; outdated technology; transportation costs; replenishment rates; insupportable debt-equity ratios; interest rates.

CONTACTS

- Canadian Forestry Association
  #203, 185 Somerset St. West,
  Ottawa, ON K2P 0J2 Tel. 613-232-1815 Fax: 613-232-4210
- Canadian Institute of Forestry
  #1005, 151 Slater St.,
  Ottawa, ON K1P 5H3 Tel. 613-234-2242 Fax: 613-234-6181
- Canadian Pulp & Paper Association
  Sun Life Building,
  1155 Metcalfe St.,
  Montreal, PQ H3B 4T6 Tel. 514-866-6621 Fax: 514-866-3035
- Forest Engineering Research Institute of Canada
  143 Place Frontenac,
  Pointe Claire, PQ H9R 4Z7 Tel. 514-694-1140 Fax: 514-694-4351

almost double the Amazon's reserves. This will create many job opportunities for those wishing to work in the CIS.

Employment in the industry is being further undermined by automation. Today, one harvester operator can replace an entire crew of lumberjacks with chainsaws, and labour-saving technology continues to overtake lumber mills.

Mining

Canada's research and development in mining is 0.5 percent of gross domestic product compared to over two percent for Finland, Germany, France, Britain, Sweden, and the U.S. According to the Mining

Association of Canada, investment in the Canadian mining sector fell by 50 percent between 1981 and 1991. "If this decline in investment continues," says Louis Gignac, chairman of the national mining association, "over 150 mining communities with a total population of one million could lose their main source of employment and economic livelihood. About 100,000 direct mining jobs and 300,000 related jobs are at stake." Total industry employment fell four percent in 1992 to 338,000 for the third consecutive year of employment reductions. The 28 closures or temporary shutdowns of mines in 1992 were only offset by eight openings, resulting in the loss of 5,800 jobs.

Inco has a 25 percent market share in the world nickel market. Although the company forecasts consumption increases of two percent to three percent annually over the long run, it has been hurt by the recession and by the dramatic increase in shipments of secondary nickel from Russia, which includes scrap nickel and nickel smuggled out of the country. Inco decided on a nickel production cutback in 1993, yet also reported that its productivity improved by 20 percent in1992 because of better ore grades and better mining techniques. The combination of reducing output but increasing productivity, means layoffs. To cut back production, Inco shut down its Sudbury mines for five to ten weeks over the summer of 1993 and production at its high-cost Levack Mine was to be suspended.

Inco announced that its future lies outside Canada. Since the company's laterite ore reserves in Indonesia, New Caledonia, and Guatemala exceed its Canadian sulphide deposits, it will expand in these countries. Clearly, Inco understands that surviving in the global market means going after the big, high-grade ore deposits.

Alcan Aluminium Ltd. has not made a profit since 1990 because the CIS flooded the market with aluminum. In 1993, one million tonnes of CIS aluminum appeared on world markets. Currently, there is a worldwide five-week inventory supply of aluminum and excessive smelting overcapacity with no smelters shutting down so far. Prices are at the lowest level in history, once inflation is factored in. Alcan has improved its productivity by cutting its work force by 23 percent since 1985. The good news is that no new production will come on-stream between 1994 and 1996. Since 1991, the prices of aluminum, zinc, lead, tin, and nickel have all fallen below their cost of production.

BULLETIN BOARD

CONTACTS
- Canadian Institute of Mining, Metallurgy and Petroleum
  Xerox Tower,
  #1200, 3400 de Maisonneuve Blvd. West,
  Montreal, PQ H3Z 3B8 Tel. 514-939-2710 Fax: 514-939-2714
- Mining Association of Canada
  #1105, 350 Sparks St.,
  Ottawa, ON K1R 7S8 Tel. 613-233-9391 Fax: 613-233-8897

Chile's large, high-quality ore reserves, stable economy, and attempts to generate foreign investment have attracted 22 Canadian mining companies over the past few years. Inco, Falconbridge Limited, Rio Algom Ltd., Cominco Ltd., Lac Minerals Ltd., and Placer Dome Inc. have invested $2.3 billion in gold and copper projects in Chile. The country's tax and regulatory environments are friendlier to mining companies and the cost structure is such that, even were copper prices to drop 50 percent, the Chilean projects would still be profitable. Noranda Aluminum Inc. is planning to build an aluminum smelter and hydroelectric dam at a cost of $1.7 billion. Although Chile does not have any bauxite—aluminum's raw material—the country can provide inexpensive electricity, which represents the largest cost in producing aluminum.

The major mining companies are planning to move into Mexico, Venezuela, and Bolivia next, and eventually Brazil, Cuba, and Argentina if conditions are favourable. In the long run, these companies will develop mines in China. At the moment, costs are so low in China that it mines and produces finished tungsten used for drill bits and incandescent light bulbs at less than the cost of just mining it anywhere else in the world. Not surprisingly, then, between 1986 and 1991, Canada didn't attract a single new mining project with a capital cost in excess of $250 million, yet Latin America had five. The decision to compete in mining on the basis of cost as opposed to non-ferrous metal product development, as in Japan, will eventually eliminate much of the mining industry in Canada.

In the long run, robots will assume all dangerous functions and the traditional miner will disappear. Job seekers are not encouraged to pursue a career in mining unless they are involved in designing or engineering advanced methods of ore extraction or refining.

Fishing

The fishing industry as traditionally practised is dying. Government announcements indicate that cod stocks have fallen from 323,000 tonnes in 1986 to 22,000 tonnes. Unfortunately, the future of the northern cod depends on the number of young fish spawned in 1986 and 1987, few of which have survived. In 1993, the Newfoundland fisheries minister, Walter Carter, announced that the number of fish old enough to spawn is less than two percent of the 1.2 million tonnes needed to sustain traditional fish catches in Newfoundland. Despite the federal government's offer of $50,000 for anyone from Newfoundland willing to leave the full-time fishing profession—other Maritime cod fishers are not eligible—few have accepted the offer. Other offers include early retirement and retraining packages. The most optimistic projections for a restoration of cod fishing say a restoration is five or six years away, and there is a good chance that the cod will never return. Since sooner or later the entire fishing industry is likely to come to this pass, it does not make sense to look to this industry for a sustainable job future.

Canadians have always had to pay 100 percent more than the world competitive price for catching the same fish in the same location—for example, the Norweigian or Icelandic fishing fleets fishing off the Grand Banks—because of the inherent inefficiencies in traditional fishing methods. Modern methods which would have lowered the price of fish to consumers, such as using large trawlers, were curtailed or forbidden. In the future, we will see more fish and seafood farming. The world's oceans provided 88 million tonnes of fish for the third year in a row, but there is some doubt that they will ever again reach the record 1989 peak harvest of 90 million tonnes.

Aquaculture or fish farming will grow in significance. Although only a $48 million industry in 1987, it now represents $260 million of Canada's $1.6 billion fishing and shellfish harvest industry. Approximately 20 percent of all the world's fish and shellfish consumed is now produced in this way. According to the United Nations' food and agricultural organization, by the end of the decade over 40 percent of all international fish revenues will come from fish farming and approximately 25 percent of

BULLETIN BOARD

CONTACTS

- Aquaculture Association of Canada
  c/o Biological Station,
  Fisheries and Oceans Canada,
  St. Andrews, NB E0G 2X0 Tel. 506-529-4766 Fax: 506-529-4274
- Canadian Centre for Fisheries Innovation
  Ridge Rd.,
  PO Box 4920,
  St. John's NF A1C 5R3 Tel. 709-778-0517 Fax: 709-778-0516
- Fisheries Council of Canada
  #806, 141 Laurier Ave. West,
  Ottawa, ON K1P 5J3 Tel. 613-238-7751 Fax: 613-238-3542

all worldwide fish production by weight will be through aquaculture. Job seekers interested in this industry are encouraged to look to this area for a career future.

Agriculture

Farming as traditionally practised is slowly disappearing, though perhaps less conspicuously than the fishing industry. In the last century, agriculture accounted for 80 percent of all jobs in Canada, whereas it employs only three percent today. In total, there are 247,000 farms in Canada with 50 percent of each farmer's income, on average, coming from government subsidization. Such a distortion of the natural economy is bound to come to an end sooner or later.

Under the GATT, Canada will not be allowed to impose its usual quotas on the import of chicken, dairy products, turkeys, and eggs. Import bans and quotas are to be gradually replaced by tariffs of up to 351 percent ensuring that marketing boards will survive till 2010. NAFTA, however, requires an elimination of all tariffs on these products by 1998 with respect to trade with the U.S. and Mexico. Regardless of the GATT accord, the agreement with the U.S. allows for duty-free importation of processed food products into Canada as of 1998. Thus, some food production would move to the U.S. if Canadian farm product prices are not

245

competitive by then.

Canada's ability to compete in international markets is hampered by a number of factors. According to the Canada Grains Council, between 1985 and 1990, U.S. government policies cost Canadian wheat farmers $2.47 billion. The U.S. upped its export subsidies beyond the Canadian treasury's ability to keep pace in order to match the European Economic Community (EEC) subsidies and began to pay farmers for leaving their land idle. Ironically, just as the world demand for wheat dissipated, all nations with subsidized farmers increased their wheat production as prices kept falling in a vain effort to sustain income levels. Consequently, Europe, which used to import wheat, became a net exporter of wheat.

While the high interest rates and burdensome debt loads of Third World countries curtailed their ability to buy wheat in the 1980s, in the 1990s, the former Soviet Union, which was a major wheat customer, can no longer afford to import wheat now that the free market pricing of wheat in the CIS has rendered bread unaffordable to most members of the CIS. Should the CIS and Eastern European private sector economies develop, they will become major grain exporters even though nuclear testing has rendered 50 percent of the CIS's arable land infertile. Even in India and China, wheat production grew by 15 percent between 1987 and 1992. Although world wheat production is likely to grow by ten percent by the year 2000, Canada's output is expected to stay static. With grain growers now getting half of what they were in 1982 and their production costs—fuel, machinery, fertilizer—rising, something has got to give. Moreover, with input costs—labour, land, fertilizer, machinery— for growing wheat lower in the EEC and Argentina, the inevitable will occur

---

WHERE HAVE ALL THE FARMERS GONE?

Despite all efforts to sustain the current marketing board supply management approach—what is produced is not controlled by consumer demand and competitive pricing—the number of farmers continues to dwindle. In Ontario, in 1983, there were 11,135 dairy farmers; now, there are about 8,500. By the year 2000, there will likely be fewer than 6,300. In 1991, 25 percent of all farmers were over 60, compared with 19 percent in 1981, and the percentage of farmers under 35 fell to 16 percent in 1991 from 21 percent in 1981.

BULLETIN BOARD

- **Job demand factors**: organically grown produce.
- **Job growth areas**: specialty farming for local markets; agricultural research.
- **Job reduction areas**: all traditional farming areas.
- **Growth limiting factors**: increasing worldwide wheat production at a cheaper cost than possible in Canada; the GATT; the Free Trade Agreement (FTA); small farm inefficiency; marketing boards; interest rates.

CONTACTS
- Agricultural Institute of Canada
  #907, 151 Slater St.,
  Ottawa ON K1P 5H4 Tel. 613-232-9459 Fax: 613-594-5190
- Canadian Federation of Agriculture
  #1101, 75 Albert St.,
  Ottawa, ON K1P 5E7 Tel. 613-236-3633; -9997 Fax: 613-236-5749
- Canadian Organic Growers
  PO Box 6408, Stn. J,}
  Ottawa, Ont. K2A 3Y6
  Tel. 613-395-5392 Fax: 613-395-0367
- Canadian Society of Agricultural Engineering
  PO Box 306, Sub Post Office 6,
  Saskatoon, SK S7N 0W0 Tel. 306-966-5335 Fax: 306-966-5334

and wheat sales could decrease because Canadian wheat would be too expensive. The recent drop in the dollar, however, should benefit the wheat farmer in the short run. Another note of optimism for Canada's wheat production is that, although world grain production increased one percent in 1992, it has fallen eight percent since reaching a high in 1984. The Canadian Wheat Board is also pinning its hopes on the developing countries which increased their per capita wheat consumption by 60 percent from 1970 to 1990. The GATT will also allow Canadian wheat farmers to compete more effectively against European wheat and U.S. growers now that export subsidies are being reduced.

The Farm Credit Corporation is urging farmers to diversify out of agriculture and is willing to sponsor the process through loans. According to former agriculture minister William McKnight, "This will help encourage diversification, value-added processing, and the development of niche markets for farmers. The continued viability of family farm businesses, the agri-food sector, and rural communities depend on the ability of farmers to develop new markets." This approach has been most successful near large urban centres where organic farmers have grown to meet the demands of restaurants, chefs and high-quality local food processors. Organic markets have become viable alternatives in a more health and quality-conscious aging society.

The agriculture industry must develop new products if it hopes to survive. There are jobs in the research end of the industry for individuals wishing to work on developing new or better growing techniques or strains of seeds.

Federal and provincial ministers of agriculture are optimistic that Canada's annual food exports will increase by 50 percent to $20 billion by the year 2000. Food exports to the U.S. are expected to rise nine percent a year over the long term, having reached a record $5.9 billion in 1992. Exports to Japan have grown by three percent a year and shipments to Latin America have been increasing six percent annually. Total exports of food last year were a record $13.3 billion.

Governments are proposing to loosen interprovincial trade barriers, provide easier access to government services, sponsor aggressive promotional campaigns, and transform the farm subsidy program into a national whole-farm income protection policy which would protect farmers during downturns, yet not violate trade agreements.

Oil and Gas

Natural gas accounts for a larger share of energy consumption than oil. Its low cost, flexibility, and cleanliness have made it particularly appealing to the consumer. Although oil reached its structural peak in 1973, it is difficult to predict when gas will reach its peak, since the amount of gas available is yet to be determined and its many uses not fully exploited. Canada has a proven 20-year supply of gas reserves as opposed to the nine-year gas reserve supply in the U.S.

According to Ted Eck, chief economist at Amoco Canada Petroleum Company Ltd., the demand for natural gas-fed electrical power plants and cars will cause a 25 percent rise in U.S. gas consumption by the year 2000 with gas-fed co-generation plants responsible for four percent of gas usage as environmentally unfriendly coal-burning plants are converted to this process. U.S. legislation has committed its federal government to buy at least 50,000 gas-fed vehicles in the next five years. State and municipal governments are expected to help realize this mandate as well. In fact, by the year 2000, four percent of gas sales will likely be for such vehicles. The Big Three automakers have already begun mass- producing gas-powered vehicles. Natural gas prices are not expected to increase until 1995, so the industry will probably stay in its retrenchment phase until then.

Employment in the oil industry fell by 3,591 between 1983 and 1992. With oil prices expected to rise only slightly by the end of the 1990s, there will be some but not many jobs created in the industry in the short term. Given increasing demand in the U.S. and the developing countries, drilling, employment, and supply activity should remain stable throughout 1994 and may improve. Most growth will likely take place in the CIS whose oil reserves rival Saudi Arabia's. Eventually, Iraq and Kuwait will be back to pre-Gulf War production levels, if not higher.

Technology is dramatically improving the production aspects of the industry. In the areas of oil exploration and drilling methods, for example, it is now possible to put a three-dimensional model of the potential oil field on a computer screen and drill as many "theorctical" wells as desired. The oil industry in the U.S. has doubled the amount spent on gathering and processing data between 1987 and 1992 to $3.2 billion (U.S.). Since being out by as little as 65 feet can make the difference in striking enough oil to recover a company's costs or not, this new accurate imaging is proving invaluable. Innovative oil drilling methods such as horizontal drilling have recently led to the one millionth barrel of oil extracted by this technique in Saskatchewan.

Unfortunately, the ratio of knowledge workers in the oil and gas industry—engineers, geologists, scientists, and technicians—has fallen drastically since 1988 from 43 to 38. As more sophisticated technology becomes available, it is likely that fewer, but more specialized knowledge workers will be needed. Traditional oil- and gas-knowledge jobs should grow in the Middle East and the CIS, as these countries try to increase production.

Although there are five Canadian companies in the CIS which have exported oil worth $287 million, it is risky at present to look to this coun-

BULLETIN BOARD

- **Job demand factors**: world economy; environmental factors favouring natural gas; political developments increasing need for foreign currency; megaprojects; better technology reducing exploration and drilling costs.
- **Job growth areas**: experts in new geological software and newer drilling techniques; Russian republics eventually; specialty consulting areas such as tapping oil and gas in fractured rock formations.
- **Growth limiting factors**: political support for megaprojects such as Hibernia; Middle Eastern and Russian politics; world economy; alternative energy sources; cost of drilling and extraction; interest rates.

CONTACTS

- Canadian Association of Drilling Engineers
  #800, 540 - 5 Ave. SW,
  Calgary, AB T2P OM2 Tel. 403-264-4311 Fax: 403-263-3796
- Canadian Association of Petroleum Producers
  First Canadian Centre,
  #2100, 350 - 7 Ave. SW,
  Calgary, AB T2P 3N9 Tel. 403-267-1100 Fax: 403-261-4622
- Canadian Gas Association
  55 Scarsdale Rd.,
  Don Mills, ON M3B 2R3 Tel. 416-447-6465 Fax: 416-447-7067
- Canadian Society of Petroleum Geologists
  #505, 206 - 7 Ave. SW,
  Calgary, AB T2P 0W7 Tel. 403-264-5610 Fax: 403-264-5898

try for jobs, as CIS authorities have recently suspended oil exports from these joint ventures, owing to allegations of fraud regarding all foreign oil firms in the country. This market is unlikely to flourish until there is clearly defined ownership of the oil and natural gas resources by means of contract law, equity purchases by foreign companies allowed, free market pricing and free movement between the republics. Since the U.S. would to like to develop CIS oil supplies so as to reduce western dependence on the politically unstable Middle Eastern countries, expect many jobs to eventually emerge in Canadian or U.S. companies operating in Russia once a market economy becomes more entrenched in the republics.

Job Survival in the Old Economy

Job growth areas within old economy industries tends to be in the service or research aspect of the sector. Design, research, and engineering play a major role in any industry that makes use of new technology. The "smart" products, like computers, will usually involve the customer in the design of the product. The need to anticipate and solve the problems of customers—self-diagnostic elevators or the fully automatic, self-propelled lawn mower that uses three navigation systems and a computer to tell it where to cut, turn, slow down or stop—requires the building-in of the service or convenience component into the product itself. These higher value-added functions are invariably service functions, and it is in this realm that most of the old economy industries will be hiring. Mature industries are in need of innovative products or processes so as to distinguish themselves from their competitors' more common or commodity-like products, whose sale is based on price alone or whose process methods are less efficient. Any mature industry that hopes to expand, or survive, must move into the higher value-added end of the market, become more efficient, or diversify into other growth areas. Individuals looking for employment in the old economy are advised to apply to companies that are pursuing these strategies. Companies that are not doing so will most likely be out of business before the turn of the century.

CHAPTER SIX

HOW COMPETITIVE IS THE CANADIAN ECONOMY?

- **The Made-in-Canada Recession**
- **Canada's Social Adjustment Programs**
- **Immigration**
- **Education, Training, and Career Awareness**
- **Technology, Foreign Ownership, and Research and Development**
- **Management, Productivity, and Labour Relations**
- **Government Regulation**
- **Finance and Competitive Infrastructure**
- **Free Trade, NAFTA, and GATT**
- **What Does It Mean for You**
- **Canada's Strengths**

It would be a big mistake to believe that Canada's basic competitiveness problem would be solved if only the dollar were at 78 cents (U.S.) and interest rates were at U.S. levels. The fundamental issues relate to investment, productivity, R&D, adding value to resources and equipping our population with the skills that will be needed in the future.

CEDRIC RITCHIE, CHAIRMAN, BANK OF NOVA SCOTIA

When the most recent recession began, many of us assumed that though we might suffer some financial pain, after a few years we would experience the usual prosperous renewal. That's what had always happened before. The advent of the global economy, however, requires a Copernican revolution in economic thinking. Canada can no longer afford the illusion that the sun, moon, and stars revolve around the North American economy. So long as the United States was the uncontested economic leader of the world, Canadians felt confident that once the American economy picked up, everything would return to "normal," with promotions and jobs for all who sought them. Ironically, even the Americans are now forced to reevaluate their ability to control world economic events.

In a global economy, competitiveness will become the primary basis for all corporate decision making. Canada must regain its competitive edge; if we don't, we will not attract investors, and those who have already set up shop here will phase out their Canadian operations or reduce their scope significantly. It is more than industry's future that is at stake; it is the very standard of living most Canadians have come to take for granted. If we fail to retrieve that edge, the consequences will be serious: falling social benefits and escalating taxes, social and economic dislocation, rising crime rates, hopelessness and cynicism as the government seems ever more powerless to control the situation.

Given these possibilities, you may want to consider pursuing employment outside Canada temporarily or even permanently. You need to look at your country as if you were an investor: is this really the best place to put your energy and hopes and talent for the future? Of course, there are other issues as well—emotional attachments, family responsibilities, nationalism. But keep an open mind. Before you make your decision, you should weigh each of the competitive factors that shape the Canadian economy to see how they might affect the career areas you're pursuing. And you should use these same criteria to evaluate any other countries you think might offer career opportunities.

The globalization of trade will increase the mobility of labour to an extent never before contemplated. If you doubt this might apply to you, just imagine that you have been approached by a company that offers you a job in your chosen field paying $20,000 (U.S.) more than you are earning now, with full benefits and better opportunities for professional

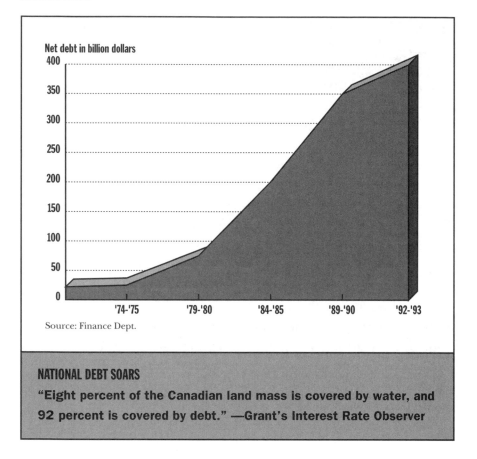

Net debt in billion dollars

NATIONAL DEBT SOARS

"Eight percent of the Canadian land mass is covered by water, and 92 percent is covered by debt." —Grant's Interest Rate Observer

growth, in Sundance, Utah, which has an extremely low crime rate, wonderful recreational and cultural facilities, and beautiful weather....

Chapter 7 will briefly outline career opportunities in other countries that may surpass those in Canada in the foreseeable future. In the meantime, brace yourself for a sobering view of where Canada now stands competitively.

The Made-in-Canada Recession

The overwhelming factor in the recent recession has been debt—personal, business, and government debt. Between 1989 and 1992, the economy grew by six percent; business debt by ten percent; household debt by 21 percent; federal government debt by 26 percent; and provincial government debt by 35 percent. Canadian households are emerging from the current recession with more debt than when they entered it. Since spending by consumers accounts for about 60 percent of Canada's economic output, that helps to explain the sluggishness of the recovery.

During the 1981-82 recession, households dramatically increased their savings in order to pay off their debts. Once those debts were reduced, consumers began to spend again, thus fuelling the recovery. But in our current situation, despite lower interest rates and the reduced cost of processing loans, debt levels for households are still high. And since consumers also have fewer savings to pay off that debt, it's not likely that it will fall any lower. More people now own homes and they tend to be paying higher mortgages than in the past. With government taxes increasing, there's little chance people will have more money to pay off their debts, let alone make new purchases.

Corporations, on the other hand, have been aggressively improving their debt situation recently by issuing new shares and converting short-term debt into long-term obligations. While this is good news, in that these corporations will eventually crawl out of debt, it also means that they're not putting as much money into expansion, hiring new employees, and other measures that would spur economic growth.

Meanwhile, the Canadian government is also heavily in debt. The money it has borrowed from both Canadians and others outside the country by selling them bonds and treasury bills as investments currently amounts to 92 percent of our gross domestic product, the value of all the goods and services the country produces. That high percentage—the U.S. debt is only 51 percent, for example—makes Canada the second largest debtor nation of the major industrialized countries, next to Italy.

The problem is not restricted to the federal government. Among the world's states, four Canadian provinces are the top four borrowers in the world, and if cities and regions are included as well, 11 of the top 22 borrowers in the world are Canadian! Indeed, Ontario by itself ranks fourth in the world among the largest borrowers, coming behind the European Investment Bank, the Kingdom of Sweden and the World Bank.

What makes our federal debt even more alarming is the percentage of it that's owed to foreign investors: over $300 billion or more than 45 percent of gross domestic product, compared to 5.3 percent of gross domestic product for Italy and 2.4 percent of gross domestic product for the U.S. At least if all of our debt was owed to fellow Canadians, we could comfort ourselves that that money would eventually flow back into the Canadian economy.

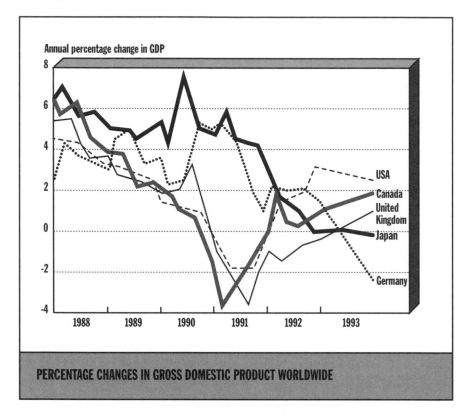

Annual percentage change in GDP

USA
Canada
United Kingdom
Japan
Germany

PERCENTAGE CHANGES IN GROSS DOMESTIC PRODUCT WORLDWIDE

As it is, our dependency on foreign lenders makes Canada extremely vulnerable. If our dollar drops for any reason, that makes our bonds less valuable. Foreign creditors would tend to dump their Canadian government bonds—which would cause even more worries about our economy and a further drop in the dollar—unless the government responds by driving up the interest rates on the bonds so that it won't lose money as the value of the dollar decreases. Higher interest rates would then put a damper on our economic growth, which in turn could affect the dollar, and round we go again.

Since 1986, Canadian borrowers have had to pay 20 percent higher interest rates than in the U.S.—a difference that puts us at a distinct disadvantage in our most important market. (The U.S. accounts for 70 percent of our export market or 20 percent of our gross domestic product.) If Americans are paying five percent to borrow money, Canadians are probably paying six percent. This discrepancy also happened during the 1975-77 period, when Canada's inflationary growth exceeded the rate in the U.S. by one-third. But this time, the premium paid by Canadian borrowers reflected not inflation, but Canada's growing national debt and increasing indebtedness to foreigners, as well as political instability surrounding Quebec.

Our troublesome debt is not only large, it's growing. The national deficit in 1992 was almost double the 1991 figure, indicating that the debt growth level was heading out of control. In 1989, the total deficit was three percent of gross domestic product, but in 1992, it soared to 6.4 percent of gross domestic product in the first three quarters alone. Were the debt level to continue to grow at this rate, Canada would be bankrupt by 1998. Fortunately, the growth of our debt will slow as the economy picks up; however, even if the economy grows by four percent a year with

---

SPENDING vs INVESTING

As frightening as our debt, deficit, and the resulting economic problems may be, we need to be careful not to focus too narrowly on simple goals. Our problem is not just the amount of money that's being spent, but *where* it's being spent. According to economist Robert Reich:

■ Over the long term, a large deficit may retard growth, but it's not the biggest drag on it. That distinction goes to failure to invest adequately in training, education, roads, bridges, water systems, and other foundation stones of a modern economy.

■ There's a key distinction between spending and investing in both the private and public spheres. Mere spending does not increase future productivity; investing does.

■ When the government finances criminal justice, national defence, jobless insurance, welfare, mental health services or farm price supports, for example, it maintains the safety and economic security of citizens here and now.

■ When it funds education, worker training, and building roads and bridges, it enhances the ability of our citizens to be productive in the future. The distinction bears directly on the deficit. Borrowing from future generations in order to invest in their capacity to be more productive is surely more justifiable than borrowing from them in order to make today's citizens safe and happy.

■ The former generates economic growth, which enables future generations to pay off the loan and enjoy its fruits. The latter simply burdens them, without growth.

---

two percent annual inflation over the next six years, we'll still be paying $22 billion per year to foreign investors. Part of the problem is that at the same time that the government has to face reduced revenues, it is also having to pay high interest rates on old bonds that investors bought when interest rates were much higher.

They were higher not just because of worldwide economic factors but because of a deliberate policy of the Bank of Canada. With its "zero inflation policy," the Bank tried to slow inflation to a virtual standstill by imposing high interest rates. While the Bank did manage to slow inflation, the policy also raised interest rates to very high levels which raised bond rates, inflated the value of the dollar well beyond its real worth, chased many businesses out of the country, and bankrupted countless numbers of remaining companies and individuals in the process. This zero inflation policy produced the aptly termed "made-in-Canada" recession and robbed Canada of ten percent of its economic output or $70 billion a year. Although low inflation and low interest rates were achieved, it's possible that Canada will never recover from the damage inflicted on the economy. By keeping interest rates unnecessarily high, the zero inflation policy increased the national debt, put Canadian industries and companies at a competitive disadvantage, effectively slowing the economy to a crawl and thereby reducing tax revenues. This was happening at the same time as our economy faced the major adjustments of a free trade agreement.

So how can we reduce this debt? Where is the fat in our spending that we can cut? The short answer is that there isn't any. Indeed, over one-third of Ottawa's revenue is devoted to paying off the debt itself, making this the biggest spending program of all. While the cost of government bureaucracy can be decreased, it accounts for only 13 percent of federal spending. The only areas for major savings are in our social programs, education, medicare or old age pension programs. Yet the political unpopularity of cutting these has sent us even further into debt. Not only does this situation place a horrible burden on future generations, we are seriously undermining our ability to pay in the long run for the very services and benefits that we are trying to protect.

How does this affect Canada's competitiveness? It's difficult for investors to have faith in our economy when we're so heavily in debt. That makes the value of our dollar unstable. Investors will still be interested in buying our bonds and treasury bills if we offer them higher interest rates. But higher interests will inhibit economic growth; we need low interest rates to encourage business and consumer spending, which in turn will lead to higher government tax revenues as income and spending increases. Moreover, as the value of our dollar drops, it becomes more expensive to buy goods and services from other countries—such as the imported technologies we need to enhance our competitiveness.

The one benefit of a drop in the dollar's value is that our goods will become cheaper for others to buy and so we'll sell more exports. However, exports only account for 30 percent of Canada's gross domestic product. And because interest rates are higher, all of us—governments, companies, and individuals—will have to pay more interest on existing debt. That puts Canadian companies at a competitive disadvantage as they try to pay off their old large debts and at the same time purchase expensive new technology. All of these factors could force us to go even further into debt.

Unless our export growth is strong enough to stabilize the dollar's value so we can keep interest rates at a reasonable level, we're in danger of entering a vicious economic circle as the debt level completely spins out of control. Many economists predict that export growth will pull us out of our economic mess as world economies slowly stagger to their feet once again. Other economists are less confident that governments can cut back on their health care, welfare, and other social programs, which are dragging us further into debt.

The government's 1994 budget fell on the confident side, avoiding major cutbacks on expenditures, raising taxes slightly in the name of "fair taxation," and trusting that the recovery would obviate the need for drastic government action. The immediate result was a significant drop in the value of the Canadian dollar, a sign that foreign markets were beginning to lose faith in our ability to manage our debts. If interest rates rise because the U.S. economy heats up or the Germans increase their rates or our economy falters for any reason, we will pay a steep price.

However, the various levels of government are making an effort. Nine provincial governments froze their health care expenditures in 1992 for the first time since 1965-66. Public service wages and welfare and unemployment insurance distribution payments are about to undergo review by all levels of government. So far, however, these cuts have not matched attempts by other countries in similar situations: Sweden plans to halve its government deficit which is running at eight percent of gross domestic product, while Italy hopes to cut its 11 percent deficit to five percent of gross domestic product over two years. For Canada to match Italy's reduction in its deficit, we would have to eliminate all of our yearly budget deficits in just two years; that is, Ottawa would have to reduce its expenditures by over 50 percent. The short-term political cost of such a measure makes this option unlikely, yet we are under greater pressure to do this, because no other industrialized country is so burdened by foreign debt. In other words, the people and institutions outside the country who loan us the money we need to function—foreign bond and treasury bill investors—will demand it.

The situation is serious. Otherwise, we would not see New Democratic Party governments engaging in what looks like political suicide by rolling back the wages of public service workers, whose unions are traditional backers of the party. In short, expect a prolonged period of government austerity, regardless of which political party is in power.

The cost of our debt also has long-range implications for Canada's business competitiveness in a global market. As mentioned in Chapter 3, investing in research and development to develop new products will be crucial to the country's success. But research and development is expensive and it is often a long time before there is any financial payoff. If interest rates are high, research and development will be even more expensive. Part of the reason the Japanese were able to gain their great competitive advantage was that Japanese banks cooperated with Japanese companies to keep interest rates on commercial loans artificially low. Since borrowing money for research and development was relatively cheap, it was possible to engage in research for a product that might not reach the market for thirty years. In Canada, unless a product can be developed within two years, it is unlikely that a company can afford the research and development necessary to complete the process.

Meanwhile, because of our economic and competitive difficulties, the investment that could help us is dropping. Business investment is not expected to keep pace with inflation in the next few years. Private investment has fallen in the space of a generation from 12 percent of gross domestic product to three percent and is dropping further. Industries that need major investment, such as the resource-based and mature man-

BULLETIN BOARD

- Canada's national debt is the second worst among all the major industrialized countries.
- Canada's foreign debt is by far the worst of all industrialized countries and poses a significant threat to Canadian sovereignty.
- Governments that increase deficit spending in order to maintain the standard of living as opposed to investing in the future are likely headed toward bankruptcy or Third World economic status; recent Canadian governments have tended to choose the latter route.
- Regardless of which political party is in power, government austerity will be unavoidable for some time to come; all government services will be affected.
- The high cost of borrowing money is affecting research and development investment and impairing Canada's ability to compete in the future and pay off its debt.
- Canadian exports should do well, but the domestic economy will be increasingly subject to the effects of consumer and government austerity.

ufacturing companies, are finding it difficult to pay for the modern technology they need.

One way to pay down the debt would be to raise taxes. But individuals and companies simply can't afford to pay higher taxes. The net result would be more companies and individuals leaving Canada or going bankrupt, and increased growth in the underground economy, which already is worth over $100 billion or 15 percent of gross domestic product, according to McGill economist Reuven Brenner. Statistics Canada reports that the government lost $4.8 billion in GST collection in 1991 and 1992 as a result of tax evasion. In the Ontario home renovation market, 48 percent of renovations are nonrecorded cash payments costing governments $2,820 on every $10,000 spent on renovations, housing economist Frank Clayton states. An even more dramatic example of a country in which higher taxation doesn't work is Sweden, which once had a 90 percent tax rate and has since moved it back to 50 percent, largely because of the destructive and evasive practices that evolved.

Another popular remedy for our sluggish economy is to spend our way out by initiating infrastructure rebuilding programs. We do need to upgrade our infrastructure, and if it weren't for our high debt levels, this would be a reasonable and perhaps appealing alternative. But once a deficit is high, boosting spending would only be throwing more money at a problem that calls for major rethinking of how our government, society, and businesses operate. According to the OECD, as much as 75 percent of North America's budget deficit and two-thirds of Europe's is structural and will continue even when their economies are going full steam. Even if we achieve some temporary relief from our current crises, we will still have the problems of large public spending for health care and pensions for an aging population, combined with a constantly increasing debt. In the long run, increasing our spending will only add to these problems.

Ultimately, our very sovereignty is at stake. If the debt spiral continues, Canada could be forced to go to the International Monetary Fund (IMF) with cap in hand as it did in 1962 and 1968 after a run on the dollar. The IMF could impose a drastic austerity plan similar to those imposed on Third World countries and, more recently, Britain.

So unless major changes take place, Canada could become a "failed nation." With foreigners controlling so much of our debt, which is already beyond what we can afford, we are extremely vulnerable to developments outside Canada. As the international economy improves, overseas investors may prefer to spend their money elsewhere. Others may decide that other countries offer better investment opportunities. Already, many Canadian investors are investing in foreign mutual funds that pay attractive rates of return and that have more promising long-term potential. At the moment, we need to generate $30 billion in trade surpluses per year just to service our accumulated foreign debt and offset the money we spend outside the country in tourism and travel. An even larger surplus is needed should we ever wish to pay down our debt.

Quebec separation, if it happens, could create one more downward push. On the whole, overseas investors have seemed puzzled by our constitutional wranglings. But actual separation could transform those emotions to stronger reactions. It's estimated that uncertainty about Canada's future unity already costs Canadians $4 billion in extra interest payments each year. Research by the Royal Bank shows that the breakup of Canada or even the threat of breakup might cause a significant fall in real estate values and other assets, a postponement of investment, a departure of capital, and the migration of more Canadians to the U.S. During the referendum campaign of October 1992, Canadians switched $2 billion from Canadian dollar bank accounts to U.S. dollar bank accounts to shelter themselves against the weakening currency.

It is worth remembering that in the early part of this century, Argentina was one of the world's richest countries, until an enormous debt threw it into political and economic chaos, from which it has not yet recovered. Indeed, it takes decades to solve a debt problem. Without a national consensus on how Canada should address the need to meet its financial obligations, the country may plunge into similar chaos.

Canada's Social Adjustment Programs

The figures are daunting: as of 1993, more than 2.3 million people were living on welfare in Canada. Ontario alone had over 500,000 unemployed and more than one million people receiving welfare. The cost of supporting the unemployed through unemployment insurance and welfare benefits reached a record high of $19.3 billion in 1992, up 9.1 percent from 1991.

There is substantial evidence that although the jobless rate may

---

THE SWEDISH EXPERIENCE

Steven Murray, author of *Losing Ground,* challenges the wisdom of welfare policies, which he believes encourage the poor to give up responsibility and assume a life of dependency, robbing them of self-esteem and the will to make positive changes. Sweden serves as a textbook example of the result of such policies. According to the *Economist,* "To pay for its [Sweden's] welfare state, taxes are the heaviest in the world. High taxes and benefits killed the incentive to work. Growth suffered. Once one of the richest countries, today its per capita income is below the OECD average." Sweden has also had the highest absenteeism (12 percent before recent welfare cutbacks) and unemployment growth problem among the industrialized nations. Many companies had to overstaff by 25 percent to ensure that enough people would show up for work. Every aspect of the Swedish welfare system is up for review and will be dramatically overhauled.

BULLETIN BOARD

- In recent years, the number of those on social assistance has risen regardless of the official level of unemployment.
- Unless Canada's social adjustment policies become part of a viable industrial strategy, many companies will leave Canada.
- Preserving regional jobs and lifestyles through tax incentives, grants, and concessions has increased the debt burden significantly without increasing competitiveness or saving jobs over the long term.

---

decline, the numbers on the welfare rolls do not. Research by Patricia Evans of York University's School of Social Work indicated that when unemployment decreased from 12 percent in 1981 to 7.5 percent in 1983, the number of people on welfare increased from 735,000 to 985,000. After six years of economic expansion and unemployment still at the 7.5 percent level, the number on social assistance rose to over one million. By 1991, the caseload number reached 1.2 million. Statistics Canada found that spending on all social programs in Ontario doubled in 1992-93 to $13 billion from the amount spent in 1988-89. Although Ontario held welfare rate increases to one percent in 1993, social expenditures will jump by 18 percent by 1995-96. The reasons for these increases include more family breakdowns, a majority of unmarried mothers keeping their children (as opposed to five percent in the 1970s), more disabled people living outside institutions, former unemployment insurance recipients joining the ranks of welfare recipients once premiums are exhausted, and an increasing number of immigrants on assistance rolls.

Clearly, present policies regarding welfare will be untenable in the long run. Experts expect that in 1995, Ottawa will eliminate the Canada Assistance Plan, which pays 50 percent of welfare costs in most provinces. Unless people on unemployment insurance and welfare have access to quality training that can actually get them jobs, and their payments are tied to marks, punctuality, and attendance in these training courses, Canada will be well on its way to becoming a Third World country. Indeed, few companies will want to stay in any country that progressively increases its taxes to cover social policies that are not designed to reduce the number of social assistance recipients. Perhaps another way of looking at the problem will put the matter in perspective: each unemployed worker would have produced $37,000 of gross domestic product if that worker had a job; a million extra workers would have added $37 billion to Canada's economy in 1992.

Unlike Canada, other countries offer labour adjustment programs that emphasize appropriate training or getting back to work rather than simply maintaining the unemployed person's income. Workers in Japan are given a substantial "re-employment bonus" if they find a new job promptly. In Germany, workers receive a ten percent unemployment insurance premium for enroling in training courses. Sweden devotes 69 percent of its unemployment insurance funds to training compared with Canada's ten percent. Both Germany and Denmark spend roughly three times as much as Canada (as a percentage of gross domestic product) on programs that actively help workers get back to work. Business, unions, government, and educational institutions have worked together to create these programs.

In Canada, however, unions and businesses are often in an adversarial relationship, with both sectors at odds with provincial and federal government educational, training, and unemployment policies. In view of the enormous cost to Canada's workers, business, and society of high rates of illiteracy, dropout, and unemployment, it would seem reasonable to spend more funds and energy on trying to integrate the various stakeholders and institutions involved. The alternative is to see these costs directly and indirectly increase as Canada loses its few remaining advantages and opportunities. According to the 1988 Canadian Task Force on Literacy, the direct cost of illiteracy to business is $4 billion per year and to society, $10 billion. Since illiterate people will comprise the largest portion of the social assistance population, it makes more sense to teach them skills that will make them employable rather than create an unemployment lifestyle.

The unwise use of public funds extends to the corporate world as well, where governments are prone to bailing out failing industries in the interest of preserving regional jobs and maintaining ever-precarious harmony among the provinces. Usually, these industries are on the way out regardless of any short-term assistance, so the money is essentially wasted and market forces distorted as companies resort to investment decisions based on tax incentives and grants rather than solid business strategy. For example, Curragh Inc. received $100 million in federal and provincial backing for its Westray mines in Nova Scotia, which closed amid accusations of unsafe practices after a cavein in 1992. According to Moncton University professor Donald Savoie, Ottawa gives out $20-25 billion each year to the private sector via guaranteed loans, grants, and tax concessions, up from $18 billion in 1984. Had these provisions been directed toward making Canada more competitive and saving jobs over the long term, there would be some justification for such generosity. Unfortunately, the result is an extra $16 billion added to the deficit every year. Attempts to protect the family farm have proven equally costly. Canadians pay $3.5 billion in higher-than-necessary food prices and an additional $7.5 billion in the form of direct government assistance, since farmers now receive roughly half their income from government support. The fishing industry also represents a lifestyle subsidized with little effect on the overall competitiveness of the industry as fish populations dwindle drastically.

Immigration

Ideally, immigration enables a country to import workers with skills that are in short supply so it can optimize its economic competitiveness. Although every country accepts refugees and immediate family members on compassionate grounds, from an economic point of view a country's primary focus should be on attracting the best and the brightest in areas of labour shortage. The importance of doing so increases dramatically each year as the information technology-based economy takes hold. With approximately 800,000 high-skilled positions that cannot be filled because of a shortage of qualified applicants, we need to import the necessary talent.

How does Canada rate in using its immigration policies to maximize its global competitiveness? According to the 1986 Census, immigrants were three times as likely to be functionally illiterate as native-born Canadians. Compare that figure to 1971, when immigrants were three times as likely to have a higher level of education than the average Canadian. What happened? At the moment, fewer than 15 percent of our immigrants are selected on the basis of their ability to contribute productively; in 1971, productive immigrants comprised 32 percent of those accepted. Business immigrants, including investors and entrepreneurs, make up only 7,000 of the 250,000 immigrants accepted annually.

The change came in 1978, when the Immigration Act was revised and job availability rather than formal education became the basis for acceptance. This quickly turned into a growing emphasis on family-class immigration, as family members "promised" jobs to their relatives. According to Don DeVoretz, an expert on immigration economics at Simon Fraser University, "These less-trained immigrants are falling further behind similarly trained Canadians with each year of residence." The disappearance of unskilled and low-skilled jobs is only making this situation worse. David Foot, an economist and demographer at the University of Toronto, asserts that accepting 250,000 immigrants annually in the midst of a recession is "insane." Communication skills are becoming an essential part of the information technology era, yet less than 50 percent of the immigrants speak English or French and it will take them up to ten years to become fluent in these languages.

To their credit, Canadians feel they want to do their share in resettling the dispossessed of the world. But according to the United Nations High Commissioner for Refugees, only 42,290 refugees needed resettlement in 1992. In 1992, Canada accepted 58,000 refugees. Informal Consultants, a Geneva-based secretariat supported by 16 industrialized nations, found that only 14 percent of those applying to these countries as refugees actually qualified as such. Canada accepted 89 percent of all refugee claimants in 1989, but now accepts 50 percent, which is by far the highest rate in the world, especially when compared with the acceptance rate for Australia (seven percent), Finland (less than one percent), Denmark (ten percent), and Sweden (five percent). According to *Toronto Star* feature columnist Daniel Stoffman, "The appeal of Canada's refugee system is so strong that it pulls people who otherwise would have stayed at home."

There are those who believe that there is a direct relationship between economic growth and size of population. Canadian economist Pierre Fortin, in a study for the *Demographic Review,* found that amongst the 22-member OECD countries there was no correlation between population size and economic growth. Indeed, if there were true correlation, both China and India would be world economic leaders; Hong Kong, with its six million inhabitants, outperforms India with its 850 million population. Were immigration to remain at 250,000 per year, unemployment in Canada would rise progressively for the rest of the decade, since even the most optimistic annual job creation forecast couldn't absorb the number of immigrants plus those entering the work force for the first time. Instead, we would see our standard of living decline further. The immigrants we really could use are those who could fill the 800,000 high-skill jobs that are going begging. If they took up residence in Canada, companies that might otherwise leave the country or cut back on expansion would benefit, as would the Canadian economy as a whole.

Until recently, it cost $50,000 per claimant, including legal aid and welfare, before a refugee claim was heard; refugee claimant determination cost Canada an estimated $1 billion per year. Fortunately, refugee claimants are now allowed to work—though it's questionable how many will be able to find jobs. Of those whose claim is rejected, 48 percent go into hiding and continue to collect welfare rather than leave the country as required.

Immigration could be contributing to Canadian competitiveness if we put more emphasis on importing workers with the skills industry needs. Moreover, immigrants with languages and knowledge of other cultures could be a major help in our attempts to do business with the rest of the world. Instead, through immigration we have increased Canada's population without increasing its productivity.

Education, Training, and Career Awareness

Education will likely become the deciding factor in the global competition among nations. And so the educational status of Canada's work force will play a considerable role in defining Canada's future.

As evidenced by those 800,000 vacant jobs, Canada is currently suffering from a mismatch of jobs and skills. Most people laid off from the goods-producing sectors, such as manufacturing, have intermediate-level skills that will be of little use in the service sector, which is where they will most likely end up. Given that most of the people who comprise the work force at the moment will also be working 15 years from now, there is an urgent need to retrain workers for those areas experiencing labour shortages.

The majority of Canadian workers are not recalcitrant lemmings, rejecting training to rush blindly into a jobless future. Rather, it's difficult for them to find training that they believe will actually lead to employment. Often, poorly designed training policy actually keeps workers from getting what they need.

For example, most employers are reluctant to hire students who don't have any prior experience; at the moment, it is extremely difficult even for university and college graduates in the software areas to find jobs, unless their program included a co-op component. Yet while the Unemployment Insurance Commission will often pay for in-class training, it will not sponsor anyone in programs that involve on-the-job experience. Even in-class training is not assured; in one case where 3,500 uranium workers were permanently laid off between 1990 and 1992, many of the unemployment insurance claimants were prevented from upgrading their basic skills because they had to remain at home and be "job-ready." Another case cited by a Canadian Labor Force Development Board report concerned older laid-off workers who had to wait until their severance pay ran out (as long as 18 months) before they were allowed to sign up for community college while on unemployment insurance. Unfortunately, since the severance pay was gone at this point and the unemployment insurance payments were insufficient to cover course costs, most were forced to drop out. Clearly, Canada's labour adjustment policies have failed to meet the educational and training needs of those displaced by the inevitable economic restructuring that is now well underway.

Even the young people who are currently making their way through the education system are not educating or training themselves in areas where the greatest labour shortages will likely arise. For example, although university enrolment rose 12 percent between 1986 and 1990, those studying history increased by 59 percent, and sociology by 31 percent, whereas enrolment in chemistry dropped by 7.7 percent and enrolment in computer sciences courses fell by 35 percent. The percentage of high school students taking technology courses dropped from 82 percent in 1980 to 57 percent in 1986. The same decline is occurring in high school math, physics, and chemistry courses, particularly among female students. College dropout rates in applied arts, business, and technology are roughly twice that of other areas. Percentage enrolment choices of students in university math, science, and engineering programs fell from 31 percent in 1983 to 24 percent in 1988, with women conspicuously absenting themselves from these areas, despite the fact that women made up most of the 30 percent increase in university and college enrolments between 1980 and 1988 and earned over 50 percent of the bachelor's degrees in the past ten years. Even the industrial apprenticeship group constitutes only 19.6 percent of total apprenticeships, with women once again noticeably absent. Women comprise only three percent to four percent of apprenticeship programs, most of them in hairstyling and cooking.

Our failure to encourage women to choose careers in the science, technology, or computer fields poses a serious labour shortage problem, since one of the few factors offsetting the coming decline in entry-level workers is the increase in female labour participation rates. Women's participation in the work force increased from 35 percent in 1951 to 55 percent in 1985, with 72 percent of the increase attributable to women between 25 and 34 years of age. According to the government publication "Apprenticeship: A New View of the Future," among 13-year-old girls who expressed an interest in going to university, 63 percent became hairdressers, airline stewardesses, secretaries, or store clerks. As a result of these choices, many women will likely be ghettoized in low-income jobs and will experience frequent and long periods of unemployment. Although 66 percent of all women do not plan to return to the work force after their first child, the hollowing-out of the middle class in our society will likely make the two-income family an unavoidable necessity. The picture is even darker for women with low-tech skills who head single-parent families, especially if government support services are cut back.

High-skill jobs, however, do not necessarily mean only college and university training. The U.S. and Canada graduate a far larger percentage of college- and university-trained workers than any other industrialized countries, yet both are outperformed economically by countries with superior secondary educational systems, notably Germany and Japan. According to Lester Thurow, "Japanese high school students come near the top in any international assessment of achievement, and its [Japan's] ability to educate the bottom half of the high school class is unmatched anywhere in the world." This is illustrated in the fact that the math abilities of the top ten percent of graduating U.S. high school students are only as good as the bottom ten percent of their Japanese counterparts.

Canada's educational disadvantage is exacerbated by a 33 percent dropout rate compared to Germany's less than five percent and Japan's two percent.

Canadians comfort themselves that at least their education system is superior to that in the U.S. But Canada's 11th place showing in the 1993 *World Competitiveness Report*—an international survey of CEOs conducted by the World Economic Forum in Geneva—compared to the U.S. 15th place is misleading. First, while Canada was ahead of the U.S. in some categories, in company training Canada ranked 22nd compared to the U.S. at 16th. Second, educational quality is not consistent throughout each nation. For example, you may get a better education in Ontario than in much of the U.S. But in 1991, only 75 percent of Ontario's high school students graduated compared with 90 percent in Massachusetts, 88 percent in Michigan, and 86 percent in California. While 17 percent graduated from university in Ontario, 28 percent graduated in California, and 21 percent in both Michigan and Massachusetts. Although many Canadian companies might find education levels too low in Georgia, Tennessee, or Kentucky to relocate to these areas, it is clear that California, Michigan, and Massachusetts have a more educationally competitive work force than Ontario does.

Canada's apprenticeship program also needs work to make it more comprehensive and more accessible. Canada's apprenticeship program is grossly inadequate and its training policies piecemeal. Compare it to Germany's. Germany has five times as many apprentices as the Canadian average, with 16 as the average age for a German apprentice versus 26 for a Canadian apprentice. Their programs use more up-to-date equipment and texts than ours and last three years, while ours have lower standards and are up to five years in length. Whereas their dropout rate is negligible, ours is roughly 50 percent, just as it is with our colleges and universities.

Because it was relatively easy to attract sufficient numbers of European tradespeople to satisfy Canada's industrial needs following World War II, there has been no direct industrial pressure to develop an effective training culture, resulting in curriculum and content that is largely out of date. As it now stands, the apprenticeship system is in many ways divorced from industry and the education system. There is no visible connection between apprenticeship programs and college technology programs, whereas one should ideally be an extension of the other; nor are colleges themselves meaningfully connected with university or other forms of private training. It is not surprising, therefore, that a Canadian Federation of Independent Business survey found that 68 percent of businesses were dissatisfied with apprenticeship programs, 52 percent with community colleges, and 36 percent with private training institutions. Although many changes have been proposed to rectify this situation at both the college level and apprenticeship level, it is likely a matter of too little too late, as far as improving Canada's competitiveness before the end of the decade.

Business itself has little to boast of in this field. For the 83 percent of the Canadian work force that leaves school largely untrained, on-the-job training would help improve their lot considerably. Unfortunately, in 1991, Canadian business only invested 0.25 percent of gross domestic product in training. This amounts to less than $100 per worker, unlike the U.S., which invested over twice as much; Australia, which invested three times as much; Japan, which invested five times as much; and Germany, which invested eight times as much. Indeed, only 31 percent of all Canadian companies (mainly large companies) offer training and even those companies only provide three days of training on average per employee, per year, with most of this training devoted to managers and other professionals and not to frontline workers.

One of the reasons private industry does not invest in its workers by training them is their fear that if they invest in employee training, other companies that don't offer it will use the money they save to offer these already trained employees higher wages. In the 1990 Ontario government report entitled "People and Skills in the New Global Economy," 58 percent of high technology companies in Ontario reported having problems of this sort. Other countries have avoided this phenomenon through legislation that makes companies either provide training or contribute to a training fund. Since 1985, all Japanese companies with profits over a certain level are obliged to put ten percent into a training and research and development fund; the United Kingdom employs a grant-levy system; and Sweden's government-sponsored training programs serve the same purpose with the extra advantage of allowing small companies that cannot afford training costs to benefit as well. This is of particular importance since virtually all new job creation springs from small businesses; indeed, 50 percent of all jobs created in Canada between

BULLETIN BOARD

- People in the work force today will still comprise the majority of workers 15 years from now; the knowledge and skills of these workers will largely determine Canada's economic fate for the foreseeable future.
- Because its education system fails to prepare students for the working world, Canada continues to pay an ever-increasing economic price through unemployable dropouts, individuals making poor career choices, and graduates without appropriate experience or training.
- Since high-paying industries will only locate in countries where there are sufficient numbers of highly trained personnel, Canada must meet those requirements or see its high-paying industries leave the country along with knowledge workers who will go where the best career opportunities lie.
- Unless there is a massive retraining effort made by business and government, Canadians will see their standard of living drop substantially, especially since Canada is in last place among industrialized nations in terms of worker training.
- Women who do not focus their ambitions on nontraditional jobs will likely be the biggest victims of changes in skills requirements.

1979 and 1987 were in companies employing less than five employees.

Business, government, and labour need to play a larger role in the education process. Considering the academic direction in which most students are headed, there seems to be a conspicuous lack of appropriate career guidance. Career confusion is dramatized by the sad fact that five years after graduation from a post-secondary institution, a majority of graduates engage in careers unrelated to their major. Given that it costs $25,000 on average to recruit, select, and train an employee for an intermediate-skill job to full productivity, it has been estimated that at least $7.5 billion is lost by Canadian employers each year as a result of people making bad career choices. A 1992 Conference Board of Canada study predicts that the 137,000 1989 dropouts will lose more than $4 billion over their working lifetimes; $2.7 billion would be lost income and other benefits, while the remaining $1.3 billion would be added social costs, such as crime, additional health care expenses and unemployment insurance benefit administration. This does not take into account the lost productivity of people in jobs they are unhappy with but can't get out of because of midlife commitments, poor career choices, or inadequate preparation. The lack of continuity within the education system between school, apprenticeship programs, community colleges and universities, and its disconnectedness with the working world result in individuals making poor career choices.

Perhaps the greatest irony is that governments are decreasing their disbursements to colleges and universities which are consequently turning away countless qualified applicants who have finally realized how essential it is to get more sophisticated training.

When you consider that the work force grew by 3.6 percent annually in the 1970s, and that it will grow by 1.3 percent in 1996, it's clear that those now entering the work force, regardless of their level of education, will form only a small part of the Canadian work force. In the past eight years, the number of 15- to 24-year-olds joining the work force has fallen by more than half a million, and another half-million drop is expected over the next couple of years. By the year 2000, 57.4 percent of all new jobs will require more than 12 years of training and 40 percent of all new jobs will require a minimum of 17 years of education, as opposed to the 23 percent which now do. Either the existing work force is retrained to meet these educational requirements, or there will be many Canadians in low-paying, dead-end service jobs. The task ahead is enormous, maybe even impossible. Most of those laid off often need training in basic literacy and numeracy skills and will therefore probably not attain the level of education needed for work in a high-tech era. That the CEOs surveyed for the 1993 *World Competitiveness Report* dropped Canada's ranking of government effectiveness from sixth to eleventh place was partly due to growing pessimism that Canada would improve its education system and worker training programs. A glimmer of hope lies in the fact that 4.8 million adults are currently enroled in upgrading programs of one kind or another. Much of our economic survival depends on enough workers becoming trained in areas of skills shortage instead of in professions such as medicine and law, which are already overrepresented.

Technology, Foreign Ownership, and Research and Development

In a world where the high-tech market is highly competitive, a country must either develop superior technology or use its technology in innovative ways. Compared with the technologies of other countries, Canada's standing is poor. The 1993 *World Competitiveness Report* ranked Canadian production technologies 15th, saying they were outdated compared to those of its competitors. In the effectiveness of its technology strategies, Canada ranked 16th. (While the *Competiveness Report* is essentially an opinion poll, rather than an objective, factual assessment, it does reflect the opinions of the people Canada will be selling to, so their perceptions are important even if they are not always totally well-informed.)

A 1993 study conducted by the OECD confirmed our low standing by looking at Canada's use of 17 advanced technologies in five key industries: 58 percent of Canadian companies used at least one of the 17 technologies, while the U.S. percentage was 74 percent. These significant differences existed regardless of the size of the company or industry involved. From 1987 to 1991, Canada ranked 21st out of 22 countries in its investment in machinery and equipment as a percentage of gross domestic product. According to a 1990 discussion paper from the federal Department of Industry, Science and Technology, only three percent of manufacturing companies have any research capacity and 70 percent do not employ a single engineer. Moreover, most did not have any staff sufficiently qualified to competently identify or acquire the technology needed. Over the past 30 years, aside from having invested a lower proportion of gross domestic product in new machinery and equipment than any other industrialized country, Canada also graduated fewer scientists and engineers per capita. It is no wonder that an OECD study, "Technology in a Changing World," placed Canada among the middle-technology countries such as Mexico and India. Such findings do not augur well for the long-term competitive survival and growth of Canadian manufacturers who are about to take on the challenge of the North American Free Trade Agreement (NAFTA).

Unfortunately, Canada's research and development record is equally discouraging, since research and development are telling indicators of investment in high technology. Research and development spending, as a proportion of gross domestic product, has been flat-to-declining over the last six or seven years. In relation to other countries, Canada spends roughly half as much (as a percentage of gross domestic product) as other industrialized countries, notably in chemicals, pulp and paper, steel, and food processing. In 1983-91, Canada ranked 17th in research and development spending growth and 17th in research cooperation between universities and companies. Canada is also weak in the amount and quality of the technology it buys, technological cooperation between companies, and spending on technological development within companies. The low level of research and development is reflected by our 16th-place showing in number of patents; Switzerland had approximately ten times the number of patents on a per capita basis. Among the Canadian patents, only six percent were submitted by Canadians or Canadian companies; 45 percent were filed by the U.S.; 20 percent by Japan; and European countries largely accounted for the remainder. Canadian managers and investors have even passed up opportunities to exploit valuable research from Canadian inventors. In his book *Ideas in Exile: A History of Canadian Invention,* J. J. Brown lists hundreds of inventions developed in Canada or by Canadians—including the electron microscope, the automatic mail sorter, the electronic organ, safety glass, the paint roller, and the first commercial jet in North America—which had to find commercialization opportunities in other countries.

The high cost of borrowing money for investment in research and development is part of the problem. A federal report entitled "Underfunding the Future: Canada's Cost of Capital Problem" revealed that in Canada research and development projects must earn a return of 20 percent on the money invested in order to be economically viable, which is double the rate of return required by a Japanese or German company. Of the 11 industries examined in the study, Canadian companies in ten of the industries faced higher capital costs than their competitors. Government policy hasn't helped. In its 1992 budget, the federal government chose to eliminate the Science Council of Canada and the Economic Council of Canada, two organizations that studied policies affecting science, technology, and innovation—precisely the areas in which Canada is particularly vulnerable. Moreover, in its 1987 budget, the government eliminated many of the research and development tax deductions.

Foreign ownership plays a major role in keeping Canada's research

BULLETIN BOARD

- Canada is considered a middle-technology country, along with Mexico and India.
- Canada's investment in research and development and deployment of technology is among the worst of all industrialized countries.
- Foreign ownership has seriously impaired the diffusion of technology in Canada and accounts for the fact that much of the research and development we use is being done elsewhere.

and development to a minimum. According to Statistics Canada, by the end of 1990, foreign-owned companies owned 52 percent of Canadian manufacturing and 43 percent of Canadian natural resources, whereas the highest level of Canadian-controlled companies were all in the declining industries facing competition from developing countries, such as furniture, clothing, shoe and leather industries, steel and other primary metals. No other major industrialized country is in the same position.

Since most of the research and development is carried out in the head office country, Canadian companies tend to acquire their technology from outside the country. While it is true that technology can be spread very quickly this way—even more quickly than buying the technology—these foreign multinationals tend to purchase items needed for their business outside Canada rather than buying from Canadian suppliers, which means there is less pressure on the Canadian suppliers to develop state-of-the-art technology. This structural problem helps explain why technology spreads more slowly in Canada than in other industrialized countries. For instance, in the automotive industry, which is Canada's largest manufacturing sector, almost all research is done elsewhere (we do only ten percent as much research in this area as other countries do). Subsidiary plants are typically responsible only for producing products, not for creating new products. The lack of research opportunities in Canada will likely send talented Canadians elsewhere, particularly to the U.S. This, in turn, will undermine both our ability to compete and our attractiveness to multinationals, which will want to locate where there is a highly trained work force. It's another vicious economic circle.

The government must play a stronger role in research and development support, particularly in basic precompetitive research projects that companies cannot afford to mount because of the large sums needed for investment and the lengthy time necessary to complete the research. In Japan, the government plays a large coordinating and subsidizing role in research and development, making Japanese companies more competitive. Canada's non-tax and government grant monies amounted to 12 percent of industrial research and development support as opposed to 35 percent for the U.S., according to a 1989 study by the Canadian Manufacturers' Association. Not surprisingly, the Canadian Institute for Advanced Research which, among many other projects, has set up a consortium of 38 companies to share research on artificial intelligence and robotics, faces a constant challenge to find funding. The combined effect of foreign-owned subsidiaries more likely to import technology, excessive government debt keeping interest rates at unusually high real rates, which crowd out research and development investment because of the high cost of capital, and the failure of the Canadian government to support research and development for Canadian-owned companies, will lead to significant decline in our long-range productivity.

According to a Canadian Manufacturers' Association strategy paper, "Canada will become a Third World country by the end of this century if we continue to rely primarily on resources and fail to strengthen our ability to compete in technology." Since 1989, only Britain, out of the 22 industrialized countries, has suffered more deterioration of its manufacturing base. Not all news is bad news, however. In 1992, manufacturing productivity rose by 4.2 percent (versus only three percent in the U.S.), the goods-producing sector by 2.9 percent, and the service sector by 2.2 percent. Multifactor productivity, however, which measures how efficiently companies use both capital and labour, showed no rise, suggesting that our productivity gains were the result of replacing workers with technology, not workers working more effectively with better technology.

Management, Productivity, and Labour Relations

The *World Competiveness Report* gives Canada a very low rating in the area of management: Canadian managers ranked 16th in innovation and entrepreneurship, the mastery of which are key for a country to survive in the new economy; the Canadian reward system was seen as encouraging extremely short-term thinking, giving Canada a ranking of 21st in this

BULLETIN BOARD

- The short-term thinking of Canadian managers, largely a result of a branch-plant economy geared mainly to reducing expenditures of all kinds, including research and development and investment in technology, has undermined our ability to improve productivity over the long term.
- Without improvements in productivity on a par with other industrialized nations, Canada's standard of living will continue to fall.
- Without good labour relations, significant gains in productivity will not be possible unless companies fully automate; yet, once most companies automate, competition will have to move to a higher value-added level, requiring the innovation that can only be provided by motivated personnel and a sufficient investment in research and development.
- Governments must keep the cost of equity and capital as low as possible in order to encourage research and development; Canada's taxation policies keep the cost of equity two to three times that of competitor nations.

area, the price/quality ratio of Canadian-made products put Canada in 17th place, while we ended up in 13th place on our attempts to provide customer service and satisfaction. In addition, Canadian managers ranked 12th in social awareness and 14th in their labour relations.

Foreign ownership is one of the reasons for our poor performance in the management category. Since most of our large companies are foreign-owned, most of the management responsibilities and decision making are assumed in the home country. Canadian executives have little opportunity to learn strategic management. To a large extent, they are merely carrying out production orders issued abroad.

Canada's productivity has fallen behind all of the industrialized countries, with the exception of the U.S., over the past 45 years. This is largely because we've had the lowest rate of investment in machinery and equipment among all the G-7 countries over the past 30 years. Canadian managers have tended to pursue a low-cost strategy, which meant minimizing all expenditures, including research and development and investment in technology. While such a strategy works well in the short term, especially if your competition employs a similar strategy, you cannot help but lose in the long run if any of your competitors are sacrificing current profits for future market share through investing in research and development and technology. As it turns out, every other competing country has had a longer-term perspective, so Canadian companies have paid the unavoidable price for short-term thinking.

Lester Thurow underscores the importance of investing in productivity-boosting technology and research and development by referring to Japan's rise to economic power, "In just 20 years, Japan has gone from having a per capita GNP [gross national product] only half that of the U.S. to one that is now 22 percent greater....Plant and equipment investment per employee in three times as high as America's and twice that of Europe; civilian R&D [research and development] spending as a fraction of GNP is 50 percent above that of the U.S., slightly above that of Germany, but far above that of Europe as a whole." Japan's existing high technology and the country's investment in research and development makes it possible for the Japanese to price their products competitively without sacrificing quality.

Obviously, labour relations also play a role in productivity. The more closely labour and management work together to help make a company more competitive, the more productivity is likely to rise. Profit sharing, total quality management, work teams, and performance or incentive pay are all efforts to improve productivity. When management is willing to delegate responsibility and power so that workers can organize their tasks in the most effective manner, productivity usually improves quite noticeably. Regrettably, unions and management in Canada have typically worked at cross-purposes to the detriment of both. Regardless of which side might win the struggle at any given moment, the victory has always been a Pyrrhic one as far as Canada's competitiveness was concerned. Wages either rose to uncompetitive levels internationally, or strikes, lockouts, increased absenteeism, or worker slowdowns undermined productivity. Rarely was a bargaining agreement arrived at that satisfied both sides and improved competitiveness at the same time.

In many ways, the military-type chain of command with its emphasis on control demanded the subordination of workers to specific, detailed, and narrow tasks. This created alienation at the lower levels and led to an adversarial approach, since employees were merely viewed as interchangeable factors of production, and certainly not trusted members of the company team who all shared in the decision making and ultimately in the prosperity of the company. As information technology alters the structure of organizations and the way in which work is carried out, significant changes are in store for both unions and management. Failure to adapt to the new realities by either party will lead to unemployment for workers and management, but particularly for workers, since ultimately companies can always pick up and leave.

Canada faces a challenge from two directions in its use of labour. No matter how much effort we make to keep wages reasonable, countries such as Mexico, South Korea, Brazil, Taiwan, China, and India, with their massive work force, will always be able to undercut us. Meanwhile, other developing countries will begin to automate, moving on to more sophisticated products in order to remain competitive. By improving labour relations and by training and trusting workers more, we can justify higher wages through product innovation, increased productivity, and better customer satisfaction.

Government Regulation

Governments play an essential role in determining Canada's future competitiveness. We have already examined how government overspending

---

GLOBAL RED TAPE

Bureaucracies are typical signs of bloated government and overregulation. Canada, with 27 million people, has had up to 32 federal government departments and 35 cabinet ministers, though the number of departments is in the range of 25 at the moment. Germany, with 80 million people, requires only 22 federal departments and the same number of cabinet ministers; France, with 57 million people, has 21 departments; while the U.S., with 252 million people, has 20 departments; and Britain, with 58 million people and no provincial or state departments, has 25 departments and ministers. With cabinet posts acting as political rewards and departments designed to serve special interest groups, there is evidence to suggest that Canadians are worse off than they were with significantly fewer departments and ministers.

BULLETIN BOARD

- Government has become an unwieldy bureaucracy that creates competitive problems for businesses and encourages them to move elsewhere.
- Interprovincial trade barriers create extra costs and are preventing companies from growing to the size necessary for global competition.

has created a debt level that has crippled the government's ability to deal with the problems facing us.We've also mentioned the government's role in education, social adjustment policies, and research and development. The 1993 *World Competitiveness Report* saw Canada's ranking for government contribution to competitiveness drop from sixth to 11th place, largely as a result of rising personal income tax and lack of control over government expenditures.

But there are many other ways in which government affects Canada's economic health. And not necessarily for the better. For example, over 50 percent of small businesses surveyed in 1993 by the Arthur Anderson Enterprise Group for the *Financial Post* indicated that, along with taxes, government regulation was by far their most serious concern. In fact, 46 percent claimed that government policies led them to contract the size of their businesses.

When the government acts as a regulatory agency, prices tend to rise. For example, in 1991 regulated prices rose by 9.2 percent on average, excluding the GST's effect. Such increases often have a direct impact on business. For example, Ontario Hydro raised its rates by 11.8 percent in 1992, an increase that may have been partly responsible for many of the layoffs at General Motors by increasing plant operating costs.

Environmental policies are another instance of overregulation—not that environmental regulations are bad, but because the way they're written and implemented binds corporations in so much red tape. For example, the Ontario Waste Management Corp. first began looking for a location site ten years ago. The company conducted detailed studies leading to a six-volume draft assessment which first had to be reviewed by 29 different government agencies. If the red tape gets thick enough, companies that have the option will simply move to other countries where approval processes are more efficient. Fortunately for us, our nearest competitor, the U.S., is equally burdened by the bureaucratic process, particularly in California. In Los Angeles, a company needs permission from eight different agencies to plant a tree and 47 more permits to chop it down. This frustrating regulatory environment is one reason a large number of California companies are relocating outside the state, with 21 percent of these firms moving to Mexico. According to the *Economist*, 708 large manufacturers either left or expanded outside the state; this exodus resulted in 107,000 manufacturing jobs lost between 1987 and 1992. Overly complex environmental regulations have had similar effects in Canada in the mining and forestry industries.

The problem of overregulation extends to intergovernmental affairs. In Canada, interprovincial trade barriers cost roughly $6 billion in economic output, the Canadian Manufacturers' Association reports. A Conference Board of Canada study indicated that 25 of 55 companies had to use inefficient production methods to bypass internal barriers, usually in the form of operating a larger number of small plants at a greater cost. For example, there are currently 16 plants across Canada producing telecommunications wire cable because provincial phone companies are required to buy locally, yet three or four world-competitive wire plants could serve Canada's market and export as well. Companies were also prevented from using national marketing strategies, something which strongly affected retailers and pharmaceutical manufacturers. Ontario pulp and paper companies cannot procure power from Manitoba, thereby upping the cost to their customers. Other barriers include restrictions on out-of-province workers, government procurement policies, liquor board marketing, farm marketing boards, beer and wine pricing, and lack of national standards or regulations. The Canada West Foundation estimates that if the four western provinces coordinated government administrative and economic policies, they would realize an annual saving of $5 billion. Projecting this saving nationally, Canada-wide cooperation would lead to an $18 billion saving or $650 per person. It should be remembered that the commerce clause in the U.S. Constitution forbidding tariffs or trade barriers among states gave the U.S. a 200-year competitive start over the rest of the industrialized world.

For Canada to compete globally, Canadian companies must grow large enough to enter foreign markets. Interprovincial trade barriers have kept Canadian businesses strictly provincial, denying us the export activity we need to balance our ever-growing trade deficit from all the imported products we love to purchase or trips we take abroad. As it stands now, many businesses find it easier to do business with the U.S. than with other parts of Canada. Fortunately, provincial and federal politicians have promised to make this a high-priority agenda item in the near future.

Finance and Competitive Infrastructure

Financial institutions play a major role in the success of companies and industries. In Japan, the banks hold minority share positions in most large companies, which means those companies have access to loans at favourable terms—including loans for all-important research and development. Japanese *keiretsus* play a similar role, allowing companies to band together for mutual benefit and to share resources. They also invest in one another as a way of maintaining commitment and of improving the competitive position of each company within its industry. Manufacturing and supplier firms are often entwined in such relationships. One day per month, the presidents of 26 companies from the Mitsui *keiretsu*, all with subsidiaries in North America, sit down to talk about joint strategy. Such communitarian business practices are in sharp contrast to the competitive individualism of the U.S. and Canadian markets. While they have the potential to degenerate into complacency and dependency, so far the Japanese *keiretsus* have by and large managed to avoid this pitfall and they have won significant economic gains for their country.

With the globalization of trade, more North American companies are recognizing the need to form joint ventures and alliances. Trade on a global level requires commitments on such a scale that it is often impossible for any one firm, even a multinational, to go it alone. So the move to partnerships is an inevitable stage in economic evolution. Asian businesses were just the first to capitalize on this strategy. Trade agreements in Europe and North America are the initial step in this direction at a national level. The growing importance of G-7 summits and tariff and trade agreements is further testament to the importance of coordinating economic strategies.

Within Canada, however, it's difficult to create the kind of corporate cooperation that works so well in Japan. Not only do banks maintain arm's length distance in most transactions, but there is also a shortage of well-integrated supplier firms for our manufacturing and natural resource industries. The main reason for this is foreign ownership.

As mentioned in our discussion of research and development, the problem is that head office frequently requires their Canadian subsidiaries to purchase supplies—the materials and services necessary to produce their product—outside the country, instead of buying from local suppliers. Head office either wants to buy from the cheapest supplier— seldom Canadian—or from an allied company in the home country. Indeed, much of Canada's trade consists of transactions between Canadian affiliates and their head office in another country or other subsidiaries in other countries. This would not be a problem if Canada were also the homebase of many multinationals, or if so much of Canada's economic wealth were not owned by foreign interests. No other country's economy is so controlled by foreign ownership as the Canadian economy. Canada is home to only three of the top 100 multinationals: The Thomson Corporation, Alcan Aluminium Limited, and The Seagrams Company Ltd. Sweden, with 8.6 million people, hosts five such transnational corporations, as does Switzerland with seven million people. Thus, Canada imports more materials and services for supplies on average than any other country in the world. An OECD report reveals that Canada imports 50 percent of these supplies, unlike France, Germany, and Britain, which are in the 35 percent to 40 percent range; the U.S., which imports 13 percent; or Japan, which source only seven percent from outside the country. Foreign part importation was greater than domestic part production in six out of ten industries examined in Canada, compared with two for Britain, one for France and Germany, and none for Japan and the U.S. The industries most strongly affected include the auto industry, which consumes five times as many foreign parts as its counterparts in other industrialized countries; the computer industry which takes in 3.2 times as many foreign parts; the aerospace industry, which brings in 2.1 times as many foreign parts; the communications and semiconductor equipment industry, which imports two times as many foreign parts; the instrumentation industry, which uses 1.4 times as many foreign parts; and the nonelectrical machinery industry, which consumes 1.3 times as many imported parts. You will notice that most of these industries are part of the new economy which will be vital to Canada's future.

BULLETIN BOARD

- Excessive levels of foreign ownership in vital Canadian industries undermine competitive networking of supplier and medium-sized companies that could support one another, because foreign-owned firms tend to source materials outside the country and are generally interested in only serving the domestic market.
- Canada's smaller high-tech firms are in need of assistance from the financial community to become larger exporters which would form the basis of a competitive, networking supplier and exporter infrastructure.
- Traditional infrastructure facilities are readily available in Canada, but at very uncompetitive prices compared with the U.S., which will cause problems as trade becomes increasingly north-south.

This heavy outsourcing is one reason that Canada has relatively few medium-sized corporations: there are 100 times as many medium-sized companies in the U.S. which has only ten times our population. And to be a supplier to a multinational, or to export your own products directly to the rest of the world, you must be at least a midsize company because of the volume of product required. You also need a healthy supply of local competing suppliers, to keep prices low and quality high. Even when Canadian companies do manage to grow to medium size, they are typically bought out by a multinational that spirits away the research and development functions and patents to the home country and leaves the company to operate on a more local or less value-added level. This process, which has repeated itself over and over again in Canada, limits the extent to which the Canadian economy can grow and helps explain why so many who graduate from engineering programs often have trouble finding work. With most of the research and development functions transferred to home countries and few domestic suppliers, there's less need for engineers. Since foreign-owned companies are not as likely to enter into joint ventures and alliances in foreign markets, the entire supporting supplier network that would grow as the company expanded, were it not foreign-owned, never gets off the ground. This situation prevents Canada from becoming a world competitor and limits the number of high-paying, knowledge-intensive jobs in Canada.

Meanwhile, the financial community, particularly the banks, have been loathe to provide the needed funds to allow Canada's small high-tech companies to become competitive. Because these firms don't have the solid assets of traditional businesses, bankers feel uncomfortable with the risk factor. And there are few medium-sized, established companies that small, start-up firms can turn to as allies. In general, Canadians seem hesitant to gamble on more adventuresome businesses. According to Peter Farwell, Ernst & Young's director of national manufacturing and high technology, "For many Canadian electronics firms, the biggest obstacle to success is raising enough capital to compete in an increasingly complex global market."

Although Canada's financial community ranks third in the world according to the *World Competitiveness Report*, it needs to change its attitude in order to play a role in helping Canada's smaller export firms grow into medium-sized companies that can support a broader network of supplier companies and form alliances with other smaller high-tech operations. Government taxation and subsidization policies could also help. Canadian high-tech firms have one advantage over many in the U.S.: given our smaller domestic market, they're forced to become global competitors sooner. Consequently, high-tech firms are big supporters of agreements such as NAFTA, especially with Mexico representing one of the fastest-growing markets for electronic goods.

Other aspects of Canada's infrastructure are in a reasonably sound competitive position, accounting for our fifth place standing in this category. Our plentiful airports, roads, electrical power, telephones and other telecommunications and transportation facilities make Canada a well-developed country. Unfortunately, our costs for these services are not as competitive as they should be. All of the above infrastructure components are significantly more expensive in Canada than in the U.S. Anyone familiar with the woes of Canada's transportation industry (see Chapter 5), will understand the difficulty of trying to compete against American carriers, especially as trade moves increasingly in a north-south direction.

Free Trade, NAFTA, and GATT

Freer trade has been a hotly contested issue and will probably continue to be controversial as the Canadian economy struggles for survival.

Regardless of one's position on the matter, freer trade in some form or other is inevitable. We cannot shut out the developing world forever. The primary issue is not whether we negotiated the best possible deals so much as the overall direction in which economic forces are pushing us and how we make use of the opportunities freer trade does provide.

What effects has freer trade had so far? Despite our fears and the genuine risks, entering a trade deal with Mexico and the U.S. is not going to cause immediate business failures or mass layoffs in any of the signatory countries. Indeed, a KPMG Peat Marwick Thorne poll of executives from Canada's largest 1,000 companies found that 90 perent favoured NAFTA and only two percent opposed the deal. In a review of all studies done on the Free Trade Agreement (FTA), Professor Leonard Waverman of the University of Toronto's Centre for International Studies found that a maximum of 15 percent of the jobs lost during the recession could be attributed to the FTA adjustment process. The open question is how many jobs would have been lost in the long run had we *not* entered the FTA and continued to avoid the challenge of becoming more competitive. Since exports increased by 10.5 percent to the U.S. after the introduction of the FTA, it is possible that the agreement may have prevented the loss of more jobs. So far as Mexico is concerned, it's important to remember that Mexico's imports are growing at a faster rate than its exports, so it also offers opportunities for us to increase our exports.

Despite problems Canadian companies may have had in adjusting to

---

THE COST OF PROTECTIONISM

Freer trade creates more jobs in the long run. As GATT director-general Peter Sutherland forcefully asserts, "Using trade barriers to protect jobs can cost several times the job's actual wage through the extra burden the barriers lay on consumers and producers. Nations do not prosper by paying $100,000 a year to protect a $15,000 job. We need reminding that industry is a consumer too. Protective measures on steel or semi-conductors raise input costs, restrict supplies and ultimately hurt the ability to compete globally. Industries affected in this way may in turn demand increased protection, spreading the problem from input to finished product. This is not just a vicious circle; it is a downward spiral to extinction."

the FTA, 51 percent of large companies and 58 percent of small companies polled felt the trade agreement had had a positive effect on their businesses. One of the advantages of the FTA is that it has forced smaller firms—a potential growth sector of the Canadian economy—to become more competitive, thus allowing us to wean ourselves from dependence on other, declining sectors of the economy. Most of the losers in the FTA were sunset industries such as clothing, furniture, and various household products. These sectors were vulnerable over the long term regardless of any new trade agreements.

So far, the FTA has not had a disastrous effect on U.S. investment in Canada, which is still the top investment destination for U.S. manufacturing (although, as discussed above, U.S. investment has its downside). In 1991, the U.S. acquired 74 Canadian companies, entered six joint ventures, began building three new plants and expanded one plant, according to a study by Ernst & Young. Mexico, however, was also a popular target for U.S. investments—56 all together, including 12 new factories and 22 expansions. The net effect was a preservation of jobs in Canada, but a creation of jobs in Mexico.

Contrary to many people's fears, it's unlikely that freer trade will allow other countries to suck jobs out of Canada simply because they have lower wages. In fact, wages and labour costs are not as crucial as some think. In the KPMG Peat Marwick Thorne poll, the executives rated what they considered the most important components in an investment decision: first, the level of taxation; second, availability of skilled employees; third, value of currency; fourth, quality of communication and transportation facilities; fifth, market proximity; sixth, interest rates; and seventh, proximity of quality educational institutions. Later on the list was wages and last was labour costs. Wages rise and fall over time to appropriate levels, as economic factors change. What's really important are government and national debt, education and training, infrastructure, and geography and demographics. This is where freer trade can really hurt us—if we fail to initiate those government policies that will bring us investment and jobs. For example, the U.S. has introduced a series of taxation measures that offer relief and encouragement to business. Meanwhile, taxes in several Canadian municipalities, such as Metro Toronto, have become the highest in North America.

Freer trade will certainly present Canada with some geographical and demographic difficulties. With Mexico joining the trade agreement, the flow of North American trade will increasingly shift north and south. California and Texas are already establishing links with bordering Mexican states. To some extent, Canada will suffer in this transformation process mainly because of our small population relative to Mexico. Mexico represents not just another country, but the doorway to trade with the rest of Central and South America. With Mexico's population expected to reach 100 million by the turn of the century and 140 million by 2025, it is clear that Mexico will surpass Canada in importance as a U.S. trading partner, even though it is not quite 40 percent the size of Canada's economy at the moment. This applies equally to Latin America whose current 440 million population is expected to reach 760 million by 2025. Although these large populations will translate into wonderful market opportunities, it will make more sense to produce in the U.S. or Mexico from a distribution point of view. Some regionalization and rationalization of scale of production has already been taking place, and is part of the reason that the manufacturing capacity of 75 percent of U.S. subsidiaries operating in Canada has been reduced and many of their functions have drifted back to their parent corporations. IBM has taken some of its sales, service, and marketing function to the U.S., and General Motors has shifted its purchasing operations from Ontario to Michigan.

Canada needs to respond to the challenge from Mexico by moving into higher value-added areas of employment. Since NAFTA sets the year 2003 as the date for fully eliminating duties, there is a reasonable amount of time to accomplish this. In competing with Mexico in U.S. and world markets and in Mexico itself, Canada does have a number of advantages. Although Canada's wages are obviously higher, so is its productivity—estimated at 6.5 times higher than Mexico's. (However, the fact that wages are 7.5 times greater in Canada suggests that low-skilled workers in Canada will see their wages diminish significantly.) The average level of education in Mexico is only 6.5 years. But this will change over time: there are 300,000 engineering students in Mexico versus the 80,000 in Canada. With 57 percent of its population under the age of 30, there will be plenty of talent available for companies that do invest in Mexico.

Still, like all developing countries, Mexico will experience unavoidable economic growing pains and obstacles. Transportation and distribution costs are high. Social security contributions and special payroll taxes are demanded by various levels of government. Workers are frequently transient, unused to working in industrial settings, and badly in need of training. The Mexican people are experiencing major social and political problems as they move from rural to urban life, and much unrest remains over past injustices that have been conveniently ignored. Business life is fraught with inefficiency and corruption. For example, it can take a month to cash a personal cheque at a Mexican bank. And property rights are not yet legally entrenched. None of these factors will disappear in the short term. While this makes the country less competitive with our own, it also makes it a less secure place for Canadian investment.

Not that Canadians have much experience with Mexico. Our current trade with this exciting new partner is less than two percent of our overall world trading. While U.S. exports to Mexico rose from $12.4 billion to $40.6 billion between 1986 and 1992, Canadian exports rose from $403 million to only $771 million. Between now and the year 2000, the U.S. and Canada will likely be relatively slow- growing economies, yet Mexico is expected to grow considerably, given that 20 million of its 85 million people have significant purchasing power. Quebec has risen to the challenge with a $3 million project aimed at promoting its exports in Mexico and already has an office in Mexico City comparable to its offices in Paris, London, and New York.

In general, for a nation that depends so much on trade, Canada shows a disturbing reluctance to pursue opportunities, despite the Canadian Export Development Corporation's $500 million line of credit to companies interested in procuring foreign contracts. As far as our international trading is concerned, we remain mired in 20th place because of our myopic focus. So far, we've tended to ignore even our most important trading partner. For example, while approximately 50 percent of Ontario's exports go to the state of Michigan, and 25 percent of its imports come from Michigan, Ontario had only a single office in Chicago, Illinois, which was expected to serve a 12-state region in the Midwest—until it closed in July 1993. Conversely, there are nine U.S. states, including Michigan, with offices in Toronto. Many American interests are coming to Canada to try to spirit away our businesses to various cities and regions that have developed an economic focus geared to specific industries. For example, the Mid-South Common Market, which is centred in Memphis but also comprises parts of Tennessee, Arkansas, and Mississippi, has already attracted 25 Canadian companies. Canadian cities must develop a similar economic focus and aggressively promote whatever they have to offer, just as Hong Kong has decided to become the gateway to South China with respect to business services, shipping, telecommunications, finance, trading and high technology, and Vancouver is positioning itself for trade with the Pacific Rim. Should anyone doubt the importance of city economies, remember that roughly 60 percent of the drop in the federal revenues caused by the recession was the result of the downturn in Toronto's economy.

At the time of writing, Mexico was the only developing country to have entered a trade agreement with developed countries. But others will quickly follow. If we can widen our focus, this trend offers tremendous opportunities for Canada. Developing countries are always short of capital goods such as resource extraction technology, commuter aircraft, and electrical equipment. Infrastructure projects are always in progress in any rapidly developing country, so opportunities exist in the areas of transportation networks, housing, energy generation and distribution systems, and construction in general. According to Everett Santos of the International Finance Corp., a division of the World Bank, developing countries are expected to spend $200 to $220 billion (U.S.) per year on infrastructure improvements during the rest of the decade and well into

---

TRADE INSTEAD OF AID?

It is estimated that restricted access to world markets is costing developing nations $500 billion per year in lost income, a figure that is roughly ten times more than what they receive in foreign aid. According to Lewis Perinbam, Commonwealth of Learning adviser, "The poor nations of the South transfer annually more than $50 billion (U.S.) more to the rich countries of the North than they receive in aid and investment....The World Bank says a 50 percent cut in trade barriers by the EC [European Community], the U.S. and Japan would raise exports from developing countries by $50 billion a year—about equal to the total foreign aid to the poor countries. The North, too, would gain. Clearly, the world will not be safe or sustainable as long as it consists of islands of affluence in a sea of poverty."

the next century. By area, $100 billion will be spent annually on electric power systems, $70 billion for water and waste facilities, $30 billion for telecommunications, and $20 billion for highway improvement. Environmental technology will be needed in all developing countries before too long, as will more sophisticated financial services. Were Canada to privatize some of its infrastructure services, Canadian companies would be able to take advantage of these opportunities as British and French privatized companies are already doing.

It is pointless to rail against free trade; these changes were inevitable as the continentalization of trade began to emerge. The lesson here is that economics will always dictate what changes will take place over the long term. As Cedric Ritchie, chairman of the Bank of Nova Scotia asserts, "The continued growth and prosperity of Canada must be linked to a philosophy of looking outward. Canadians must embrace globalization despite its challenges, if for no other reason than there is no alternative for a trade-dependent nation like ours with barely the economic weight of California."

In the immediate future, virtually all developing countries will try to challenge the rest of the world in competitiveness. If NAFTA were not in place, the Japanese and Europeans would still invest heavily in Mexico, something they are already doing. In other words, Mexico represents a key component in a global strategy for economic development. Whichever countries develop the strongest foothold in Mexico are best positioned to expand into the rest of Latin America. Consequently, you will find the major multinational firms expanding their presence in Mexico; Volkswagen AG, for example, plans to increase its production to 380,000 vehicles from its current 200,000. Meanwhile, Japan is creating the same sort of trading bloc in Asia, shifting much of its labour-intensive activity to developing countries.

The recent conclusion of the General Agreement on Tariffs and Trade (GATT) talks may partially offset some of the undesirable aspects of the FTA or NAFTA, since most of the U.S. "country of origin" or "dumping" restrictions will have to be considerably liberalized. Indeed, in general, the GATT appears to be very good news for Canada. Much of the worry for dairy, poultry and egg farmers has been quelled, since quotas will be replaced with tariffs that reach as high as 351 percent on butter. Although the tariffs will be reduced slightly over a six-year period,

---

BULLETIN BOARD

- Trade patterns are shifting to a north-south focus, with trade regionalizing according to geographic and demographic economic competitive advantage, i.e., business is moving south.
- NAFTA will not be fully phased in until 2003 and a recent GATT agreement should help minimize most of the negative features of NAFTA for Canada.
- Regions will need to develop economic focusses and actively market their advantages abroad.
- Seek work in expanding export industries located in areas with strong competitive infrastructures.

---

beginning in 1995, marketing boards will continue until 2010, when all tariff barriers will be eliminated.

Among the key winners in Canada are fishing, electronics, construction equipment, chemicals, non-ferrous metals, and forest products. Pulp and paper tariffs are to be phased out in Japan and Europe and lumber tariffs reduced to five percent. Chemical tariffs will drop to six percent from the current 12 percent to 15 percent, while manufacturers of mining, industrial, agricultural and contruction equipment will see tariffs completely eliminated. The GATT also opens up the $1 trillion market for telecommunications and urban transit companies, and opportunities for service sector industries such as computer software, management consulting, engineering, insurance, and banking. The tradeoff developing countries accepted in exchange for access to industrialized markets was a recognition of patents and copyrights, which should help protect entertainment products—compact discs and videocassettes, for example—software, seed patents, and pharmaceutical companies. However, the textile industry gets no relief, since these products can be cheaply manufactured in developing countries.

Fortunately for Canada's entertainment and cultural industries, France was able to prevent an open market for the U.S.'s multimedia products, which have already successfully penetrated most foreign markets. Nonetheless, much of the growth in Canada's entertainment industries will come from marketing our talents to U.S. consumers, who are devoting an increasingly larger portion of their disposable income to entertainment.

Peter Passell, writing in the *New York Times*, nicely sums up the essence of the GATT agreement: "Countries ready to grow may be more inclined to gravitate toward open trade. More specifically, the cultural values that seem to underpin growth—thrift, rule of law, respect for property rights, fiscal discipline—may also create political systems that are better at defending the interests of efficient, export-minded producers against those of groups demanding a free economic ride." Since the only way to reduce unemployment is through economic growth, Canada's unemployment future rests squarely on our response to this challenge. With the GATT expanding world trade by up to $5 trillion over the next ten years, Canada's expertise in importing and exporting could really pay off if we can respond to the challenge.

These forces have specific implications for job seekers, who should plan on seeking work in a growth export industry located in an area of the country that is strategically focussed on attracting and supporting such businesses. An alternative is to seek work in a company that is expanding beyond Canada, since it will have many career growth opportunities worth pursuing. The remaining option, which the next chapter will discuss, is to leave the country for work in one of the expanding economies.

What Does It Mean For You?

The foregoing information, much of it disturbing, is not intended to discourage you but to point out the factors in our economy that you need to take into account when planning your career. While Canada's current economic and competitive situation is serious, we don't know what the final outcome will be. Perhaps government and business will make all the right moves. Even if they don't, the resulting economic dislocation and unemployment won't create career crises for everyone. Some workers will do quite nicely and even prosper in difficult circumstances.

The following scenarios are presented to help you understand the factors you should be watching. Even if the situations presented don't match your goals and circumstances, they will help get you started on the kind of thinking you'll need as you plan your career.

Scenario A:

Suppose you've been studying mechanical engineering with the goal of pursuing a career in a high-tech manufacturing industry. But while you are in school, the country's economic problems have continued to worsen and the Canadian dollar has dropped in value. This isn't necessarily bad news. The manufacturers that have survived so far will have a strong export focus, so a devaluation in the dollar should help them by increasing exports. They will only profit, however, so long as most of the raw materials necessary for production can be acquired within Canada at stable prices and the countries that import the products can continue to afford them. A lower dollar does mean that these manufacturing companies will have to pay more for imported technology. But in the long run, if they reinvest the profits made from the increased sales that a lower dollar brings them, keep product prices competitively low, continue to innovate, and expand their export markets, these companies should prosper despite Canada's other economic problems. If, on the other hand, the companies you're considering are more short-sighted in their strategies, you might want to make plans that would eventually take you to a country whose high-tech industry is wiser.

Scenario B

Suppose your chosen field is environmental cleanup, but you find that declining government revenues have put a lot of environmental projects on hold for lack of funding. Despite economic worries, environmental groups continue to warn of environmental damage, and citizens will insist that government take action. In plannning your strategy, try to assess which environmental areas will most likely draw the greatest public scrutiny. You might also want to consider switching your specialty from cleanup to prevention. Smart corporations realize that, even in times of cutbacks, it's cheaper to prevent the problem now than clean it up later. You may be able to find employment with one of these companies. The same principles hold true for people who want to enter the civil engineering field. Many infrastucture projects have been delayed owing to declining tax revenues, and many civil engineers graduating with master's degrees are currently unemployed. However, there's a limit to how long municipalities and governments can postpone major overhauls. According to the Federation of Canadian Municipalities, 40 percent of

BULLETIN BOARD

- Even in tough times, not all job markets will suffer.
- Making a career plan involves putting the pieces of an economic puzzle together. You don't need to have all the pieces, just the ones that could affect the areas that interest you.
- Keep your eye on how economic issues will affect several career areas that could be relevant for you. The more alternative strategies you have, the more options you will have even if things don't turn out the way you forecast.
- Remember that different regions of the country may be affected differently by Canada's economic situation. Stay open to the idea of moving.

roads, 29 percent of sewer-and-water networks, 21 percent of water and sewage treatment, and nine percent of bridges are in need of repairs worth over $20 billion just to bring them up to minimum standards. To put it in perspective, most underground water and sewer pipes were installed just after World War II and in many cases, as in Montreal's, 18 percent of water mains were installed over 80 years ago. So while times may be rough initially, eventually there should be work for civil engineers.

Scenario C

If you want to be involved in the mining industry, then you should be concerned that a lot of mining is moving to South American and Asian countries. You could revise your choice of career or consider joining a multinational working in those countries. Or you could plan to specialize in gold extraction. If the world economy continues to lurch from crisis to crisis, the value of gold will increase since it becomes a stable international form of currency. Even if the world economy improves, gold should also rise in value for purely commercial reasons that will likely continue into the foreseeable future. In future, as now, the demand for gold will likely exceed the supply, so the Canadian gold mining industry will flourish over the long haul regardless of economic circumstances.

Scenario D

Suppose you and your fiancé are both training in Ontario to be health professionals. While you, as a physiotherapist interested in treating arthritic patients, have a potentially rosy future because of our aging population, your fiancé, a young doctor planning to specialize in obstetrics, should be worried. As governments are forced to cut back on health costs, routine medical care will be taken away from expensive specialists and handed over to cheaper medical professionals with only the essential skills. Many of your fiancé's potential clients will go to midwives instead. Try to convince your intended to switch to a more promising field, such as geriatrics. In that case, you may want to consider moving to British Columbia, where it's predicted many aging boomers will retire. If you stay in Ontario, be grateful if health care costs in the U.S. continue to rise and the Ontario government refuses to pay for them. That will keep your snowbird clients at home.

The above scenarios demonstrate that, while there's much to be worried about in Canada's competitive situation, keeping your eye on economic, business, demographic, and regional factors can help you make more realistic career plans.

Canada's Strengths

Even though our competitiveness may be deteriorating significantly, there is still much to be thankful for and appreciative of in the Canadian economy. We have an elaborate infrastructure of roads, highways, airports, hospitals, railways, office buildings, residential neighbourhoods, retail outlets, serviced land, and telecommunications that all growing Asian countries are rapidly trying to emulate. Our proximity to U.S. markets and our trade agreement with the U.S. is the envy of all developing countries. Even though many of our natural resources may command less value in world markets at the moment and are becoming scarcer or harder to access, we still have a significant amount of natural resources to exploit, something most other countries lack. As the world's population expands, the demand for natural resources, particularly water, will grow accordingly. And even though the agriculture industry has not been prosperous for some time, food is not a product that will ever go out of style.

Canadians enjoy a high standard of living in terms of health care, entrenched democratic and legal rights, reasonable accommodation, and excellent recreational facilities. Our low crime rate in our big cities—while still high compared to most other industrialized nations—is something Americans can only dream about.

The economic adjustment pain we have experienced is partly a result of Canadian companies becoming more competitive through the incorporation of computer technology into all business activities. The increase in computer literacy both on the job and at home is a positive sign for our competitiveness in an age ruled by information technology. While roughly one-third of all Canadians and Americans own a home computer, personal computers are virtually unheard of in Japan. We have a decided leg up on many other nations in this respect.

Our education system does not suffer from the problems that have effectively turned many American schools into correctional institutes. In addition, our post-secondary education system is much better than that found throughout much of the developing world and in Asian countries; indeed, they send their students to Canada for graduate school. As long as we guide our students into university and college programs that are likely to lead to jobs—as well as attract the kinds of businesses that will hire people with those skills—we will see our knowledge industries flourish. If we can improve both our apprenticeship programs and adult reentry programs, we will gain some competitive ground against Japan and Germany.

Financially, we have evolved well beyond the mercantile economies of many of the developing nations, where an often complex and corrupt legal system fails to guarantee the right to own and convey private property. Our financial institutions are among the world's best.

Although our manufacturing industries have deteriorated, it is important to realize that consumers in 20 nations ranked Canadian manufactured goods sixth among 12 nations in a 1993 study conducted by Bozell Worldwide Inc. and the Gallup Organization. We are still in the running. Canada's problem is that we are not capitalizing on our many advantages and risk losing the ones we do have. While rating sixth in the world in manufacturing may sound good, we need to see the differences that exist between first and sixth place. Thirty-nine percent of the respondents rated Japan's products as "excellent" or "very good," whereas only 18 percent rated Canada's products as meeting this level of quality.

It's important to remember that we're not the only ones in trouble.

BULLETIN BOARD

- Despite its problems, Canada still has many competitive advantages: a well-formed infrastructure, stable financial institutions, a high standard of living, good post-secondary education, and sizable natural resources.
- At least some of our current economic pain reflects the fact that we have already undertaken some of the restructuring that many of our competitors have yet to initiate.
- Our current export strength and growth rates give us one last chance to get our economic act together.
- Canada's economic situation and the changes it requires can be seen as a challenge and an opportunity. Use your energy and creativity to create various strategies, rather than dwell on the negatives.

TIPS

➤ Follow the stocks of companies you're interested in and invest imaginary money in them. You'll soon learn how national and global economic developments can affect an industry and a company.

Both Japan and Germany are momentarily crippled by disadvantages that will significantly undermine their ability to compete over the next few years. Both will have to undergo a radical economic restructuring to get their economies back on track, and for the moment Canada has the edge because it's already started on this process. Both Japan and European countries are hampered in their restructuring by long-standing traditions or powerful unions. Until they manage to overcome these obstacle as well as other structural problems specific to each country—such as the lack of a more open market economy within Japan or Germany's assimilation of East Germany—they will lose competitive advantage.

Canada is at an economic crossroads at the moment. We have one last chance to get in the game and succeed. Canada suffers from interprovincial barriers, social adjustment policies that make minimum wage employment unattractive, and immigration policies that do not take economic reality into account. Coupled with a growing deficit, we are increasingly trying to compete internationally as an economically challenged nation.

Despite this, there is still room for hope thanks to the growing market of emptynesters, the increasing tendency of developing countries to import high-tech products and natural resources, and the cumulative competitive benefits of restructuring and widespread adoption of high-tech in Canada and the U.S. With the trade surplus expected to reach $12.1 billion in 1993 and $14 billion in 1994, the highest it's been since 1985, there are grounds for optimism. Our industrial output led the world in 1993. We are now witnessing a spurt of economic activity that will allow Canada to lead the major industrialized world in economic growth during 1994—growth that will give us one last chance to get our economic and competitive house in order. With some three billion people now joining the world economy from places as diverse as India, China, Vietnam, Latin America, Eastern Europe, and the former Soviet Union, we need to learn how to take advantage of the growth opportunities provided, particularly in the infrastructure areas, and avoid trying to compete with them in the low cost manufacturing areas they will come to dominate. The global competitive race is on in earnest and nice nations such as Canada, unless they learn to compete effectively, will suffer significant declines in living standard. While our standard of living is unlikely ever to deteriorate to the level of the former Soviet states, thanks to our proximity to the U.S., we could see the country break up and our much-touted generosity become a tale told to our grandchildren.

GLOBAL CAREER MARKETS

- **The World of the Multinational**
- **Career Markets Outside Canada**
- **Doing Your Homework**

We are not a nation so much as a world.

HERMAN MELVILLE

The choice that confronts western industry is to automate, emigrate, or evaporate.

JAMES BAKER,
FORMER EXECUTIVE VICE-PRESIDENT,
INDUSTRIAL SYSTEMS SECTOR,
GENERAL ELECTRIC COMPANY

n order to plan a successful career, it is crucial that you understand the competitive strengths and weaknesses of the country where you'll be building that career. Job seekers must look at a country as if it were a stock they were planning to invest in: does it offer opportunity, prosperity, and long-term job security? As we saw in the previous chapter, for many of us Canada may not be the best possible investment. Moving to another country, even temporarily, may be the only way you can acquire work or gain more marketable skills in your area of expertise. And even if you don't feel it's necessary to move right now, your being aware of the possibilities offers you a backup strategy in case your industry or the Canadian economy as a whole experiences another downturn.

Working outside Canada will also help you understand the new global realities of business. Since the most successful businesses in the future will be export-oriented, we need to develop an international view of competition and economic development. Colleges and universities are helping students do just that by offering courses that have a global focus. For example, the University of Western Ontario offers programs in international business and cross-cultural management, and Dalhousie University teaches international transportation and banking. International exchange programs are part of the curriculum at the universities of British Columbia, Western Ontario, McGill, Saskatchewan, Queen's, and Montreal's Ecole des haute études commerciales. The student-run LEADER program at York University and Western sends Canadian M.B.A. students to Eastern Europe to help businesses there solve problems. The Royal Bank sponsors internships for York University I.M.B.A. (International Masters of Business Administration) students in its Paris and Tokyo offices.

The World of the Multinational

If the idea of working in a foreign country appeals to you, how do you go about acquiring a job abroad? While you may be offered an opportunity to work directly for a foreign company, chances are your best strategy will be to look for a position with a multinational, even a small one, that exports to the country or region in which you may be interested.

This could be a wise move in any case—depending on your career and goals—because even though strategic alliances and joint ventures among smaller companies are increasing, the international economy is still dominated by multinationals. The top one percent of the world's multinational corporations own 50 percent of the foreign-owned sub-sidiaries and affiliates worldwide.

The success of multinationals has made them a major source of employment for Canadians in the past. One of the business advantages of multinationals is that they have the ability to move operations anywhere in the world, depending on what's most advantageous to them. As the availability of skilled, cost-effective labour has increased in developing nations, this flexibility has meant job losses for western workers. For example, Swissair Transport Co. Ltd. has sent much of its accounting function to India, and Apple, Motorola, Intel Corporation, and Texas Instruments Incorporated have located high-tech subsidiaries in India to take advantage of low costs in that country. Political instability, tough envi-ronmental or labour legislation, high interest rates—all can send a multi-national packing. Which means that if you work for a multinational, you may not only find it *easier* to work overseas, you may be *required* to do so.

A job at your multinational of choice will give you the opportunity to learn more about the countries you're interested in and determine if that's really where you want to go. If the answer is yes, then once you get to know the company and the company gets to know you, you can begin to apply for postings. For example, if you have a diploma in construction technology or experience as a computer programmer/analyst, you might try to get a job with Computer Methods Corporation, a company that provides software for the construction industry worldwide. Seventy-five percent of its sales are attributable to exports, and the company is involved in many foreign contracts and international joint ventures. So, assuming that all goes well in your work at the home office, your job at Computer Methods could offer you many opportunities to transfer to other countries, particularly in the Pacific Rim.

The problem is, multinationals are not hiring the way they used to. You may have to establish yourself at a domestic company or an export-ing company that offers you the training and experience that you can then use to win a job at the multinational of your choice.

Just as you'd analyze any company you were planning to work for in Canada, you should also consider the long-term prospects for any over-seas division you're planning to join. What are the signs of a healthy, overseas operation? Make sure that the division is involved in one of the company's core businesses and that it has a clear advantage in its market. The division must have enough funding from head office to become established over the long term. And while it should be subject to strong financial controls by head office, the local managers should have enough power to make the decisions necessary for success.

For example, Bombardier, the highly successful Canadian company that grew out of the snowmobile business, has a reputation for making shrewd decisions in its expansion outside Canada. Among the companies they've acquired are Short Brothers PLC, an aircraft company in Belfast, and Learjet Corporation in the U.S. Both were a fit with Bombardier's core business, transportation, and in both cases Bombardier made an investment that was substantial enough to give these companies a better than average chance of succeeding. These kinds of acquisitions proved to be 88 percent more profitable than other acquisitions that were unrelated to Bombardier's core business. On the other hand, both Canadian Tire Corporation and Dylex Ltd., the fashion retail company, showed less wisdom when they ventured into U.S. markets. Neither company did sufficient research. As a result, they failed to assess the nature and strength of their competition and didn't offer their U.S. customers anything they couldn't already find elsewhere. Obviously, looking for a company that is expanding outside of Canada is not enough; you need to find one that's doing its homework and making smart, strategic decisions.

As well as considering the chances for success of the overseas company, you should also examine the health of the economy where it operates. When Canadians think of working outside the country, we tend to think automatically of the U.S. It's interesting to note, therefore, that Canadian companies located in foreign countries other than the U.S. have been 50 percent more profitable than those located in the U.S. That's primarily because most of the growth in the recent past has been outside the U.S. or Canada. And most forecasters think that will hold true for the rest of the decade. (Ironically, however, the vast majority of Canadian exporters have targeted only U.S. markets. Perhaps Canada's smaller companies will increase their export activity to the developing countries now that the Canadian Export Development Corporation has upped its financial assistance to exporters by 50 percent, so that a company can now borrow up to 15 times its equity.)

So when you're thinking about what other parts of the world you

BULLETIN BOARD

- Develop an international outlook by learning as much as possible about the country or countries in which you may want to pursue a career.
- Look for positions with exporting companies, especially those exporting to developing countries that are growing at the fastest rates.
- Canadian companies exporting to countries other than the U.S. are 50 percent more profitable than companies that focus strictly on exporting to the U.S.
- Keep an open mind about which countries may offer the greatest opportunities. But remember, you—and your family, if you have one—will have to live as well as work there.

TIPS

➤ For more information and advice on moving overseas with your family, see *Relocating Spouses Guide to Employment* by Frances Bastress.

might want to work in, don't fall victim to stereotypes. Developing countries have experienced remarkable progress in the past 25 years and now vigorously compete with industrialized countries in manufacturing and other "value-added" areas. In other words, they no longer simply ship out raw materials, but use knowledge and skill to transform those raw materials into a product: they've "added value" to the raw material. For example, one-third of Latin America's exports are manufactured items. Average per capita consumption in developing countries has risen by 70 percent, life expectancy has increased from 51 to 63 years, and elementary school enrolment is 89 percent of the eligible population. There are now 350 million middle-class people in these rapidly growing countries—a 50 percent increase over ten years ago; and another 250 million middle-class consumers are expected to emerge by the end of the decade. The economies of developing countries are anticipated to grow by 4.7 percent annually over the next ten years, up from 2.7 percent per year over the past decade.

North Americans tend to lump all developing countries together.

These countries are very different from one another economically, politically, culturally, and it is important to take these differences into account when you're thinking about where to relocate. Economically, one difference is in the growth in gross domestic product per capita since 1970. In Asia, gross domestic product grew from $100 to $250 (U.S.) in 1992, but in Africa's developing countries, gross domestic product per capita dropped from the original $100 in 1970. Since 1965, the gross domestic product has increased three times as fast in South Korea, Japan, Taiwan, Thailand, Indonesia, Malaysia, and Hong Kong as in Latin American countries and the U.S., and over 20 times as fast as developing countries in Africa.

One last point before we consider the individual regions: while working overseas may sound exciting, romantic, and good for your career, it can also mean major adjustments, especially if you have a family. Before making any plans or decisions to locate in another country, you'll want to consider a wide range of issues. How comfortable will you feel living there? Will you be required to learn a new language? Is the country relatively safe and politically stable? Is there adequate health care? Can your children get a good education? Will your spouse be able to work there? What visas and work permits are required? These are key issues, and it's just as important to research them as it is to look into the career prospects of working outside Canada. Fortunately, there are numerous sources of information available that focus on living and working in a foreign country.

Career Markets Outside Canada
LATIN AMERICA AND THE CARIBBEAN

Despite its history of political and economic problems, there are many signs that Latin America is on the verge of realizing a healthy economic future. Import growth in Latin America increased by more than 20 percent in 1991 and, according to the World Bank, will begin accelerating again after 1994, outdistancing world trade growth over the next decade. Foreign investors certainly have confidence in the area. In 1991, for example, 7.4 percent of Mexico's domestic investment came from foreign sources—more than any other developing country received. While there are still serious problems in Latin America, many of its countries have escaped the burden of huge debts and are now experiencing greater political stability and improved standards of living. In 1994, the income per person is expected to grow by 3.5 percent, and every major Latin American country, with the exception of Argentina, will have a presidential election. Voters are demanding a better standard of living and an improved educational system.

Many of the Latin American countries are banking on an extension of NAFTA or another such arrangement to expand their trade horizons. However, the Americans will likely need a prolonged cooling-off period, considering the political fireworks created by the passage of NAFTA. The American public will not want to leap into another such agreement with other Latin American countries for some time, so unless they make an effort to begin exporting outside the Americas, they will have to funnel their products through Mexico.

Moreover, according to an econometric study by the Institute of Public Policy Studies at the University of Michigan completed in 1994, the effects of a NAFTA-like deal would be minimal. The net benefit of a comprehensive agreement would spur growth in Canada by 0.3 percent; Mexico, by 1.2 percent; U.S., by 0.2 percent; Chile, by 2.1 percent; Argentina, by 0.5 percent; Colombia, by 1.5 percent, and Brazil, by 0.3 percent. The sooner any of the Latin American countries enter the agreement the greater the benefit, however. Nonetheless, it should be clear that the economic consequences of joining a broader agreement will mean little dislocation or transition for the countries involved since the gains are somewhat marginal. It will make more sense for Latin American countries to pursue trade opportunities globally as Chile has done, particularly in the Pacific Rim.

In the meantime, they have already created numerous multilateral trade pacts among themselves: Mercosur (Brazil, Argentina, Paraguay, Uruguay); the Group of Three (Venezuela, Colombia, and Mexico); a Mexican-Andean pact; a revived Andean pact (Bolivia, Colombia, Venezuela, Peru, Ecuador); a Central American Common Market aligned with Mexico; and Caricom, a Caribbean free trade agreement.

Currently, the countries that have the strongest links with North America are Mexico and Chile. Both countries have experienced substantial economic growth and also have strong trading links with their neighbours, so for the near future they will probably act as conduits of trade between Latin America and North America. If you're interested in Latin

America, your best bet is to find a job with a Canadian company located in either Mexico or Chile.

Mexico

Mexico sends 74 percent of its total exports to the U.S., where the other Latin American countries only send 28 percent.

Big exporters can also afford to be big importers of goods, technology, and services. Already, Mexico's imports exceed its exports as it brings in new technology, such as software and telecommunications, to improve its competitiveness and assure its growth. That offers opportunities not only to Canadian exporters but to Canadian companies that want to set up business in Latin America. Transnational companies have tripled their investment in Mexico and other Latin American countries to take advantage of the anticipated growth.

Companies that are in the best position to profit from the coming boom in Mexico's economy made sure they had established a presence in the country by the mid-1980s. Government, business, and consumers are expected to spend about $2 billion on telecommunications in Mexico in 1992, with the amount increasing in subsequent years. Not surprisingly, Northern Telecom and SHL Systemhouse have been among the small number of Canadian companies that got into Mexico in the 1980s and so have been successful in making an early start in capturing parts of this market.

Other Canadian companies with a presence in Mexico include Magna International Inc. (auto parts), McCain Foods Limited, Royal Bank of Canada, Bank of Nova Scotia, Bombardier, Berclain Group (factory automation software), Dare Foods Limited, Connors Bros. Limited (fish and shellfish products), and Laidlaw Inc.(waste management).

As pointed out in Chapter 6, however, Mexico continues to have many business disadvantages: too many monopolies (62 vacant television frequencies were given to Televisa, a monopoly, without tender in 1993); poor infrastructure that forces up the cost of transport and energy; a slow pace of deregulation; an education system that's neither universal nor high in quality; political injustice and instability. The economy grew by only 0.5 percent in 1993. Mexico's real growth rate will have to be five percent or six percent annually in order to provide employment for the one million workers who enter the work force every year.

Chile

In the course of its struggle for greater political freedom and stability, Chile has become a successful exporting nation. Unlike other Latin American economies, which only export five to ten percent of their gross domestic product, Chile exports $10 billion worth of goods, which amounts to one-third of its gross domestic product. In 1991, Chile had 6,300 exporting firms producing 2,700 different items for 131 foreign markets, compared to 160 exporting firms in 1975 exporting 500 products to 50 markets.

One of the secrets of Chile's success has been a decentralization process that has evolved under the Allende, Pinochet, and Aylwin governments. In 1990, municipalities financed 60 percent of their own expenditures from money raised locally. Consequently, the number of professional and technical staff increased significantly at local levels from eight percent to 33 percent between 1975 and 1988. The federal and local governments have tried to make the country inviting to foreign investors by privatizing public companies such as gas, electricity, telephone, airline, steel and oil companies. Such widespread privatization has brought in well over $3 billion in foreign revenue and encouraged further investment, particularly in mining, given the strong natural resource base found there. At the same time, Chile has wisely expanded its export focus beyond North America to Europe and the Pacific Rim. Chile has forged direct links to the rest of the world with 32 percent of its $10 billion in exports going to Europe, 30 percent to Asia-Pacific, 18 percent to North America, and 14 percent to other Latin American countries.

For Canadians, the best job prospects will lie with the companies, typically North American, that either bought or served as consultants when the industries listed above were privatized.

Argentina

Although Argentina's economy suffered a significant setback during the 1980s, the reforms attempted since then by the government are beginning to pay off now that the government has simplified its regulations, lowered tariff barriers, privatized industries, and stabilized its currency. The country raised $7.5 billion by selling 51 companies between 1989 and 1992 and plans to completely divest itself of almost all its public sector. The privatization effort, which includes telephone, iron, and steel companies, has attracted large numbers of foreign investors who now anticipate that Argentina will join Chile as a booming South American country.

Brazil

Brazil's 160 million people comprise one-half of South America's population, making it one of the ten largest economies in the world, larger than the rest of the continent combined. While Brazil was plagued by debt in the 1980s, the economy grew by four percent in 1993, which was twice the rate of Mexico's growth.

Beginning in 1990, Brazil introduced a number of reforms such as trade liberalization and deregulation, reduced tariffs and import licencing restrictions, opened up to foreign investment and technology transfer, simplified government paperwork, introduced competitive retail pricing, eliminated the domestic wheat monopoly, and began the privatization process. The government has been eager to privatize, since public sector companies were responsible for over half of its budget deficit. The faster Brazil is willing to privatize its public sector, the better the economy will perform; however, political forces have made this a rather slow, lengthy process so far.

Venezuela

Because of the current political and economic turmoil, Venezuela is best avoided as a potential job market at this time. President Rafael Caldera has set the country back 33 years by once again suspending the economic rights promised in the country's constitution. In January 1994, Venezuela's second largest bank, Banco Latino, collapsed. Over 50 percent of government revenues are now needed just to pay the interest on the national debt. Its economic prospects for 1994 are discouraging since its recession will likely worsen.

Peru

In the fall of 1993, 300 U.S. bankers and investors gave President Alberto Fujimori a standing ovation after a speech in New York in recognition of the remarkable turnaround in his country's economy. Peru is staging a significant comeback only two years after the U.S. cut off aid to the country. In 1992, Peruvian stocks, particularly mining stocks, rose 125 percent in value, making it the world's second best performing stock market.

BULLETIN BOARD

- Best job prospects for working in Latin America would be for a Canadian company located in Mexico or Chile.
- Mexico will become the springboard to trade in the other Latin American countries.
- Mexico's growth will outpace that of the rest of the world for the next ten years.
- Canadian firms that located in Mexico in the mid-1980s are best positioned to reap the benefits of growth there.
- Argentina, Peru, Colombia, and Costa Rica may also provide good opportunities in the near future.

TIPS

➤ Seneca College of Applied Arts and Technology, Toronto, Ontario, has agreed to train Mexican students in Mexico and will provide an introduction and orientation service for Canadian companies in Mexico. Job seekers interested in working there should contact the college (tel. 416-493-4144)

Foreign investment has quadrupled because of several important government initiatives: the restructuring of the country's $7 billion in bank loans; reduction of state control over the economy; and the permission granted to foreign investors to bid freely on 200 state-owned companies auctioned off in 1992. In 1994, Peru will privatize 35 percent of its telecommunication company ENTEL, as well as sell off oil and electricity companies, thereby offering further opportunities. Inflation has been reduced from 7,650 percent in 1990 to an expected 30 percent in 1994.

Colombia

Although most Canadians are familiar with Colombia's reputation as one of the two largest coffee exporters in the world along with Brazil, few are aware that it is the world's second largest exporter of cut flowers. In the U.S., 80 percent of all carnations and 33 percent of all roses come from Colombia. However, Colombia exports only ten percent of the world's flowers (Holland controls 60 percent of the market), and its share is being slowly eroded by competitive exports from Costa Rica, Ecuador,

Kenya, and Turkey. Colombia will have to improve its infrastructure to remain competitive in the flower industry. Fortunately, unlike other South American countries, it did not saddle itself with debt during 1970s. Its average annual growth in gross domestic product between 1965 to 1980 was 5.7 percent and 3.7 percent from 1980 to 1990. The country's economic health, coupled with the recent discovery of oil deposits there, which are expected to be worth $5 billion per year by 1997, will allow the country to initiate the necessary infrastructure improvements. Moreover, the country's excellent education system and its artisan tradition will help it during the privatization process that has now begun in earnest and that hopes to attract investment and encourage trade.

Central America

With the exception of Costa Rica, the Central American countries are not a good bet for Canadian job seekers because of the political, social, and economic upheaval still going on there. However, there are some positive signs for the future: Guatemala, El Salvador, Honduras, and Nicaragua have started to reduce trade barriers, agreed to a common low tariff on import, and have initiated free trade discussions with Mexico, Venezuela, and Colombia. Costa Rica, which enjoys political stability and relative prosperity, has an unemployment rate of four percent unlike its northern neighbour, Nicaragua, with a 60 percent rate. To stem a potential flood of unemployed from surrounding countries, Costa Rica has avoided economic integration with the other Central American countries. Instead, it has tried to establish its own bilateral treaties with the U.S. and Mexico. Recently, the country has been hurt by a European quota on banana exports, which account for 40 percent of the country's exports.

Many retiring Canadians have become Costa Rican snowbirds; it costs less to spend the winter there than in the U.S., especially with our devalued currency. This trend plus the interest in "environmental tourism," could provide jobs for Canadians.

Bahamas and the Caribbean

The best job prospects in this region will be in tourism. A good source of specific information is the latest edition of Jeffrey Maltzman's *Jobs in Paradise* which covers this and other notable tourist areas around the world. Pay particular attention to cruise ship tourism, which has become a mass market industry. Even though Caribbean hotels had occupancy rates of only 65 percent in 1992, ocean cruise liners were 87 percent full, up nine percent from the previous year. The most favourable projections see eight million cruise passengers annually by the year 2000. The Caribbean does not have any significant competition in the cruise realm thanks to its natural advantages: many attractive islands not too far apart and close to Miami.

Cuba remains the most interesting wild-card country in the area with the anticipated fall of Castro—or at least the evaporation of his influence—imminent. In expectation of this, foreign investment has already risen from less than $1 million in 1989 to over $35 million by 1990. With the country's external debt equal to 148 percent of its gross domestic product, the country will collapse unless bailed out by foreign investors.

PACIFIC RIM COUNTRIES

By now, we're all aware of the inspiring developments in the economies of the Pacific Rim. This is not just an historical inevitability, but the result of a keen entrepreneurial spirit and a lot of hard work. In most of the Pacific Rim countries, unemployment is never above three percent and their work week varies from 52 hours in South Korea, 49 hours in Singapore, 48 hours in Taiwan, 47 hours in Hong Kong and the Philippines, to 41 hours in Japan. While these countries, like Canada, certainly have their problems, they also have some compelling competitive advantages, such as an education system that is in many ways superior to North America's, a low national debt (with a few glaring exceptions), and a population that's expected to reach five billion by 2050—approximately five times greater than the European Community's and six times greater than North America's. Economic growth rates for 1993 were 6.5 percent for South Korea, 7.5 percent for Thailand, 11.4 percent for Malaysia, 6.3 percent for Taiwan, 12.1 percent for China, 6.1 percent for Indonesia, 5.2 percent for Hong Kong, and 9.2 percent for Singapore. The Asian Development Bank estimates that by the year 2000, the Asian economy will grow by $5 trillion. This is roughly the equivalent of adding another United States to the world economy. Small wonder that the U.S. is anxious to develop formal ties between NAFTA and the ASEAN free trade area.

But the U.S.—indeed, all western nations—have found themselves dealing with a far more confident region, less dependent on and less impressed by their western neighbours. The nations of Southeast Asia now look to Japan for their economic prosperity. In 1988, they supplanted North America as Japan's biggest trading partner, and they now represent 41 percent of total world trade—as opposed to North America's 30 percent. In recent years, investors, disenchanted with the slumping U.S. and Japanese economies, have been happy to pour funds into the Pacific Rim nations. In 1992, China—along with Mexico—received the largest amount of foreign investment by multinational corporations. These countries have a lot to be confident about, and they know it.

Because of the rapid growth in their economies, Pacific Rim countries need to develop their infrastructure. It's estimated that between now and the end of the century, Asia as a whole will have spent $2.5 trillion on roads, airports, railways, telecommunications systems—all the basic equipment that makes a modern economy possible. Over the next five years, Thailand alone plans to spend $47 billion (U.S.) on its infrastructure with money borrowed from local banks—an indication of savings levels unparalleled by those in North America.

This represents an unprecedented growth opportunity for Canada, since we are a world-class exporter of the goods and services necessary to build infrastructure. It's good news for natural resource companies that supply lumber, steel and oil, as well as companies that supply prefabricated housing, road, bridge, and hotel construction, telecommunications, and transportation systems. Already Northern Telecom is the largest supplier of computer network equipment to China and has installed 1.6 million phone lines in the country, 142 digital microwave systems, and over 140 switching systems. Since that still leaves only one phone line for every 100 people in China compared with 58 lines for every 100 Canadians, the potential for increased growth in the area of telecommunications is enormous. It will take approximately $400 billion in telecommunications expenditures to bring the Asia-Pacific region, including India and China, to a "teledensity" of ten lines for every 100 inhabitants. The International Telecommunications Union reports that telecommunications services have already increased by 70 percent in the Pacific Rim, with three million cellular telephone subscribers and 11 million radio pager users throughout the region. Another company helping China solve its communications problems is CANAC/Microtel of Coquitlam, British Columbia, which has built and installed toll highway communications systems.

In construction, China is rapidly becoming the biggest market in the world, currently spending six to eight percent of its gross national product on housing—more than any other country. A number of Toronto architecture firms have won contracts in China totaling over $500 million: Bregman and Hamann Architects, Webb Zerafa Menkes Housden Partnership, Murray Marshall Cresswell Architects and Planners, Kirkland Partnership Inc., and Petroff Architects. In the Pudong region of Shanghai, $60-$70 billion in commercial and industrial development is expected over the next ten years. Even a small Canadian company such as TS Aluminum, with its reusable aluminum concrete forming capacity, has been contracted to build 7,000 units in Iraq, Egypt, and Malaysia, and is hoping to break into the Chinese market. These projects should provide overseas opportunities for Canadians in civil engineering, construction supervision, sales, and consulting.

Altogether, there are 210 technology-intensive projects in China worth $30 billion and yet to be assigned to interested foreign companies. Canadian companies planning to take advantage of these opportunities include Ontario Hydro, Quebec Hydro, B.C. Hydro, MacDonald Dettwiler and Associates (earth stations), Power Corporation, Westcoast Energy Inc.(co-generation plant), Simpson Power Products Ltd. (power systems), General Electric Canada Inc. ($180 million project secured), and Glenayre Electronics Ltd. (paging systems). China represents Canada's fourth largest export market ($2.1 billion or ten percent of our exports) and the $600 million increase in exports in 1992 created 18,000 jobs in Canada.

Canadian companies typically need to form strategic alliances with one another or with Asian partners in order to succeed in the Pacific Rim markets. This is partly because major lenders have stipulated that there can only be one bidder from each country for a contract, and also because of the obvious advantages of cooperation on large-scale projects in foreign countries. For example, the Asia Marketing Group located in Manila, Philippines, consists of engineering and environmental companies brought together by the British Columbia Trade Development Corporation for common marketing purposes.

Canadian companies forming partnerships with foreign companies include Endeco International Ltd., Calgary; Wolcott Gas Processors Ltd.,

Calgary; and TransCanada Pipelines Ltd. which joined British Gas PLC, Singapore, and Mitsui and Co., Tokyo, in tendering bids in Vietnam. Stanley International Group, Edmonton, has joined forces with EPS Ltd., Victoria, Agrarund-Hydrotechnik, Essen, Germany, and Knight-Piesold, London, England, to develop a large China river-basin study which involves economic development and environmental feasibility. Ports Canada has been asked by Saigon Port to coordinate companies as part of a single bid to renovate its harbour. Needless to say, a wide variety of jobs in engineering and environmental areas will be created as these companies win lucrative bids abroad.

Job seekers interested in working for companies exporting to Asia, most of which will probably end up establishing overseas offices, would be well advised to look for them in British Columbia, since 35 percent of that province's exports are shipped to the Pacific Rim. The Pacific Rim represents a motherlode of opportunities for Canadian high-tech and environmental control and clean-up companies. While local workers will likely fill most positions in all of these industries, companies will still require a certain number of home office specialists to fulfil such functions as installation, training, sales, and ongoing monitoring.

Japan already has an excellent infrastructure, and since it continues to suffer through its worst recession in fifty years, opportunities for Canadians will be limited there in the near future. In order to recover, Japan must radically restructure its economy. The necessary changes, however, tend to go against the Japanese tradition—much the way Canada's need for budget cuts goes against its social support values. The Japanese government is propping up banks that should be allowed to go bankrupt; banks are continuing to prop up companies they have a vested interest in but which should also be allowed to go bankrupt. In addition, workers will need to be let go in large numbers and real estate values allowed to fall much further.

Unfortunately, Japan is excessively overregulated, which makes change difficult. Over 10,000 regulations act as barriers to competition— the ones the Americans always complain about. Unless Japan finds the willpower to make the necessary changes, many Japanese companies will simply leave Japan.

Even if Japan has change forced upon it by a financial collapse, it will still remain in a superior competitive position because it is unencumbered by government debts, enjoys leading-edge technology and research, well-established worldwide markets, and a well-trained and educated work force.

For the moment, Japan's economy remains becalmed and will probably grow by only 0.3 percent in 1994 and 2.1 percent in 1995. In the near future, aside from their teaching English, Canadians will find it difficult to get work there—but not impossible. Despite its current problems, Japan is Canada's second biggest trading partner, purchasing more of Canada's exports ($7.4 billion) in 1993 than Germany, France, and the United Kingdom combined. Not surprisingly, many Canadian companies have started to locate in Japan, and this should create overseas career opportunities in marketing. Indeed, many U.S. companies, fed up with local marketers and distributors, are setting up their own marketing operations or buying out Japanese firms. Nike International Inc. and Mattel, Inc., were successful in doing this in 1993, and many more companies—Canadian companies included—will likely follow suit. This will create employment opportunities for Canadians with marketing and management expertise, especially those who speak Japanese. A variety of Canadian companies are already active in Japan. The Molson Companies Limited owns Nippon Diversey in Japan, suppliers of commercial and industrial cleaning and sanitation equipment to airlines, hospitals, restaurants, and hotels, and from 1990 to 1992 has seen its sales rise from $28 million to $40 million. Other Canadian exporters successful in penetrating Japanese markets include Pacific Edge Trade Group Japan (sporting goods), Moore Business Forms & Systems (business forms), Dylex (clothing), George Weston Limited (food products), Drummond Brewing Company Ltd., McCain Foods Limited, Maple Leaf Foods Inc., Clearly Canadian Beverage, and Telesat Canada.

While working for a multinational is probably the easiest route to career opportunities in East Asia, don't rule out the possibility of working directly for a local company. One advantage North Americans have over the Japanese is that North Americans graduate three times as many college and university students as Japan, and while our high school standards suffer by comparison to those in much of East Asia, our postgraduate education is, on the whole, superior. So, for example, individuals trained at the masters level in high-tech areas will likely be able to find work in Japan. Indeed, University of Waterloo graduates with masters degrees in computer engineering or computer sciences are actively sought by Japanese companies. And if you have accounting certification, remember that China, a country with 1.2 billion people, has only 13,000 accountants. Taking advantage of these overseas opportunities will almost certainly require learning the appropriate language or dialect.

But while China, with its huge market, and Japan, with its competitive advantages, tend to dominate Canadians' thoughts of the East, it is worthwhile to note that many other East Asian countries offer career opportunities and a pleasant, intriguing way of life. Let's take a closer look at some of these.

Singapore

This English-speaking nation's economy will likely grow by at least seven percent in 1994, making it the growth leader among the young "dragons." Its main strengths are in electronics, computer and telecommunications equipment, chemicals, machinery and transport equipment. Currently, almost 50 percent of foreign investment is in manufacturing and the rest divided between financial and business services. Singapore is emerging as the financial and marketing capital of the area, thanks to its all-around competitive strengths. Many foreign companies are using the country as a gateway to other Asian countries. Since Singapore trades mainly with India, Southeast Asia and Indochina, it is immune from a possible downturn in the Chinese market should that country's economy overheat. Singapore is currently spending $60 million to upgrade its ports, and plans to add a third runway at Changi airport by 1997-98.

For Canadians looking for employment in the Pacific Rim, Singapore is the ideal country. Besides English being its main language, the 1993 *World Competitiveness Report* ranks Singapore as far and away the number-one developing country overall and specifically in terms of domestic economic strength, internationalization, government, finance, infrastructure, science and technology, and work force. In comparison with the other Asian dragons, Hong Kong ranks second; Taiwan, third; Malaysia, fourth; and Korea, sixth. To put these comparisons in a North American context, Mexico ranks eighth. The high standard of living enjoyed in the country has provided food marketing opportunities for President's Choice products, Catelli Ltd. of Toronto, Ontario, and McCain Foods. Singapore is eager to recruit skilled workers from around the globe and has even sought prospective employees in former Soviet states. Engineering graduates, international business specialists, and construction personnel should definitely explore the employment prospects available here.

South Korea

Korea's main exports are cars, electronics, and chemicals. Its rapid rise in economic strength has so increased wages that many of its manufacturing industries are now shifting production to other lower-wage countries. The ongoing reform of South Korea's political practices and financial system—including an attack on its underground economy, which is even larger than Canada's—should bring it further prosperity, to the point that it will rival Singapore in economic growth.

Continued growth will provide the funding for a $65 billion infrastructure program that will include $12 billion for upgrading and building ports and $950 million for Atomic Energy of Canada Candu reactors. Canadian companies, such as Scott Associates Architects, designer of Pearson International's Terminal 3 in Toronto, have already bid on the $6 billion Kaohsiung International Airport expansion and a high-speed rail system. SHL Systemhouse has set up a joint venture in data-systems software with Samsung Co. Ltd.

The political disintegration of North Korea following the eventual passing of Kim Il-Sung's regime will pose both a challenge and an opportunity for South Korea. If the two nations can avoid war, a reunification similar to that in Germany will probably follow. South Korea will be able to combine cheap labour in the north with its own technology. For Canadian companies, the reunification could offer further opportunities to help with infrastructure planning and construction.

Taiwan

To get a grasp on how big Taiwan's export activities are, consider that its $120 billion in foreign currency reserves are the largest in the world compared with $80 billion held by Germany and Japan. Taiwan is shifting its economic focus from electronic and electrical goods and is concentrating on the technology- intensive aspects of the chemical industry and knowledge-intensive aspects of finance and insurance. These changes mark the country's economic evolution from a low-wage manufacturer to a higher-skilled, technology-based economy.

Taiwan's economy is expected to grow by at least six percent in 1994, much of the growth stemming from the resolution of Taiwan's peculiar love-hate relationship with its long-time enemy and natural business ally, China. Despite barriers to cooperation, Taiwan's investment in China exceeds $10 billion, and those barriers are gradually being removed. Chinese workers are already permitted to visit Taiwan for training. Chances are, Taipei's embargo on direct shipping and transport to China will be lifted some time during 1994, especially now that China has replaced the U.S. as Taiwan's biggest trading partner. Many Canadian companies are taking advantage of this route into China's markets by forming strategic alliances with Taiwanese companies.

However, foreign investment and export growth are threatened by poor infrastructure, which has prompted Taiwan to launch a $400 billion infrastructure program aimed at improving its telecommunications system, highways, and power-generating facilities. Pollution is also a major problem in Taiwan—sulphur dioxide emissions in Taiwan are five times greater than those found in Los Angeles. This presents opportunities for environmental companies, such as Alberta Special Waste Management Corporation and MBB-Trecan Inc. of Mississauga, Ontario. Among other Canadian companies selling their services and equipment to Taiwan: Lovat Tunnel Equipment Inc. of Toronto sold the Taiwanese tunnel boring equipment for a light-rail transit system; Canada Post has been hired to set up five mail distribution systems there; Ebco Technologies Inc. and Nordion International are building commercial cyclotrons in Taiwan; Macdonald Dettwiler and Associates will be supplying all the hardware and software for a Taiwanese space ground station; Quadrant Development of Vancouver has begun to build wood-frame housing in Taipei, taking advantage of the fact that Taiwan is the West Coast timber industry's third largest export market after Japan and Britain; Canadian Airlines has joined forces with Mandarin Airlines to exploit Taiwan's tourism potential; Scintrex Ltd. is providing safety shutdown systems and other similar equipment to the South Korea Power Commission Corporation which has purchased Candu nuclear reactors.

Hong Kong

Now that its position as the sole conduit to business with China is being challenged by South Korea and Japan, which are using Shanghai and

---

BULLETIN BOARD

- The Asia-Pacific region will spend $2.5 trillion on infrastructure by the turn of the century, representing an unprecedented opportunity for Canadian companies and individuals specializing in these areas.
- Over $400 billion will be spent on telecommunications alone in the Pacific Rim.
- Given the high growth rates and rate of return on investment among the Pacific Rim countries, a substantial amount of investment has moved into these countries.
- Numerous Canadian companies have successfully penetrated Asian markets.
- Australia and New Zealand offer many opportunities to both companies and job seekers who want to take advantage of the Asian market without the attendant culture shock.

TIPS

- ➤ For more information about Canadian companies in Japan, consult Michelle Brazeau's *Directory of Canadians Doing Business in Japan.*
- ➤ For more information about opportunities in the Pacific Rim, consult the *Pacific Rim Almanac* by Alexander Besher, the magazine *Asia Inc.*, or Robert Sanborn's *How to Get a Job in the Pacific Rim.*
- ➤ Seneca College of Applied Arts and Technology, Toronto, Ontario, serves as liaison between Canadian businesses and the Chinese business market. Job seekers interested in working in China may inquire about companies located in China through Seneca (tel. 416-493-4144)

---

other northeastern ports, Hong Kong is beginning to concentrate on developing economic ties with South Asian countries. Nonetheless, Hong Kong entrepeneurs have started up more than 40,000 factories in southern China over the years and they will continue to exploit these opportunities even while exploring other Asian markets. The return of many former residents who had fled in fear of 1997, when Hong Kong reverts to Chinese rule, suggests that China will likely remain very much a market economy even after Deng Xiaoping dies. The rush is on to secure as much of the Chinese market as possible before other foreign investors stake their claims.

Meanwhile, the colony is spending $28 billion on port, airport, tunnel and highway development, and private construction is also booming. The focus of foreign investment in Hong Kong is in the labour-intensive aspects of electronic and electrical goods production and the clothing industry. Other prominent export areas include chemical products, printing, publishing, toys, watches and clocks, and imitation jewelry.

Thailand

While Thailand has had some success in its main export industries—which include electrical appliances and chemicals—the country continues to be held back by a variety of political, social, and economic problems. Its mounting infrastructure problems and rising wages are causing many investors to shift their investments to other countries in the area, especially to China and Vietnam. A low level of education and undersupply of technically trained workers, such as engineers and computer scientists, will hamper its evolution to a knowledge-based economy, leaving it more of a low wage economy in many respects. Thailand desperately requires a large investment in its infrastructure. Consequently, there is currently a $2 billion telephone installation project underway, $2.5 billion is being spent on an elevated transit system in Bangkok, and an additional $3.5 billion is going towards the upgrading of the airport at Nong Ngu Hau. By 2001, 59 new power plants costing $27 billion are scheduled for completion. Serious water shortages in the country may present employment opportunities for foreigners in the area of water conservation.

Malaysia

Malaysia specializes in labour-intensive exports in the auto parts and electronic component industries as well as in the forest products, metal products, and chemical, and petroleum industries.

Beginning in the early 1980s, the government began liberalizing foreign investment laws, reformed and simplified its tariff and tax system, and privatized many state enterprises. Since 1991, many more industries have been privatized, including a cement factory and a shipyard. Plans are underway to privatize both water and telecommunications, areas responsible for 15 percent of the country's gross domestic product. The government has also launched a major infrastructure program, including the $1.2 billion Pergua dam, already under construction and scheduled for completion in 1996; a fiber-optic cable installation project worth $6.4 billion; and a gas pipeline that will cost $1 billion. However, the country suffers from a shortage of Malaysians capable of speaking English well enough to conduct business internationally. Anyone interested in gaining employment teaching English in Malaysia will likely receive a warm reception.

Indonesia

Indonesia shifted from a plantation-based economy in 1966 when foreign investment laws were liberalized. Between 1967-1985, foreign investors poured billions of dollars into the country, 70 percent of these funds going to the petroleum industry. Since 1987, there has been considerable investment in manufacturing, particularly in the textile and electrical equipment industries which are labour-intensive and export-oriented.

Among its infrastructure projects, Indonesia is undertaking expansions in telephone cabling, switches, and buildings worth $260 million; a power transmission facility upgrade on the islands of Java and Bali worth $640 million; and the $150 million Madura Island bridge project.

Philippines

Along with its ongoing political problems, the Philippines faces constraints on economic and export growth. U.S. economic support will decline as military bases there are closed. Work is desperately needed on the former colony's infrastructure, particularly an increase in power generation capability. Buildings damaged by the 1990 earthquake are still being reconstructed. Only two percent of the population have telephones and there is often a five-year waiting period before installation can be completed. With telecommunications improvement a necessity in a global economy, you can expect investment and job creation to occur in this area. There is also a $200 million water diversion project—the Umiray River basin to Manila—planned.

Vietnam

Since 1989, the government has shifted to market pricing, legalized private enterprise, reformed the tax system, lifted domestic trade controls, decreased subsidies, decentralized government control, introduced a stock exchange, and allowed its currency to float internationally. The freeing up of the economy has led to a revival in many craft industries such as tailoring, shoemaking, furniture making, silk weaving, and ceramics. Liberalization in agriculture has also helped spur growth in this large sector of the economy. Vietnam is expected to be the next big growth area as it sets out to repair the damage left by the civil war.

Anyone interested in working in Vietnam should contact one of the Canadian consulting firms brought together by ACS Canada Group of Companies, Vancouver, to bid on Vietnamese contracts: Stanley International Group, Edmonton; Associated Engineering International Ltd., Burnaby; Klohn-Crippen Consultants Ltd., Richmond, British Columbia. The group hopes to use their complementary skills and experience in resource development, transportation, and water and sanitation to get an early start on opportunities in Vietnam.

Australia and New Zealand

Job seekers who prefer a Western lifestyle, but are intrigued by emerging career possibilities in the Pacific Rim, should scout out Australia and New Zealand.

Australia sends 53 percent of its exports to the Pacific Rim, competing with Canada to sell minerals, pulp and paper, energy products, and agricultural products to this area. For example, it has been actively pursuing projects to exploit the large oil, gas and mineral reserves found in Vietnam, as well as its agricultural business. (All Australian trade with Vietnam is coordinated through Ernst & Young Australia.)

Eager to exploit its relationship with Pacific Rim countries, Australia is offering incentives for foreign companies to locate their regional headquarters in Australia. Many large American firms have initiated takeover bids of Australian companies as a means of gaining a foothold in the Australasia area. With incentives in place to encourage foreign investment, expect to see many job opportunities in agriculture, natural resources, and software as more and more companies set up springboard operations to the Asian countries via Australia. Australia has just begun a 12-year campaign aimed at making 60 percent of its students proficient in Asian languages, particularly Indonesian, Mandarin, and Japanese. Economic growth for 1994 is expected to be around four percent, possibly higher than Canada's, and 3.4 percent in 1995.

New Zealand has already gone through much of the economic

restructuring Canada is now embarking upon. Indeed, its current economic success is the result of nine years of restructuring that rivals that of any of the OECD countries. Businesses are attracted to New Zealand because of its stable economy, flexible immigration and labour laws, functional infrastructure, high productivity rates, and competitive wage structure for skilled workers.

The country has long been famous for meat and forestry exports, but tourism now brings in as much money as either of these industries. Visits by Taiwanese and South Korean tourists have risen by 80 percent annually since 1991, with the overall number of tourists expected to double by the year 2000. As a result, there should be job opportunities in tourist activities such as skiing, birdwatching, and sightseeing, and in preserving New Zealand's environmental beauty.

OTHER ASIAN COUNTRIES
India

With its large domestic market and low wages, India holds many attractions for investors. It also has an established stock market and in recent years, has welcomed foreign investment and attempted to liberalize trade. Nevertheless, investors have been reluctant because of significant infrastructure problems, high taxes on exports and profits, regulatory restrictions, and difficulties in redeeming dividends and royalties. Moreover, while the country has a well-developed, impartial legal system, it also has such a backlog of court cases, it would take until the end of the next century to hear them all, according to *The Economist*.

Of the foreign investment that has taken place, the bulk is devoted to the manufacturing sector, which includes industrial machinery, transport equipment, electrical equipment, and chemicals. And although misgivings about India's political and currency instability remain, foreign capital is beginning to find its way to India thanks to a ten-year reform program established in 1991. Public enterprises, which account for 20% of India's non-agricultural gross domestic product, will be privatized. The electronics industry has already benefitted from delicencing and reduction in export and import duties, and other industries will eventually share in these reforms. The rupee is now partially convertible and the austerity reforms induced by the International Monetary Fund have led to a trade surplus. Liberalization of trade, however, has hurt the inefficient agricultural industries.

As the reforms are more fully implemented toward the end of the decade, India is expected to enjoy the economic growth rates of the Asian "dragons." Until then. it should grow at a respectable four percent. Foreign institutional investors have responded enthusiastically, buying up $1.6 billion of Indian shares during the financial year of 1993-94, mostly in the power and telecommunications areas. However, it is not certain that India's reforms are irreversible. If political instability worsens, the budget deficit could rise dramatically as the government tries to buy off lobby groups. Some lobby groups might insist that reforms unfavourable to their industries be reversed, so stay tuned.

Despitc India's drawbacks as a place to do business, large multinationals operating there may offer opportunities for Canadians with engineering and technological training.

Pakistan

Political instability and large government deficits have produced a rather grim situation in Pakistan. The country is extremely dependent on foreign crcdit and external funding for capital spending, making it extremely vulnerable to a withdrawal of needed funds. In short, Pakistan is not a good prospect for career opportunities.

THE MIDDLE EAST

Peaceful relations in the Middle East will have a major effect on the economic success of these countries—not to mention its desirability as a place to live and work! At time of writing, the prospects looked good— not for a total peace perhaps, but at least for more cooperation. If you are considering working in the Middle East, however, it's important to remember that there is a long history of hostility and political uncertainty in the area which will not be easily or soon resolved.

Saudi Arabia

Since the 1970s, the Saudi government has spent whatever was required to maintain a modern industrial economy, and Canadian companies have benefitted from that resolve. Saudi Arabia is Canada's largest trading partner in the Middle East, with trade between the two countries amounting to $1 billion. Over 20 Canadian trade delegations were sent to Saudi

BULLETIN BOARD

- India presents many business disadvantages—poor infrastructure, a highly litigious and bureaucratic society. However, its large workforce, low wages, and a series of business reforms have already lured many foreign investors, creating some opportunities for technical staff with multinational corporations. Pakistan, however, does not offer much in the way of employment opportunities.
- The Middle East has good business potential in natural resources and infrastructure, as well as tourism and some high-tech industry in Israel. However, growth in these industries—and your comfort level while living there—are highly dependent on the region's political future.

Arabia in 1993, and there are permanent offices for 18 Canadian-Saudi joint venture companies and over 200 Canadian companies.

At the moment, telecommunications and airplane fleet expansion have gained the attention of Bombardier, Northern Telecom, Al Babtain LeBlac Telecommunications Systems Ltd., Bell, and Allied Mechanical Contracting/ Twaik Establishment, all of which have offices in Riyadh. Northern Telecom is seeking a telephone expansion contract worth roughly $3 billion.

Israel

Israel is typical of many modern industrialized nations with services accounting for 51 percent of gross domestic product; construction and manufacturing, 44 percent; and agriculture, five percent. A poll by *The Economist* in 1993 rated Israel as having a higher overall quality of living than Canada. In recent years, the country has made significant economic and business advances. Its foreign debt has declined from 80 percent of its gross domestic product in 1985 to 25 percent in 1993, and although 20 percent of the gross domestic product is accounted for by government-owned companies, privatization plans are beginning to come into effect. Reductions in tariffs barriers, with the exception of textiles, and liberalization of investment markets are helping the economy. Although the influx of Russian immigrants caused the country's unemployment rate to rise to 11 percent in 1993, it also led to a significant rise in house building. Fortunately, most of the newcomers are highly skilled: technicians, architects, doctors, nurses, engineers, and scientists.

Peaceful relations with its neighbours, if sustained, should increase tourist trade to Israel as well as to the entire Middle East. Peace would also lead to increased foreign investment and trade with India and China which have boycotted Israel for political reasons. Multinationals, though, are likely to hold off situating in Israel because of government red tape, trade unions, and the absence of cheap labour. If peace continues, the economy will benefit from the diversion of military expenditures into the market economy.

While Israeli labour may be expensive, it is also highly educated. Fifteen percent of the work force are either engineers or technical specialists, supplying staff for the more than 40 high-tech Israeli companies that are listed on the U.S. stock exchanges. U.S. defense manufacturer Fairchild Industries and Japan's Kyocera have stepped up research and development efforts in Israel. Eastman Kodak, Apple, and Baxter Medical are planning to establish operations in Israel as well.

Syria

Syria represents a significant opportunity for Canadian companies in the Middle East. The country is currently expanding its telecommunications network by 930,000 lines and its international exchange lines will be increasing tenfold. In addition, there are plans to upgrade and expand its power generation and distribution systems. Also in the works is an agriculture modernization program and a conversion of its railway locomotives to western electric and diesel locomotives. Already, a number of Canadian companies have service contracts worth $65 million in Syria's oil industry in such areas as drilling, oil and gas plant design and construction, pipeline engineering and construction, and the treatment of heavy oil and sour gas.

Jordan

Jordan is already beginning to reap some of the benefits of a more peaceful Middle East. Jordanian companies have sought Israeli expertise in oil shale development, electric grid linking, overland pipelines for natural gas, and drip irrigation technology. The country now benefits from Israeli tourists visiting Amman and the red rocks of Petra.

Egypt

Egypt's conciliatory attitude in Middle East political matters has potential benefits for its economy but has also led to some internal problems. Egypt's tourism, responsible for 50 percent of its gross national product, is down by 66 percent, thanks to the terrorist activities of Islamic fundamentalists protesting Egypt's position toward Israel. On the plus side, talks are underway between Egypt and Israel to exploit natural gas deposits found under the Nile Delta and to link up electricity grids. The government will likely have to pass through a strict authoritarian period in order to quell the internal dissent. If successful, the return of tourism combined with growing ties with Israel should encourage foreign investment.

AFRICA

While one might imagine that foreign investors would be attracted by the cheap labour available in Africa, they are, in fact, discouraged by a number of serious problems in the country. Many African countries are experiencing crises because of political, economic, and social instability, disease and natural disasters. Unfortunately, those countries that are trying to make an effort to improve circumstances—Ethiopia, Eritrea, Ghana, Namibia, and Uganda, for example—are surrounded by countries full of political strife that inevitably spills over their borders. In countries such as Zaire, tribal violence is widespread, its copper mines worth $1.4 billion are flooded and will not open in 1994, its main port is no longer functional, and its trains are running once a week at best. Throughout much of the continent, business law, including contracts and private land ownership, is often unenforceable. According to a World Bank report entitled "Adjustment in Africa," released in March 1994, "With today's poor policies, it will be 40 years before the region returns to its per capita income of the mid-70s."

From a strictly business point of view—though certainly not from a moral one—South Africa has long been the most successful African country. It is rich in natural resources, with 82 percent of the world's manganese, 64 percent of the world's platinum, and 44 percent of the world's diamond reserves. The burning question is whether the move to genuine democracy can be accomplished without massive disruption and bloodshed. Unemployment is currently running at 50 percent and may

BULLETIN BOARD

- The African continent faces major political and social problems. Generally speaking, job seekers should avoid Africa unless they are extremely familiar with the political, economic, and social circumstances surrounding any potential employment area.

get worse, thus adding to the tension. However, if the transition period is successfully managed, large sums of money from ethically sensitive mutual and pension funds will likely find their way to South Africa, possibly allowing the economy to grow by four percent later in 1994. Despite a population growing by 2.7 percent a year, a high level of illiteracy (only 50 percent of blacks have had a formal education), and a rising government deficit, 29 of the 200 American companies that withdrew in protest between 1985 and 1990 have returned, though almost all are distributors.

EUROPE

While its problems do not approach the level of tragedy found in Africa, with a few exceptions Europe is almost as unlikely a place to go job searching in the immediate future. The International Monetary Fund has predicted that of the 32 million unemployed among the industrialized nations in 1994, 18 million will be in Europe. According to a 1993 unemployment study by the OECD, hardly any new jobs have been created outside government over the past 20 years. Roughly 50 percent of those unemployed in Europe have been without a job for over a year. Given this state of affairs, it is no wonder companies have experimented with ideas like job sharing. Unfortunately, these experiments have largely failed: even with wages dropping by 20 percent to accommodate a four-day work week, employers' non-salary costs for benefits have risen and efficiency has fallen.

With the exception of Britain, most of the European industrialized nations have yet to go through the necessary economic restructuring—essentially the dismantling of the welfare state and a reduction of union power and wages. According to a 1994 projection by Salomon Brothers for *Fortune Magazine*, by the year 2000, government debt levels for

European nations are expected to rise to the highest levels since World War II—90 percent of gross domestic product in France and 130 percent for Sweden and Italy. With an aging population demanding more in the way of health care and pension payouts, there are serious questions about whether European governments can meet these future obligations. In addition, much of Europe is involved in medium technology industries that are slow-growing—autos, steel, and heavy machinery, for example. European reluctance to match the U.S. in restructuring these industries has led to higher sustained levels of unemployment.

Meanwhile, all of Europe and North America is paying the price of Germany's reunification. In order to raise the $100 billion per year it costs to restore what once lay behind the Berlin Wall, Germany has kept its interest rates high, which in turn has depressed economic activity throughout the continent. And since Europe is the world's largest trader, that has in turn caused a slowdown in worldwide trade. So long as wages remain uncompetitive with workers in the Far East, Europe will continue to have relatively high rates of unemployment.

Because Europe has lost its competitive edge over the U.S. and Japan, protectionist policies will likely emerge, keeping unemployment levels high, but increasing trade within Europe. Unfortunately, many of the EEC proposals to allow job seekers to move freely among countries have not lived up to their promise and may be withdrawn as a means of curbing the flow of East European and African refugees and the expansion of Italian drug trade crime across borders.

Despite the gloomy news, there is still great economic promise in Europe, especially if the problems of cooperation through the EEC are resolved. A united European community, however, is still very much a dream. European negotiations frequently get bogged down in conflicting self-interest, mutual suspicion and concerns about sovereignty.

Given the current malaise, only highly skilled workers in the knowledge industries will likely find anything more than temporary work in Europe for some time to come. However, since much of the economic activity in Europe will probably come from joint ventures among companies in different countries, there may be job opportunities in coordinating these activities. Anyone who is knowledgeable about international business and speaks more than one European language should consider this possibility.

Germany

Unemployment rates still tell the tale of two countries: western Germany had an unemployment rate of 8.8 percent in January 1994, while eastern Germany suffered a 17 percent unemployment rate. With average hourly wages and benefits of $36, payroll taxes set at 40 percent of basic wage, and severance packages required by law costing as much as $36,000, German workers are in danger of pricing themselves out of the global job market. No wonder Volkswagen AG reduced its work force by a third or 38,000 jobs in the course of 15 months. Mercedes-Benz and BMW AG are looking to move operations to low labour-cost countries such as Poland, the Czech Republic, Russia, Portugal, China, Mexico, and even the U.S. Since Germany is only now beginning to restructure its economy, unemployment rates will remain high and relationships between banks, businesses, and unions, once the traditional source of economic strength, will be reassessed and strained during the adjustment period. Indeed, a double-dip recession is a very real possibility, especially since social spending now accounts for a third of Germany's gross domestic product. It's estimated that these reunification and restructuring problems are costing the country $100 billion annually, and the German economy is expected to grow by only 0.4 percent in 1994 and 1.8 percent in 1995. The economic price of absorbing East Germany will continue into the next century with government debt likely to reach 80 percent of gross domestic product by then.

Nonetheless, economically Germany remains a formidable and highly efficient country whose strength lies in the application of high technology to medium technology industries. In technological innovation, however, Germany now lags behind the U.S. and Japan. Its future likely lies in the opportunities created by economic reforms in the Eastern European countries. In the meantime, unemployment will probably rise slightly in western Germany during 1994 and bottom out in eastern Germany. Reunification will create infrastructure opportunities for Canadian companies: rebuilding plans for eastern Germany include a $450 billion transportation project over the next 18 years, with $200 billion allocated for 3,220 kilometres of high-speed rail development and 2,415 kilometres of road improvement.

France

France will continue to offer poor prospects for job seekers. Unemployment is expected to rise in 1994 from 11.3 percent to 11.5 percent in 1994, according to the International Monetary Fund. Though the economy is expected to begin picking up in the last quarter of 1994 and continue throughout 1995, the growth rate is expected to be only 0.9 percent in 1994 and 2.5 percent in 1995. Burdened by one of the highest tax rates in the world, excessive regulation, and protectionist tendencies, France will take longer to emerge from the recession and will require a growth rate of at least three percent in order to create jobs; in other words, twice the growth rate needed by a country with fewer economic constraints. With a presidential election in 1995, it is unlikely that politicians will adopt the aggressive economic strategies needed to restructure the country's economy. If, on the other hand, France adopts the four-day work week that is being contemplated, up to 2 million jobs could be created.

France is unpromising territory for Canadian job seekers unless you are approaching a Canadian company expanding in France. However, those who are interested in the telecommunications industry might approach Alcatel Cable, the world's largest manufacturer of telecommunications, systems, and cable. It specializes in electrical equipment, electrical power plants, high-speed trains, and shipbuilding. Asia, which now accounts for roughly 25 percent of France's market, is buying the country's high-speed rail and power products. The Asian market is serviced through Alcatel's Australian branch.

Italy

The Italian economy, which continues to be plagued by unemployment, political turmoil, corruption, and a large government debt, is forecast to grow by 1.1 percent in 1994 and 2.5 percent in 1995. Unless the new Italian government begins to tackle these pressing economic matters, the north, which is eager to take advantage of the European Community, will definitely drift toward separation. As the *Economist* recently stated, "If there is a single, recurrent, almost obsessive theme in the political history of post-war Italy, it is that of the need for reform and of the failure to achieve it." However, perhaps change will finally be forced by the public's anger at corruption, estimated to account for 15 percent of the government's debt, which itself is expected to rise to a monstrous 113 percent of gross domestic product in 1994.

If you are looking for work in Italy, concentrate on the north, where the standard of living is among the highest in the world and unemployment rates are significantly lower. Italy's chief industries are steel, machinery, autos, textiles, shoes, machine tools, and chemicals. Best bets for foreign job seekers are likely fashion, textiles, and shoes, since Italy excels in these areas. But get a diploma or degree in fashion or fashion management as well as some Canadian experience before pursuing employment here. Kraft General Foods Canada Inc. is involved in the Italian food processing industry and may offer some opportunities for Canadians. Since a lot of natural gas underlies much of the Northern Plain and parts of Sicily, Canadians with expertise in gas exploitation may find work in this area. Anyone with expertise in plastics, fertilizer, and synthetic rubber production from natural gas would also stand a reasonable chance of finding a position. And since Italy has always relied on its large and profitable tourist industry to offset its ongoing trade deficit, there will always be jobs in this area.

Britain

Of all the large European countries, Britain has the best long-range job prospects. It has already passed through much of the painful restructuring that other European countries are only now experiencing. By the end of the decade, Britain is forecasted to have by far the lowest government debt burden as a percentage of gross domestic product and will be the first country to emerge from the recession with the economy growing by 2.6 percent in 1994 and 2.8 percent in 1995.

Nevertheless, unemployment remains at the ten percent level. Britain is a year behind the recovery in the U.S., with investment stagnating as companies try to bring down their high debt loads before reinvesting profits in corporate investment. Look for a turnaround in the automotive industry; Britain will probably become a net exporter of automobiles in the next two or three years. By 1995, Britain should see its unemployment levels begin to fall once investment takes off. Career opportunities for Canadians may arise then, particularly in the finance field, which is Britain's main competitive strength.

Spain

Although Spain has now surpassed Canada as one of the largest industrialized countries, it offers few opportunities to its own citizens, let alone to outsiders. Spanish labour law and practices make it extremely difficult to lay off workers or keep wages in check; consequently, companies are over-staffed and production extremely inefficient. Pension and health care now constitute 60 percent of the government's budget. Crime rates have risen in major cities since unemployment remains so high. As a result, the black market economy accounts for 20 percent to 30 percent of gross domestic product. Even the tourist industry will offer few jobs, now that the Olympic festivities are long over. Spain's economy should grow by 0.6 percent in 1994 and 2.2 percent in 1995.

Portugal

Portugal's traditional industries, textiles and clothing, will likely suffer in 1994 as they are forced to compete with more technologically advanced foreign competitors. However, its modernized car and electrical machinery component sectors should do well, and its political stability and pro-business pragmatism should allow it to survive the transition to greater competitiveness.

As the poorest country is Western Europe, Portugal is eligible for $240 billion in aid from the European Community over the next six years, along with another $25 billion awarded to Spain, Portugal, Ireland, and Greece as a means of catching up with other European Community nations. As a result, Portugal will be launching a number of competitive changes requiring the help of highly educated consultants and staff. This, combined with Portugal's economic strengths, is good news for Canadians interested in Portugal, since only ten percent of Portuguese students go beyond high school, thus creating a shortage of the highly educated workers needed to make these changes.

Greece

The Socialist government in the 1980s was responsible for a quadrupling of the government debt, which reached 120 percent of gross domestic product in 1992. Greece now has the lowest productivity, largest external debt, highest inflation, biggest underground economy, and lowest income per person of all European countries and the situation is worsening. Although reforms have been instituted, Greece risks complete loss of control over its finances unless it takes serious measures to deal with its Sisyphisian debt.

Sweden

With a budget deficit of around 14 percent in 1993, Sweden has suffered considerably. Its banks are in trouble and its building industry stagnant. Sweden has been willing to forego growth in the short term in order to get its economic house in order. Plans for 1994 included eliminating 80,000 public service jobs, cutting back on housing subsidies and sickness benefits, and shifting the old age pension starting date to 67 years of age. Many companies, such as SAAB Automobile AB and Volvo Car Corporation, are also restructuring and laying off in preparation for entering the European Community. Unemployment was eight percent at the end of 1993, up from 5.5 percent in 1992. The economy is expected to grow by 1.6 percent in 1994 and 2.4 percent in 1995. Hold off as yet in seeking employment here.

Finland

Finland, with an unemployment rate of 20 percent in 1994, is also unpromising. The country's gross domestic product fell 14 percent between 1990 and 1993 once trade with Russia collapsed. This has put 100,000 people out of work, raising unemployment to 20 percent roughly and the budget deficit to 14 percent of gross domestic product. Over that same time period, the gross domestic product per person dropped 40 percent, representing a substantial drop in the standard of living for Finlanders. Virtually all the banks are in trouble, although a currency devaluation in early 1993 helped exports grow by 26 percent. Low world prices for paper have hurt its pulp and paper industry. One bright spot is that the Finnish company Nokia now controls 17 percent of the world's cellular phone market. Politically, Finland remains undecided about its future, but is contemplating joining the European Community and trying to sort out its relationships with Russia and the CIS.

Norway

Thanks to the discovery of North Sea petroleum and gas in the late 1960s, Norway manages to enjoy one of the highest standards of living in the world. Petroleum and natural gas exports now account for more than 40 percent of its export market. Meanwhile, Norway's hydroelectric power has become a serious rival to France's nuclear power in supplying the rest of Europe with electricity. It is estimated that by the turn of the century, the export of hydroelectric power could bring in as much revenue as the oil and gas industry.

Unfortunately, Norway's non-oil economy has not grown since 1989 which accounts for the country's nine percent unemployment rate. So far, oil and gas wealth has allowed Norway to maintain a high level of social support payments. Spending on disability and rehabilitation rose by 80 percent between 1980 and 1990. But unless steps to reform welfare policies are undertaken, most of the rest of the country's economy will continue to languish.

With economies beginning to pick up slightly in 1994, the oil, gas, and hydroelectric industries should prosper, meaning opportunities for Canadians with expertise in these areas. However, Norway's high level of social support payments and state control is a matter for concern. Moreover, there's a good chance Norway will not join the European Community, since that would mean dismantling much of its state-controlled economy.

Denmark

Most people are unaware that in 1993, Denmark ranked third in the world in competitiveness, just ahead of Switzerland and Germany. Despite setbacks during the recession, when currency fluctuations made its exports more expensive and its major customer, Germany, cut back its spending, Denmark has extremely good long-range potential, given its strong international orientation. Denmark has one of the world's best infrastructures and work forces. Its managers are ranked second in the world. Despite its being a social democratic country, Denmark has avoided most of the social support excesses of its Nordic brethren, so it has not had to devalue its currency yet. Nevertheless, Denmark is embarking on a job creation program in 1994 aimed at creating 42,000 jobs and costing 1.2 percent of gross domestic product. Other taxes are expected to rise as the deficit grows to six percent of gross domestic product to cover the government's shortfall in revenue. The Danish economy should grow by 2.1 percent in 1994 and 2.5 percent in 1995.

- Although Europe may eventually become a unified trading bloc, it will be beseiged, for some time to come, by debt, unemployment and the need for economic restructuring.
- Since Europe's unemployment levels rival Canada's, it offers few opportunities for Canadians, with the exception of specific industries or multinationals, which are succeeding despite the general malaise.

Denmark's main industries are industrial and construction machinery, textiles, furniture, and electronics. Food processing is also a large part of its export market. Those with electronic engineering and computer backgrounds could contact such well known multinational industrial manufacturing companies as Unisys, Control Data Systems Ltd., General Dynamics, Amdahl Canada Limited, Raytheon Co., IBM, Hewlett Packard, Motorola, Philips Electronics, and Analog Devices, all of which operate in Denmark. Denmark's North Sea oil drilling has attracted Imperial Oil Limited and Goodyear Canada Inc.

The Netherlands

The Netherlands are also in a good long-range competitive position, ranking sixth compared to Sweden, France, and Italy, which held the ninth, tenth, and twentieth spots respectively. The Netherlands' strengths lie primarily in finance, its managers, and its domestic economy. Its economy will likely grow by 1.0 percent in 1994 and 2.2 percent in 1995. Dutch industries that are prospering and could offer opportunities to Canadians include oil, electronics, and metal and chemical manufacturing.

Belgium

The situation is less positive in Belgium, where the unemployment rate was 12.1 percent in 1993 and is expected to rise to 13.2 percent in 1995. Its net public debt has reached 129 percent of gross domestic product, which will leave the country poorly equipped to meet the pension needs of its aging population. Its economy is expected to grow one percent in 1994 and two percent in 1995, which is not enough to solve its debt and unemployment problems. Avoid Belgium for job opportunities in the near future.

Switzerland

Switzerland will continue to be the stable country it has always been. According to a 1993 *Economist* poll, it enjoys the highest overall quality-of-life rating among the industrialized nations. Although higher taxes have curbed growth somewhat, reforms to eliminate price-fixing agreements in the public and private sectors should help spur growth to 1.1 percent in 1994 and 2.0 percent in 1995. The best employment opportunities for foreigners will be in the pharmaceutical industry and in Switzerland's famous financial industry, which may benefit from continuing economic and political instability elsewhere in the world.

Austria

The Austrian economy should grow by 1.5 percent in 1994 and 2.2 percent in 1995. Because a large part of Austria's economy is controlled by state enterprises, there is some trepidation about joining the European Community. Along with Germany, Austria is well situated to trade and compete with the emerging Eastern European countries. Its domestic economic strength, strong international focus, and highly educated work force (99 percent literacy) will help it make the necessary transitions that all European countries are going through.

The Austrian government is about to devote a considerable amount of money to infrastructure in order to maintain its construction industry, and it will continue to promote tourism to stabilize its currency. Either of these areas could offer opportunities to Canadians.

Russia, the Republics, and Eastern Europe

If you're interested in Russia and the newly emerging republics, bear in mind that political conditions there are still volatile. And the economy is still in crisis. Crime, corruption, and government instability and interference have created a drag on economic development. Russia's 1993 national production and spending fell 15 percent in 1993 and is expected to fall by seven percent during 1994. Its current economy is approximately 35 percent to 45 percent smaller than in 1989. Canada, with one-fifth as many people, exported three times as much as Russia in 1992. And, as far as standard of living is concerned, the Great Depression of the early 1930s was mild in comparison to the deprivation facing Russia today.

BULLETIN BOARD

- If they can overcome political and social instability and make a successful transition to a market economy, Russia and its former republics and allies offer exciting opportunities for Canadian companies and job seekers.

- In the near future, infrastructure and natural resource development will likely provide the first major job opportunities for foreign workers, since the latter will help pay for the former. Raising capital will also become a major preoccupation, creating opportunities for those who have financial consulting and banking expertise and can speak the appropriate languages. Given the dire state of the environment, there will be opportunities in that field eventually. However, for the moment, pure economic survival industries will take precedence over environmental concerns.

The business news is mixed, however. While production in areas where Russia has no competitive advantage, such as steel, shoes and VCRs, has fallen drastically, the production of television sets and refrigerators was up by ten percent. In 1993, oil exports increased by 21 percent. Meanwhile, it is impossible to predict accurately what will happen politically.

However, if Russia and the republics can make a successful shift to a market economy, there will be opportunities for Canadian companies that can help exploit the rich natural resources in this region. For example, according to a Strategic Investments newsletter, Russia may privatize 60 percent of its oil and gas industry over 1994-95—a significant opportunity since Russia's oil reserves are equal to those of Saudi Arabia. Oil production has diminished considerably since 1989 and is in need of $12 billion investment capital to restore existing production facilities, and another $10 billion to improve production. Given Canadians' expertise in oil recovery, this should offer significant employment opportunities.

Another area of opportunity for Canadian companies is in environmental and health industries. According to Vladimir Pokorovsky, head of the Russian Academy of Medical Sciences, "We have already doomed ourselves for the next 25 years. The new generation is entering adult life unhealthy. The Soviet economy was developed at the expense of the population's health." With half the drinking water and a tenth of the food supply contaminated in Russia, and many of its former republics and allies suffering similar problems, there should be work for environmental specialists.

Some Canadian companies have already made the leap into Russia, including Patriot Computer Corp. of Richmond Hill, Ontario, which has sold up to $1 million worth of computers per month to Russia, and Soapberry Shop, of Toronto.

The now-independent republics and former Soviet allies offer the same combination of economic potential and political uncertainty. Kazakhstan is rich in oil and gold, Turkmenistan in oil and gas, and Azerbaijan has one of the largest unexploited oil reserves in the world. Many foreign companies have already entered Kazakhstan, which has welcomed privatization.

Estonia has 4,000 foreign-owned companies, half of which have Finnish partners. The Swedes have invested even more. The country's well-educated work force, inexpensive labour, and stable government are earning it the title "Hong Kong of the Baltic." Many Finnish companies have moved to Estonia because total factory production and management costs are typically a third of Finland's. However, the situation is less optimistic in Ukraine, despite its agricultural resources. At time of writing, Ukraine's economy was very near financial collapse with inflation running at 50 percent each month.

Among the former allies of the USSR, Hungary is particularly well positioned, since it started its transition to a market economy before the other Eastern European countries and thus avoided the economic shocks its neighbours are now experiencing. The only thing holding Hungary back from economic recovery is the extremely slow pace of privatization. The country's main competitive economic strengths lie in its well-educated work force and its strong science and technology focus. Since 75 percent of Hungary's work force has been trained in technical colleges, Ikea, Ford, Philips Electronics, and Suzuki have set up factories there.

Poland seems to have passed through its transitional period and, at the moment, is growing faster than any other European country. In 1994, western commercial banks agreed to a reorganization of the country's debt that reduced the amount owed by 40 percent. Besides increasing the country's access to western capital markets, the agreement will allow the government to go ahead with power plant renovations and road construction—an important development, since Poland's decaying infrastructure has been an impediment to western companies with plants and distribution requirements there. Unemployment should remain level over the next few years at 20 percent.

The Czech Republic also offers relative political stability and a quick transition to a market economy. Unemployment has been high, at eight percent, and will probably increase, largely because of privatization. But already Czech exporters are earning 80 percent of their revenues in western economies, with Germany absorbing 30 percent of these exports. One Canadian company that has given the Czechs a vote of confidence is Bata Industries Limited, which returned to the republic in 1991 and now has a manufacturing plant and 43 stores located there. The company is able to compete in the European import market against other low-priced exports from the Pacific Rim, Portugal, and Italy.

Slovakia, on the other hand, has not fared well after the breakup since it has suffered most from the collapse in trade among former Communist countries. Its slow rate of privatization and large government debt will give it an 18 percent unemployment rate in 1994 and 1995.

THE UNITED STATES

Most Canadians, not willing to go far afield for employment, will look south, to the U.S. While there has been considerable focus on the flaws of the U.S. economy in the past decade, we are now beginning to appreciate some of its strengths. As Canada and Europe struggled with high unemployment, the U.S. rate has dropped far more quickly as it eases out of the recession. The key to low unemployment is flexibility: the ability to easily hire workers when needed and to lay them off or reduce their worktime or wages when the economy is performing poorly. In addition, minimum wages must be low enough that employers will continue to hire people instead of automating, but not so low that people will prefer to go on social assistance. Because the U.S. has this kind of hiring and wage flexibility, companies have been able to undergo the necessary restructuring essential to becoming globally competitive. Japan and Europe have rather rigid policies with respect to hiring and wages so that any economic adjustment period is likely to be longer and more painful. For this reason, the U.S. will always be an economic contender even if it must

---

BULLETIN BOARD

- Continuing growth as the U.S. economy recovers should provide job opportunities for Canadians, particularly in the entertainment and health care fields.

TIPS

➤ For an outline of the best places in the U.S. to weather an economic downturn, refer to the appendix of *The Great Reckoning* by James Davidson and Lord Rees-Mogg.

---

inevitably share its past supremacy with the Pacific Rim and Europe.

In general, the U.S. has always had a flexible, innovative approach that has allowed it to get a head start on its competitors. Although the U.S. has many social problems that will challenge its future economic ambitions, it will emerge a strong economic nation so long as it refrains from taxing employers excessively in order to subsidize entitlement programs. Assuming the U.S. does bite the bullet on entitlement programs, politically unpopular though such a move will be, the next question is what are the promising job areas in the U.S. over the long haul.

There should be a shortage of engineers who are familiar with integrated manufacturing, electronics, computer engineering, robotics, and telecommunication systems. In other words, look for jobs in the new economy areas which will hire a greater percentage of qualified applicants because of the large number of medium, large, and multinational companies located in the U.S. In 1993, consumer spending on motor vehicles increased by 19 percent, second only to entertainment. In 1994, the U.S. is expected to overtake Japan as the world's largest vehicle producer for the first time in 13 years. Look for jobs in the design end of the business which is less susceptible to automation, economic downturns, and consumer buying patterns.

If President Clinton's infrastructure promises materialize, there should also be many jobs for civil engineers, highly skilled construction workers, and architects over the next few years. Natural disasters such as floods, hurricanes, and earthquakes will continue to fuel building starts and repairs for some time to come.

But the biggest growth industry of the 1990s in the U.S. should be the entertainment industry, which along with recreation created 200,000 new jobs in 1993, representing 12 percent of all new jobs, surpassing the health care industry which was the biggest job creator in the 1980s. A total of $450 billion (Canadian) was spent on entertainment in 1993, which represents an after-inflation increase of 13 percent since 1991 or twice the growth rate of consumer spending overall. Over $17 billion is being spent by Blockbuster Entertainment, MCA, and The Walt Disney Company to develop theme parks, casinos, theaters, and ballparks. Once again, the baby boomers, who tend to be the biggest spenders on entertainment, are responsible. Areas of expansion will include both traditional entertainment plus new technology.

While rising productivity is expected to increase U.S. wages and discretionary spending, rising health care costs could put something of a damper on entertainment spending. But this inevitable rise will constitute another job opportunity area for Canadians. Similar opportunities to those mentioned in the section that discusses jobs in Canada's health care industries will flourish; however, the U.S. will have more jobs in pharmaceuticals, biotechnology, and medical equipment.

As always, Canadians who want to work in the U.S., with the help of their prospective employers, will have to convince the government that they offer invaluable skills. But with the demand for knowledge workers increasing as the U.S. economy picks up, this should not be too difficult to do.

Doing Your Homework

While the foregoing discussion should give you a general idea about which areas of the world might be of interest to you in your job search, it is important to do thorough research—especially since conditions are changing constantly. The *Economist* magazine, arguably the best newsmagazine of its type in the world, is an excellent source of information, as is the World Bank's annual edition of *Global Economic Prospects and the Developing Countries* and *The World Competitiveness Report*. World Trade Centers located in each of Canada's major cities are open to inquiries from individuals wishing to investigate career possibilities in foreign countries. Very useful is Jean-Marc Hachey's *The Canadian Guide to Working and Working Overseas for Entry-Level and Seasoned Professionals*, which contains over 900 documented international job resources.

Moreover, the following international trade associations are also happy to provide information to interested job seekers:

☛ ASEAN-Canada Business Council
  The Canadian Chamber of Commerce,
  #1160, 55 Metcalfe St.,
  Ottawa, ON K1P 6N4 Tel. 613-238-4000 Fax: 613-238-7643

☛ Asia Pacific Foundation of Canada
  #666, 999 Canada Pl.,
  Vancouver, BC V6C 3E1 Tel: 604-684-5986 Fax: 604-681-1370

☛ Canadian Exporter's Association
  #250, 99 Bank St.,
  Ottawa, ON K1P 6B9 Tel. 613-238-8888 Fax: 613-563-9218S

☛ Canadian International Trade Association
  World Trade Centre,
  60 Harbour St.,
  P.O. Box 38,
  Toronto, ON M5J 1B7 Tel. 416-651-2220 Fax: 416-651-2519

☛ Federation of Export Clubs Canada
  #1402, 67 Yonge St.,
  Toronto, ON M5E 1J8 Tel. 416-364-4112 Fax: 416-364-4074

CHAPTER EIGHT

CAREER SURVIVAL FOR CANADIANS IN THE NEW GLOBAL ECONOMY

- **Planning**
- **Flexibility and the Ability to Deal With Stress**
- **Communication and Interpersonal Skills**
- **Entrepreneurship**
- **The Last Word**

We've broken the whole mummy and daddy syndrome. Nobody is responsible for your happiness. You have to see yourself as a business. That's *your job.*
WILLIAM MORIN, CHAIRMAN, DRAKE BEAM MORIN U.S. INC.

If money is your hope for independence, you will never have it. The only real security that a man can have in this world is a reserve of knowledge, experience and ability. HENRY FORD, U.S. AUTOMOBILE MANUFACTURER

The job market of the future will be very different and your strengths tested in ways that may at times be quite trying. As you move from contract to contract, learn to work at home, consider the competitive outlook for Canada, wonder if you should take a job in Mexico, or weigh the value of various training courses, what personal characteristics will you need to adapt and prosper?

There are four skills categories that have always been useful in building a career but that will become even more important in the future: *planning; flexibility and the ability to deal with stress; communication and interpersonal skills;* and, *entrepreneurship.* A career plan has always been key, but in a time of economic restructuring, planning will become an even more sophisticated exercise. In addition, you'll need the flexibility and emotional resilience to modify those plans and adapt to new working situations quickly. The changing structure of work and the increased emphasis on competitiveness means we will all have to become entrepreneurs, whether we are employees, contract workers, or running our own businesses. And in a fast-changing, service-oriented environment, communication and interpersonal skills will be indispensable.

Planning

Career survival in the new global economy requires careful thought and planning. You must evaluate how realistic your career choice is and determine what skills you need and how to get appropriate training.

Fortunately, there are plenty of resources available to help you plan, including books, courses, and counselling services. If you're a student, you can probably take advantage of free career counselling services. Otherwise, a reputable counselling service will help you decide where your strengths and weaknesses lie. As part of the process, you should take evaluative tests that identify and measure your abilities, aptitudes, personality traits, learning style, interests, and values. They will also match your attributes with those required in certain categories of work. These categories may include not only jobs you've already considered but related careers that might not otherwise have occurred to you. Even if the testing process confirms what you already know—that you are ideally suited to be an accountant, engineer, or social worker, for example—the results can be remarkably reassuring at time when you are inclined to doubt your choice. And if your chosen career disappears in a fast-changing economy, you have information about related careers that you can use to make new plans. Many of the tests typically used in career counselling can also tell you a lot about your working style—whether you prefer to work independently or as part of a team—which is also important in planning your career.

Once you've identified a career, learning about it firsthand will help you determine if you have, in fact, made the right decision and it will clarify how you should pursue that goal. One approach is to work as a co-op student in the career you've chosen to pursue. Whether you are allowed to perform the work you eventually want to do full-time or simply observe others as a junior employee, a co-op position will give you an up-close look at the realities of your chosen career. There's no point spending years training for a job, only to discover you don't like it once you've been hired. A stint as a co-op student also acts as a kind of prolonged job interview during which the employer can more accurately assess your suitability, and this could eventually translate into a job. So, as a co-op student, you may acquire a future job prospect, a potential positive reference, or at the very least, information about other companies that are hiring in your area of interest. Almost all colleges and universities offer co-op programs, which typically place the student in at least three different work settings, each paying a weekly salary of between $400-500. As a rule, co-op students will always be hired before non-co-op students According to the director of recruitment and college relations for General Mills, "About a third of our offers to new grads go to people who've already worked for us as interns. We plan to raise that to between 40 percent and 50 percent."

Unfortunately, given the current unemployment rate, even co-op students can't always find short-term work. A variation of the co-op experience is "job shadowing," which allows you to follow around a professional for a week or two. Even though you won't be paid, this approach could lead to a job referral and, as with the co-op experience, offers you an excellent opportunity to solicit feedback from people already employed in the field. To arrange a job shadowing opportunity with an appropriate company, call the human resources department of a company, the department you're interested in, or, if it's a small company, the president, and explain what you want to do. Try your luck with smaller companies since employees perform a wider variety of functions, giving you a more

BULLETIN BOARD

TIPS:

➤ For valuable assistance in charting a future course among many possible futures, refer to Peter Schwartz's book, *The Art of the Long View: Planning for the Future in an Uncertain World.*

➤ Cut out want ads in career areas that interest you over time and date them. This will give you a feel for hiring and qualification trends.

➤ Look for *Profit* magazine's list of the 100 fastest growing Canadian companies with the best five-year growth in revenues (usually the June issue) and list the companies by industry to determine which industries and companies are performing well.

➤ There are a variety of books and magazines that predict trends. Three very reliable sources are *The Futurist* magazine, which publishes articles on the changing economic scene; *Future Survey*, which reviews books devoted to various aspects of the future; and *The Futures Research Directory*, which lists the various organizations and publications devoted to future research. *The Economist, The World Competitiveness Report, The World Investment Report, Global Economic Prospects and the Developing Countries,* and *World Employment Outlook* are excellent tools that will help you assess the competitiveness of a company, industry, or country. For anyone with a computer and a modem, on-line information services—Internet, CompuServe, Prodigy, and America On-line, for example—provide access to a wide variety of resources.

complete picture of a job's responsibilities.

Another way of finding out what a career is really like is through volunteer work. Many charitable organizations are short of funds these days and eager for volunteers. They are also taking an increasingly serious approach to volunteer management, hiring and training volunteers as if they were paid staff. Look for an organization that has a well-managed volunteer program and is interested in helping you gain the experience you want. Volunteer work is especially useful for acquiring managerial, project management, teamwork, and interpersonal skills. Don't forget that since many highly placed people spend time working with non-profit organizations, volunteer work can be an opportunity to make contacts and demonstrate your abilities. Moreover, as part of your role as a volunteer, you'll probably be called upon to contact other organizations, both profit and non-profit—yet another chance to network and investigate the job market.

You can also learn about a specific career by joining a trade or professional association, attending their meetings, seminars, or trade shows, and introducing yourself to members and association executives. Many people find useful job-hunting information through networking—who is hiring and who is not, what skills an employer is looking for, and so on. Association journals and newsletters will inform you about job opportunities, current developments in the profession, and the relative competitiveness of the companies you're interested in working for.

Even in more stable times, career planning was never a once-only event. It is an ongoing process. As you grow and change, your goals and expectations change as well, and these changes must be taken into account when developing a career strategy. And as economic realities shift, you must be ready to respond, constantly keeping an eye on shifts in your field and related businesses, always keeping contingency plans in more than one back pocket.

Your career survival depends upon your knowing how to market yourself effectively, and to do that, you must have a clear sense of your values, strengths, weaknesses, and career and life goals. You'll also need to understand how your skills and qualities can be transferred to new work situations. Personal and professional security—a strong sense of who you are and what you want—will take the place of job security. As well as knowing what you want—including what you expect—from any organization you work with, you must understand who your clients are within as well as outside of the organization. Only by learning to balance your own needs with these other, sometimes competing needs can you maintain the enthusiasm, motivation, and attitudes necessary to survive in a highly competitive environment. Job seeking is no longer just a brief activity undertaken until work is secured, but the very real task of negotiating your own personal identity and psychological stability.

Persistence will also be crucial. In many ways, we're all embarking on a competitive job marathon, and many will drop out along the way. The biggest challenge will be to maintain your determination and drive regardless of how disappointing or frustrating your job—or jobless—situation gets. If you're unemployed, getting a job must become a full-time occupation. If you try often enough, you'll not only succeed in eventually landing a job, but your ability to persevere will make you successful in the long run.

Flexibility and the Ability to Deal With Strees

Flexibility is essential when facing an uncertain future where the only constant is change itself. Mergers and acquisitions will upset the career plans of those who never anticipated that their company might be

---

PORTRAIT OF THE FLEXIBLE WORKER

The U.S. Congress's Office of Technology Assessment (1988) has developed the following list of "adaptive skills":

- *Skills of Problem Recognition and Definition:*
  - recognizing a problem that is not clearly presented;
  - defining the problem in a way that permits clear analysis and action;
  - tolerating ambiguity.
- *Handling Evidence:*
  - collecting and evaluating evidence;
  - working with insufficient information;
  - working with excessive information.
- *Analytical Skills:*
  - brainstorming;
  - hypothesizing counter arguments;
  - using analogies.
- *Skills of Implementation:*
  - recognizing the limitation of available resources;
  - recognizing the feedback of proposed solution to the system;
  - the ability to recover from mistakes.
- *Human Relations:*
  - negotiation and conflict resolution;
  - collaboration in problem solving.
- *Learning Skills:*
  - the ability to identify the limits of your knowledge;
  - the ability to ask pertinent questions;
  - the ability to penetrate poor documentation;
  - the ability to identify sources of information.

---

bought by or merged with another company. The end result could include a location transfer, more responsibility, or even a demotion. Employees will need to learn to expect change— changes in the company's values, their jobs, and their co-workers. The ability to adapt and clearly demonstrate your contribution to the company will become necessary survival skills.

In the new flattened organization, where information flows freely and strategies, procedures, and products are constantly changing to meet the customer's needs and challenges from competitors, you will have to be flexible to survive. As your job or job description changes constantly, you'll be required to learn new sets of skills. You'll be expected to juggle different functions and responsibilities. For example, you may have to learn a new job while training someone else to do your former job. Working in teams will also require flexibility and may mean your having to learning new skills—the interpersonal ones.

These changes in the workplace have the potential to create enormous anxiety at a time when life is already stressful. According to the 1993 "World Labor Report" by the United Nation's International Labor Organization, "Stress has become one of the most serious health issues of the twentieth century." Today's economic realities are only adding to it. A 1993 study of 12 large Canadian companies by Bryan Downie and Mary Lou Coates of Queen's University's Industrial Relations Centre, cites "incredible change, uncertainty, reorganization, and the fear of job loss" as significant stress-producing factors. One of the human resources professionals interviewed for the study compared this environment to "being told you're going whitewater rafting forever."

There are certain resources that people can use to deal with stress. There are plenty of books and magazine articles on the subject, suggesting strategies such as exercising, meditating, watching your diet, attending counselling sessions, moving closer to work to avoid long commutes, and changing attitudes and behaviour. Beyond this, you should make sure there's a comfortable fit between your needs, abilities, and expectations and the career you pursue. As your working situation changes and becomes less secure—if you are working at home, working on contract, or self-employed—it's more important than ever to build both personal and professional support networks. Form alliances with others working in the same or related fields to share work, information, and provide a sympathetic ear and sound advice during difficult times. You may also consider forming partnerships or group benefit programs, since knowing that you're not properly insured can be a major source of stress. As always, make sure you have contingency plans for tough times.

Fortunately, companies are already acknowledging the relationship between stress and reduced or sluggish productivity and are beginning to focus on ways of relieving stress for their workers. Companies may introduce flextime, job sharing, a partnership approach to management, or job redesign. Some companies even hire someone to take care of daytime errands for workers.

Why this sudden concern from employers? Their interest likely stems from their need for employees who will remain enthusiastic, committed, and trustworthy, even though for these workers there are few, if any, opportunities for promotion and little job security. In an increasingly competitive business environment, companies need dedicated employees who can be trusted to make their own decisions and thus foster the success of the company. As Matthew Barret, chairman of the Bank of Montreal, puts it, "It is innovation that is crucial to staying ahead and this relies on people and the effectiveness of their managers. This implies giving heavy weight to development of human resources. Not the least benefit from investing in employees is what it does for their commitment to the firm. If they know you value them enough to invest in them, they develop confidence in their ability to make a difference. That is the real meaning of empowerment. Empowerment, if it is not to be anarchy, has to take place within an understood framework of controls. The combination is the basis for a relationship built upon trust, fairness, openness, and recognition of achievement. And it helps make a firm a living culture rather than a lifeless organization chart."

The smartest employers will not only want to know what you can do for them, but also what they can do for you. Whether you're on staff or on contract, good companies will want to reduce your stress by clarifying where you fit into the company's overall objectives, and helping you develop skills that not only meet the company's goals but are consistent with your career strategy. Of course, this means that you must be clear about your career objectives.

Marti Smye, chairwoman of People Tech Consulting Inc. in Toronto, describes how the Co-operators Group Ltd., a major insurance company, began a career planning process for its managers at all levels 15 years ago. A week was spent with each employee every year and everyone was assigned a peer mentor. The approach worked. Employee turnover dropped and lateral career moves tripled in the first three years. According to Smye, "People changed more than their jobs. They said their personal relationships improved, they undertook health and fitness programs and generally felt happier. By finding a meaning in life, people found meaning in work."

In the corporate environment Smye describes, managers will be like coaches who help you see that your skills offer a number of career opportunities either with the company or with other companies. That, in turn, should give you a greater sense of control over your life and career. If disaster does come, at least you will have prepared alternatives. In fact, don't be surprised if companies start trading workers willing to move, much the way professional sports teams trade players in order to create the most effective team. Most athletes realize they will only play for a given team for a short period of time, yet they also know that the new team that acquires them will genuinely value their talents and will want to develop their skills. By understanding your own strengths, weaknesses, and career objectives, you have a better understanding of just how well you will fit in to any given work environment.

Not all companies will be this smart, however, and even those with good intentions will take some time to reach this nirvana of employee empowerment. For many who are employed, the roles that will be demanded of them will be very stressful. And a company's good intentions can vanish in the crunch—during mergers and acquisitions, for example. In *Working Scared,* Kenneth Wexley and Stan Silverman list typical sources of stress as corporations are bought and sold in the new global economy: getting saddled with too many responsibilities by your mean-and-lean company; uncertainty over what your role is; conflict over how you should do your job; fear of losing your job; concern about where your career is going; politics and power struggles; little or no feedback on your performance; autocratic and distant leadership. In such situations, your focus must remain steadfastly on how you can make the best of a bad situation. Prepare yourself for the possibility of extra responsibility, demotion, or transfer. Threatening as they may sound, all such changes can offer important career development opportunities, as long as you keep your head. More than ever before, it's necessary to keep a positive outlook and prove your worth by staying visible, performing well, and

---

TESTING YOUR PERSONALITY

One way to acquire objective information about yourself is through personality assessments. The following are just a few of the most widely used assessments, divided into two categories: *overall* and *career-specific.*

These *overall* personality tests are useful in career planning:

- the 16PF measures 16 dimensions of personality;
- the California Psychological Inventory measures managerial potential, work orientation, leadership potential, social maturity, and creative potential;
- the Personal Style Inventory is designed to empower individuals by helping them achieve greater personal flexibility, increasing their respect for individual diversity and their responsiveness to change;
- the Wonderlic Personnel Test assesses an applicant's ability to learn, solve problems, adapt, and understand instructions;
- the Meyer-Kendall Assessment Survey measures personal attributes related to work performance, especially in an office setting;
- the Supervisory Practices Inventory reveals the way people are being supervised versus the way they would like to be supervised;
- the Personnel Performance Problems Inventory focuses on responsibility, authority, accountability, results, and conditions;
- the Time Problems Inventory, Time Use Analyzer, and the Time Perception Inventory deal with time management related issues;
- the Leadership Ability Evaluation measures leadership abilities, behaviour, and style;
- the FIRO-B predicts and explains personal tendencies in team situations and projects, leader and subordinate roles, supervision and delegation, and conflict and communication;
- the Myers-Briggs Type Indicator is an easy-to-understand assessment that divides people into 16 different types and is commonly used with the Strong-Campbell Vocational Interest Inventory.

High school, college, or university career counselling departments also use many strictly *career-related* assessments. These assessments do not reveal your personality so much as match up your personality with career areas.

promoting and documenting your accomplishments. And, of course, what was true in the past will be even truer in the future: you should always be upgrading your skills and have on hand an updated resumé, a large network of contacts, and a contingency plan.

Losing your job can be devastating, but when it does happen, try to remain positive. Concentrate on looking for new opportunities and finding appropriate training. The new global economy is knowledge-based and therein lies future job security. As Dian Cohen notes, "In a knowledge-based economy, people have again become assets. The more they know, the more valuable they are." If you find training that takes you in the same direction as the market, you'll eventually find employment.

Communication and Interpersonal Skills

Working effectively with others has always been key in any career. Even those who work primarily on their own need to be able to relate to others at certain times. Many a brilliant career has been undermined because of personality or communications problems, while others with weaker ideas or less ability forge ahead because of their skill at getting along with people.

Qualities such as leadership, effective communication, empathy, and cooperation will be even more important in the workplace of the future. Since many companies are restructuring and job descriptions are in a constant state of flux, there is bound to be considerable conflict, confusion, and misunderstanding amongst workers. You'll need to be able to deal with these situations if you want to survive and thrive. According to Jerald Hage and Charles Powers, the authors of *Post-Industrial Lives: Roles and Relationships in the 21st Century*, work in the future will involve constantly shifting goals for which no set of rules or procedures can be specified in advance. Although relationships on the job will become less routine and more personalized, they will also become more conflict-ridden, because without specific rules and guidelines, disagreements over what is expected are bound to occur.

In order to work successfully in a team, you'll need strong communication skills so that you can explain to your team members exactly what you're doing and really hear what they're telling you. To ensure that the group functions with a minimum of conflict, you and your co-workers will need to show mutual respect, criticize constructively and reassuringly, and display empathy. Everyone needs to be both a leader and a follower in order to get the job done. Team members should be able to ask managers or other team members for clarification; they should feel comfortable about speaking frankly and tactfully about any reservations they have about a project. They will also need to develop tolerance for "diversity"—a popular buzzword that recognizes that successful companies must focus on finding the best person for the job, regardless of race, gender, disability, lifestyle, or personal beliefs.

PORTRAIT OF AN ENTREPRENEUR

According to Dorothy Leeds, author of *Marketing Yourself,* the most successful workers of the future will be those who apply marketing principles to their careers. Leeds identifies the following as the ten marketable skills that characterize the "career entrepreneur."

- *Adaptability:* "An effective marketer isn't resistant to change, but views it as a challenge and an opportunity";
- *Commitment:* "With so many similar products and services today competing for the same markets, the commitment of the salesperson is often the deciding factor";
- *Communication:* "Increase your selling power by improving your communication: Be sure your message is received the way that you sent it and meant it";
- *Creativity:* "Selling is a creative problem—how best to get what you want while giving the customer what he or she needs";
- *Decision making:* "Marketing often requires quick and confident decisions. That doesn't mean you have to be right all the time—we learn from all of our decisions",
- *Evaluation:* "The best sales question you can ask yourself is, 'How can I do better next time'";
- *Foresight:* "Marketing must be consistently future-oriented for a product or service to survive in a rapidly changing world";
- *Independence:* "The more we rely on our own sales and marketing abilities, the more self-assured we become";
- *Team Playing:* "Interdependence and trust are the essential relationship builders";
- *Value-Added Marketing:* "Knowing what people want and giving them more than they expect."

Of course, every team will have its power struggles and conflicts. But ultimately, each team member will need to learn how to build trust, confidence, and commitment in their fellow team members so they can work together to get the job done.

In a 1993 *Harvard Business Review* article, Peter Drucker predicted that these skills will soon become just as important as the more traditional requirements in hiring decisions:"Being an educated person is no longer adequate, not even educated in management. One hears that the [U.S.] government is doing research on new job descriptions based on subject

---

BASIC AND ADVANCED CAREER SURVIVAL SKILLS

According to "Learning Well, Living Well," a consultation paper produced for the federal government's Prosperity Initiatives Program that addresses Canadian educational issues, the following are the *basic skills* workers of the future will need:

- the ability to learn;
- reading, writing, and computation skills;
- speaking and listening skills;
- skills and values needed to achieve high self-esteem, motivation, and goal setting;
- career development skills;
- interpersonal skills;
- an understanding of how the organization that employs them functions.

The following *advanced skills* are critical to an employee's becoming a successful "insider" in a business organization:

- the ability to apply mathematical and scientific principles;
- the ability to adapt to and operate comfortably in a rapidly changing technological environment;
- the ability to operate effectively in team environments, which often comprise people of diverse social and cultural backgrounds;
- the ability to work effectively in both official languages and in the languages of competitor nations, and to be sensitive to the history and culture of other parts of Canada and other countries;
- the ability to be entrepreneurial and innovative in many areas—not only in design and research and development, but in the management of people and information.

---

knowledge. But I think that we can probably...leap right over the search for objective criteria and get into the subjective—what I call *competencies*. Do you really like pressure? Can you be steady when things are rough and confused? Do you absorb information better by reading, talking, or looking at graphs and numbers? I asked one executive the other day: 'When you sit down with a person, a subordinate, do you know what to say?' Empathy is a practical competence. I have been urging this kind of self-knowledge for years, but now it is essential for survival."

How well do your interpersonal skills stack up? Just as you analyzed your strengths and weaknesses in choosing your career and planning your job search strategy, you'll need to understand where you're already successful and where you need help. In order to accomplish this ego-challenging task, you'll have to find out what other people think of you. You might go so far as to ask a trusted friend to collect anonymous character reports from workers and other friends as though the friend were a human resource specialist carrying out a reference check. At a minimum, make sure you get continuous feedback on your performance from your supervisors and other team members. Difficult as it may be, try to look at the information objectively rather than become defensive. Think of it as helpful information that lets you know where you stand and what you need to do in order to achieve your goals. By learning to help yourself improve, you'll also learn how to help others, which is the essence of leadership. Even if you've been playing the mentor role yourself, make sure you have someone to act as *your* mentor. No one is ever too old to learn, even from those who are younger.

Entrepreneurship

The final skill that will be crucial for survival in the future job market is entrepreneurship. Given the high job turnover expected in the future, everyone will have to learn to market themselves. A 1992 U.S. Labor Market report predicts that college graduates will change jobs 7.5 times over the course of their working lives, with four of these changes being involuntary. Job seekers will need to continually refine their interview skills, improve their business network connections, and expand their resumés. Assertiveness and hustle will have to become second nature. Since most employment in the future will be contractual, the ability to sell yourself will be critical. Even if you spend most of your career in a

BULLETIN BOARD

- Traditional tools, such as testing, can help you choose and plan a career. But be prepared to constantly revise your strategy.
- Co-op programs are a crucial part of landing a job, particularly in high-tech industries. If co-op work isn't an option, get experience and make contacts any way you can.
- Never stop marketing yourself, even when you have a job.
- The ability to adapt to constant change and deal with the resulting stress will be crucial to your career success and personal happiness. Look for employers who recognize the problems of stress and address them in their workplaces.
- Interpersonal skills will be crucial. Get help in evaluating and developing yours.
- Use your entrepreneurial skills not only for your employer but for yourself. Your career success will depend on your ability to market yourself.
- Keep one eye on your bank account and one eye on the skills listed in your resumé. The two are closely related.

more traditional employer-employee relationship, corporate structures of the future will require that you become a more independent worker who thinks constantly in terms of selling to the customer. As Jim Hansberger, senior vice- president at Shearson Lehman Hutton puts it, "People who recognize it's salesmanship that distinguishes them from the competition are the ones who are going to forge ahead. To make it successfully into the 21st century, we must be market-oriented and sales-minded."

Whatever your career strategy and situation, you'll need to manage and market yourself as though you were a small business. This means you will need a marketing plan that aggressively promotes the product that you should know everything about—yourself. Like any company, you will need to know your industry and its future opportunities and challenges. With this information at your fingertips, you can make sure your product—you—undergoes appropriate improvement on an ongoing basis so that you will always have buyers interested in your product. Knowing your

BULLETIN BOARD

TIPS

The following books offer practical and psychological insights that will help you in your career planning.

➤ *Future Edge,* by Joel Barker, describes the psychological paralysis that prevents us from responding to change.

➤ *The Learning Enterprise,* by Lewis Perelman, advocates an openminded and optimistic approach to the economic uncertainties of the future.

industry will also tell you how you can make yourself stand out against your competitors.

In short, you need to look at your career as a business. And as a business, your bottom line is simple: the more marketable skills you have, the more choice you will have; the fewer marketable skills you have, the less choice you will have. To start with, your English and math skills must be excellent and you must know how to translate technical information or raw data into everyday language, measure productivity, compile statistics, and organize and balance budgets.

To increase your chances of acquiring a stable career, when you're job hunting, think about your resumé as well as paying your rent. Look for jobs with companies that will help you develop the skills you'll need for your career of choice. If you choose jobs because of salary alone, you may be cheating yourself in the long run. You may have to take on various jobs that are lower-paying along the way, but these can prepare you for taking greater responsibility and may enhance your resumé overall.

The company that hires you will evaluate you from a cost/benefit perspective. It's unlikely that you'll be hired unless you can convince management that you will improve their competitiveness and productivity. Your payment level will reflect their opinion of how well you can do that. Companies will need to be flexible, requiring employees to do a wide variety of tasks. For example, the factory workers at Krueger International Canada Inc., a contract furniture manufacturer, must be able to read and understand balance sheets and financial statements, use a computer, drive a forklift, participate in collective decision making, conduct interviews of prospective employees, and lead a work team. So, the more skills you offer, the more valuable you'll be.

Entrepreneurship may ultimately extend to starting your own business. With companies of all sizes outsourcing or contracting out peripheral functions to small businesses, there will be a growing demand for small firms that can provide the latest services at competitive rates. More and more people are taking this route and many of them are prospering. Statistics Canada reports that in 1990 self-employed workers in incorporated firms in the service industries earned 35 percent more than paid workers, and self-employed workers in unincorporated businesses took home 14 percent more in pay. Women are gravitating toward self-employment in increasing numbers. Between 1971 and 1991, the number of self-employed women increased by 265 percent in Canada.

As Dorothy Leeds, author of *Marketing Yourself*, explains, the new economy is creating a cultural shift to a more entrepeneurial society. While that shift may at times be frightening, it also has its rewards. "There is a new spirit that's revitalizing the way we work in this country. It has nothing to do with mysticism or spiritual rebirth. It has to do with what we want out of work, what we chose to do with our lives, and how, when, and where we chose to do it."

The Last Word

Prospering in the job market of the future will call for our having a greater degree of awareness and flexibility than most of us have ever experienced in our working lives. Cultivating these survival qualities is particularly important given the troubling state of our nation, as summed up by Judith Maxwell, head of Queen's University's Policy Studies: "Canada, in 1993, is a country with many of the earmarks of a war-shattered economy. We have a mountain of debt; discredited political institutions; a lost generation of young people who cannot find work; industry that is only slowly shifting to the new knowledge base; a growing underground economy; a social safety net that is tilted toward the poverty trap; and an extraordinary degree of discord... There are many people in leadership today who seem overwhelmed by this. They see their job as short-term survival: steering the ship away from the closest reef. They are so focussed on the reefs that they are not trying to turn the ship around and head for the open sea."

Given even the most optimistic scenario for the Canadian economy, we must all develop the skills necessary to survive and prosper in an extremely competitive era as developing countries demand their fair share of economic prosperity. With 100 million migrants worldwide at the moment and an additional 47 million job seekers entering the world labour market every year, the only security will reside in what you know and what you are capable of achieving. The good news is that if you plan your career strategically, you can not only survive during any period of change, but ride the crest of global opportunities and choice, which will be both more challenging and more rewarding than anything we have yet witnessed.

APPENDIX: CAREER PROSPECTS

"Career Prospects," reprinted from *Prospects Canada*, Fall 1993, by permission of Career Information Partnership Canada. The economic factors discussed in this book should be taken into consideration when analyzing the government projections contained in this appendix.

Occupations are listed alphabetically. A brief work description is provided for each.
Employment: Refers to the industries where the occupation can be found.
Education and Training: Describes the educational and training requirements of the occupation.
Subjects: Suggested fields of study related to the occupation.

Salary: The annual average salary for the occupation (based on 1986 Statistics Canada Census; adjusted to 1992 using Consumer Price Index).
Outlook: Arrow indicates the projected growth rate (1900-2000) for the occupation: ↑ =high growth; ↗ =moderate growth; → =stable; ↘ =moderate decrease; ↓ =strong decrease; (based on Canadian Occupational Projection System, and Immigration Canada, 1992).

OCCUPATIONS	WHAT YOU NEED	OUTLOOK & SALARY	
BUSINESS, FINANCE AND ADMINISTRATION			
ACCOUNTANTS Work as Chartered Accountants (CAs), Certified General Accountants (CGAs) or Certified Management Accountants (CMAs) in a number of areas, such as auditing, taxation, external reporting, insolvency and reconstruction, management accounting and financial accounting (treasury). **Employment:** Medium- or large-sized firms, government.	**Education and training:** Secondary school graduation (or equivalent) plus mature student status (for CGA candidates); university degree (for CA and CMA candidates); completion of formal studies and practical experience, with periodic examinations; registration, certification or licensing requirements in most provinces and territories; professional accreditation. **Subjects:** business, accounting, law, economics.	↗	$41,152
AUTO PARTS CLERKS Receive and sort incoming stock of automotive parts and supplies, maintain inventory of stocks, sell stock to customers and requisition or order stock as required. **Employment:** Retail stores, wholesalers, repair shops.	**Education and training:** High school completion is usually required; automotive parts apprenticeship (3 to 4 years); or several years experience in auto parts stores plus college parts clerk course; Red Seal certification (interprovincial) is available. **Subjects:** Auto, business.	↗	$26,572
BOOKKEEPERS Maintain complete sets of books or records of financial transactions carried out by businesses or other establishments. May use computer software accounting packages to perform bookkeeping activities. **Employment:**	**Education and training:** High school completion is required plus courses in accounting or bookkeeping; or several years experience in financial, bookkeeping or accounting work; or college program in accounting or related	↗	$24,705

Banks, insurance companies, wholesalers.

Occupation	Salary
CLAIMS ADJUSTERS/INVESTIGATORS — Investigate insurance claims for damage or loss. Determine the amount of damage or loss and whether the policyholder is covered. **Employment:** Insurance firms. **Education and training:** Secondary school completion is required; a bachelor's degree, college diploma or some post-secondary education or several years of experience is required. **Subjects:** Business, law.	◄ $29,011
DESKTOP PUBLISHING OPERATORS OR SPECIALISTS — Operate electronic publishing and word-processing equipment to design, lay out and produce camera-ready copy for brochures, manuals, bulletins, books, newsletters, in-house and other publications. Use computer graphics software to provide illustrations for publications. **Employment:** Typesetting firms, newspapers. **Education and training:** High school completion is required; college graphic arts program; or training in computer typesetting or desktop publishing or typography is usually required. **Subjects:** Art, English, graphics, visual arts.	◄ $25,778
GENERAL OFFICE CLERKS — Record and process information. Type and file correspondence, reports and other materials. Answer telephones and attend to counter inquiries. Operate photocopiers and perform other clerical activities. **Employment:** Public and private sectors. **Education and training:** High school completion is preferred; business or high school commercial courses may be required; typing or word-processing skills may be required. **Subjects:** Business, English.	◄ $25,111
HOSPITAL ADMINISTRATORS — Are responsible for the general administration, including financial controls, of a hospital or other health care institution. Develop policies to set the direction and goals of the hospital/health care institution and usually report to a board of directors. **Employment:** Hospitals, health care institutions. **Education and training:** University degree or college diploma in business or hospital administration or related discipline is usually required; extensive experience (10 to 15 years) in subordinate positions in hospital/health administration is usually required. **Subjects:** Business, English, family studies.	◄ $73,919
HUMAN RESOURCES/PERSONNEL MANAGERS — Develop and put into place programs for hiring and training employees. Classify jobs and install pay and benefits procedures. Organize and may conduct employee information sessions and develop management training programs. Also attend to many other personnel problems and details. **Employment:** Medium- or large-sized firms, government. **Education and training:** University degree in business administration, industrial relations or a related field; or professional development program in personnel administration plus extensive experience as a personnel officer. **Subjects:** Social studies.	◄ $48,073

LOAN OFFICERS

Interview persons who want loans or credit, and evaluate their financial and credit status and their ability to repay the loans. Can authorize loans or credit up to an amount set by the institution or recommend approval of larger amounts to a loan manager. **Employment:** Bank, trust companies, credit unions.

Education and training: High school completion plus several years general banking experience; or university degree or college diploma related to commerce or economics; internal loan or credit training program (6 to 12 months) is usually provided. **Subjects:** Business, mathematics.

▲ $41 152

MEDICAL RECORDS TECHNICIANS

Process, code, store and retrieve medical records and statistics of medical patients. Usually operate computerized record-keeping systems. **Employment:** Hospitals, health care institutions.

Education and training: High school completion is required; college medical records technician course (1 to 2 years); or Canadian Hospital Association correspondence course plus work experience in medical or other record keeping. **Subjects:** Mathematics, keyboarding, business, health care.

▲ $23,127

PURCHASING OFFICERS

Purchase the goods, materials, supplies and services needed to operate a business. Determine requirements, negotiate prices and delivery. **Employment:** Retail stores, government offices.

Education and training: A bachelor's degree or college diploma in business administration, commerce or economics is usually required. **Subjects:** Business, marketing, retailing.

▲ $38,544

RECEPTIONISTS

Greet people entering offices or reception areas and direct them to appropriate persons or services. Answer telephones, take messages and schedule appointments. May type data. Perform other clerical duties. **Employment:** Public and private sectors.

Education and training: Some high school, but high school completion is preferred; specific typing speed or word-processing experience may be required. **Subjects:** Office procedures, word processing.

◄ $21,060

SECRETARIES

Type correspondence, reports and other data. Arrange and schedule appointments, meetings and business travel. Operate word processors, typewriters, microcomputers and other electronic office equipment. May take dictation using shorthand. Perform many other clerical and administrative duties. **MEDICAL AND LEGAL SECRETARIES** usually have specialized training, and **EXECUTIVE SECRETARIES** usually have considerable secretarial experience. **Employment:** Public and private sectors.

Education and training: High school completion is usually required; college secretarial program (1 to 2 years); or previous clerical experience including typing or word processing; college legal or medical secretarial program (1 to 2 years) is usually required for these specializations. **Subjects:** English, office procedures, word processing.

▲ $23,584

	Salary
SHIPPERS AND RECEIVERS Record and ship parts, supplies, equipment and other materials from manufacturing plants, wholesale and retail warehouses and other storage facilities. Inspect and record goods received. May pack, unpack, load or unload goods, move goods into storage or route goods to storage areas. May also operate computerized inventory systems. **Employment:** Retailers, wholesalers, manufacturing companies.	**Education and training:** High school completion and some warehouse experience are usually required. **Subjects:** Business.	↑ $26,430
STOCKBROKERS Advise clients on investment opportunities, and buy and sell mutual funds, bonds, stocks, commodity futures and other securities on clients' behalf. May work for individual investors or institutions. **Employment:** Investment and stockbrokerage firms.	**Education and training:** University degree in economics, business administration or a related discipline; or high school completion plus extensive experience; Canadian Securities Commission examination; licensing. **Subjects:** Business, mathematics.	↖ $64,556
TELLERS Serve customers at banks or other financial institutions. Process customers' cheques or cash deposits, withdrawals, credit card payments and other banking transactions. Calculate foreign exchange currency. Perform related clerical duties such as balancing cash and preparing and filing statements. **Employment:** Banks, credit unions, trust companies.	**Education and training:** High school completion is required; on-the-job training is provided. **Subjects:** Accounting, keyboarding.	↖ $18,677
WORD PROCESSOR OPERATORS Type correspondence, reports, financial statements, charts and other data. Operate word processors, typewriters and microcomputers. Also usually perform some clerical duties such as photocopying and filing. **Employment:** Public and private sectors.	**Education and training:** Some high school, but high school completion is preferred; word processing course certificate may be required; specific typing speed is usually required. **Subjects:** Word processing, business, English, graphics.	← $22,532

NATURAL AND APPLIED SCIENCES

	Salary
AIR PILOTS Operate airplanes to transport passengers and cargo to and from scheduled destinations and to provide services such as aerial surveying, spraying and crop dusting, and search and rescue. Also operate helicopters. **Employment:** Crop spraying companies, flying schools, airlines.	**Education and training:** High school completion; flying school certification; or aviation school completion; commercial pilot's licence; Canadian restricted telephone certificate (Department of Transport Canada); Department of Transport Canada special ratings or endorsements for flying different types of aircraft. **Subjects:** Mathematics, sciences, geography.	→ $72,553

AIR TRAFFIC CONTROLLERS

Direct air traffic within a particular airspace to ensure safe landings and takeoffs of aircraft and to control the activities of all moving aircraft and service vehicles on airport tarmacs. Observe aircraft from airport towers. Watch radar and other monitors. Operate radio and other communications and electronic equipment. **Employment:** Federal government, airlines.

Education and training: High school completion; Department of Transport Canada's air traffic controller's training program completion; telephone operator's licence; air traffic controller's licence. **Subjects:** Mathematics, sciences.

➤ $47,343

ARCHITECTS

Design buildings and develop plans regarding design specifications, materials, cost and construction time. May specialize in designing residential, industrial, commercial, institutional or public buildings (for example, fire stations, airports, museums, galleries). **Employment:** Architectural firms, government, construction.

Education and training: University degree in architecture; or 8 years on-the-job training with registered architect plus syllabus of studies from the Royal Architectural Institute of Canada; provincial/territorial examinations; internship (2 years). **Subjects:** Mathematics, sciences, art, graphics.

➤ $43,877

BIOLOGICAL TECHNOLOGISTS AND TECHNICIANS

Conduct laboratory tests and analyses, field surveys, and perform other technical activities for scientists and engineers. Work in areas such as agriculture, resource management, plant and animal biology, microbiology, cell and molecular biology; health science, and in fish hatcheries and greenhouse and livestock production programs. (Technologists perform their duties under general supervision, often independently, while technicians usually work under the direct supervision of professionals or technological staff.) **Employment:** Laboratories, chemical companies.

Education and training: College technologist's diploma (2 to 3 years) or technician's (1 to 2 years) in a field related to agriculture, biology, microbiology, wildlife or resource management. **Subjects:** Biology, chemistry, mathematics.

➤ $33,957

BIOLOGISTS

Conduct studies to extend knowledge of living organisms, their characteristics and behaviours. May specialize in a particular field such as zoology, botany, virology, microbiology or entomology. Often work in laboratories or in field settings. **Employment:** Universities, hospitals, government.

Education and training: University degree in biology, biochemistry or a related natural science; master's or doctorate degree is usually required for research scientists. **Subjects:** Mathematics, chemistry, biology, physics.

➤ $44,617

BIOMEDICAL TECHNOLOGISTS

Install, calibrate, test, modify and repair electrical, electronic and electro-mechanical medical equipment in hospitals and other health care institutions. Usually instruct nursing and other staff in the use of monitoring or

Education and training: College electronics or electrical engineering technologist's diploma (2 to 3 years) plus experience in hospital biomedical department or courses in biomedical engineering technology. **Subjects:**

➤ $33,957

Occupation and description	Education and training	Average salary
other patient care equipment. **Employment:** Communications, electrical and electronics industries.	Mathematics, technical studies.	
CHEMICAL TECHNOLOGISTS AND TECHNICIANS Perform various technical functions for scientists or other professionals involved in areas such as chemical and biochemical research and analysis, industrial chemistry, chemical engineering and environmental monitoring. (Technologists perform their duties under general supervision, often independently, while technicians usually work under the direct supervision of professionals or technological staff.) **Employment:** Hospitals, government, food processing companies.	**Education and training:** College technologist's program (2 to 3 years) or technician's program (1 to 2 years) in chemical, biochemical, chemical engineering or related discipline is usually required; university degree in chemistry or biochemistry may be required for chemical technologists. **Subjects:** Mathematics, chemistry.	↑ $38,417
CHEMISTS Conduct basic research into the chemical properties, composition and structure of substances, and conduct applied research to develop new or improved materials, compounds and substances for industrial, commercial or other purposes. Carry out quality control programs in manufacturing plants, investigate chemical aspects of drug action and perform other research and development activities. May specialize in areas such as biochemistry and analytical or physical chemistry. **Employment:** Scientific firms, mining companies, hospitals.	**Education and training:** University degree in chemistry, biochemistry or a related discipline; master's or doctorate degree is usually required for research chemists; licensing may be required. **Subjects:** Mathematics, chemistry, physics.	↘ $42,821
CIVIL ENGINEERS Plan, design, develop and manage projects for the construction or repair of structures such as bridges, dams, ports, water and waste management systems, pipelines, roads and buildings. Also conduct feasibility, traffic pattern, environmental impact and other studies for construction proposals, and make recommendations. **Employment:** Railways, construction, electrical utilities.	**Education and training:** University degree in civil engineering or a related engineering discipline; registration as a professional engineer is often required. **Subjects:** Mathematics, sciences.	↘ $53,771
COMPUTER ENGINEERS Plan, design, develop and test computers and related equipment for applications in process and machine control, robotics, instrumentation, environmental monitoring, remote sensing and related engineering and scientific applications. Also design and develop computer software. **Employment:** Banks, insurance firms, software companies.	**Education and training:** Bachelor's degree in computer or electrical or electronics engineering or engineering physics, computer science or mathematics or a related discipline; registration as a professional engineer may be required. **Subjects:** Mathematics, computer science, business.	◀ $41,957

COMPUTER PROGRAMMERS

Write detailed step-by-step instructions or programs that tell a computer what it must do to solve a problem. May work as application programmers and write programs or software for specific jobs such as accounting and inventory control, or as systems programmers who write programs for software that controls the operation of an entire computer system. **Employment:** Banks, software companies, government.

Education and training: Bachelor's degree in computer science or related discipline such as mathematics or commerce; or college computer science diploma; post-secondary study or experience in science, engineering or other technical areas is usually required for application programmers in those fields. **Subjects:** Mathematics, computer science, business.

◄ $41,957

COMPUTER SYSTEMS ANALYSTS

Analyze business, scientific, engineering or other technical requirements or problems, and design computer systems to meet clients' needs. Write specifications for computer programmers to implement and follow. Plan and implement computer security systems. Develop computer languages or software packages. **Employment:** Insurance and software companies, government.

Education and training: Bachelor's degree in computer science, mathematics, commerce, business administration or engineering; or college computer science diploma plus extensive experience in computer programming; post-secondary study or experience in science, engineering or other specialized technical areas may be required. **Subjects:** Mathematics, computer science, business.

◄ $41,957

DRAFTSPERSONS

Prepare accurate working or detailed drawings for construction, engineering, manufacturing, mapping, machinery installations and other purposes. Work from notes, sketches, calculations, specification sheets and other data. Usually operate computer-aided drafting and design systems (CAD/CAM). **Employment:** Construction, manufacturing, engineering.

Education and training: High school completion is usually required; college drafting diploma; or apprenticeship (4 years) in drafting or several years related experience plus college or industry drafting courses. **Subjects:** Mathematics, sciences, industrial drafting and design.

◄ $35,252

ELECTRICAL AND ELECTRONICS ENGINEERING TECHNOLOGISTS

Develop and test power equipment and systems; industrial process control systems; telecommunications, broadcasting and recording systems; computer systems and networks; and computer software. Conduct or supervise the installation and operation of electrical and electronic equipment and systems, and perform many other technical functions. Work under the general direction of engineers or other professional staff. **Employment:** Airlines, government, radio and TV networks.

Education and training: College electrical or electronics engineering technologist's diploma (2 to 3 years). **Subjects:** Mathematics, physics, electronics.

◄ $40,103

ELECTRICAL AND ELECTRONICS ENGINEERS

Design, plan and evaluate electrical and electronics equipment and systems, and direct or supervise installations, testing, inspection and maintenance activities. Specialize in many areas such as electrical power generation and transmission, communication systems, instrumentation and control systems, computer applications and software design. **Employment:** Communications, engineering, electrical utilities.

Education and training: University degree in electrical or electronics engineering or an appropriate related engineering discipline; registration as a professional engineer is usually required. **Subjects:** Mathematics, physics, electronics.

$52,767

FOREST TECHNOLOGISTS AND TECHNICIANS

Conduct and supervise forest inventories and surveys. Assist in the preparation of forest management and harvesting plans. Monitor activities of logging companies. Supervise and participate in tree seeding, planting and nursery operations and other forest preservation activities. **Employment:** Forest industry, government, consulting firms.

Education and training: College forestry technology course (1 to 3 years) is usually required. **Subjects:** Agriculture (resources), biology.

$35,046

GEOLOGISTS

Conduct exploration and research programs to extend knowledge of the structure, composition and processes of the earth and surface and subsurface waters; to locate oil, natural gas and mineral deposits; and to plan the extraction or exploitation of those resources. Also advise in areas such as waste management and selection of sites for construction purposes. **Employment:** Mining companies, government.

Education and training: University degree in geology or a related discipline. **Subjects:** Mathematics, sciences, geography.

$61,275

HOME ENTERTAINMENT EQUIPMENT TECHNICIANS

Diagnose problems and repair radios, TVs, VCRs, tape decks and compact disc players. **Employment:** Retailers, wholesalers, engineering.

Education and training: Completion of a college program (2 to 3 years) in electronics or completion of a 4-year apprenticeship program in electronics servicing and repair. **Subjects:** Mathematics, physics, business, electronics.

$29,234

INDUSTRIAL DESIGNERS

Develop designs and prepare specifications for a wide variety of products to be manufactured (such as furniture, electronics, keyboards, mechanical products). **Employment:** Manufacturing, design firms.

Education and training: University degree in industrial design, architecture or engineering; or college industrial design diploma plus work experience in industrial design; portfolio. **Subjects:** Physics, art, graphics.

$29,369

INDUSTRIAL ENGINEERS

Determine the most effective and efficient ways for an organization to use the basic elements of production – people, machines, materials, informa-

Education and training: A bachelor's degree in industrial engineering or in a related engineering discipline is required; registration as a professional

$47,540

tion and energy. **Employment:** Manufacturing, transportation, engineering.

LANDSCAPE ARCHITECTS

Plan and design the landscaping of parks and other public areas, subdivisions, buildings and building grounds, private residences and other areas. Plans include features such as trees, shrubs, gardens, walkways, patios, lighting and fences. **Employment:** Architectural and landscaping firms, development agencies.

Education and training: University degree in landscape architecture is usually required; extensive (minimum 7 years) landscaping experience plus college landscape architecture diploma may be accepted; licensing may be required. **Subjects:** Mathematics, sciences, art, construction, agriculture.

$43,877

MARINE ENGINEER OFFICERS

Operate the main engines of ships and other water transport vessels, as well as the machinery and auxiliary equipment such as boilers, steering and deck machinery, motors, pumps and generators. Also supervise the engine room crew. **Employment:** Marine transportation, government, Canadian Forces.

Education and training: High school completion is required; marine engineering cadet program (3 years); or 30 months engine room crew sea service plus 6 months approved formal training in marine engineering institute; or 30 months experience as a mechanic plus minimum 6 months sea service. **Subjects:** Physics, technical studies.

$47,648

MECHANICAL ENGINEERS

Research and design machinery and systems for heating, ventilating and air conditioning, power generation, transportation vehicles, processing and manufacturing and other activities. Also perform functions related to the installation, operation and maintenance of machinery and systems. **Employment:** Engineering, manufacturing, mining companies.

Education and training: University degree in mechanical engineering or in a related engineering discipline; registration as a professional engineer is usually required. **Subjects:** Mathematics, sciences.

$52,237

METEOROLOGISTS

Analyze and interpret information received from meteorological stations, satellite imagery and computer models to forecast the weather. Research weather patterns and climates, and the transportation of pollutants by the atmosphere. **Employment:** Broadcasting universities, research laboratories.

Education and training: Bachelor or Master of Science degree in meteorology or a closely related field; doctoral degree is usually required for research scientists in meteorology; formal training is provided by the Atmospheric Environment Service (up to 6 months). **Subjects:** Mathematics, physics, geography.

$51,323

PHARMACOLOGISTS

Study the actions and effects of drugs and other substances on human and animal cells, tissues, organs and life processes. Test drugs for medicinal use dosages. **Employment:** Government, pharmacies, health clinics.

Education and training: Master's or doctorate degree in pharmacology or a related biological science is usually required. **Subjects:** Biology, chemistry, mathematics.

$44,617

PHYSICISTS

Conduct research to extend knowledge of natural phenomena and to develop innovations in fields such as electronics, communications, power generation and distribution, aerodynamics, optics and lasers, remote sensing, and medicine and health. **Employment:** Research centres, universities.

Education and training: Master's or doctorate degree in physics, engineering physics or a closely related field. **Subjects:** Mathematics, physics.

$53,661

SURVEYORS

Conduct surveys of land and establish the legal boundaries and ownership of land. Prepare and maintain the associated records and drawings or maps. Operate electronic and non-electric survey equipment to measure distances, angles and land elevations. **Employment:** Private sector land surveying, government

Education and training: University degree in survey science or civil engineering; or college survey technology diploma; articling period; licensing. **Subjects:** Mathematics, physics.

$36,625

URBAN AND LAND USE PLANNERS

Prepare plans for zoning, transportation, public utilities, community facilities, parks, housing and related services for cities, towns and rural areas. Also prepare and recommend plans for the provision of wildlife preserves, national and provincial parks, protection of watersheds and the prevention of soil erosion. **Employment:** Government, land developing, engineering.

Education and training: University degree in urban design, planning, geography, engineering or a related discipline; graduate degree in regional and urban planning, design and environmental planning, architectural engineering or a related discipline is usually required; association membership is usually required (Canadian Institute of Planners). **Subjects:** Geography, social studies.

$49,101

HEALTH

AUDIOLOGISTS

Diagnose hearing problems using specialized audiometric equipment and plan and implement rehabilitative programs for patients, including the selection and fitting of hearing aids or devices. **Employment:** Hospitals, schools, rehabilitation centres.

Education and training: University degree in audiology; certification with Canadian Audiology and Speech Language Pathology Association is mandatory. **Subjects:** Social sciences, sciences.

$40,341

CHIROPRACTORS

Diagnose patients' conditions. Adjust and manipulate the spinal column and other parts of the body. Employ massage, heat, electrical and other therapies to treat patients' disorders. **Employment:** Private practice.

Education and training: 4-year program at an accredited chiropractic college after 2 year undergraduate studies in science; examination; licensing. **Subjects:** Sciences, social sciences.

$55,884

Job	Description	Education and training	Salary
COMMUNITY AND HOSPITAL PHARMACISTS	Prepare and dispense pharmaceuticals according to doctors' prescriptions. **INDUSTRIAL PHARMACISTS** formulate and test newly developed drug products. **Employment:** Drugstores, hospitals, large supermarkets.	**Education and training:** A Bachelor of Science in pharmacy; supervised practical training for community and hospital pharmacists; licensing for community and hospital pharmacists. **Subjects:** Chemistry, mathematics.	► $44,971
DENTAL ASSISTANTS	Assist dentists during the examination and treatment of patients. Sterilize and maintain instruments and equipment. Take X-rays and perform routine laboratory procedures and other duties as directed. **Employment:** Dental clinics.	**Education and training:** High school completion is preferred; college program (3 months to 1 year); or on-the-job training; certification required for intra-oral duties. **Subjects:** Dental assisting, office procedures.	► $24,000
DENTISTS	Diagnose and treat diseases, injuries, malformations and other disorders of the teeth, gums and surrounding tissues, and prescribe and administer preventive procedures. May specialize in areas such as orthodontics periodontics, endodontics and dental surgery. **Employment:** Private practice.	**Education and training:** Dentistry degree; licensing (general practice); licensing (dental specialization). **Subjects:** Mathematics, chemistry, physics.	◄ $66,992
DIETITIANS	Plan, administer and supervise food preparation and service programs in commercial establishments, hospitals, schools and other educational institutions. Act as consultants to private companies, government and individuals in the areas of nutrition, diet and food selection. Also plan special therapeutic diets and menus for hospital patients and others. **Employment:** Hospitals, personal care homes, government.	**Education and training:** Bachelor's degree in dietetics, nutrition or a related science such as food and nutritional science or biochemistry; 1 to 2 years supervised practical training; certification (Canadian Dietetic Association). **Subjects:** Chemistry, home economics.	◄ $37,729
EMERGENCY MEDICAL TECHNICIANS (PARAMEDICS)	Provide emergency medical care to sick or injured persons until and while they are transported to hospitals or other medical facilities. Administer cardio-pulmonary resuscitation (CPR) and oxygen. Connect equipment for persons with ventilation or circulation complications. Provide other life support care. Apply bandages and splints. Also care for patients during air ambulance flights. **Employment:** Hospitals, government, manufacturing.	**Education and training:** High school completion is preferred; college, hospital-based or other recognized emergency medical technology program (up to 24 months); or courses in emergency health care plus supervised practical training; certification; emergency vehicle licence. **Subjects:** Health care, sciences.	◄ $25,587

Occupation		Salary
MEDICAL LABORATORY TECHNOLOGISTS Conduct laboratory experiments. Test and analyze human blood, tissue or other samples to assist in the diagnosis, treatment and prevention of disease. **Employment:** Hospitals, clinics, laboratories.	**Education and training:** Bachelor of Science degree or equivalent; or college medical laboratory technologists program (2 to 3 years) plus supervised practical training; certification (Canadian Society of Laboratory Technologists) is usually required. **Subjects:** Mathematics, chemistry, biology.	◄ $34,108
NURSES (RNs) Provide nursing care to patients in hospitals, clinics and other health care agencies, in doctors' offices and in private homes. Also provide nursing services to students in schools and to employees in government offices, industrial plants and other establishments. May specialize in hospital units such as cardiology, surgery or obstetrics; in public, occupational or industrial health; or as consultants or researchers. **Employment:** Hospitals, schools, health clinics.	**Education and training:** College nursing program completion; or Bachelor of Science degree in nursing; or regional hospital or independent school of nursing diploma; registered nurse certification; additional education, nursing courses or training are required for specializations. **Subjects:** Mathematics, chemistry, English, biology, health care.	◄ $33,380
NURSES AIDES AND ORDERLIES Assist with the care of patients in hospitals, nursing homes and other health care facilities. Perform activities such as feeding patients, transporting them in wheelchairs or on stretchers, lifting them, bathing and dressing them, and taking and recording their temperatures. **Employment:** Hospitals, nursing homes.	**Education and training:** Some high school, but high school completion is preferred; college or institution nurse aide, health care or long-term aid program (3 to 5 months); or college nursing orderly program (10 to 12 months); or on-the-job training. **Subjects:** Mathematics, sciences, English, health care.	↖ $23,939
OCCUPATIONAL THERAPISTS Plan and carry out specially designed activities for patients with physical or mental health problems to enhance or help patients regain their ability to care for themselves and to engage in work and recreational pursuits. Advise on health risks in the workplace or other environments, and on the modification or addition of equipment to assist persons with disabilities. **Employment:** Hospitals, rehabilitation services, nursing homes.	**Education and training:** Bachelor of Science degree in occupational therapy or rehabilitation; period of field work; national certification examination; licensing or registration. **Subjects:** Chemistry, physics, English.	◄ $32,719
OPTICIANS Fit clients with prescription glasses or contact lenses. Help clients select frames and order the lenses. May grind, polish, cut, edge or otherwise finish lenses and fit lenses into frames. Instruct clients on the use of contact lenses. **Employment:** Optical retail outlets, optical dispensing firms.	**Education and training:** College program (2 to 3 years) and apprenticeship; or night school program (2 to 3 years) plus supervised practical experience; or 2-year correspondence course plus supervised practical experience; licensing is usually required. **Subjects:** Physics.	↖ $29,439

PHYSICIANS AND SURGEONS Conduct physical examinations of patients. Prescribe laboratory and other tests. Make diagnoses. Prescribe medicines and treatments for diseases, disorders and injuries. Perform surgery. Advise patients on preventive medicine techniques. May specialize in a particular type of medicine such as family practice, cardiology, orthopaedics, neurology or obstetrics. **Employment:** Hospitals, clinics, government.	**Education and training:** Bachelor of Science degree plus medical degree; internship or residency program is required for family or general practitioners; internship plus residency plus lengthy training (up to 7 years) including subspecialty training are required for specialists. **Subjects:** Sciences, mathematics, English, health care.	◄ $72,280
PHYSIOTHERAPISTS Plan and carry out physical treatments to maintain, improve or restore the physical functioning of patients with muscle, bone, nerve or joint problems. Use equipment such as ultrasonic and microwave machines, infrared and ultraviolet lamps, laser and other electrotherapeutic equipment, as well as massage and therapeutic exercises. **Employment:** Hospitals, physiotherapy clinics.	**Education and training:** Bachelor's degree in physiotherapy; supervised clinical practice; registration. **Subjects:** Chemistry, physics, biology, physical education.	◄ $35,581
RADIOTHERAPY TECHNOLOGISTS Administer radiation treatments to cancer patients as prescribed by physicians called **RADIATION ONCOLOGISTS**. Operate and monitor specialized radiotherapy equipment. May also help prepare sealed radioactive substances to apply to the patient's body. **Employment:** Hospitals, X-ray clinics.	**Education and training:** High school completion; college, hospital school or other approved program (2 years) in radiation therapy plus supervised practical training. **Subjects:** Mathematics, physics, chemistry, biology.	◄ $35,143
REGISTERED NURSING ASSISTANTS (RNAs) Assist registered nurses in providing nursing care to patients. RNAs with operating room technician's training set out surgical instruments and perform other activities to assist surgical teams. RNAs who obtain a specialized certificate may assist in dispensing drugs and medications to patients. Are sometimes called certified or licensed nursing assistants or licensed practical nurses. **Employment:** Hospitals, nursing homes, clinics.	**Education and training:** College- or hospital-based RNA diploma; additional academic training or on-the-job training is required for operating room technicians; licensing is usually required. **Subjects:** Mathematics, chemistry, biology, health care.	◄ $25,091
RESPIRATORY THERAPISTS Operate and monitor specialized medical equipment to treat patients with breathing difficulties caused by disorders such as asthma, emphysema, bronchitis, pneumonia and heart disorders, or to treat heart attack victims or patients experiencing complications after surgery or other medical	**Education and training:** High school completion; college or hospital respiratory therapy (2 to 3 years) including clinical training; licensing may be required. **Subjects:** Mathematics, chemistry, biology.	◄ $35,411

problems. Also provide home care. **Employment:** Hospitals, health care institutions.

ULTRASOUND TECHNOLOGISTS (MEDICAL SONOGRAPHERS)
Operate and monitor specialized equipment that produces and records images of the body's internal parts. Record the imaging on film, tape or computer. Report the results to physicians to assist them in diagnosing patients' conditions. **Employment:** Hospitals, clinics.

Education and training: Completion of an approved allied training program such as diagnostic radiology, nuclear medicine or nursing plus college- or hospital-based program (1 year) in diagnostic medical sonography and supervised practical training; certification and registration are usually required. **Subjects:** Technical studies.

▲ $26,073

VETERINARIANS
Diagnose and treat diseases and disorders in animals. Inoculate animals, set bones and perform surgery on animals. Advise owners of animals on feeding, hygiene, preventive measures against disease and general health care of animals. **Employment:** Veterinary clinics, private practice.

Education and training: Preveterinary university undergraduate studies (2 to 4 years) or CEGEP health science program diploma in veterinary medicine; national certification examination; licensing. **Subjects:** Chemistry, mathematics, physics.

↘ $44,777

SOCIAL SCIENCE, EDUCATION AND GOVERNMENT SERVICE

EARLY CHILDHOOD EDUCATORS/PRESCHOOL TEACHERS
Plan, organize and lead children in activities, such as indoor and outdoor games, crafts, singing and music sessions and story times, to help the children develop intellectually, physically and emotionally. **Employment:** Daycare centres.

Education and training: Bachelor's degree or college diploma in early childhood education; or Bachelor of Education degree. **Subjects:** Child care, family studies, social studies.

↘ $40,039

ECONOMISTS
Research and analyse economic data and prepare estimates, forecasts and reports on the basis of past and current economic trends. This information is used by governments, educators, businesses, industries and others to help them in planning their future activities and projects. **Employment:** Government, banks investment companies.

Education and training: Bachelor of Economics degree (minimum); graduate degree in economics is usually required. **Subjects:** Mathematics, economics, political studies, computer science, history.

↘ $50,506

ELEMENTARY SCHOOL TEACHERS
Plan lessons that are appropriate for the particular grade or grades being taught according to approved curricula. Teach subjects such as reading, writing, arithmetic, social studies, natural science and computer operation. In senior elementary grades, may specialize in particular subjects such as

Education and training: Bachelor of Education degree; undergraduate degree; provincial/territorial teaching certificate. **Subjects:** Mathematics, sciences, English.

↘ $40,039

music, physical education, mathematics or science. **Employment:** Elementary schools.

ESL/FSL TEACHERS (TEACHERS OF ENGLISH OR FRENCH AS A SECOND LANGUAGE)

Teach English or French to civil servants or teach immigrants and others who wish to learn either of Canada's official languages. (To teach in educational institutions, ESL and FSL teachers require the same qualifications as other teachers.) **Employment:** Government, specialized schools.

Education and training: Bachelor's degree with a specialization in education, linguistics or a related area is usually required; ESL or FSL certification is usually required; teaching experience is usually required. **Subjects:** English/French, family studies.

$46,407

HIGH SCHOOL TEACHERS

Prepare lessons according to approved curricula and teach academic subjects such as mathematics, music, science, history and literature; technical and vocational subjects such as auto mechanics, machine shop, drafting and hairdressing; or business subjects such as typing and accounting. Pupils include high school students and adults. **Employment:** Junior and senior high schools.

Education and training: Academic teachers – undergraduate degree plus Bachelor of Education degree (1 year course) or a Bachelor of Education degree (3 to 4 years). Technical/vocational/business teachers – Bachelor of Education degree; high school completion or college diploma plus specific number of years experience in subject(s) taught; provincial/territorial teaching certificate. **Subjects:** Mathematics, sciences, English, family studies, social studies.

$46,407

HOME ECONOMISTS (HUMAN ECOLOGISTS)

Provide information and advice to individuals, groups and the general public on subjects such as food and nutrition, family relations and studies, housing and interior design, clothing and textiles, and other consumer products. Teach in schools and also work in many different areas such as food or consumer products testing, journalism, marketing and product development, and food service. **Employment:** Government, consulting firms, schools.

Education and training: Degree in home economics/human ecology. **Subjects:** Family studies, social studies, home economics.

$36,100

LAWYERS

Interpret the law and advise clients on legal matters. Plead cases and conduct prosecutions in law courts. Draw up legal documents such as contracts and wills. Represent clients at courts or other assemblies. Lawyers may specialize in areas of law such as criminal, corporate, commercial, real estate, family, estate and labour law. **Employment:** Law firms, government.

Education and training: Bachelor's degree in law; articling period; bar admission course; bar exam; licensing. **Subjects:** Law, English, social studies.

$53,247

MARKET RESEARCH ANALYSTS Conduct research on market conditions in local, regional or national areas to determine the sales levels for particular products or services and to assess potential markets and future trends. **Employment:** Government, marketing firms, business associations. **Education and training:** University degree in economics, commerce or a related discipline is usually required. **Subjects:** Business, social studies, mathematics.	◄ $50,506
PARALEGALS Research records and court files and prepare legal documents, court and other reports and affidavits. Interview clients. Perform other activities to assist lawyers in law firms or in legal departments of companies or governments. **Employment:** Law firms, government. **Education and training:** University degree in law; or college legal assistant or law clerk program; or paralegal in-house training in a law firm or other legal establishment. **Subjects:** English, mathematics, keyboarding, law.	◄ $32,307
PROBATION AND PAROLE OFFICERS Provide general supervision of criminal offenders serving probationary terms or serving the remainder of sentences after being released into the community on parole. **Employment:** Government, community centres, correctional centres. **Education and training:** Bachelor's degree in social work, criminology, psychology or other related social science is required. (Note: For parole officers, experience plus passing a university equivalency test may substitute for formal education requirements.) **Subjects:** Social studies, law, family studies.	◄ $34,440
PSYCHOLOGISTS Study or diagnose behavioural, mental and emotional disorders. May work in clinical practices and provide counselling and therapy to clients to help them overcome or adjust to personal, marital, social, vocational or other problems. **Employment:** Schools, hospitals, community health facilities. **Education and training:** Doctoral degree in psychology is preferred; master's degree in psychology may be acceptable; licence to practise is usually required. **Subjects:** English, social studies, family studies.	◄ $42,091
RECREATION AND SPORTS PROGRAM DIRECTORS/SUPERVISORS Plan, organize and supervise various sports programs (such as swimming, aerobics and fitness, gymnastics, tennis and team sports) or recreational activities (such as arts and crafts, drama, teen clubs, camping and outings) for senior citizens and persons with disabilities. Recruit and train full-time staff, volunteers and part-time leaders and instructors. May instruct or lead groups themselves. **Employment:** Municipalities, community or professional athletic organizations. **Education and training:** University degree in physical education, recreology, sports administration or related disciplines; or college diploma in recreation plus experience in recreation and sport activities. **Subjects:** Languages, business, social studies, physical education.	◄ $27,062

Occupation	Description	Education and training	Salary
REHABILITATION TEACHERS	Teach blind or sight-impaired students to read and write braille. Instruct deaf or hearing-impaired students in lip reading, finger spelling and sign language and help them develop the ability to speak. Teach physically disabled students to use aids that lessen the effects of their disabilities. Teach in elementary and high schools and may also teach school curricula. Are often called special education teachers. **Employment:** High schools, elementary schools.	**Education and training:** Bachelor of Education degree; teaching certification; certificates/diplomas in special education programs. **Subjects:** Social studies, family studies, physical education.	$29,220
SCHOOL AND GUIDANCE COUNSELLORS	Advise students on course selection and career planning. Counsel students regarding personal and social issues such as family problems, self-esteem, drug and alcohol abuse and depression. **Employment:** Schools, counselling centres, government.	**Education and training:** Bachelor's degree in education; graduate courses in counselling usually required; teacher's certificate is required; some teaching experience is usually required. **Subjects:** Family studies, community services, social studies.	$44,832
SOCIAL WORKERS	Help people who have personal, financial, medical, housing, marital or other problems. Provide counselling to individuals and groups, and may refer them to other professionals or social services for assistance. May specialize in a particular age group or area such as adults, youth, geriatrics or clinical social work. **Employment:** Community services, hospitals, correctional facilities.	**Education and training:** Undergraduate degree in social work; graduate degree is preferred. **Subjects:** Family and community services, languages, social studies.	$34,440
SOCIOLOGISTS	Study the origins, development and activities of human society. Also study the family, community, education, industrial relations, crime, politics, poverty and other social issues. Conduct surveys, analyze data and present their findings, which are often of interest to the general public. **Employment:** Government and private sector.	**Education and training:** Master's or doctoral degree in sociology is usually required. **Subjects:** Family studies, social studies, history.	$40,930

ART, CULTURE, RECREATION AND SPORT

Occupation	Description	Education and training	Salary
ANNOUNCERS AND BROADCASTERS	Introduce programs, interview guests and read the news, weather and traffic conditions, commercials and other announcements for radio and television. May specialize in broadcasting sports activities, weather reports, film	**Education and training:** High school completion; college radio or television arts program is usually required; auditions are required. **Subjects:** Dramatic arts, English.	$37,610

Occupation	Education and training	Salary
reviews or other subject matter. **Employment:** Radio and TV stations, advertising firms.		
AUDIO AND VIDEO RECORDING TECHNICIANS Operate specialized electronic equipment to record stage productions, live programs or events, and studio recordings. Edit and reproduce tapes for compact discs, records and cassettes, for radio and television broadcasting and for motion picture productions. **Employment:** Film, video and concert production, sound recording firms.	**Education and training:** High school completion is usually required; college or other program in recording engineering or audio-visual production; or experience in a recording studio as an assistant. **Subjects:** Music, electronics.	▲ $34,982
COMMERCIAL ARTISTS/GRAPHIC DESIGNERS Create graphics, illustrations and other artwork for magazines, advertisements, films, posters, signs and various publications. May also create logos for companies, organizations or individuals. **Employment:** Printers, publishers, graphic design firms.	**Education and training:** University degree or college diploma in visual arts with a specialization in commercial or graphic arts or photography; or high school completion plus on-the-job training in commercial or graphic arts; portfolio. **Subjects:** Art, commercial art, graphics.	↖ $31,221
CONSERVATION AND RESTORATION TECHNICIANS Clean dirt, paint, varnish and other substances from museum or gallery exhibits. Make minor repairs to paintings or other works of art. Apply preservatives and perform other tasks to conserve or restore exhibits. Work under the direct supervision of a conservator who may specialize in a particular field. **Employment:** Museums, art galleries.	**Education and training:** High school completion; college museum or conservation technology program completion; or extensive technical training with a conservator. **Subjects:** Technical studies.	↖ $29,916
EDITORS AND WRITERS Review, evaluate and revise or edit books, magazines, journals, manuals, press dispatches, scripts, newsletters, pamphlets and other material. Work in many different settings such as newspaper offices, publishing houses, radio and TV stations or may work freelance. **Employment:** Newspapers, magazines, publishing houses.	**Education and training:** University degree in journalism, literature, history or a related field is usually required (i.e., science degree for editors of scientific publications). **Subjects:** English, journalism, word processing.	▲ $39,628
FILM AND VIDEO CAMERA OPERATORS Use cameras and related equipment to record scenes for motion pictures, TV and video productions or to film news events, field assignments or other programs. **Employment:** TV networks, video production companies.	**Education and training:** High school completion is usually required; college program in film and video or a related field such as broadcasting is usually required; some on-the-job training; motion picture camera operators require considerable experience. **Subjects:** Art, graphics, technical studies.	↖ $31,675

	Salary
INTERIOR DESIGNERS Develop plans for the use of interior space in offices, public buildings, homes and other establishments. Prepare detailed sketches and three-dimensional models showing the arrangement of walls, lighting and other fixtures, and estimate costs and amounts of materials needed. **Employment:** Architectural firms, interior design firms, retail stores. **Education and training:** University degree in interior or architectural design; or college interior or architectural design diploma plus work experience in interior design; provincial/territorial association registration may be required; portfolio. **Subjects:** Art, graphics, visual arts.	$29,369
JOURNALISTS AND REPORTERS Conduct research, interview people and visit particular locations to collect background material about newsworthy events or topics of interest. Prepare stories for newspapers, other print media, radio, TV or film. May report the material on TV or in other media. Journalists and reporters may also travel to other countries as foreign correspondents to report on political unrest, wars or other news stories. **Employment:** Radio and TV networks, newspapers, magazines. **Education and training:** University degree or college diploma in journalism is usually required. **Subjects:** English, social studies, history.	$39,625
LIBRARIANS Develop, organize and maintain library collections of materials such as books, magazines, films, videos and reference publications and assist library users in locating and using these materials. Develop and operate computerized information systems to organize library collections and to locate or borrow requested items from other libraries. **Employment:** Libraries, universities, schools. **Education and training:** Master's degree in library science; librarian accreditation/certification is usually required. **Subjects:** English, social studies, keyboarding.	$35,580
LIBRARY TECHNICIANS Assist librarians in cataloguing new library books, manuscripts and other materials and in conducting reference searches. Assist library users in locating books, articles or other materials. Also operate computerized library systems and perform other library duties. **Employment:** Libraries, archives, schools. **Education and training:** High school completion is required; college library technician (1 to 2 years), or CEGEP certificate is usually required. **Subjects:** English, social studies, keyboarding.	$29,916
PHOTOGRAPHERS Operate still cameras to take pictures of people, events, scenes, products and many other subjects. May specialize in portraits; in commercial, industrial, medical or scientific photography; or in police work or photojournalism. **Employment:** Photography studios, magazines, newspapers. **Education and training:** Bachelor's degree in visual arts (specialization in photography); or college photography program; or extensive experience plus on-the-job training in photography; portfolio demonstrating creative and technical ability. **Subjects:** Art, graphics, visual arts, technical studies.	$31,675

PUBLIC RELATIONS CONSULTANTS

Organize and implement publicity or information campaigns designed to promote products, clients and services. Often represent clients in dealings with radio, TV and other media. **Employment:** Government, business associations.

Education and training: University degree or college diploma in public relations; communications, journalism or a related discipline is usually required. **Subjects:** English, social studies.

◀ $42,769

TRANSLATORS

Translate written documents from one language into another. May specialize in translating scientific, medical, legal or other technical documents. **INTERPRETERS** translate speeches, proceedings and individual conversations as they take place. Some interpret for people with hearing impairments, translating speech into sign language and vice versa. **Employment:** Translation and interpretation agencies, government, media.

Education and training: Bachelor's degree in translation with specialization at the graduate level is usually required for translators; college diploma in interpreting is the minimum requirement for interpreters; certified translator diploma may be required (Canadian Translators and Interpreters Council); knowledge of three languages may be required for translators and interpreters; knowledge of sign language may be required. **Subjects:** Languages, English.

◀ $40,162

SALES AND SERVICE

ADVERTISING MANAGERS

Direct and manage the activities of advertising departments or agencies which develop advertising and promotional programs to promote productions or services. **Employment:** Marketing and public relations companies, government.

Education and training: University degree or college diploma in public relations, communications or a related field such as public relations, are usually required. **Subjects:** Business, English, visual arts.

◀ $41,018

AIRLINE PASSENGER AND TICKET AGENTS

Issue tickets and assign or reserve seats. Check passengers' baggage. Prepare boarding passes. Announce flight information. Tend boarding gates and assist passengers who are preboarding. May look after baggage and cargo shipments and other duties at small airports. **Employment:** Airline companies.

Education and training: High school completion is usually required; formal on-the-job training is provided. **Subjects:** Keyboarding, languages, hospitality.

◀ $27,662

BAKERS

Prepare and bake bread, rolls, muffins, pies, cakes and other baked goods. **Employment:** Bakeries, grocery stores, hotels.

Education and training: Some high school, but high school completion is preferred; apprenticeship; or on-the-job training; trade certification may be required. **Subjects:** Baking, cooking.

◀ $23,537

BARBERS AND HAIRDRESSERS Cut and style customers' hair. May wave or colour hair, shave beards, shampoo hair and apply scalp treatments. **Employment:** Hairdressing salons, barber shops.	↖ $17,677*
Education and training: Some secondary school education is required; completion of an apprenticeship (2 or 3 years) or completion of a college program in hairstyling combined with on-the-job training is required. **Subjects:** Cosmetology.	
BARTENDERS Mix and serve alcoholic and non-alcoholic beverages to customers or prepare beverages for serving staff. **Employment:** Hotels, restaurants, clubs.	← $15,911
Education and training: Some high school, but high school completion is preferred; college bartending course; or mixology course; or on-the-job training. **Subjects:** Hotel/hospitality, business.	
BUYERS Select and buy merchandise to be sold in retail and wholesale stores. Study market reports and sales promotion materials, attend trade shows, visit factories and showrooms, and negotiate prices, shipping arrangements and other details to meet the stores' merchandise requirements. **Employment:** Wholesalers, retail stores.	↑ $35,641
Education and training: High school completion is usually required; university degree or college diploma in business, marketing or a related area is usually required; sales experience is required. **Subjects:** Business, family studies, marketing, retailing.	
CHEFS Plan menus and estimate food requirements. May supervise other chefs and cooks. May also prepare and cook food. Executive chefs in large hotels, restaurants, hospitals and similar establishments spend most of their time in administration and supervision activities and may cook only for special guests or occasions. **Employment:** Hotels, restaurants, clubs.	↖ $19,321
Education and training: Some high school, but high school completion is preferred; apprenticeship; or other formal training; 3 to 6 years commercial food preparation experience (additional cooking and supervisory experience are required for executive chefs); trade certification may be required. **Subjects:** Cooking, food services, home economics.	
COOKS Prepare and cook food in many different settings and have varying levels of responsibility. May cook complete meals or short-orders, or prepare special dishes or ethnic foods. May prepare menus, estimate food costs and order supplies or work under the direction of a specialist chef in a large hotel or restaurant. **Employment:** Airlines, hotels, restaurants, clubs.	↖ $19,321
Education and training: Some high school, but high school completion is preferred; apprenticeship; or 2 to 4 years commercial cooking experience; or on-the-job training; trade certification may be required; Red Seal certification (interprovincial) is available. **Subjects:** Cooking, food services, home economics.	
CORRECTIONAL SERVICES OFFICERS Guard prison inmates and detainees, and maintain order in penitentiaries, jails and other correctional institutions. **Employment:** Government, correctional facilities, juvenile institutions.	↑ $27,771
Education and training: High school completion is required; college program for correctional workers may be required. **Subjects:** Family and community services.	

Occupation	Education and training	Salary
FIREFIGHTERS Control and extinguish fires, conduct fire prevention programs and assist in other emergencies. **Employment:** Government, large industrial establishments.	**Education and training:** High school completion is required; firefighters training course is provided; specific physical requirements. **Subjects:** Technical studies, physical education.	↑ $45,756
FLIGHT ATTENDANTS Explain safety procedures to passengers and make announcements. Serve food and beverages. Attend to passengers' needs during flights. **Employment:** Airline companies.	**Education and training:** High school completion is required; Department of Transport Canada training program. **Subjects:** English, languages, hospitality, social studies.	↖ $32,805
FOOD SERVICE SUPERVISORS Direct, supervise and co-ordinate the activities of workers preparing and serving food in food service business. **Employment:** Cafeterias, catering companies, hospitals.	**Education and training:** High school completion is usually required; college food service administration or hotel and restaurant management or a related program; or several years experience in food preparation and service including some supervisory functions. **Subjects:** Home economics, food services, business.	↘ $25,111
HOTEL FRONT DESK CLERKS Register guests, assign rooms and issue room keys. Answer inquiries about hotel services. Compile and present bills to departing guests. Accept payments and prepare related records. May make reservations. Usually operate computerized hotel registration and accounting systems. **Employment:** Hotels, motels, resorts.	**Education and training:** High school completion is required; college front desk operations or hotel management program may be required. **Subjects:** English, languages, hospitality, keyboarding, social studies.	↑ $18,065
HOTEL MANAGERS Plan, direct and control the operations of hotels, motels, resorts or other lodging facilities. **Employment:** Hotels, motels, resorts.	**Education and training:** University degree or college diploma in hotel management or a related discipline; or several years experience working in various hotel positions including administrative and supervisory functions. **Subjects:** English, languages, family studies, food and hospitality, business.	↖ $29,471
INSURANCE AGENTS Sell life, fire, accident, automobile, endowment, marine and other types of insurance to clients. Calculate rates or premiums from charts and other predetermined data and arrange for payment schedules. Also attend to clients regarding insurance coverage after car accidents, fires or other calamities. **Employment:** Insurance companies.	**Education and training:** High school completion; industry-sponsored insurance training course is required; provincial/territorial licensing. **Subjects:** Marketing, business, social studies.	↘ $37,852

INTERNATIONAL MARKETING SPECIALISTS Conduct research on international markets and prepare marketing plans and strategies. Attend world and other fairs to market Canadian products and services. Travel to other countries to negotiate sales of products and services. **Employment:** Public and private sectors.	**Education and training:** Undergraduate degree in business administration, economics, commerce, marketing or a related discipline; specialization in international marketing may be required; MBA may be required; knowledge of a particular foreign language or languages may be required; foreign travel experience is an asset. **Subjects:** Business, social studies, geography, marketing.	➴ $50,506
JANITORS, CARETAKERS AND BUILDING SUPERINTENDENTS Clean and maintain offices, apartment houses, shopping malls, schools and similar establishments. Make minor repairs to plumbing, heating and electrical systems, and perform other maintenance activities such as painting, cutting grass and shovelling snow. May also advertise and show apartments, collect rents and supervise other workers. **Employment:** School boards, hospitals, shopping malls.	**Education and training:** Some high school, but high school completion is preferred; previous cleaning and maintenance experience may be required.	⬆ $22,932
MANUFACTURERS' AGENTS AND SALES REPRESENTATIVES Sell products in an allotted region to stores, wholesalers, professionals or manufacturers. Find new customers, quote prices, arrange delivery and keep up with new products. **Employment:** Wholesalers, manufacturers.	**Education and training:** Completion of secondary school is required; a university degree or completion of a college or other program may be required; experience in sales or in an occupation related to the product is usually required. **Subjects:** Retailing, marketing, business.	➴ $41,055
MEAT CUTTERS Cut meat carcasses into large portions for processing or packaging, and cut portions into steaks, chops, roasts and other specific cuts to be shipped to institutional, commercial or wholesale customers. **RETAIL BUTCHERS** prepare cuts of meat, poultry, fish and shellfish for sale in grocery stores, butcher shops and supermarkets, and often serve customers and cut meat to order. **Employment:** Meat packing plants, grocery stores, meat markets.	**Education and training:** High school completion may be required for retail butchers, college program in industrial meat cutting or retail meat cutting may be required; on-the-job training is usually provided for retail butchers.	⬆ $27,029
POLICE OFFICERS Detect and investigate crimes and arrest criminal suspects. Provide testimony in law courts and information on crime prevention and safety. Perform other activities to maintain law and order. Also patrol assigned areas on foot, motorcycle, horseback, bicycle, cruiser car or other vehicle. **Employment:** Government, Canadian Forces.	**Education and training:** High school completion is required; police training program is provided; specific physical requirements; college program or university degree in law and security is an advantage. **Subjects:** Languages, social studies, family studies, community services.	⬆ $47,215

REAL ESTATE AGENTS

Buy and sell houses, apartments, commercial and industrial buildings, land and other properties on behalf of clients. Estimate selling prices. Advertise and list properties. Arrange for clients to see properties. Advise clients on market conditions, mortgages and related matters. Draw up sales agreements. **Employment:** Real estate agencies, housing developers.

Education and training: High school completion is usually required; real estate training course is required; provincial/territorial licensing. **Subjects:** Retailing, marketing, business.

▲ $40,200

RESTAURANT AND FOOD SERVICE MANAGERS

Plan, direct and manage the operations of establishments serving food and beverages to ensure that good service is provided and that budgets are maintained. **Employment:** Hotels, restaurants, self-employment.

Education and training: High school completion; college restaurant management program; or several years experience in the food service sector including administrative and supervisory functions. **Subjects:** English, food and hospitality, home economics, business.

▲ $29,471

SALES CLERKS

Help customers select products and either receive payments of direct customers to cashiers. May need to be knowledgeable about the product if selling products such as fine china, yard goods, cameras, computers, hardware and building supplies, automobiles and motorcycles. **Employment:** Retail stores, wholesalers, other industries.

Education and training: High school completion is preferred; demonstrated sales ability and product knowledge are usually required for selling certain products. **Subjects:** Business, retailing.

▲ $26,572

SALES MANAGERS

Direct and manage sales departments or groups of salespersons directly or through subordinates. Approve or establish sales territories, sales quotas and objectives. Confirm or assign salespersons to territories. May determine prices, advertising and promotional activities. **Employment:** Retail stores, wholesalers, other industries.

Education and training: University or college program in business administration with a specialization in sales or marketing plus extensive sales experience is usually required. **Subjects:** Business, retailing, marketing.

◄ $41,018

SECURITY GUARDS

Watch entrances to plants or other buildings and issue passes. Perform security checks of passengers and luggage at airports. Patrol buildings and outside properties to guard against theft, vandalism, illegal entry and fire. May work as armoured car guards and pick up and deliver money and other valuables to stores, banks and other establishments, and must carry firearms to protect themselves and their cargo. **Employment:** Retail stores, wholesalers, other industries.

Education and training: Some high school, but high school completion is preferred; training is usually provided; firearms licence may be required.

▲ $27,771

Occupation	Education and training	Average income
TECHNICAL SALES SPECIALISTS Sell technical goods and services such as scientific and industrial products, electricity, telecommunications and computer services. May specialize in selling a particular line of goods or services. **Employment:** Manufacturers, pharmaceutical companies, computer service firms.	**Education and training:** High school completion is required; university degree or college diploma in a program related to the product or service is usually required; previous sales experience or experience in a related technical occupation is usually required. **Subjects:** Technical studies, business, marketing.	◄ $45,283
TRAVEL COUNSELLORS Provide information to clients on trip costs and schedules. Plan itineraries and reserve hotel rooms or other accommodation. Prepare air, train or other tickets. Receive payments and attend to other travel details for clients. **Employment:** Travel agencies.	**Education and training:** High school completion; college travel and tourism program may be required. **Subjects:** Geography, keyboarding.	◄ $27,662
VISITING HOMEMAKERS Look after individuals and families during times of illness, convalescence or some other family disruption. May look after infants and children or persons who are chair- or bedridden. Perform routine housekeeping duties and prepare meals. **Employment:** Government, home care agencies, self-employment.	**Education and training:** Some high school, but high school completion is preferred; certification may be required. **Subjects:** Family studies, health care, home economics.	◄ $27,062
WAITERS/WAITRESSES Take orders from customers and serve food and beverages to them. May also prepare and serve flambés and other specialty foods at customers' tables and recommend wines. **Employment:** Restaurants, hotels, clubs.	**Education and training:** Some high school, but high school completion is preferred; minimum of 6 months to 1 year experience is usually required for formal/French service. **Subjects:** Food services, hotel/hospitality, business.	▲ $14,190

TRADES, TRANSPORT AND EQUIPMENT OPERATION

Occupation	Education and training	Average income
AIRCRAFT MECHANICS Maintain, repair and overhaul, modify and install aircraft mechanical systems. **AIRCRAFT INSPECTORS** certify aircraft for airworthiness when the mechanical systems have met established standards for safety and performance. Some inspectors work as mechanics as well as being responsible for inspections. Aircraft inspectors are usually called aircraft maintenance engineers. **Employment:** Air transport firms, aerospace manufacturers.	**Education and training:** High school completion; college/CEGEP aircraft maintenance course (1 to 3 years) may be required; training of several years provided; licence (aircraft maintenance engineer) plus endorsements for specific aircraft and systems from the Department of Transport Canada are required for aircraft inspectors. **Subjects:** Mathematics, sciences, mechanics, electronics.	◄ $38,263

389

AIR TRANSPORT RAMP ATTENDANTS

Drive and operate vehicles and equipment such as food service trucks, aircraft-towing tractors, de-icer sprayers and lavatory service trucks at airports. Handle baggage, load and unload freight and perform other ground support duties. **Employment:** Airlines and air services, federal government.

Education and training: High school completion is usually required; driver's licence is usually required. **Subjects:** Technical studies.

$35,768

APPLIANCE SERVICERS/TECHNICIANS

Repair household electrical appliances such as refrigerators, stoves, washers, dryers and window air conditioners. May repair the appliances in customers' homes, in repair shops or in repair and service departments of companies. **Employment:** Repair shops, retail stores, wholesalers.

Education and training: High school completion is preferred; apprenticeship (3 years); or college program in appliance repair; trade certification may be required. **Subjects:** Technical studies, electrical, business.

$37,960

AUTO BODY REPAIRERS

Replace and repair damaged fenders, hoods, bumpers, doors, glass and other exterior parts of motor vehicles. Straighten bent frames and remove dents. Sand and paint motor vehicle bodies. Also repair and replace seat frame assemblies, upholsteries, floor coverings and other interior furnishings. **Employment:** Auto body repair shops, auto dealerships.

Education and training: Some high school, but high school completion is preferred; apprenticeship (4 years); or college automotive body repair technology program plus several years experience in auto body repair; trade certification may be required; Red Seal certification (interprovincial) is available. **Subjects:** Mathematics, auto body repair.

$29,152

AUTO MECHANICS/ TECHNICIANS

Repair and service the mechanical, electrical and electronic systems and components of cars, trucks and buses. May take extra training to specialize in a particular area of repair or to obtain special knowledge of cars from a particular manufacturer to repair and service them properly. **Employment:** Auto dealerships, service stations, truck transportation.

Education and training: High school completion is preferred; apprenticeship (4 years); or college automotive technology program (2 years) plus 2 years experience in automotive repair; trade certification is usually required; Red Seal certification (interprovincial) is available. **Subjects:** Mathematics, sciences, mechanics, electronics.

$29,152

BRICKLAYERS

Lay concrete blocks, bricks, precut stone and similar materials to construct or repair walls, foundations, fireplaces, chimneys, smokestacks and other structures. Line or reline furnaces, kilns and similar installations. Some bricklayers specialize in stonework and are called stonemasons. **Employment:** Construction contractors, self-employment.

Education and training: High school completion is preferred; apprenticeship (3 to 4 years); or 4 years experience in the trade plus college or industry courses in bricklaying; trade certification is usually required; Red Seal certification (interprovincial) is available. **Subjects:** Building construction, technical studies.

$31,937

Occupation	Education and training	Salary
BUS DRIVERS Operate buses and receive money, tickets or passes. **TRANSIT OPERATORS** operate subway trains and light rail transit vehicles to transport passengers over established routes. **Employment:** Urban transit systems, school divisions.	**Education and training:** Some high school, but high school completion is preferred; on-the-job training including formal instruction is provided; driver's abstract/record; age requirements; minimum 1 year driving experience is required; experience as a public transit bus driver is usually required for subway/transit operators.	$34,387
CABINETMAKERS Construct and repair cabinets, furniture, fixtures and similar products using mainly wood and wood-veneer materials. May construct built-ins or other special cabinets for custom orders. **Employment:** Furniture manufacturers, construction.	**Education and training:** High school completion is preferred; apprenticeship (3 to 4 years); or 4 years experience in the trade plus college courses in cabinetmaking; trade certification is usually required; Red Seal certification (interprovincial) is available. **Subjects:** Carpentry, technical studies, woodworking.	$23,861
CARPENTERS Construct, erect, install, renovate and repair buildings and other structures made of wood, wood substitutes and other materials. May specialize in residential, commercial/institutional, industrial, maintenance or restoration and renovation carpentry. **Employment:** Construction, wood products manufacturers.	**Education and training:** High school completion is preferred; apprenticeship (3 to 4 years); or 4 years experience in the trade plus college or industry courses in carpentry; trade certification is usually required; Red Seal certification (interprovincial) is available. **Subjects:** Building construction, carpentry, technical studies, woodworking.	$29,850
COMMERCIAL DIVERS Search for drowned persons, submerged watercraft, automobiles and other articles. Perform underwater construction activities such as welding, drilling and placing explosives. Perform many other activities using cameras, sonar and related equipment and cutting torches. **Employment:** Commercial diving, shipping and marine construction.	**Education and training:** Some high school, but high school completion is preferred; scuba certification; commercial diver's licence is usually required; provincial blaster's licence is usually required for setting and detonating explosives; medical certificate. **Subjects:** Technical studies, physical education.	$21,892
CONSTRUCTION MANAGERS Plan and supervise construction of roads and bridges, hydro-electric dams and buildings. Prepare cost estimates and timetables, arrange loans and co-ordinate work of construction trades. **Employment:** General contractors.	**Education and training:** A university degree in civil engineering or a college diploma in construction technology is usually required; several years experience in the construction industry, including experience as a construction supervisor or field superintendent, is usually required. **Subjects:** Construction, business, technical studies.	$52,162

Occupation	Education and training	Outlook	Salary
CONSTRUCTION MILLWRIGHTS Engage in the initial installation of machinery and mechanical equipment in industrial plants. **INDUSTRIAL MECHANICS** maintain and repair machinery and mechanical equipment, and usually operate machining tools to make replacement or other parts. **Employment:** Construction, industrial plants.	**Education and training:** High school completion is preferred; apprenticeship (3 to 4 years); or over 5 years experience in the trade plus high school, college or industry courses in millwrighting or industrial machinery repair; trade certification is usually required; Red Seal certification (interprovincial) is available for industrial mechanics (millwrights). **Subjects:** Industrial mechanics, technical studies, mathematics.	▲	$40,026
CRANE OPERATORS Operate cranes to lift, move, position or place machinery, equipment and other large objects at construction or industrial sites, ports, railway yards, offshore drilling rigs and other locations. Operate cranes equipped with dredging attachments to dredge waterways and other areas. **Employment:** Construction, industrial cargo handling companies.	**Education and training:** Some high school, but high school completion is preferred; apprenticeship (1 to 3 years); or college or industry courses in crane operating; or on-the-job training; trade or company certification is usually required; Red Seal certification (interprovincial) is available for mobile crane operators. **Subjects:** Construction.	◢	$39,691
DELIVERY DRIVERS Drive light trucks, vans or other motor vehicles to pick up and deliver various products such as newspapers, dairy products, drugstore items, dry cleaning, pizzas and groceries. **Employment:** Dairies, drugstores, newspapers.	**Education and training:** Some high school, but high school completion is preferred; 1 year driving experience is usually required; licence for type for vehicle driven.	◢	$28,431
DIESEL ENGINE MECHANICS Repair and maintain diesel engines in industrial, farm, construction and transportation equipment. **Employment:** Major trucking firms, railways.	**Education and training:** Some secondary school education is required; apprenticeship (4 years) or a combination of over 4 years of work experience in the trade and some high school, college or industry courses in heavy equipment repair is usually required to be eligible for trade certification. **Subjects:** Mathematics, mechanics, electrical.	▲	$28,431
DRYWALL INSTALLERS AND FINISHERS Measure, cut and install drywall sheets to form walls and ceilings in buildings and other structures. Install acoustic and other special ceilings. Apply careful finishing techniques to the seams so the seams won't show after they are painted. **Employment:** Construction contractors, self-employment.	**Education and training:** Some high school, but high school completion is preferred; apprenticeship (3 to 4 years); or over 3 years experience in the trade plus college or industry courses in drywall installing and finishing; trade certification may be required. **Subjects:** Construction.	◢	$30,348

Occupation	Education and training	Salary
ELECTRICAL POWER LINE AND CABLE WORKERS Erect and maintain poles and towers. Install overhead and underground power lines, cables, insulators, conductors, switches, transformers and other associated equipment. Work at heights from ladders or hydraulic lifts, or in confined spaces such as trenches and tunnels. May also work in isolated areas and rough terrain. **Employment:** Electrical utilities, construction.	**Education and training:** High school completion is required; government-regulated or internal company apprenticeship (4 years) is required; or college or CEGEP electrical technology/electricity courses plus 4 years experience in the trade; Red Seal certification (interprovincial) is available. **Subjects:** Mathematics, electrical.	▲ $49,287
ELECTRICIANS Install, test, troubleshoot and repair electrical wiring, fixtures, control devices and related equipment in houses and other buildings and structures. Often called construction electricians. **Employment:** Construction, industry.	**Education and training:** High school completion is usually required; apprenticeship (4 to 5 years); trade certification is usually required; Red Seal certification (interprovincial) is available. **Subjects:** Construction, mathematics, electrical.	▲ $38,075
ELECTRONICS EQUIPMENT SERVICE TECHNICIANS Install, service and repair home and office equipment such as stereos, TVs, VCRs, computers, printers and photocopiers. Work either at the customer's premises or remove the equipment to shops for testing and further repair. **Employment:** Public and private sectors.	**Education and training:** High school completion is usually required; apprenticeship (4 years); or college program in electronics (2 to 3 years); or college or technical school training in electronics servicing and repair plus on-the-job training. **Subjects:** Technical studies, electrical/electronics.	◄ $29,237
FLOOR COVERING INSTALLERS Install carpeting, wood flooring, linoleum, vinyl and other resilient floor coverings in residential, commercial, industrial and institutional buildings. **Employment:** Construction, floor-covering and carpet outlets.	**Education and training:** Some high school, but high school completion is preferred; apprenticeship (1 to 3 years); or over 3 years experience in the trade; trade certification is required. **Subjects:** Construction.	◄ $29,156
FORKLIFT OPERATORS Drive industrial trucks equipped with various attachments to move materials to and from storage areas and to place materials in designated locations. **Employment:** Retail stores, wholesalers, warehouses.	**Education and training:** Some high school, but high school completion is preferred.	◄ $33,622
GAS FITTERS Install, test and repair gas lines, meters, regulators, heating units and appliances in residential, commercial, institutional and industrial establishments. **Employment:** Gas utilities, gas servicing companies.	**Education and training:** High school completion is preferred; apprenticeship (3 years); or 2 to 3 years experience in the pipe fitting trade plus college or industry gas fitter program; trade certification is usually required; gas fitter licence is usually required. **Subjects:** Construction.	▲ $36,656

393

GLAZIERS Prepare, install and replace glass in residential, commercial and industrial buildings; on exterior walls of buildings and other structures; and in vehicles, furniture and other products. **Employment:** Construction, glass installation, retail services.	**Education and training:** High school completion is preferred; apprenticeship (4 years); or over 4 years experience in the trade plus college or industry courses for glaziers; trade certification is usually required; Red Seal certification (interprovincial) is available. **Subjects:** Construction.	◄ $28,953
HEAVY-DUTY EQUIPMENT MECHANICS Repair, overhaul and maintain heavy mobile equipment used in construction (such as bulldozers, cranes, graders and backhoes) as well as heavy mobile mining, forestry, material-handling, land-clearing, farming and similar heavy equipment. **Employment:** Heavy construction, construction equipment dealerships.	**Education and training:** High school completion preferred; apprenticeship (4 years); or over 4 years experience in the trade plus high school, college or industry heavy equipment repair courses; trade certification is usually required; farm equipment repair certification; mine equipment repair certification. **Subjects:** Mathematics, mechanics, auto.	▲ $40,026
HEAVY EQUIPMENT OPERATORS Operate backhoes, bulldozers, graders, dredgers, pavers, compactors, power shovels, side-booms and similar equipment used in the construction and maintenance of roads, bridges, airports and gas and oil pipelines; in the construction of buildings and other structures; in mining and quarrying activities; and in material-handling work. **Employment:** Construction, public works, pipeline industry.	**Education and training:** Some high school, but high school completion is preferred; apprenticeship (1 to 2 years); or college or industry courses in heavy equipment operation; or on-the-job training; trade certification may be required. **Subjects:** Construction, auto.	↖ $35,571
INDUSTRIAL PAINTERS Operate spray-painting, dip-painting or flow-painting equipment or systems, and painting machines, or use brushes or hand-held spray guns to apply various paints, lacquers and coatings to surfaces of equipment, parts and other items in manufacturing and industrial plants and other establishments. **Employment:** Construction, painting, building maintenance.	**Education and training:** High school completion is usually required; college or other training in automated painting systems may be required. **Subjects:** Construction, visual arts.	▲ $28,374
IRONWORKERS Assemble, join and erect structural ironwork, precast and reinforced concrete components, curtain walls and other metalwork used in the construction of buildings, bridges, tanks and other structures. Make, install and repair ornamental and other structures such as metal stairways, railings and power doors. May work at great heights. **Employment:** Construction, ironwork contractors.	**Education and training:** High school completion is preferred; apprenticeship (2 to 3 years); or over 3 years experience in the trade; trade certification is usually required; Red Seal certification (interprovincial) is available. **Subjects:** Construction, technical studies.	▲ $38,133

Occupation	Education and training	Salary
JEWELLERS Make and repair jewellery. Design special jewellery mountings or settings for custom orders. Use fine precision instruments. **Employment:** Jewellery, clock and watch manufacturers.	**Education and training:** High school completion is usually required; apprenticeship (3 to 4 years); or several years on-the-job training plus college jeweller's program; trade certification may be required. **Subjects:** Art, visual arts.	↙ $23,030
MACHINISTS Set up and operate various machine tools, including computerized numerically controlled tools to shape metal parts or products of precise dimensions. The machine tools are used for milling, boring, planing, drilling, precision grinding and other operations. **Employment:** Metal fabricators, machinery manufacturers.	**Education and training:** High school completion is preferred; apprenticeship (4 years); or 4 years experience in the trade plus college or industry courses in machining; trade certification is usually required; Red Seal certification (interprovincial) is available. **Subjects:** Mathematics, industrial drafting and design.	↙ $34,028
MATERIAL HANDLERS Load and unload products and materials to and from warehouses, railway cars, trucks and other transportation vehicles, containers and areas. Move loads by hand or using equipment such as hand trucks, dollies, forklift trucks, winches, tractors and loaders. Also operate equipment for handling liquid and bulk materials. **LONGSHORE WORKERS** work at ship- and docksides and may operate cranes to handle the cargoes. **Employment:** Transportation, storage and moving companies.	**Education and training:** Some high school, but high school completion is preferred.	↑ $31,794
PAINTERS AND DECORATORS Apply paint and other finishes to interior and exterior surfaces of buildings and other structures. Apply wallpaper and other coverings to interior surfaces of buildings. **Employment:** Construction contractors, self-employment.	**Education and training:** High school completion is preferred; apprenticeship (2 to 3 years); or over 3 years experience in the trade; trade certification is usually required; Red Seal certification (interprovincial) is available. **Subjects:** Construction, visual arts.	↑ $28,374
PLUMBERS Install and repair piping and fittings for water distribution and waste disposal in homes and commercial, institutional and industrial establishments. Install domestic fixtures such as sinks, toilets, bathtubs and specialized industrial and commercial fixtures. **Employment:** Construction contractors, self-employment.	**Education and training:** High school completion is preferred; apprenticeship (4 to 5 years); or over 5 years experience in the trade plus high school, college or industry courses in plumbing; trade certification is usually required; Red Seal certification (interprovincial) is available. **Subjects:** Construction, technical studies.	↙ $36,656

PRINTING PRESS OPERATORS ▲ $33,004

Set up and operate sheet web-fed and offset presses to print on paper, plastic, sheet metal and other materials. **Employment:** Printing and publishing firms.

Education and training: Completion of secondary school is usually required; completion of a college program in printing technology; an apprenticeship in printing (4 years) or on-the-job training is usually required. **Subjects:** Mathematics, graphic arts, production arts.

PUBLIC WORKS EQUIPMENT OPERATORS ◀ $32,017

Drive heavy street-cleaning and snow removal equipment, garbage trucks, salting and sanding trucks and other vehicles to clean and maintain streets and highways. **Employment:** Public works, private sectors.

Education and training: Some high school, but high school completion is preferred; driver's licence (appropriate for vehicles driven); on-the-job training is provided.

REFRIGERATION AND AIR CONDITIONING MECHANICS ▲ $37,960

Install, maintain, repair and overhaul central air conditioning systems in private homes, commercial and industrial refrigeration and air conditioning systems and combined heating and cooling systems. **Employment:** Air conditioning and refrigeration equipment dealers.

Education and training: High school completion is preferred; apprenticeship (4 years); or 5 years work experience in the trade plus college or industry courses in refrigeration and air conditioning; trade certification is usually required; Red Seal certification (interprovincial) is available. **Subjects:** Mathematics, electrical/electronics, technical studies.

ROOFERS ↖ $29,254

Install and repair all types of non-metal roofs. Replace coverings such as hot asphalt-saturated felt or waterproof sheet materials on flat roofs, and asphalt and wood shingles or shakes (roofing tiles) on steep roofs. **Employment:** Roofing contractors, self-employment.

Education and training: High school completion is preferred; apprenticeship (2 to 3 years); or several years experience in the roofer trade; trade certification may be required; Red Seal certification (interprovincial) is available. **Subjects:** Construction.

SHEET METAL WORKERS ▲ $33,517

Make, install and repair sheet metal products such as ventilation shafts, eavestroughs, air and heat ducts and sheet metal buildings. Also specialize in installing and repairing metal roofs. Operate various types of machines and equipment to perform cutting, drilling, shaping and other functions to make sheet metal products. **Employment:** Construction and aircraft manufacturers, railways.

Education training: High school completion is preferred; apprenticeship (3 to 4 years); or over 4 years experience in the trade plus high school, college or industry courses in sheet metal working; trade certification may be required; Red Seal certification (interprovincial) is available. **Subjects:** Mathematics, machine shop, industrial drafting and design, construction.

SHOE REPAIRERS ↖ $18,207

Replace heel lifts, soles and other parts of shoes, boots and other footwear. Stitch or otherwise repair the upper parts of footwear. Repair purses and

Education and training: Some high school, but high school completion is preferred; apprenticeship (2 to 3 years); trade certification may be required. **Subjects:** Technical studies.

other leather products. May make custom or orthopedic footwear if they are very experienced or have extra training. **Employment:** Shoe repair shops, custom shoemaking establishments.

SMALL ENGINE MECHANICS

Test, repair and service gasoline- and diesel-powered small engine equipment such as outboard motors, air-cooled engines, lawn mowers and similar equipment. **Employment:** Dealership service shops.

Education and training: Some high school, but high school completion is preferred; apprenticeship (3 to 4 years); or several years small engine repair experience plus college courses in small engine equipment repair; trade certification may be required. **Subjects:** Auto, technical studies.

▲ $33,246

STATIONARY ENGINEERS (POWER ENGINEERS)

Operate, monitor and maintain stationary engines and auxiliary equipment such as boilers, turbines, generators, compressors and other equipment to provide heat, ventilation, refrigeration, light and power for buildings, industrial plants and other sites. **Employment:** Industrial and manufacturing plants, hospitals.

Education and training: High school completion is preferred; apprenticeship; or on-the-job training plus correspondence or college program in stationary engineering; trade certification (1st, 2nd, 3rd and 4th class) is usually required. **Subjects:** technical studies.

▲ $39,684

STEAM FITTERS AND PIPE FITTERS

Install, repair and service high- and low-pressure piping systems carrying steam, water, oil and other liquids and gases used in heating, cooling, and lubricating systems. SPRINKLER SYSTEM INSTALLERS install, test and maintain piping and fixtures used in automatic sprinkler systems for fire protection in buildings. **Employment:** Maintenance departments of factories, pipe-fitting and sprinkler system contractors.

Education and training: High school completion is preferred; apprenticeship (4 to 5 years); or over 5 years experience in the trade plus high school, college or industry courses in steam fitting, pipe fitting or sprinkler system installation; trade certification as steam fitter/pipe fitter or sprinkler system installer is usually required; Red Seal certification (interprovincial) is available for both trades. **Subjects:** Technical studies.

▲ $34,180

TILE SETTERS

Apply ceramic, marble, quarry, mosaic and terrazzo tiles on interior and exterior walls, floors and ceilings of buildings and on other surfaces to provide a protective finish and a decorative appearance. **Employment:** Construction companies, masonry contractors.

Education and training: Some high school, but high school completion is preferred; apprenticeship (3 to 4 years); or 3 to 4 years experience in the trade plus college or industry courses in tile setting. **Subjects:** Construction.

▲ $31,937

TOOL AND DIE MAKERS

Set up and operate machine tools to make, repair and modify custom-made tools, jigs, fixtures and gauges. Compute dimensions and tolerances from specifications. **Employment:** Aircraft manufacturers, metal fabricators.

Education and training: High school completion is preferred; apprenticeship (4 years); or over 5 years experience in the trade plus college or industry courses in tool and die making; trade certification is usually required. **Subjects:** Mathematics, machine shop, industrial drafting and design.

▼ $39,706

TRACTOR-TRAILER DRIVERS
Operate tractor-trailer combinations to transport goods and materials within or between cities, towns, and rural areas, between provinces and over international boundaries. Operate two-way radios or other communication systems to maintain contact with dispatchers, or may operate on-board computers. May carry hazardous or dangerous goods. **Employment:** Truck transport companies, wholesalers, retail stores.

Education and training: Some high school, but high school completion is preferred; tractor-trailer driver's licence and permit; driver's abstract/record is usually required; certificate for transportation of dangerous goods may be required. **Subjects:** Technical studies.

▲ $32,212

WELDERS
Operate welding equipment to fuse metal parts together. May specialize in particular types of welding such as aerospace precision welding, pressure vessel welding, pipeline construction welding or custom welding. May require experience welding certain types of metals such as stainless steel, titanium and zirconium. **Employment:** Metal fabricators, machinery manufacturers, transport companies.

Education and training: High school completion is preferred; apprenticeship (3 to 4 years); or over 3 years experience in the trade plus college welding courses; trade certification is usually required; Red Seal certification (interprovincial) is available. **Subjects:** Mathematics, welding, machine shop.

▲ $33,572

PRIMARY INDUSTRY

AQUACULTURE WORKERS
Assist in the operation of fish hatcheries and fish or aquaculture farms. Perform activities such as feeding stock, culling unsatisfactory stock and marking or banding stock. Also maintain and clean aquaculture enclosures, pumps, filters and other equipment. **Employment:** Public or private fish hatcheries.

Education and training: Some high school, but high school completion is preferred. **Subjects:** Biology, technical studies.

◀ $28,452

FARM WORKERS
Plant, cultivate and harvest crops, and raise livestock and poultry. Operate equipment such as tractors and trucks; seeding, cultivating and harvesting equipment; haying and foraging equipment; and automated feeding, watering, egg-gathering, milking, manure and storage-handling systems. Perform many other activities that involve physical labour. May also maintain and repair farm equipment and buildings. **Employment:** Crop, livestock and specialty farms.

Education and training: Some high school completion is preferred; farm experience is preferred; driver's licence may be required. **Subjects:** Technical studies.

↘ $15,814

LANDSCAPE WORKERS

Plant trees, flowers, shrubs and hedges. Sod lawns, install walkways, patios and decks. May perform related maintenance work. **Employment:** Landscaping and lawn care companies, cemeteries.

Education and training: Some high school, but high school completion an asset; licence required if applying chemical herbicides and pesticides. **Subjects:** Botany, technical studies.

$25,745

MINERS

Work in underground and surface (or open pit) mines. Work in either soft rock mining (coal, potash, salt) or hard rock mining (iron ore, nickel). Operate various machines such as diamond, long hole and rotary drilling machines, haulage equipment and front-end loaders. Handle explosives and must be very safety-conscious. **Employment:** Mining companies.

Education and training: Some high school, but high school completion is preferred; safety and other training is usually required; blaster's licence is usually required; miner certification may be required; mine hoist operators require a hoist operator's licence. **Subjects:** Technical studies.

$42,215

OIL WELL DRILLING CREWS

Assist in drilling for oil or natural gas and work under the general direction of supervisors called tool pushers. Operate stationary engines and oil drilling machinery; guide drills into place and perform various other activities. Drill wells of different depths on land and offshore from semi-submersible platforms, barges or other sea drilling rigs. **Employment:** Petroleum companies, drilling and well services.

Education and training: Some high school, but high school completion is preferred; training is provided; various certificates (blowout prevention, safety, first aid, etc.) are usually required. **Subjects:** Technical studies.

$41,800

PROCESSING, MANUFACTURING AND UTILITIES

AIRCRAFT ASSEMBLERS AND AUTO ASSEMBLERS

Assemble, fit and install aircraft skins, frames and other structural parts on aircraft in addition to mechanical systems such as flight controls, rigging and hydraulics. Work at benches or directly on aircraft and use hand and power tools. AUTO ASSEMBLERS assemble and install engines, transmissions, door and instrument panels and other parts. Operate hand and power tools, robotic and other automated assembling equipment, hoists and other specialized equipment. **Employment:** Aircraft manufacturers, auto manufacturers.

Education and training: High school completion; college or CEGEP aircraft manufacturing course (1 to 3 years) may be required for aircraft assemblers; on-the-job training plus formal classroom training is usually provided for aircraft assemblers; on-the-job training is provided for auto assemblers. **Subjects:** Technical studies, auto, mechanics.

$34,539

ELECTRONICS ASSEMBLERS

Assemble by hand various electronic components such as resistors, transistors, capacitors and other parts and solder them to printed circuit boards, or operate automatic and semi-automatic machines to position and solder

Education and training: Some high school, but high school completion is preferred. **Subjects:** Technical studies, electrical/electronics.

$25,501

...the parts to circuit boards. May also assemble microcircuits requiring the use of microscopes and fine-hand assembly. **Employment:** Electronics manufacturers.

FURNITURE ASSEMBLERS

Operate hand and power tools to assemble furniture and fixtures made of wood, metal, cane, plastic and other materials. **Employment:** Furniture manufacturing companies.

Education and training: Some high school, but high school completion is preferred. **Subjects:** Technical studies, woodworking.

↑ $23,861

PHOTOGRAPHIC FILM PROCESSORS

Operate automatic equipment to develop negatives and slides; to print black and white and colour photographs; and to develop motion picture film. Retouch photographic negatives or original prints to correct defects. Workers in retail photo-finishing outlets operate automatic equipment that develops colour negatives, prints and slides. **Employment:** Film processing laboratories, retail photo-finishing.

Education and training: High school completion is usually required; college or CEGEP program (2 years) is required for photographic and film laboratory processors; or extensive experience; usually no previous experience is required for workers in retail photo-finishing outlets. **Subjects:** Graphics, visual arts, technical studies.

↖ $25,008

WOODWORKING MACHINE OPERATORS

Set up and operate saws, routers, planers, drills, sanders and other woodworking machines to make or repair wooden parts for furniture. **Employment:** Furniture, fixture and wood products manufacturers.

Education and training: Some high school, but high school completion is preferred. **Subjects:** Construction, woodworking.

→ $24,580

SELECT BIBLIOGRAPHY .

BUSINESS:

Ambry, Margaret, and Cheryl Russell. *The Official Guide to the American Marketplace.* Ithaca: New Strategist, 1992.

Boyett, Joseph, and Henry Conn. *Workplace 2000: The Revolution Reshaping American Business.* New York: Plume, 1991.

Clemmer, Jim. *Firing On All Cylinders: The Service/Quality System for High-Powered Corporate Performance,* 2nd ed. Toronto: Macmillan Canada, 1992.

Hammer, Michael, and James Champy. *Reengineering the Corporation.* New York: Harper Collins, 1993.

Senge, Peter. *The Fifth Discipline: The Art and Practice of the Learning Organization.* New York: Doubleday, 1990.

Sharwood, Gordon. *At the Threshold: Canada's Medium-Sized Businesses Prepare for the Global Marketplace of the 90s.* Toronto: Sharwood and Company, 1989.

CANADA'S ECONOMIC FUTURE:

Beck, Nuala. *Shifting Gears: Thriving in the New Economy.* Toronto: Harper Collins, 1992. Highly recommended as introduction to the changing economy.

Canada. Employment and Immigration Canada. *Success in the Works: A Profile of Canada's Emerging Workforce.* Ottawa, 1989.

_____*Job Futures: Occupational Outlooks,* Vol. 1. Ottawa: 1990.

_____*Software and National Competitiveness: Human Resource Issues and Opportunities.* Ottawa, 1992.

C. D. Howe Institute. *Canada at Risk? Canadian Public Policy in the 1990s.* Toronto, 1991.

Cohen, Dian, and Guy Stanley. *No Small Change: Succeeding in Canada's New Economy.* Toronto: Macmillan Canada, 1993.

Crane, David. *The Next Canadian Century: Building a Competitive Economy.* Toronto: Stoddart Publishing, 1992.

Ernst & Young. *Canada's Technology Industries in the 1990s: How to Win in a World of Change.* Toronto, 1990.

Lipsey, Richard. *Economic Growth: Science and Technology and Institutional Change in the Global Economy.* Toronto: Canadian Institute for Advanced Research, 1991.

Luciani, Patrick. *What Canadians Believe, But Shouldn't About Their Economy.* Toronto: Addison-Wesley Publishers, 1993.

Mansell, Jacquie. *Workplace Innovation in Canada.* Ottawa: Economic Council of Canada, 1987.

Porter, Michael. *Canada at the Crossroads: The Reality of a New Competitive Environment.* Ottawa: Monitor Co., 1991.

Slater, David. *The Contribution of Investment and Savings to Productivity and Economic Growth in Canada.* Ottawa: Investment Canada, 1992.

CAREERS:

Adams Job Almanac. Holbrook: Bob Adams Inc., 1994.

Angle, Susan, and Alex Hiam. *Adventure Careers.* Hawthorne: Career Press, 1992.

Basta, Nicholas. *Top Professions: The 100 Most Popular, Dynamic, and Profitable Careers in America Today*. Princeton: Peterson's Guides, 1989.

_____*Environmental Career Guide*. New York: Wiley, 1991.

Bolles, Richard. *The Three Boxes of Life*. Berkeley: Ten Speed Press, 1981.

_____ *What Color is Your Parachute* . Berkeley: Ten Speed Press, 1993.

Canada. Employment and Immigration. *Software and National Competitiveness: Human Resource Issues and Opportunities*. Ottawa,1992.

Career Associates. *Career Choices: Art, Business, Communications and Journalism, Computer Science, Economics, English, History, Law, Mathematices, MBA, Political Science and Government, Psychology*. New York: Walker and Co., 1990.

_____*Encyclopedia of Career Choices for the 1990s*. New York: Putnam, 1993.

The Career Directory, 1993 ed. Toronto: Edcore Publishing Co., 1993.

"Careers in ..." series, 1990-1993. *Accounting, Advertising, Business, Communications, Computers, Education, Engineering, Health Care, High-Tech, Law, Marketing, Medicine, Science*. Lincolnwood: National Textbook Co.

Centron, Marvin, and Owen Davies. *The Great Job Shake-Out: How to Find a Career After the Crash*. New York: Simon & Schuster, 1988.

Cornish, Edward, ed. *Careers Tomorrow: The Outlook for Work in a Changing World*. Bethesda: World Future Society, 1988.

Damp, Dennis. *Health Career Job Explosion*. Coraopolis: Damp Publications, 1993.

Didsbury, Howard, Jr., ed. *The World of Work: Careers and the Future*. Bethesda: World Future Society, 1983.

Farr, J. Michael, and Kathleen Martin, eds. *America's Fastest Growing Jobs: An Authoritative Information Source*. Indianapolis: JIST Works, 1991.

Feather, Frank. *Tomorrow's Best-Canadian Careers*. Thornhill: Global Management Bureau, 1987.

Feingold, Norman, and Maxine Atwater. *New Emerging Careers: Today, Tomorrow, and in the 21st Century*. Garrett Park: Garrett Park Press, 1989.

Field, Shelly. *100 Best Careers for the Year 2000*. New York: Prentice Hall/Arco, 1992.

Gale, Barry, and Linda Gale. *Discover What You're Best At*. New York: Simon & Schuster, 1990.

Glenn, Reed. *The Ten Best Opportunities for Starting a Home Business Today*. Boulder: Live Oak Press, 1993.

Harkavy, Michael. *101 Careers: A Guide to the Fastest Growing Opportunities*. New York: Wiley & Sons, 1990.

Innes, Eva, et al. *The 100 Best Companies to Work for in Canada.*. Toronto: Harper Collins, 1990-91.

Job Opportunities for Business and Liberal Arts Graduates. Princeton: Peterson's Guides, 1993.

Job Opportunities for Engineering, Science, and Computer Graduates. Princeton: Peterson's Guides, 1993.

Job Seeker's Guide to Private and Public Companies. Detroit: Gale Research, 1992.

Kavanagh, Robert. *New Scientists and Engineers from Canadian Universities*. Ottawa: Natural Sciences and Engineering Research Council, 1991.

Kleinman, Carol. *The 100 Best Jobs for the 1990s and Beyond*. Chicago: Dearborn Financial Publishing, 1992.

Krannich, Ronald L., and Caryl Rae Krannich. *The Educator's Guide to Alternative Jobs and Careers*. Manassas Park: Impact Publications, 1991.

_____*The Best Jobs for the 1990s and into the 21st Century*. Manassas Park: Impact Publications, 1993.

_____ *Careering and Re-Careering for the 1990s*. Manassas Park: Impact Publications, 1993.

Krantz, Les. *The Jobs Rated Almanac*. New York: Pharos Books, 1992.

Lewis, Adele, and Doris Kuller. *Fast-Track Careers for the 90s*. Glenview: Professional Books Group, 1990.

Mast, Jennifer. *The Job Seeker's Guide to 1000 Top Employers*. Detroit: Visible Ink Press, 1993.

Morgan, Bradley, ed. *The Career Advisory Series: Advertising, Book Publishing, Business and Finance, Health Care, Magazine Publishing, Marketing and Sales, Newspaper Publishing, Public Relations, Radio and Television, Travel and Hospitality*. Detroit: Visible Ink Press, 1992-93.

Norback, Craig. *Careers Encyclopedia*. Lincolnwood: National Textbook, 1992.

"Opportunities in..." series, 1984-1993. Over 160 titles. Lincolnwood: National Textbook Co.

Orpwood, Graham. *The Chemical Professions of Canada: Employment and Education for the Future*. Ottawa, Chemical Institute of Canada, 1991.

Petras, Kathyrn, and Ross Petras. *Jobs '94*. New York: Simon & Schuster, 1994.

Rubin, K. *Flying High in Travel*. New York: Wiley, 1992.

Satterfield, Alan. *Where the Jobs Are: The Hottest Careers for the '90s*. Hawthorne: Career Press, 1992.

Shenk, Ellen. *Outdoor Careers*. Harrisburg: Stackpole Books, 1992.

Smith, Carter. *America's Fast Growing Employers*. Holbrook: Bob Adams, Inc., 1992.

Snelling, Robert, and Anne Snelling. *Jobs! What They Are, Where They Are, What They Pay!* New York: Simon & Schuster, 1992.

Stienstra, Tom. *Careers in the Outdoors*. San Francisco: Foghorn Press, 1992.

U.S. Department of Labor. *Occupational Outlook Handbook*. Washington, 1993.

Wegman, Robert, et al., eds. *Work in the New Economy: Careers and Job Seeking into the 21st Century*. Indianapolis: JIST Works, 1989.

Wright, John. *American Almanac of Jobs and Salaries*. New York: Avon, 1990.

DEMOGRAPHICS:

Barna, George. *The Invisible Generation: Baby Busters*. Barna Research Group, 1992.

Dychtwald, Ken, and Joe Flower. *Age Wave: The Challenge and Opportunities of an Aging America*. New York: Bantam, 1989.

Foot, David. *The Over-Forty Society: Issues for Canada's Aging Population*. Toronto: James Lorimer & Co., 1988.

Gollub, James. *The Decade Matrix*. Toronto: Addison-Wesley Publishers Ltd., 1991.

EDUCATION:

Centron, Marvin, and Owen Davies. *American Renaissance: Our Life at the Turn of the 21st Century*. New York: St. Martin's Press, 1989.

Economic Council of Canada. *A Lot to Learn: Education and Training in Canada*. Ottawa, 1992.

National Center on Education and Economy. *America's Choice: High Skills or Low Wages*. Rochester, 1990.

Perelman, Lewis. *The Learning Enterprise*. Council of State Planning Agencies, 1985.

_____ *School's Out: Hyperlearning, the New Technology, and the End of Education*. New York: William Morrow & Co., 1993.

FUTURE TRENDS:

Abrams, Malcolm, and Harriet Bernstein. *More Future Stuff: Over 250 Inventions That Will Change Your Life by 2001*. New York: Penguin Books, 1991.

Barker, Joel. *Paradigms: The Business of Discovering the Future*. New York: Harper, 1992.

Celente, Gerald, and Tom Milton. *Trend Tracking: The System to Profit From Today's Trends*. Toronto: Wiley & Sons, 1990.

Coates, Joseph, and Jennifer Jarratt. *What Futurists Believe*. Bethesda: World Future Society, 1989.

Coates, Joseph, et al. *Future Work: Seven Critical Forces in North America*. New York: Josey-Bass, 1990.

Cornish, Edward, ed. *The 1990s and Beyond*. Bethesda: World Future Society, 1990.

Didsbury, Howard, Jr., ed. *The Future: Opportunity Not Destiny*. Besthesda: World Future Society, 1989.

_____ *The Years Ahead: Perils, Problems and Promises*. Besthesda: World Future Society, 1993.

Feather, Frank. *G-Forces Reinventing the World: The 35 Global Forces Restructuring Our Future.* Toronto: Summerhill Press, 1989.

Future Vision: The 189 Most Important Trends of the 1990s by the editors of *Research Alert.* Trabuco Canyon: Sourcebooks, 1991.

Kennedy, Paul. *Preparing for the 21st Century.* Toronto: Harper Collins, 1993.

Makridakis, Spyros. *Forecasting, Planning, and Strategy for the 21st Century.* New York: The Free Press/Macmillan, 1990.

Naisbitt, John, and Patricia Aburdene. *Megatrends 2000: Ten New Directions for the 1990's.* New York: Avon Books, 1990.

Ogden, Frank. *The Last Book You'll Ever Read.* Toronto: Macfarlane Walter & Ross, 1993.

Popcorn, Faith. *The Popcorn Report on the Future of Your Company, Your World, Your Life.* Toronto: Harper Collins, 1991.

Saaty, Thoma, and Larry Boone. *Embracing the Future: Meeting the Challenge of Our Changing World.* Westport: Praeger, 1990.

Toffler, Alvin. *Powershift: Knowledge, Wealth and Violence at the Edge of the 21st Century.* New York: Bantam Books, 1991.

Watt, Kenneth. *Taming the Future: A Revolutionary Breakthrough in Scientific Forecasting.* Davis: Contextured Web Press, 1992.

TECHNOLOGIES TRANSFORMING THE WORKPLACE:

Caudill, Maureen. *In Our Image: Building an Artificial Person.* New York: Oxford Press, 1992.

Conway, McKinley. *A Glimpse of the Future: Technology Forecasts for Global Strategists.* New York: Conway Data, 1992.

Economic Council of Canada. *Making Technology Work: Innovation and Jobs in Canada.* Ottawa, 1987.

Ernst & Young. *Canada's Technology Industries in the 1990s: How to Win in a World of Change.* Toronto, 1990.

Keen, Peter. *Shaping the Future: Business Design Through Information Technology.* Cambridge: Harvard Business School Press,1991.

Kennedy, Paul. *Preparing for the 21st Century.* Toronto: Harper Collins, 1993.

Lipsey, Richard. *Economic Growth: Science and Technology and Institutional Change in the Global Economy.* Toronto: Canadian Institute for Advanced Research, 1991.

Martino, Joseph. *Technological Forecasting for Decision Making.* New York: McGraw-Hill, 1993.

Organization for Economic Co-operation and Development.*Technology in A Changing World.* The Technology/Economy Program. Paris, 1991.

Tapscott, Don, and Art Caston. *Paradigm Shift: The New Promise of Information Technology.* Toronto: McGraw-Hill,1993.

UNDERSTANDING THE NEW GLOBAL ECONOMY:

Burrows, Brian, et al. *Into the 21st Century: A Handbook for a Sustainable Future.* New York: Adamantine Press,1991.

Carnevale, Anthony. *America and the New Economy: How New Competitive Standards Are Radically Changing American Workplaces.* San Francisco: Jossey-Bass, 1991.

Davidson, James, and Lord William Rees-Mogg. *The Great Reckoning: Protect Yourself in the Coming Depression.* New York: Simon & Schuster, 1993.

Dent, Harry. *The Great Boom Ahead: Your Comprehensive Guide to Personal and Business Profit in the New Era of Prosperity.* New York: Hyperion, 1993.

Didsbury, Howard, Jr., ed. *The Global Economy: Today, Tomorrow, and the Transition.* Bethesda: World Future Society, 1985.

Drache, Daniel, and Meric Gertler, eds. *The New Era of Global Competition: State Policy and Market Power.* Kingston: McGill- Queen's University Press, 1991.

Drucker, Peter. *Post-Capitalist Society.* New York: Harper Collins, 1993.

Figgie, Harry, Jr., *Bankruptcy 1995: The Coming Collapse of America and How to Stop It.* New

York: Little, Brown & Co., 1992.

Henderson, Hazel. *Paradigms in Progress: Life Beyond Economics*. New York: Knowledge Systems Inc., 1991.

Hoover, Gary, et al. *Hoover's Handbook of American Business* and *Hoover's Handbook of World Business*. Austin: The Reference Press, 1993.

Kester, Carl. *Japanese Takeovers: The Global Contest for Corporate Control*. Boston: Harvard Business School Press, 1991.

Malabre, Alfred, Jr. *Understanding the New Economy* . Homewood: Dow-Jones Irwin, 1993.

Porter, Michael. *The Competitive Advantage of Nations*. New York: The Free Press, 1990.

Reich, Robert. *The Work of Nations: Preparing Ourselves for 21st Century Capitalism*. New York: A.A. Knopf, 1991.

Thurow, Lester. *Head to Head: The Coming Battle Among Japan, Europe, and America*. New York: Warner Brothers, 1993.

The World Competitiveness Report 1993. Geneva: World Economic Forum, 1993.

Yoffie, David, ed. *Beyond Free Trade: Firms, Governments, and Global Competition*. Boston: Harvard Business School Press, 1993.

WORKING ABROAD:

Beckmann, David, et al. *The Overseas List*. Minneapolis: Augsburg Publishing, 1986.

Franz, Del, and Laxaro Hernandez, eds. *Work, Study, Travel Abroad: The Whole World Handbook*, 11th ed., 1992-1993. New York: St. Martin's Press, 1992.

Hachey, Jean-Marc. *The Canadian Guide to Working and Living Overseas: For Entry-Level and Seasoned Professionals*. Ottawa: Intercultural Systems, 1992.

Kocher, Eric. *International Jobs*. Reading: Addison-Wesley Publishers Ltd., 1989.

Krannich, Ronald L., and Caryl Rae Krannich. *Jobs for People Who Love Travel*. Manassas Park: Impact Publications, 1990.

_____ *The Almanac of International Jobs and Careers*. Manassas Park: Impact Publications, 1991.

_____ *The Complete Guide to International Jobs and Careers*. Manassas Park: Impact Publications, 1992.

A Practical Guide to Living and Working in Japan. Ottawa: Transglobal Publications.

Sanborn, Robert. *How to Get a Job in Europe*. Chicago: Surrey Books, 1990.

_____ *How to Get a Job in the Pacific Rim* . Chicago: Surrey Books, 1992.

MAGAZINES AND NEWSLETTERS:

Asia Inc. and *Asiaweek* provide information on Pacific Rim developments.

Canadian Business provides a good overview of various Canadian business developments.

The Economist is a must-read magazine which covers current topics in-depth including discussions of global developments affecting finance, politics, science, and economic prosperity.

Forbes and *Fortune* are the stalwart U.S. business publications along with *Businessweek*.

The Harvard Business Review provides in-depth discussion of current business issues.

Mergers & Acquisitions helps you keep up with the activities of larger corporations and industry consolidation in general.

Newsletter on Newsletters, 44 West Market St., Rhinebeck, NY 12572, helps you find newsletters on any desired topic.

World Press Review acts as a monthly digest of articles in newspapers and magazines from a worldwide perspective.

NEWSPAPERS

The Globe & Mail "Report on Business" is a dependable source of relevant daily information and industry analysis.

The Financial Post provides in-depth analysis of Canadian business and stock market activities.

The Toronto Star's business section covers many industry-related developments affecting careers.

USA TODAY is full of trend-related information.

The Wall Street Journal, along with *Barrons*, provide highly accurate in-depth reports of important business matters.

Worldwide Weeklies and Dailies of Note: *Asahi Shimbum* (Tokyo), *Berliner Zeitung* (West Berlin), *Corriere dell Sera* (Rome), *Manchester Guardian Weekly*, *Le Monde* (Paris), *The New York Times, Nikkei Weekly* (Tokyo), *Pravda* (Moscow), *La Prensa* (Mexico), *The Times* (London), and *Washington Post*.

ELECTRONIC INFORMATION SOURCES:

Besides using the information resources of reference and university libraries which have considerable information access through Internet, you may wish to use the following resources to acquire information on particular careers, job markets, and trends.

BOOKS:

Directory of On-Line Data Bases (Cuadra Associates)
Encyclopedia of Information Systems and Services (Gale Research Co.)

SERVICES:

AT&T Information Services: 1-800-567-4672
Business Information Exchange International: 1-800-263-5925
Compuserve Information Services: 1-800-544-4079
Globe Information Services: 1-416-585-5280
Infomart Online (news and business): 1-416-445-6641
Mead Data Central International Inc. (business and legal): 1-416-361-6323
SkillsLink (government training resources, products, and services): 1-800-387-1234

INDEX

Colin Campbell, author of *Where the Jobs Are*, is president of Career World, a career counselling and resume service company which offers its clients career counselling, employment prescreening assessment, and an **electronic resume hiring service**. A resume placed on Career World's database allows employers across Canada or in the United States to find qualified job seekers quickly and easily. Resumes are reviewed electronically during every hiring search, are always kept active, and can be placed in foreign employment databases or matched against the daily classified ads of the top 60 U.S. newspapers.

For more information, contact:

Career World
2032 Gerrard Street East
Toronto, Ontario M4E 2B1

Tel: (416) 690-1972 or (416) 690-8421
or 1-800-648-6705
Fax: (416) 690-9329

This book was designed and set into type by James Ireland Design Inc., Toronto.

The text face is ITC New Baskerville, a digital issue of the popular and highly readable English typeface designed by John Baskerville in the 1750s. All headings are set in Franklin Gothic and Franklin Gothic Extra Condensed, designed by American Morris Benton in 1903.